Effective Web Presence Solutions for Small Businesses:
Strategies for Successful Implementation

Stephen Burgess
Victoria University, Australia

Carmine Sellitto
Victoria University, Australia

Stan Karanasios
Leeds University Business School, AIMTech Research Group, UK

T0336172

Information Science REFERENCE

INFORMATION SCIENCE REFERENCE

Hershey · New York

Director of Editorial Content:	Kristin Klinger
Director of Production:	Jennifer Neidig
Managing Editor:	Jamie Snavely
Assistant Managing Editor:	Carole Coulson
Typesetter:	Chris Hrobak
Cover Design:	Lisa Tosheff
Printed at:	Yurchak Printing Inc.

Published in the United States of America by
Information Science Reference (an imprint of IGI Global)
701 E. Chocolate Avenue, Suite 200
Hershey PA 17033
Tel: 717-533-8845
Fax: 717-533-8661
E-mail: cust@igi-global.com
Website: http://www.igi-global.com/reference

and in the United Kingdom by
Information Science Reference (an imprint of IGI Global)
3 Henrietta Street
Covent Garden
London WC2E 8LU
Tel: 44 20 7240 0856
Fax: 44 20 7379 0609
Website: http://www.eurospanbookstore.com

Copyright © 2009 by IGI Global. All rights reserved. No part of this publication may be reproduced, stored or distributed in any form or by any means, electronic or mechanical, including photocopying, without written permission from the publisher.

Product or company names used in this set are for identification purposes only. Inclusion of the names of the products or companies does not indicate a claim of ownership by IGI Global of the trademark or registered trademark.

Library of Congress Cataloging-in-Publication Data

Burgess, Stephen, 1958-
  Effective web presence solutions for small businesses : strategies for successful implementation / by Stephen Burgess, Carmine Sellitto and Stan Karanasios.
     p. cm.
  Includes bibliographical references and index.
  Summary: "This book provides small businesses with a holistic approach to implementing their Web presence"--Provided by publisher.
  ISBN 978-1-60566-224-4 (hbk.) -- ISBN 978-1-60566-225-1 (ebook)
  1. Small business--Information technology. 2. Internet marketing. I. Sellitto, Carmine, 1957- II. Karanasio, Stergios, 1979- III. Title.
  HD62.7.B834 2009
  658.8'72--dc22
                                        2008041369

British Cataloguing in Publication Data
A Cataloguing in Publication record for this book is available from the British Library.

All work contributed to this book set is new, previously-unpublished material. The views expressed in this book set are those of the authors, but not necessarily of the publisher.

Effective Web Presence Solutions for Small Businesses: Strategies for Successful Implementation is part of the IGI Global series named *Advances in Global Information Management (AGIM)* Series, ISBN: 1935-3154

If a library purchased a print copy of this publication, please go to http://www.igi-global.com/agreement for information on activating the library's complimentary electronic access to this publication.

Advances in Global Information Management (AGIM)

ISBN: 1935-3154

Editor-in-Chief: M. Gordon Hunter, University of Lethbridge, Canada

Effective Web Presence Solutions for Small Businesses:
Strategies for Successful Implementation

Stephen Burgess, Victoria University, Australia; Carmine Sellitto, Victoria University, Australia, & Stan Karanasios, Leeds University Business School, AIMTech Research Group, UK

Information Science Reference • copyright 2009 • 400pp • H/C (ISBN: 978-1-60566-224-4) • US $165.00 (our price)

Over the past several years, a great deal of research has been devoted to the use of information technology by small businesses. One technological tool now used to boost company success is Web presence enhancement in alignment with business strategy. Effective Web Presence Solutions for Small Businesses: Strategies for Successful Implementation is the first book to provide small businesses with a holistic approach to implementing their Web presence through identification of Web site content that matches their business strategy. A valuable read for small business owners as well as academicians and researchers, this book connects the various issues involved in the planning and execution of successful Web sites for small businesses.

Handbook of Research on Information Management and the Global Landscape

M. Gordon Hunter, University of Lethbridge, Canada & Felix B. Tan, AUT University, New Zealand

Information Science Reference • copyright 2009 • 589pp • H/C (ISBN: 978-1-60566-138-4) • US $265.00 (our price)

Online collaboration is increasingly improving partnerships for organizations across the globe, strengthening existing relationships and creating new alliances that would previously have been inconceivable. Through these new global networks come significant issues, opportunities, and challenges for the consideration of researchers, organizational managers, and information professionals. Handbook of Research on Information Management and the Global Landscape collects cutting-edge studies that deliver deep insights into the array of information management issues surrounding living and working in a global environment. Collecting over 20 authoritative chapters by recognized experts from distinguished research institutions worldwide, this truly international reference work emphasizes a regional theme while contributing to the global information environment, creating an essential addition to library reference collections.

Strategic Use of Information Technology for Global Oranizations

M. Gordon Hunter, University of Lethbridge, Canada & Felix B. Tan, AUT University, New Zealand

IGI Publishing • copyright 2007 • 397pp • H/C (ISBN: 978-1-59904-292-3) • US $89.96 (our price)

The role of chief information officer (CIO) takes on many forms, and is contingent on many factors. Environmental factors such as size, industry, or organizational structure; senior management's interpretation of the value of information technology to the overall operation of the firm; and industry-based regulations, all contribute to the function of this role. Strategic Use of Information Technology for Global Organizations provides valuable insights into the role of CIO's, their necessary interaction with other parts of the organization and the external relationships with vendors and suppliers. Strategic Use of Information Technology for Global Organizations emphasizes the need for balance between management and technology in the role of CIO. It focuses on this role as not only an expert on information technology, but as a leader in the appropriate application of IT.

The Advances in Global Information Management (AGIM) Book Series is an interdisciplinary outlet for emerging publications that address critical areas of information technology and its effects on the social constructs of global culture, how information resources are managed, and how these practices contribute to business and managerial functions. The series directly addresses the world economy, its powers and implications. Big international companies are deconstructing themselves and creating new structures to survive in the new world order.

Order online at www.igi-global.com or call 717-533-8845 x100 –
Mon-Fri 8:30 am - 5:00 pm (est) or fax 24 hours a day 717-5 33-7115
Hershey • New York

Table of Contents

Section I:
Setting the Scene

Chapter I

Chapter II

Section II:
Readiness, Business Aims and Planning

Section III:
Web Presence Implementation and Evaluation

Foreword

I consider it an honour and a privilege to be given the opportunity to write the Foreword to this book, as it provides the results of many investigations into the use of the Internet by small business.

Over many years of research the authors have noted a change from basic technologies that promote a more efficient operation to now where Websites attached to the Internet are employed to engage customers and contribute to the effectiveness of the business.

Small businesses are unique (Belich and Dubinsky, 1999; and Pollard and Hayne, 1998). They contribute significantly to a nation's economy. Also, as a sector it represents the largest employer.

Yet small businesses suffer from resource poverty (Thong et al, 1994). They lack time, money, and skills. Thus, managers of small businesses tend to make short term decisions (Bridge and Peel, 1999; and Hunter et al., 2002) focusing upon minimal commitments (Stevenson, 1999). This approach seems contradictory to the decision making necessary to invest in the development of Websites. Thus, as you will find in this book, small business managers have come to recognize the benefits of both Websites and the Internet.

My own research into information systems and small business has found similar results. Pugsley et al. (2000) and later Hunter et al. (2002) determined that the adoption of information systems increased small business dependency on either an internal or external entity. Further, most adoptions of information systems have been to support efficiency of operations. These findings were further substantiated internationally (Hunter, 2005a; Hunter, 2005b; and Hunter et al, 2005).

The readers of this book will appreciate its format and organization. In Section I, the context for information and communication technologies and small business is presented via a discussion of relevant research projects and the lessons for small businesses presented throughout the book are summarised. This discussion then proceeds, in Section II, into the readiness of small business for adoption of

I consider it an honour and a privilege to be given the opportunity to write the Foreword to this book, as it provides the results of many investigations into the use of the Internet by small business.

Over many years of research the authors have noted a change from basic technologies that promote a more efficient operation to now where Websites attached to the Internet are employed to engage customers and contribute to the effectiveness of the business.

Small businesses are unique (Belich and Dubinsky, 1999; and Pollard and Hayne, 1998). They contribute significantly to a nation's economy. Also, as a sector it represents the largest employer.

Yet small businesses suffer from resource poverty (Thong et al, 1994). They lack time, money, and skills. Thus, managers of small businesses tend to make short term decisions (Bridge and Peel, 1999; and Hunter et al., 2002) focusing upon minimal commitments (Stevenson, 1999). This approach seems contradictory to the decision making necessary to invest in the development of Websites. Thus, as you will find in this book, small business managers have come to recognize the benefits of both Websites and the Internet.

My own research into information systems and small business has found similar results. Pugsley et al. (2000) and later Hunter et al. (2002) determined that the adoption of information systems increased small business dependency on either an internal or external entity. Further, most adoptions of information systems have been to support efficiency of operations. These findings were further substantiated internationally (Hunter, 2005a; Hunter, 2005b; and Hunter et al, 2005).

The readers of this book will appreciate its format and organization. In Section I, the context for information and communication technologies and small business is presented via a discussion of relevant research projects and the lessons for small businesses presented throughout the book are summarised. This discussion then proceeds, in Section II, into the readiness of small business for adoption of the necessary technology; and subsequently the strategy and planning required to prepare for the establishment of a Web presence. In Section III, the chapters discuss issues surrounding implementation and evaluation of Websites. Finally, Section IV presents comments about future innovations.

Various stakeholders will appreciate the material contained in this book. Academics will find leading edge discussion and analysis of the application of information and communications technologies to small business. Researchers will be presented with novel approaches and intriguing findings in this subject area. Students will see how small business is using information and communication technologies. This will be of interest to students of small business as well as those studying information and communications technologies. Of course, Web developers and small business consultants will discover many ideas which may be employed in their own interactions with small business. Finally, small business owners and managers will be able to determine the necessary approach and steps to be taken to ensure readiness for and the subsequent establishment of a Web presence.

The authors bring 25 years of combined experience and research into small business and the use of information and communications technologies. This represents extensive authority and significant longevity in such a new area of investigation.

As stated earlier, I am honoured to write this Foreword and to recommend this book. The issues presented and discussed here are current and provide an important context regarding small business and the use of information communication technologies to establish a Web presence.

M. Gordon Hunter
Professor Information Systems
The University of Lethbridge
Alberta, CANADA
Editor, Book Series
Advances in Global Information Management
August, 2008

M. Gordon Hunter *is a professor of information systems in the Faculty of Management at The University of Lethbridge, Alberta, Canada. He has also been appointed visiting professor, Faculty of Business, Computing and Information Management, London South Bank University. Gordon has previously held academic positions at universities in Canada, Hong Kong, and Singapore. He has held visiting positions at universities in Australia, England, Germany, Monaco, New Zealand, Turkey, and USA. During July and August of 2005 Gordon was a Visiting Erskine Fellow at the University of Canterbury, Christchurch, New Zealand. He has a bachelor's of Commerce degree from the University of Saskatchewan in Saskatoon, Saskatchewan, Canada and a PhD from Strathclyde Business School, University of Strathclyde in Glasgow, Scotland. Gordon has also obtained a Certified Management Accountant (CMA) designation from the Society of Management Accountants of Canada. He is a Chartered Information Technology Professional (CITP) and member of the British Computer Society. Gordon is also a member of the Canadian Information Processing Society (CIPS), where he has obtained an Information Systems Professional (ISP) designation. He has extensive experience as a systems analyst and manager in industry and government organizations in Canada. Gordon is an associate editor of the Journal of Global Information Management. He serves on the editorial board of Information and Management, The International Journal of E-Collaboration, and The Journal of Global Information Technology Management. Gordon is also a member of the Advisory Board for the Journal of Information, Information Technology, and Organizations. Gordon has published articles in MIS Quarterly, Information Systems Research, the Journal of Strategic Information Systems, the Journal of Global Information Management, Information Systems Journal, and Information, Technology and People. He has conducted seminar presentations in Australia, Canada, England, Europe, Hong Kong, New Zealand, Singapore, Taiwan, Turkey, and USA. Gordon's research approach takes a qualitative perspective employing personal construct theory and narrative inquiry to conduct in depth interviews. He applies qualitative techniques in interdisciplinary research such as multi-generation small business, recruitment and retention of medical doctors, and cross-cultural investigations. His current research interests in the information systems (IS) area include the effective development and* *implementation of IS with emphasis on the personnel component; the role of chief information officers; and the use of IS by small business.*

REFERENCES

Belich, T. J., & Dubinsky, A. J. (1999). Information Processing Among Exporters: An Empirical Examination of Small Firms. *Journal of Marketing Theory and Practice, 7*(4), 45-58.

Bridge, J., & Peel, M. J. (1999). A Study of Computer Usage and Strategic Planning in the SME Sector. *International Small Business Journal, 17*(4), 82-87.

Hunter, M. G., Burgess, S., & Wenn, A. (2005). The Use of Information Systems by Small Business: An International Perspective. In M. G.Hunter, S. Burgess, & A. Wenn (Eds.), *Small Business and Information Technology: Research Issues and International Case Studies.* Melbourne, Australia: Heidelberg Press.

Hunter, M. G. (2005a). International Information Systems and Small Business Project: A Western Canadian Perspective. In M. G.Hunter, S. Burgess, & A. Wenn (Eds.), *Small Business and Information Technology: Research Issues and International Case Studies.* Melbourne, Australia: Heidelberg Press.

Hunter, M. G. (2005b). Information Systems and Small Business: Stakeholder Considerations. In M. Khosrow-Pour (Ed.), *Encyclopedia of Information Science and Technology,* Volume I-V. Hershey, PA: Idea Group Publishing.

Hunter, M. G., Diochon, D., Pugsley, D., & Wright, B. (2002). Unique Challenges for Small Business Adoption of Information Technology: The Case of the Nova Scotia Ten. In S. Burgess (Ed.), *Managing Information Technology in Small Business: Challenges and Solutions.* Hershey, PA: Idea Group Publishing.

Pollard, C., & Hayne, S. (1998). The Changing Faces of Information Systems Issues in Small Firms. *International Small Business Journal, 16*(3), 70-87.

Pugsley, D., Wright, B., Diochon, M., & Hunter, M. G. (2000). Information Technology and Small Business: Listening to Voices from the Field. *Proceedings of the Administrative Sciences Association of Canada* (ASAC) Conference, July 8-11, Montreal, Canada.

Stevenson, H. H. (1999). A Perspective of Entrepreneurship. In H. H. Stevenson, I. Grousebeck, M. J. Roberts, & A. Bhide (Eds.), *New Business Ventures and the Entrepreneur,* (pp.3-17). Boston: Irwin McGraw-Hill.

Thong, J., Yap, C., & Raman, K. (1994). Engagement of External Expertise in Information Systems Implementation. *Journal of Management Information Systems, 11*(2), 209-223.

Preface

All they want to talk about is the Internet

This is actually a comment made by one of us. At the time of writing this book we are working on a project with the University of South Australia and the University of Queensland, funded by the Australian Collaborative Research Centre for Sustainable Tourism, where we are developing a toolkit to be used by small tourism businesses to help them to use information and communications technologies (ICTs) effectively. The first phases of the project involve us running focus groups and conducting interviews with small tourism business to see how they are currently using ICTs – and this is where the quote emanated from. Although we are asking the owner/managers of these businesses about their use of *all* ICTs, it is when we move to talking about the Internet and Websites in particular that they really start to get interested and involved in the discussion – if they haven't already raised it themselves beforehand. It is almost as if the other technologies that they use, including hardware (such as personal computers [PCs], printers and scanners) and software (such as word processing and accounting packages) are things that they *have to have* to improve efficiencies in their businesses. However, they see the Internet and Websites as technologies that they can use to *engage* their customers – and we have noticed the increased enthusiasm towards these technologies as we have conducted research into their use of ICTs over the years.

This book is predominantly a research book, although it does contain some insights gained by the authors in their interactions with small businesses and, in some cases, during careers as information systems academics. We believe a major contribution of the book is that it is a comprehensive attempt to draw together, in one publication, the issues faced by small business practitioners in setting up and maintaining their Web presence. Although there is a great deal of wonderful research being conducted in this arena, there has, to date, been no real attempt to consolidate the issues that are being raised in a manner that may be translated to a comprehensive set of guidelines for small businesses. Thus, we have concentrated as much on the links between the various issues we have raised as much as the discussion about the issues themselves. As such, the book is not meant to be a literature review of all leading research in the field – rather it is a compendium of those sources, research projects and experiences that have led us to this point in time. We hope, in this way, that this book acts as a starting point and the issues raised and the links between them will evolve over time. We also believe that small business researchers may find the book to be useful as a means by which they can frame their own research. Although the book is not intended to be read directly by small business practitioners (it is a bit too long and *heavy* in some content to fill that purpose), we have put together a set of lessons or tenets that may be applied by consultants or researchers to small businesses when advising them of their Web presence practices.

This book is *not* about virtual businesses – those small businesses that rely entirely on their Internet presence. It is for those small businesses that have a 'physical' presence (even if it is at home) and are looking to supplement this with a Web presence. Some of the concepts in this book can be applied to virtual businesses, but for a more complete coverage of the issues associated with virtual businesses, readers could do worse than take a look at Burn et al (2001). What types of online activities are we targeting in the book? Chaffey et al (2003) provides some useful classifications for the different types of commercial online activities that can occur. Our book is predominantly aimed at those businesses that are looking to support their *business-to-consumer* (or B2C) activities with their online presence. We are not concerned with *business-to-business* (B2B) activities (which mainly relate to the use of the Internet for supply side transactions, such as purchases of raw materials). Also, we are not concerned about *consumer-to-consumer* (C2C) activities (such as online auction sites that allows consumers to sell personal items to each other) – except where these have implications and possibilities for B2C activities in small businesses.

The interest in small business use of the Internet is not just restricted to small businesses themselves. It is becoming increasingly difficult to find literature related to the general ICTs in small businesses. In a literature review related to the use of ICTs by rural businesses, Galloway and Mochrie (2005) suggested that studies related to the use of Internet-based and 'other' networked technologies in small businesses are more prevalent than those involving other ICTs.

It is generally accepted that the rate of adoption of ICTs in small businesses is lower than that of larger businesses (Deakins et al 2004). Although it has also been recognised that higher proportions of larger businesses adopt the Internet than their smaller counterparts, the gap is narrowing. In fact, Internet penetration rates for medium sized businesses almost match those of larger businesses in most OECD countries (well over 90%). However, small businesses generally have a slightly lower penetration rate (Barba-Sánchez et al 2007).

The comparison between large and small businesses can be directly related to the human and financial resources that they have available to devote to the use of ICTs. Often there is a greater need for small businesses to search for ICT expertise from outside the business – as the resources are often not available internally. Historically, small business applications of ICTs have tended to be targeted at administrative or operational processes rather than longer-term strategic applications. Also, delays in the adoption of ICT generally have been related to a lack of appreciation by small businesses of the benefits that they can offer (Corso et al 2001).

Lockett et al (2006) suggest that basic applications like email and Internet access are now ubiquitous in small businesses. In a study of small businesses in the Northern region of the UK, Maguire et al (2007) discovered that there were more networked PCs than standalone PCs. In fact, an increasing number of small businesses are connecting their computers into networks, which allows them to improve their communication and information sharing capabilities, in addition to their raw computing power (Barba-Sánchez et al 2007).

Whilst *cost reduction* was the primary reason given for employing ICTs in Maguire et al's study (2007), it was also recognised that ICTs could be used to *improve products and services*. There was also some evidence of strategic ICTs applications, predominantly in the areas of forecasting sales and customer analysis. The traditional barriers to ICT use were identified (lack of time, lack of skills and shortage of skilled staff). Back in 2002, one of the authors (Burgess 2002) edited a book targeting the use of ICTs by small business. A theme throughout that book was that the same barriers to the use of ICTs that are listed existed then (and in previous years) and that these translated to small business use of electronic commerce.

In Australia, a study by Sensis (2007) revealed that a much higher proportion of medium-sized businesses (87%) possessed a Website than small businesses (51%). Metropolitan businesses (57%) also had a higher proportion of Websites than rural businesses (43%). Nearly two-thirds of SMEs suggested that their Website had increased business effectiveness, with small businesses (66%) representing a slightly higher proportion than medium sized businesses here (58%). The most popular reasons given for increased business effectiveness were that the Website:

- Generated more business (16%)
- Provided more exposure (13%)
- Resulted in more enquiries (13%)
- Allowed people to get information (12%)
- Provided easy access to information (11%).

The reader will note that one of the things that we repeatedly mention in the book is the need for small businesses to take a systematic approach to their presence on the Internet and to take the time out to understand the possibilities that are offered and match these to their business objectives and strategy.

The bottom line is that we feel the time is right for a book like this. The Internet and the Web presence, in particular, are becoming key aspects of small business operations. There is enough evidence to tell us that not many small businesses get it completely right, and that some do not get it right at all.

In the next section we each talk individually about what led us to write this book and a little about the experience of writing it.

SPECIFIC VIEWS

Stephen Burgess

I have been conducting research into small business use of ICTs for almost 13 years now and on their use of the Internet for about a decade. I suppose it still amazes me that with the increased attention by governments and communities worldwide on the importance of small businesses to their economies that a set of standards for small business use of ICTs has not emerged. We know the importance of small business – making up over 90% of all businesses (depending upon how you define them) and around half of the private workforce employees around the world. When we think about the importance that is placed on the ICT resource in larger businesses – with accepted practices in systems design, database design, network integration, ICT infrastructure and information architecture having been around for a long time – it seems amazing to me that very little of this has been translated down into the small business arena. Of course, not all of the practices employed in large businesses can be applied to small businesses – but some can be and we try to look at some of these in this book.

Of course, the book is specifically devoted to the small business Web presence, but that Web presence often relies on a small business having already adopted some ICTs (to access the online environment). This is where we were able to draw a parallel with larger businesses – which are used to having ICT infrastructure in place that can be used to support other business projects that use those ICTs. We also draw on some large business expertise when we refer to areas such as governance, business continuity and security.

In fact, one of things that surprised me when compiling this book was how much I had to rely on areas I had come across during my career that *were not* associated with small business and ICT research. My seven years as a cost accountant helped to form part of the content of the Web presence evaluation chapter. My years as an information systems lecturer helped to inform the content in other areas of the book.

What I expected when we initially decided to put this book together was that we would collaborate by drawing together the lessons we had learned during our (many) combined years of small business research. This has occurred, but what also happened was that as we went along we found a number of gaps that needed to be filled – where there was not a lot of research or that logically had to be included. A classic example of this is the chapter on governance. Initially, this was going to be a chapter on security and privacy issues that related to small business use of the Internet. As we were developing it (as a matter of fact, when I was writing about something as simple as backup procedures), it struck me that we cannot talk about those issues without mentioning the idea of business continuity. I had already co-authored a contribution to Standards Australia that had discussed business continuity in small businesses, so it seemed a natural to include business continuity as an area for small businesses to consider. After that, it was also a natural inclusion to talk about all of these topics under the general banner of business governance.

What I have found whilst putting together this book was that it not only gave me an avenue to bring together various disparate research studies involving small businesses that I have been involved with over the years (which I *was* expecting), it has also enabled me to place each of these in context with each other. In short, I have been able to achieve some idea of how the research that I have already conducted *fits in* to the overall picture of where I would like it to be and what I would eventually like my research to contribute.

I have previously been involved in editing and co-editing a few books in the area of small business and ICT research and also involved in co-authoring a few local textbooks (used predominantly in Australia). Thus, I thought that I had some idea of the requirements of this book and the effort that would be involved. In reality, this entire process has been more challenging, more time consuming and infinitely more enjoyable than I could ever had imagined. The cooperation of my co-authors, with whom I had worked quite a bit in the past, has made this task much easier.

Stan Karanasios

I have been conducting research into small business for four years. My main area of interest has been the adoption and use of ICT by small businesses in the context of developing countries. Recently, I have completed a PhD that set out to understand ICT adoption from the perspective of small businesses in the developing world. This involved interacting with small business owners in South East Asia and South America and provided a number of insightful experiences that have contributed to this book. Researching small businesses and ICTs from the perspective of the developing world is largely an under researched area but one that still provides a number of general lessons for small business owners worldwide. When investigating small businesses in countries where there is unreliable and inadequate telecommunications infrastructure, the cost of technology is high and an unstable political environment exists; a characteristic of many small business owners is that they manage to overcome these limitations and still make use of ICTs. Having said this, one conclusion from studying ICTs and small businesses in the context of countries such as Malaysia and Ecuador is that there are significant benefits to be potentially attained by small businesses. Just some of these are enhanced access to markets, increased sales/booking and cost savings on marketing and communication. One such example that stands out is the story of a small business in a remote mountainous region that set up a satellite dish to access the Internet and engage customers.

Further experience with small businesses and the use of ICTs came from studies within Australia that examined small business in the outer suburbs of a major city and tourism enterprises across various states. These studies showed that most small businesses have a long way to go before they can claim to operate a truly successful Web presence. One recurrent theme in these studies is that small business owners lack the necessary know-how to plan, develop and market a successful Web presence. Indeed, even though statistics suggest that roughly half of all small businesses in Australia have developed a Website and even more have adopted ICTs in the business in the same shape or form, there are large numbers of small businesses that have tried and failed to develop a Web presence and others may have a Web presence but have not enjoyed any benefit from it. From this standpoint, this book is useful for both small businesses without a Website but also for many small businesses that need adopt a holistic approach to working through the creation of a successful Web presence. Even without a crystal ball, one can predict that the Web will continue to grow in its dominance in business across the globe and that businesses without a successful Web presence will be amongst those that are likely to suffer.

In my contributions to this book, I have attempted to express much of the knowledge that I have gained from these studies in the hope of providing a somewhat global perspective. Examples from the authors in this study crisscross much of the world, and by doing so provide a relevant and extensive overview of developing a Web presence.

My view is that there are a number of different ways that a small business may approach the development of a Web presence. This is dependant on a number of decisive factors such as what the business wishes to achieve, its products and its customers. This book is useful because it merges the different elements of creating a Web presence and provides rigorous, yet flexible, guidelines for small businesses to plan the development of a Web presence.

Carmine Sellitto

My exposure to the small business area has predominately occurred in the last eight years. The first study that allowed me to develop a familiarity and understanding of small business entities was an examination of the workings of the Australian wine industry and their use of Internet technology. The Australian wine industry has been a global success story, having undergone a renaissance over the last twenty years – success that is typically linked to the leadership and innovative characteristics of the high number of small business operators that compose the industry. Much of the findings of this study that related to Internet technology were premised on how the early adopters of the technology were able to provide exemplary examples of best practice in the use of e-mail marketing, Web presence and e-business.

Further understanding of small business characteristics occurred through a study that examined the adoption of ICTs by a group of small rural medical practitioners. This study was made possible through an Australian Research Council (ARC) grant and explored Internet and ICT use by doctors from a socio-technical perspective. One of the interesting approaches of the study was to consider medical practices and their operators (the doctors) to be analogous to small business entities – a classification position that is not commonly encountered in the health literature. Indeed, medical practices do not like to be referred to as businesses, but consider themselves as health providers, with business activities having little to do with patient treatment. Consequently, the study had an unusual, but justifiable approach to investigating this group. The study postulated that many ICT applications and products, although having been developed to support doctors in various aspects of their work, were being reluctantly used. Seemingly, many of the typical challenges associated with ICT adoption that had been highlighted in the mainstream small business literature appeared to also be applicable in the small medical practice environment.

My experience and familiarity with small business entities was further strengthened through another government-sponsored study that was associated with home-based business activity. Indeed, the home-based business sector constitutes a significant proportion of the overall small business population – a population group that is prevalent in many countries. Indeed, the recent growth in home-based business activity has been fuelled by a number of factors, including rapid improvements in communication and information technology, downsizing in public and private organizations and a tendency by larger organizations to outsource non-core activities. Arguably, operating a small business from home offers lower overheads and start-up costs and the opportunity to balance work and family life more congenially. Moreover, at all levels of governments there is an increasing level of recognition of the important contribution that home-based businesses make to the economic and social development of an area – albeit urban, regional or rural.

Another set of studies that has also reinforced my understanding of the small business area has been the investigation of small to medium sized tourism enterprises (SMTEs) and their adoption of Internet technology. SMTEs are a set of important operators that can contribute significantly to a country's overall export income and prosperity. One of these tourism studies examined Web-based e-commerce with respect to SMTE business-to-business and business-to-consumer activities in both urban and regional localities. The study documented the relationship between small tourist-oriented businesses and their Website development practices. More precisely, various Website adoption and implementation processes, as well as the technical constraints to the uptake of Websites by managers of SMTEs, was recorded. An important finding showed that Website progression was not linear but typically proceeded in a stop-start manner, such that SMTEs developed different trajectories towards their Web presences.

My collective experience and involvement in these studies has confirmed to me that small businesses entities have their own peculiar needs and characteristics when it comes to ICT adoption, technology use and ongoing skills acquisition. This is even more pertinent in the Internet environment where the easy implementation of Website sales and marketing features can greatly assist all small operators with increasing their profitability. In contributing to this book, I have attempted to convey much of the knowledge that I have gained from the numerous studies I have been associated with that have exposed me to the small business environment. Invariably, many of the examples or passages I have contributed have tried to reflect some of the good or best practices activities associated with Web presence – activities that tend to reflect adaptable, efficient and strategic options that have been previously used. I am a great admirer of the capacity, resilience and innovative thinking of many small business operators and believe that these values assist many smaller operators to navigate the complexity of the ICT area – an area that is rapidly evolving and impacting on business activities.

ORGANISATION OF THE BOOK

We have specifically divided this book into a number of different sections. Figure 1 represents the basic structure of the book, with most chapters being represented there. The diagram will be discussed at length in Chapter II, but for now it will suffice to say that a small business needs to understand how ready it is to adopt a Web presence ('readiness') and then perform a business analysis to see how it is situated. After this it can consider the various aspects of its activities that relate to establishing and maintaining a Web presence.

Figure 1. Basic structure of the book

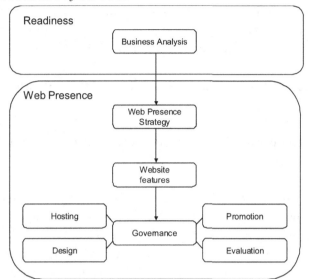

Section I: Setting the Scene

Chapter I: Introduction. In this chapter. we discuss some definitions of small business and decide upon one that we feel is suitable for this book. We then examine a few different models and frameworks, tools and even books that have been prepared to assist small businesses set up a Website. This list is not comprehensive (that would be impossible), but we believe it does serve to highlight the gap that we are attempting to fill with this book.

An important part of this chapter is that we briefly discuss a number of different research projects – examining small business use of ICTs and the Internet – we have conducted over the years. Throughout the book we refer back to these studies as examples of the points we are trying to illustrate, illustrating 'best practice' examples of what we are suggesting or, perhaps more importantly, deficiencies that we have recognised in the use of the Internet by small businesses. One of the possible limitations of this approach is that although some of our studies have been international, they have mostly been based around the Australasian region. To reduce the chance of a 'localised' view being the only view that we present, we have selected a number of international studies that we also highlight throughout the book.

Chapter II: Web Presence Lessons for Small Businesses. In this chapter we present the tenets (lessons) presented in the body of the book, as well as the lessons from earlier studies that we have conducted and others that we have reported. The idea of the chapter is to present the tenets in a manner that might be attractive to small business owner/ managers, useful to small business consultants and serve as a means for small business researchers to frame their research.

Section II: Readiness, Business Aims and Planning

This section of the book is made up of two chapters and addresses what we believe to be an important part of the process that small businesses should follow when setting up a Web presence.

Chapter III: Readiness for a Web Presence. We begin this chapter by discussing what we mean by 'Web presence'. At this early stage it is important to note that we believe that in these times a small business Web presence can typically involve more than just a Website. More on that in the chapter! We then look at some of the main barriers and drivers of ICT adoption. We then move on to examine the notion of the 'readiness' of small businesses to set up a Web presence. This is particularly important for those small businesses that have difficulty accessing the Internet. We will also examine previous studies that have examined adoption of ICTs in small businesses, for the purpose of identifying those drivers and barriers that can affect small business wishing to go down that path.

Chapter IV: Business Strategy and Planning. This chapter builds on the notion of 'readiness' identified in Chapter II to examine how a small business might prepare itself for a Web presence. We believe that small business operators/ managers should know their strategic business direction before they consider establishing a Web presence. We begin the chapter by introducing some basic business theory, discussing some well-known business strategies that have involved ICT use and how to match these to business aims. We then discuss how a business might investigate its own competitive position for the purposes of identifying a Web presence strategy.

Section III: Web Presence Implementation and Evaluation

This is the section of the book that relates to how small businesses, having determined their business strategy and competitive position, can actually determine what they want from the Web presence and how they can achieve it. As such, there are quite a variety of topics in this section of the book, from more business strategy and processes (Chapters V, VIII, and X), some technical issues (Chapters VI and VII) and a chapter that bridges both (Chapter IX).

Chapter V: Web Presence Strategy and Content. This chapter discusses how a small business decides upon it Web presence strategy and then determines what features will make up the content of its Web presence. The Web presence strategy is considered after the overall business strategy has been determined. The chapter and its associated appendix provide a useful checklist of the typical types of features that can make up a small business Web presence and how these can be linked back the Web presence strategy.

Chapter VI: Web Presence Hosting. In this chapter, we examine and elaborate on the diversity of options available to the small business operator when hosting their Web presence – hosting options that can impact Websites' features. Arguably, the appropriate use of Web hosting services has evolved to the point where they are an integral part of the Web presence experience for the small business operator. Topics in this chapter include the selection of Internet Service Providers; considerations for hosting, building and maintaining a Website; and hosting content externally from the small business Websites (such as on Web portals – or, as we call it, 'the extended Web').

Chapter VII: Website Design. This is the most technical of the chapters in this book. It is centered on Website design and is the only chapter in the book where we refer solely to the small business *Website* rather than *Web presence.* In the previous chapter we discussed how a small business, once it decides to have a Website, needs to decide where it will be hosted, how it will be built and how its content will be initially loaded and then maintained. Website design is considered at the time of building the Website and then again at any major redesign of the Website.

Chapter VIII: Web Presence Promotion. In this chapter, we discuss how small businesses can approach the task of promoting their Web presence. We discuss different approaches to online promotion and how these might be linked with traditional approaches to promotion. An important tenet from this chapter is that it is usually appropriate for small businesses to select a mix of different approaches to its Web presence promotion strategy.

Chapter IX: Web Presence Governance. We start this chapter by discussing corporate governance – perhaps considered by some to be an unusual topic for small businesses. However, there are some aspects of governance that can be applied to small business, such as business ethics and an awareness of cultural diversity. Another issue is business continuity – how a small business might continue in existence if an unexpected event occurs. Again, the idea of business continuity planning might seem a topic reserved for larger businesses – but some of the principles involved in business continuity planning and 'good' governance translate well to the small business situation. This especially the case when considering what happens to suppliers, competitors and employees if there is a problem with the Web presence, how sensitive information is kept secure over the Web presence and how the privacy of this information is maintained on the Web presence. In discussing these issues, it is necessary to talk about the use of ICTs in general in the business, not just its Web presence.

Chapter X: Evaluating Web Presence Success. This chapter examines the notion of how the success of a small business Web presence can be assessed. In doing so, there is initially a discussion of how a small business should classify its ICT expenses and attempt to match them with associated revenues. After this, the discussion moves to establishing the notion of 'success' in relation to the Web presence and considers different approaches to determining this.

Section IV: Epilogue

Chapter XI: A Look into the future. This chapter serves to raise an awareness of some of the more cutting edge Internet innovations and applications that may become viable and useful to the small business operator in future. The chapter focuses on some of the new and emerging forms of technologies that the authors have identified as potentially affecting the Web presence.

Appendix: What Led us Here?

This section tells the story of what led us to the organisation of the chapters behind the book. Throughout the book we have referred to literature from others and the results of our own research projects as we have discussed each topic.

However, one thing that we have not really discussed is how we ended up with the order of the chapters as they have emerged. The appendix provides a brief overview of each of our PhDs – all of which involved research into small business adoption and use of ICT and Internet technologies. In effect, we felt that this chapter might provide some insights into how this book has evolved and the way that the various chapters have been ordered.

Stephen Burgess, Carmine Sellitto, Stan Karanasios
August 2008

REFERENCES

Barba-Sánchez, V., del Pilar Martínez-Ruiz, M., & Jiménez-Zarco, A.I. (2007). Drivers, Benefits and Challenges of ICT Adoption by Small and Medium Sized Enterprises (SMEs): A Literature Review. *Problems & Perspectives in Management, 5*(1), 103-114.

Burgess, S. (2002). Information Technology in Small Business: Issues and Challenges. In S. Burgess (Ed.), *Information Technology in Small Business: Challenges and Solutions* (pp. 1-17). Hershey, PA, USA: Idea Group Publishing.

Burn, J., Marshall, P., & Barnett, M. (2002). *e-Business Strategies for Virtual Organizations.* UK: Butterworth-Heinemann.

Chaffey, D., Ellis-Chadwick, F., Johnston, K., & Mayer, R. (2006). *Internet Marketing: Strategy, Implementation and Practice* (3rd ed.). UK: Financial Times/ Prentice Hall.

Corso, M., Martini, A., Paolucci, E., & Pellegrini, L. (2001). Information and Communication Technologies in Product Innovation within SMEs – The Role of Product Complexity. *Enterprise & Innovation Management Studies, 2*(1), 35-48.

Deakins, D., Mochrie, R. & Galloway, L. (2004). Rural business use of information and communications technologies (ICTs): A study of the relative impact of collective activity in rural Scotland. *Strategic Change, 13*(3), 139-150.

Galloway, L. & Mochrie, R. (2005). The use of ICT in rural firms: a policy-orientated literature review. *Info, 7*(3), 33-46.

Lockett, N., Brown, D.H., & Kaewkitipong, L. (2006). The Use of Hosted Enterprise Applications by SMEs: A Dual Market and User Perspective. *Electronic Markets, 16*(1), 85-96.

Maguire, S., Koh, S.C.L., & Magrys, A. (2007). The adoption of e-business and knowledge management in SMEs. *Benchmarking: An International Journal, 14*(1).

Section I
Setting the Scene

Chapter I
Introduction

PREAMBLE

Over the last decade there has been a great deal of research into the use of Information and Communication Technologies (ICTs) in small businesses. More recently, this research has centred on the use of Internet technologies in small businesses, particularly their use of Websites for the purposes of 'e-business' or 'e-commerce'. Much of this research has examined the adoption of these technologies, including the drivers and barriers that small businesses face. Other studies have investigated models or frameworks that might help to guide small businesses to take full advantage of these technologies, particularly Websites for the purpose of conducting e-business. A great deal of this research has been admirable in that it has contributed to the body of work available in the area. Simultaneously, there has been a body of research that has focused on specific aspects of establishing a Website. These aspects can be technical in nature, addressing issues such as how to design a Website or how to identify hosting options, or business orientated, involving the identification of aspects of Website promotion and publishing. However, given the diversity of research being reported, we feel that there is a major gap in that small businesses are left without guidance in relation to how to approach *all aspects* of setting up and maintaining their Websites. The components are out there, but there is little available in relation to how a small business might access these, or even piece them all together. In fact, a little further on in this book we will suggest that these days, with the presence of many of Web services such as portals available, a small business Web presence may be even more than just a Website.

Copyright © 2009, IGI Global, distributing in print or electronic forms without written permission of IGI Global is prohibited.

THIS BOOK

In this book we will cover the major areas that a small business needs to address to be able to appropriately establish and maintaining its Web presence. The book also provides a structured approach for small businesses that leads them through the process of:

- Determining their business strategy and the commensurate alignment of this strategy with their Web presence.
- Deciding what Website features are required according to their Web presence strategy.
- Determining how best to host the Web presence, and if required, how to design a Website for maximum effectiveness.
- Understanding some governance and technical (for instance, security) aspects related to the Web presence.
- Knowing how to promote the Web presence.
- Understanding the importance of evaluating their Web presence.

Most of the chapters in this book outline some background in relation to each of these areas, as well as the results of our own, and others', small business research. More importantly, we summarise the chapters' salient points in a series of *tenets* to guide small businesses through each part of the process. The following section provides some background for material in the rest of the book.

Small Business Definitions

One of the authors published an edited book (Burgess 2002) that examined the challenges facing small businesses in their use of ICTs. At the time the observation was made that it was extremely difficult to compare and contrast different small business studies that had been carried out over time due to the varying definitions of 'small business' encountered around the world.

In 2003, the IRMA Special Research Cluster on Small Business and Information Technology examined the notion of a universal definition for small business amongst its members. Definitions for the terms 'micro business', 'small business', 'medium-sized business' and 'small and medium sized business' were found to differ amongst respondents from around the world (Australia, New Zealand, North America and Europe were involved in the investigation). Definitions tended to focus on the number of people employed by a business as a primary grouping metric, however, some countries also took into account a hybrid approach to categorising

Copyright © 2009, IGI Global, distributing in print or electronic forms without written permission of IGI Global is prohibited.

businesses using not only the number of employees but also the assets owned and annual turnover.

In this book we have a preference for using the number of employees, as it is easier to ask businesses for that information when conducting studies.

A limitation of only using employee numbers is that we end up classifying some highly successful businesses, with very large turnovers and a small number of employees, as small businesses. We are not overly concerned about this more inclusive definition, as perhaps those businesses will not be seeing a need to look at a book like this anyway!

So, what do we mean by the term small business? In the following definitions we use the number of 'regular' employees – a 'regular' employee being someone that works more than 15 hours per week on a regular basis with the business.

A **micro business** is any business with one to five regular employees.

A **small business** is any business with one to 20 regular employees. This obviously includes micro businesses

A **medium-sized** business is any business with 21-50 regular employees.

Therefore, a **small to medium sized enterprise** (SME) is any business with 1-50 regular employees.

SMALL BUSINESS WEB PRESENCE

The reason that we have written this book is that we see a significant gap in relation to how small businesses may be assisted to use the Internet and set up their Web presence effectively. Much of the research that has been published is really only of use for medium-sized businesses (the 'M' in 'SME' if you like), is not detailed enough to be effectively used by small businesses or points to areas of future research that may eventually lead to some practical outcomes.

There are many published models that document how a 'typical' small business might build its Website over time. Some of these are known as 'staged' Website development models. The idea behind these is that the development process of a Website is argued to be progressive: where the early stages of the Web presence are typified by a simple 'brochure' type Website, whilst later stages provide small businesses with advanced Website features such as enhanced publishing opportunities, improved business promotion and interactive after sales support. At the final stage, Website complexity is typically reflected by having online customer order/payment

Copyright © 2009, IGI Global, distributing in print or electronic forms without written permission of IGI Global is prohibited.

processes that can mature to become fully integrated with 'back office' systems. This actually means that the Website operations are fully integrated into the computer systems of a business, such as its customer and products databases.

We will now provide look at some of these typical staged models. Rao et al (2003) have proposed a model reflecting electronic commerce development by small and medium sized enterprises (refer Figure 1). The model is characterised by four stages:

- **Presence:** This provides for a basic 'brochureware' site. Communication is therefore 'one way' from the business to the user.
- **Portals:** This level introduces 'two way' communication via order placement and building customer profiles through communications (such as product feedback and surveys).
- **Transactions integration:** Online financial transactions are introduced. This may be facilitated by the presence of virtual communities set up around areas of common interest – encouraging online marketplaces.
- **Enterprises integration:** This is where the business processes of an organisa- tion are completely integrated with the online business so that they are virtu- ally indistinguishable, usually requiring high levels of collaboration between business partners.

For each stage of their model, Rao et al (2003) have identified a number of barri- ers and facilitators that assist the business to decide if it is logical to move to a later stage in the process. We have found that this model has been useful as a reference point for some of our previous work (some of which is described later in this chap-

Figure 1. SME e-commerce development model (adapted from Rao et al 2003)

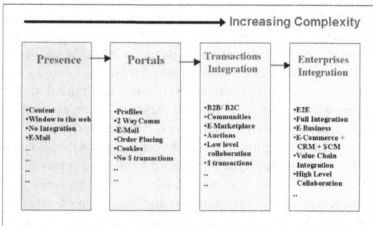

Copyright © 2009, IGI Global, distributing in print or electronic forms without written permission of IGI Global is prohibited.

ter) as it assisted in determining the particular stage of Website implementation a small business is at by examining its Website features.

Another example of a staged model is that proposed by Burgess and Cooper (2001), a Web adoption model that has been applied to various Australian industries such as tourism and metal manufacturing (This model was referred to as the '3Ps' model in Burgess et al (2005) and is used here to represent the collective stages of Website adoption). The 3Ps model proposes that Websites have three stages with appropriate content associated with each stage. The model contains the following stages:

- **Promotion stage:** This is an information stage that involves the Website detailing business contact details and providing product and/or service information that promotes the business on the Web.
- **Provision stage:** This stage adds functionality to a Website and adds features such as a catalogue or price list (not linked to a database), support for the customer in the form of frequently asked questions (FAQs) and internal site links that add value for a visitor to the site. Industry-specific information content is incorporated at this stage.
- **Processing stage:** This is the transaction phase of Website evolution and involves online ordering, processing and payment activities associated with business products or services.

Although the delineation between 'stages' in these examples is different, the similarity of approaches (from basic to advanced Websites) is obvious in both. An important point to note about these models is that they do not specifically address individual Website content, nor the strategic decisions associate with including spe-

Figure 2. Web adoption '3Ps' model (adapted from Burgess and Cooper 2001)

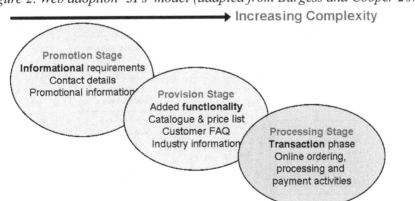

Copyright © 2009, IGI Global, distributing in print or electronic forms without written permission of IGI Global is prohibited.

cific Website material and features. These are two aspects that are important to the introduction and development of Web presence that we will address in this book.

There is some criticism of staged models. Levy and Powell (2003) assert that 'stages of growth' models for development of a business' Web presence may not hold and that few small businesses even go beyond the early stages of Website development. Alonso Mendo and Fitzgerald (2006) support this assertion and suggest that many small business Websites can remain in a 'dormant' state for months or even years. Martin and Matlay (2001) refer to these types of models as 'linear' models and also argue that they may be too simplistic due to the great diversity that small businesses exhibit - this diversity being associated with different types of business size, economic activity, location, resource availability and level of ICT adoption.

From our research, where we have matched our findings to some of these models, we have concluded that most small businesses tend to start conservatively and rarely move beyond a simplistic Web presence (the early stages of these adoption models). One important point that we will be making is that this may not necessarily be a bad thing! The level of sophistication of the Web presence needs to be related to the overall business strategy – where the business is situated and where it trying to get to.

Figure 3. Conceptual model of e-business development (adapted from Fillis et al 2004)

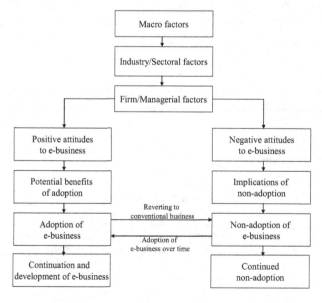

Copyright © 2009, IGI Global, distributing in print or electronic forms without written permission of IGI Global is prohibited.

More Integrated Models

Recently, Fillis et al (2004) proposed a conceptual model designed to help understand why some smaller businesses implement and develop e-business activities and others do not. Their model considers a range of internal and external factors that may impinge on attitudes to e-business and the implementation (or not) of an e-business strategy. Figure 3 depicts a simplified version of the model. Initially, the business is affected by factors such as government policy and globalisation, then industry factors. Within this environment, factors such as the size of the business, the types of products or services they offer and the set of business competencies within the business will influence either positive or negative attitudes to e-business and eventual adoption or non-adoption. The model recognises that an adopter may choose to revert back to conventional business processes, or a non-adopter may eventually become an adopter of e-business.

Chaston and Mangles (2002) propose a model to support and deliver an e-commerce marketing strategy. This is represented in Figure 4.

Decisions in this model are based on the hierarchy, with financial and operational competencies being determined by the strategic positioning options chosen by management.

Figure 4. A qualitative model of competencies to support and deliver an e-commerce marketing strategy (adapted from Chaston and Mangles 2002)

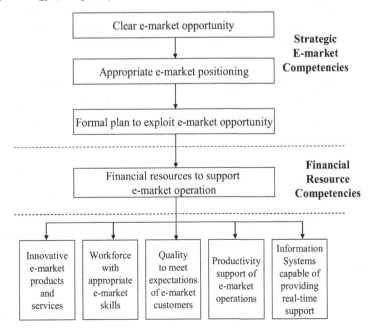

Copyright © 2009, IGI Global, distributing in print or electronic forms without written permission of IGI Global is prohibited.

Strategic Competence

Chaston and Mangles (2002) draw on the work of Ghosh (1998) who has proposed four strategic marketing opportunities for the Internet:

- Establishing a direct link with customers to complete transactions or exchange information more easily
- Bypass others in the value chain (for instance, use the Website to sell direct to customers)
- Develop and deliver new products and services
- Become a dominant online player by changing the business rules.

Financial Resource Competence

The business must be able to fund the level of investment required to support their online marketing strategy. This includes having appropriate systems, having the resources to update the Website, ensuring appropriate integration with existing business systems and ensuring that the Website is promoted at a level to attract visitors.

Operational Competencies

Once the strategy has been determined and the finances allocated, Chaston and Mangles (2002) suggest that the business needs to examine new ways of improving their Internet products and processes. Furthermore, a business should also ensure that its workforce is skilled to carry out the online plans, has a high level of quality in relation to products and services, and that an efficient customer service in relation to logistics is provided (as customers can more easily switch to other suppliers).

In testing their model, Chaston and Mangles (2002) came up with a number of recommendations, beyond marketing activities, for small businesses with an online presence. Some of these recommendations are to:

- Identify an online marketing niche
- Develop a formal-business plan to guide e-commerce operations
- Have sufficient financial resources to fund the plan
- Be innovative in the development of new products around the Internet
- Manage online service quality effectively
- Support employees by skilling them for e-commerce operations.

Copyright © 2009, IGI Global, distributing in print or electronic forms without written permission of IGI Global is prohibited.

An important component of these types of models is that they recognise that small businesses need to be aware of the environment that they are in and plan effectively for their Web presence. What is lacking in the models is some idea of *how* to achieve this once the business gets beyond the planning stage. Further examples of models that provide useful background for this book are described in Chapters III and IV.

OTHER TOOLS FOR SMALL BUSINESS

There are various information resources available to the small business operator when they wish to examine the progression or enhancement of their Web presence. These sources can include government-based publications, Web hosting services that provide information to support their products, and the traditionally published small business 'strategy' books that include a section on the benefits of having the Internet. Collectively, all these resources can be viewed as providing a valuable set of information for small business operators, assisting them with decision-making about aspects of their Web presence. Indeed, many of these third party entities provide reliable and relevant information, with some highlighting case study findings. We now will examine some examples of the types of Web presence advice or information provided by these third party entities.

Government Support

The following examples of government information support for adopting or improving small business Web presence are drawn from the United Kingdom, Australia and Canada.

Figure 5. The DTI e-adoption ladder (adapted from DTI 2002)

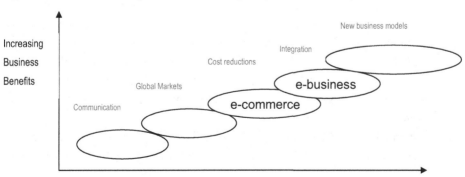

Copyright © 2009, IGI Global, distributing in print or electronic forms without written permission of IGI Global is prohibited.

United Kingdom

The United Kingdom Department of Trade and Industry (DTI) proposed an e-business adoption ladder that could be used to classify small and medium sized (SME) entities based on their degree of Internet use and business adaptability (Note: The DTI has been replaced by the Department for Business, Enterprise and Regulatory Reform).

The ladder (refer Figure 5) is similar to the various other staged adoption models and identifies the various complexities of Website and ICT adoption. The small business use of e-business and ICTs and the benefits derived are a guide that allows the business to be classified with respect to complexity and sophistication. The ladder does not address small business planning or strategic approach when it comes to having a Web presence. Indeed, there is a fundamental assumption that the small business will expand and move through these sophistication stages progressively, which (we have found) may not be the case.

Business Link (UK)

Another UK based government organisation that provides administrative support and practical advice for enterprises is Business Link (http://www.businesslink.gov. uk). Business Link is primarily supported by the United Kingdom's Department for Business, Enterprise and Regulatory Reform and offers a myriad of advice that ranges from starting up and growing a business, employing people, legal/taxation regulations and health and safety issues. Two areas that the Business Link resource provides informational support for when it comes to undertaking business online is advising on developing a Website and adopting e-commerce. With respect to developing a Website the support advice and information that is presented addresses issues associated with:

- **Best practice of Web design:** Information and advice is provided that specifies the design issues that need to be considered in order to implemented a Website. These issues embrace aspects of Website planning, technical considerations, design, navigation and designing for users.
- **The Business Website:** This uses a question and answer tool to allow a business to determine whether a Website is appropriate to implement, and whether it will increase customer access. Website content can be mapped to current business products and services.
- **Maintaining content and technology:** This provides a guide to the key phases associated with implementing a Website, including the requirement for

Copyright © 2009, IGI Global, distributing in print or electronic forms without written permission of IGI Global is prohibited.

integration with 'back-office' systems (typically existing business database systems), together with advice on the ongoing maintenance tasks that need to be undertaken with having a Website.

- **Online transactions with government:** This again uses a form of interactive question and answer tool to identify the Web-based government transaction services that can be useful for UK businesses.
- **Website hosting options:** This elaborates on the Web server issues, maintenance of files, reliability and domain name selection that is associated with the business using a hosting service to manage its Website.

Business Link also advises on the e-commerce aspects of being online. With respect to e-commerce, some of the support information addresses the following issues:

- **Planning and implementing an e-commerce solution:** The key issues that need to be examined when establishing e-commerce as part of the business are addressed.
- **Online orders and payments:** Elaborates on the online payment feature and the functionality associated with the customer delivery process after an online purchase has been made.
- **Security and legal considerations:** Advice is given on the regulations that need to be adhered to when examining e-commerce. Information is also provided on security aspects of electronic sales and ordering in the online environment.
- **Electronic marketing:** Provides advice on developing an electronic marketing plan and the associated benefits that can benefit not only for the business, but also existing and prospective customers.

The UK's Business Link information resource is primarily aimed at UK based smaller businesses and is professional, informative and comprehensive - and should be highly prized by the business user. However, some of the advice and information that is provided can be argued as being aimed at medium size enterprises, or for a business that wishes to grow - the assumption being that the business has relatively unlimited resources and deep pockets to achieve this. This is not necessarily typical of the environmental conditions that the smaller business operates in. Future business strategy or the identification of internal or external resources requirements does not appear to be directly advised on. The initial adoption or progressive diversification of a small business Web presence is partially depended on the availability of existing and future technological skills as well as management leadership - an issue that does not appear to be overtly highlighted.

Copyright © 2009, IGI Global, distributing in print or electronic forms without written permission of IGI Global is prohibited.

Australia

Australia's Department of Communications, Information Technology and the Arts (DCITA), in an endeavour to encourage small businesses to move to the online environment, has suggested a six-stage guide in promoting e-business and Website development (DCITA 2004). The six functional stages are simple, but instructive in addressing e-business issues, with the stages being:

- **Understanding:** An informative stage that expands on e-business jargon and the perceived benefits of being online. The informational source provides the small business with answers to fundamental questions such as what is e-business and what are the benefits? It also elaborates on issues associated with online trust and getting started with e-business.
- **Planning:** An instructive stage in identifying the correct level of online involvement a business should have, as well as how to research and plan the move to the Internet environment. This functional stage provides information that assists the small business to decide which one of five modes of e-business it can adopt or evolve to. These modes have a close resemblance to many of the staged adoption models that have been proposed, making the fundamental assumption that progression is linear. Modes include:
  - o **Participating:** The business simply participates in the online world (e-mail and Internet activities with no Web presence).
  - o **Supporting:** A Website is used to promote and support existing business activities.
  - o **Expanding:** The Website becomes important in allowing the business to generate new activities and growth.
  - o **Assimilating:** The business's online activities become dependant on offline activities (move to business backend integration)
  - o **Transformed:** Web presence and internet technology alters the fundamental nature of the business and the manner in which it operates.
- **Building:** Examines the business requirements relating to Website implementation, and addresses issues associated with design, marketing, e-commerce functionality and user-requirements.
- **Protecting:** Introduces the security facets of doing business online and the issues that need to be considered.
- **Managing:** The e-business venture, just like other business functions, needs to be managed appropriately allowing for maintenance, budgeting, control and strategic application.
- **Improving:** Attempts to enhance the online experience for the business by addressing the evolving and changing functional value of the adopted technology.

Copyright © 2009, IGI Global, distributing in print or electronic forms without written permission of IGI Global is prohibited.

The e-business guide also provides very good support for small business through cases studies and an interactive question and answer checklist. There is an inference that through exploring case studies and the checklist that small businesses will be will be able to determine their e-business requirements that will allow them to adopt and/or enhance their own Web presence. Arguably, the strategic information or approaches identified may not allow all small businesses to evaluate ICT readiness, technology resources and operational skills requirements associated with a successful Web presence.

Canada

Industry Canada

The Canadian Government, through the Industry Canada Department, is an important resource for small business with respect to promoting e-business activities. Industry Canada maintains an easy-to-use Website (*ebiz.enable*) directly aimed at assisting small and medium-sized enterprises to make informed decisions about e-business issues. The *ebiz.enable* Website can be found at http://www.ic.gc.ca/epic/site/ee-ef.nsf/en/home (Industry Canada 2007).

The Website is one of the better information resources aimed at small to medium size business entities. It provides a step through set of questions and answers or lessons based on e-business adoption. Four critical areas of e-business are examined and contain both general as well as specific information. The information for small business addresses:

- The characteristics on an e-business (What is e-Business?). The type of information provided for small businesses addresses issues associated with the online environment, the expected trends of e-business, benefits and return on investment (RIO).
- The increase opportunities available to small business in the Web environment. There is a focus on functional areas such as customer relationship management (CRM), competitive intelligence, human resources management and product distribution.
- Implementation of Web presence (e-business implementation). Issues such as security, privacy, technology and the legal aspects of a Web presence are addressed in this section. Website design and content are embraced under a technology section.
- E-business strategy. Identifies some of the approaches that a small business needs to consider in the online environment. Business preparedness for Web presence needs to be assessed as well as undertaking industry-wide and com-

Copyright © 2009, IGI Global, distributing in print or electronic forms without written permission of IGI Global is prohibited.

petitor investigations. Advice on project teams and performance evaluation are also covered.

Industry Canada's *ebiz.enable* information resource for business is vast and informative. If there were to be any criticism of the *ebiz.enable* site it would be that it might be overwhelming for the small business entity to explore. Arguably, some of the topics covered are aimed at medium size enterprises or presume that a small business wishes to expand - and if so, in a linear fashion. Moreover, there is an expectation that the business will have the resources in the form of money, skills and employees that allows these types activities to be undertaken (which may not necessarily be the case).

Web Hosting Services

Web hosting services tend to be a necessary requirement for the small business owner when it comes to implementing and maintaining their Web presence. Web hosting services as part of their product development and marketing will generally attempt to provide relevant and timely information to the business operator, assisting them with online related decision-making issues. An example of a professional and typical Web hosting service that provides small business information is the company WebCentral.

WebCentral

WebCental is a large Australian Web hosting service that aims at providing cost-effective Web presence solution for both large and small businesses - the WebCental homepage can be found at http://www.Webcentral.com.au/ (WebCentral 2007). The company indicates that it provides services with proposed solutions aimed at:

- The government or corporate sector that may wish to outsource some of its online activities,
- Large enterprises that require assistance with reducing risk and costs that may be associated with some of the important applications,
- Other third party IT consultants that could utilise the WebCentral services to buttress their own products or indeed, act as re-sellers and
- The small business operator, where WebCentral provides important information that addresses issues such as the selection of the business's primary domain name, Website hosting options, e-mail services and the growing importance of e-mail marketing. These hosting features aimed at small business are briefly summarised in Table 1.

Copyright © 2009, IGI Global, distributing in print or electronic forms without written permission of IGI Global is prohibited.

Table 1. Summary of features offered by WebCentral

Hosting feature	Advice and Information offered
Domain name selection	The company offers advice and background on the appropriate selection of a domain name that reflects a company's identity in the web environment. Indeed, the selection of the domain name is an important element in being able to establish a web presence.
Website hosting	A broad range of website hosting plans are offered based on the perceived needs of the small business. These plans range from the entry level economy plan that allows a small business to have a basic and static website, through to a high-powered solution that is able to withstand significant website visitor traffic, is database enabled and provides for the smaller business that requires the use of online applications.
E-mail	Small businesses are able to source e-mail services that range from a basic solution through to high volume premium services. This type of service is also packaged with WebCentral's products assist the small business to alleviate the 'junk mail' component associated with having a business e-mail account.
E-mail marketing	E-mail marketing has become popular in recent time, especially when practiced with the use of permission. WebCentral allows the small business to access affordable and template e-mail communication forms such as newsletters, surveys, invitations and special offers.

The types of services that WebCentral provides small business are commonly encountered and offered by various other hosting services in different countries. Arguably, these services assume that the small business has undertaken an examination of business requirements and the strategy that underpins their move to having a Web presence. This may not be so and although hosting services do provided an important resource for small businesses to use and access, there is an apparent gap between the small business requirements analysis with respect to understanding its level of readiness, strategy, the availability of skills and investment return when it comes to being able to select the most appropriate solution offered by hosting services.

Popular Small Business Management Books

Popular small business management books have in recent times, commenced to incorporate a section that deals with electronic business and marketing - further complementing the advice that these books have traditionally conveyed. One best seller of this type that is now in its 10th edition is the book titled *How to Organize & Operate a Small Business in Australia* by John English (2006). There will be comparable publications on small business of this type in other countries that will also enjoy similar popularity by providing advice and information based on local

Copyright © 2009, IGI Global, distributing in print or electronic forms without written permission of IGI Global is prohibited.

conditions and knowledge. The book in this instance serves as a useful resource in illustrating the type of Web information that is typically available to small businesses.

English (2006) provides most information for small businesses under the heading of Internet marketing - a common approach that is used by other writers and one that can reflect a popular business area in which the technology is employed. The books total coverage to small business adoption and use of the Internet is 11 pages - from a total number of 337 pages.

The advice and information provided by the book is broad and informative. The various areas covered include:

- **Studying other Websites:** Advice is offered on examining the Websites of other business to identify appropriate content, images, navigation and usability issues. There are numerous questions proposed that assists the small business operator on how they should address and undertake these tasks.
- **Designing the business site:** A series of topics are explored with information provided on marketing strategy for the Website, determining what the site should achieve, and implementing the Website. Ancillary areas covered include domain name registration (explained later), security and Website design issues.
- **Selecting a Web hosting services:** Advice and information is provided on the various options associated with selecting a hosting services and the features that a small business should consider.
- **Moving to e-business:** This refers to the Australian government's DCITA six-stage guide in promoting e-business and Website. No new information is provided, but the DCITA resource is championed as a resource that can be used to support small business e-business.

English (2006) also advises on the various methods that small businesses can use to promote their Website. Advice is provided on the way a Website can be use to promote the company message to target audience in order to improve Website visitor traffic. Part of the suggested promotional methods includes:

- Registration with search engines and directories
- Banner Advertisements
- Links to other Websites
- Online promotions through e-mail listings, user groups and e-newsletters
- Off line promotion through tradition publication media and business stationery

Copyright © 2009, IGI Global, distributing in print or electronic forms without written permission of IGI Global is prohibited.

English's book is an excellent source for the small business operator to gain an introduction to aspects of Web presence. However, given the complexities associated with being online, various important issues including Internet readiness, small business tools for evaluating strategy in the Web environment, resource availability that impacts on Website implementation, the availability of skills to deal with being part of the online community and salient aspects of Web design are either not commented on, or are superficially explained. But then, in 11 pages the book was not going to be comprehensive in addressing all the aspects associated with small business use of the online environment.

How this Book Fills the Gap in Understanding Small Business Web Presence

Various information forms and resources are available to the small business operator when considering their Web presence. These resource are valuable, and informative - some more so that others. The information provided by the various government Websites examined appears to be broad and inclusive, with some sites providing interactive tools or checklists for the small business operator to use. Arguably, the size and volume of information provided on government sites can pose a challenge for the small business operator when trying to identify a specific element of information. Some information provided by governments is aimed at medium size enterprises or presumes that a small business wishes to expand - and if so, in a linear fashion.

Hosting service sites such as WebCentral provide important and relevant information to support many of their products that are used by the online community. Moreover, these services have evolved to the point where they are an integral part of the Web presence experience for the small business operator. Given the highly valuable resources they provide for small businesses, there is an assumption that issues such as readiness, strategy and the availability of internal and external resources have been addressed. This may not be necessarily the case and as such the hosting service may omit or gloss over this small business requirement when it comes to the Web presence.

Other resources that can be accessed by small businesses, providing them with information on their Web presence are the numerous management books that include Internet information. English's (2006) book was used as an example of how such information can be structured to provide an important overview of the various online-related issues. English's publication may be typical of many other small business books around the world that deal with the Internet in this manner. Arguably, the eleven pages that address the Internet issues in English's book are concise, clearly written and informative. However, they need further expansion.

Copyright © 2009, IGI Global, distributing in print or electronic forms without written permission of IGI Global is prohibited.

The section does not address adequately issues including small business Internet readiness, strategy in the Web environment, resource availability, skills to deal with being part of the online community and salient aspects of Web design.

Clearly, many of the previously mentioned information resources are valuable to the small business community. However, given the diversity of small business research being reported, as well as the volume of information that has been published, we feel that there is a major gap in that small businesses are left without guidance in relation to how to approach *all aspects* of establishing and maintaining their Web presence. The information component on small business Web presence exists in the general milieu of small business books, government publications and host service support. However, the authors contend that these information elements are disparate and difficult to pinpoint by small business operators that are resource poor. This book interlinks those elements in one publication and makes an important contribution to the small business literature associated with understanding Web presence.

OUR PREVIOUS STUDIES

As mentioned earlier, this book will include references to previous small business research carried out by the authors. The purpose of this section is to introduce readers to studies we have undertaken over the past few years. Most of the studies have been researched in Australia, but some of our work does have an international focus. The studies fall into three major categories, those that have involved interviews with small businesses, those that have involved surveys of small businesses and those have involved the analysis of small business Websites. We will now provide a brief introduction to each study, as well as references to where further information about the studies can be found.

Interviews with Small Businesses

Accountant_07

This project was interesting in that the study involved the analysis of the Websites of small Australian accounting practices as well as some interviews with accounting personnel. The study was funded by the Institute of Chartered Accountants in Australia (ICAA). The overall aim of the study was to report on the use and potential applicability of Internet services amongst Australian accounting practices. Using the ICAA's member database, a random sample of 100 practices with existing Websites was constituted. Their Websites were then evaluated as to their content.

Copyright © 2009, IGI Global, distributing in print or electronic forms without written permission of IGI Global is prohibited.

From these results, a stratified sample of 20 practices was identified to participate in in-depth interviews - this sample represented firms across the various stages of Website development. The selected interviewees were also representative of firms at various stages of development of online business processes. The face-to-face interviews were used to collect in-depth data to identify key issues that could define the drivers or barriers associated with a Web-based practice model. The interviews were carried out early in 2007. Details of the study can be found in Burgess, Breen and Quiazon (2007).

Winery_case_06

The case study method was used to detail the motivations for Internet adoption as well as to document an understanding of how e-business allowed one particular small business to sell 70% of its wine via direct online sales - a technique that used e-mail permission marketing in tandem with Website ordering. The case study provides an exemplary example of how other small wineries that experience high product demand can use the Internet for direct sales activities. Furthermore, the study identified winery business characteristics - profitability, direct sale channels and product demand that were directly associated with Internet adoption. Details of the study can be found in Sellitto (2006).

Outer_06

This study was predominantly scoping in nature and was conducted by the authors in conjunction with the Centre for Community Networking Research at Monash University in 2006. The study was centered on two outer-suburban areas in Melbourne (Australia) and was used to identify how small businesses and community-based organisations (CBOs) build capacity for their use of information and communications technologies (ICTs). Interviews were conducted with 18 home based/ micro businesses and 14 CBOs. Details of the study can be found in Karanasios et al (2006).

Develop_06

This research PhD examined the use of the Internet amongst small tourism enterprises in Malaysia and Ecuador. The objective was to take into account the perspectives of metropolitan, regional and remote tourism operators. The study involved field research and discussions with the 26 tourism operators. As a result of the study an e-commerce framework was developed for small tourism enterprises in developing countries to assist them with making decisions concerning e-commerce. It was

Copyright © 2009, IGI Global, distributing in print or electronic forms without written permission of IGI Global is prohibited.

found that even though tourism operators face many challenges to adopting and using the Internet (such as inadequate and reliable infrastructure, cost of using the technology and lack of knowledge and skills) many found ways to overcome these obstacles and successfully adopt and use the Internet. Details of the study can be found at Karanasios and Burgess (2006/7).

Tourism_04

This project was sponsored and funded by the Australian Sustainable Tourism Co-operative Research Centre (STCRC). The project involved researchers from three Australian universities. The major objective was to systematically explore the nature and extent to which small and medium sized tourism enterprises are currently online in order to determine how they benefit from online technologies. Focused interviews afforded information on four different types of tourism businesses in two major categories: Accommodation (bed and breakfast establishments and backpacker lodgings) and Attractions (local tour operators and museums/galleries). There was also a concerted effort to collect data from urban areas (Sydney and Melbourne – capital cities of States of Australia) and one rural area (Bendigo, a town in the state of Victoria approximately 300 kilometres from Melbourne). The majority of the interviews were mainly carried out between October-December 2004. In all, 59 interviews were conducted and the study focussed on businesses with Websites. Details of the study can be found in Davidson, Burgess and Sellitto (2006).

APEC_02

This was a unique study, sponsored by the Asia Pacific Economic Cooperation (APEC) and was conducted in 2002. The purpose of the study was to examine six small and micro businesses in the APEC region to promote discussion and under-standing of the barriers, enablers and needs of SMEs involved in intra-regional trade and investment, particularly in relation to technological (especially e-commerce), financial and regulatory factors. Interviews were conducted with one small busi-ness in each of six APEC countries. Details of the study can be found in Breen et al (2004).

Studies Involving Surveys of Small Businesses

Wineries_survey_05

This research identified an emergent tourism focus associated with winery Websites. The Australian wine industry has been a recent global success story and wineries

Copyright © 2009, IGI Global, distributing in print or electronic forms without written permission of IGI Global is prohibited.

appear to have adopted the Website as part of an integral strategy surrounding tourism. The study captured winery owner's perceptions of how they view the benefits and features of their Websites. Winery Website adoption was found to be above the small business national average, with a high degree of features associated with tourism and direct marketing. Moreover, important competitor-to-competitor links were found on a notable number of sites in an endeavor to promote multi-winery cellar door visits. The study is significant in that it is one of the few emerging academic works dealing with the relatively new and important global industry associated with wine tourism. Details of the study can be found in Sellitto (2005).

Wineries_PhDsurvey_04

This research PhD investigated Internet adoption by small to medium size (SME) wineries and developed an e-business best practice model based on the experiences and perceptions of a group of early Internet adopting wineries. In an age were numerous generic e-business models have been proposed, very few are industry specific - indeed, the industry specific e-business practices from this research have informed Australian wineries with respect to their Internet adoption strategies. Details of the study can be found in Sellitto (2004a).

Wineries_survey_04

This project was a national study that examined Internet adoption by 225 small Australian wineries. Findings indicate that this technology has been widely embraced by the industry and that numerous perceived benefits, especially associated with e-mail marketing, are being achieved. The study identified that many wineries collected e-mail addresses for marketing purposes, whilst many engage in a high degree of direct marketing using the e-mail medium to distribute newsletters. Smaller wineries appear to be the main proponents in using the Internet, the study concluding that this group achieved the highest proportion of Website sales. A link was established between small wineries that had a high use of e-mail permission marketing and increased Website sales. Details of the study can be found in Sellitto (2004b).

Studies Involving the Analysis of Small Business Websites

Accountant_analysis_07

This study has already been discussed, as it involved both an analysis of accounting practice Websites and interviews within accounting practices. The Website analysis

Copyright © 2009, IGI Global, distributing in print or electronic forms without written permission of IGI Global is prohibited.

component involved examining the Websites of 100 accounting practices. Details of the study can be found in Burgess, Breen and Quiazon (2007).

Wineries_analysis_07

The focus of this project was on the acquisition phase associated with Website newsletter marketing. This direct marketing approach has received renewed interest from various firms and is one premised on potential customers opting to receive a marketing newsletter usually via the Website. A research evaluation framework was used to explore a set of small business Websites within an industry group that has traditionally used direct marketing as a primary sales channel. Results of this exploratory study found that individually and collectively many small businesses scored poorly in this important area of their Website e-marketing strategy. Details of the study can be found in Sellitto (2007).

CBO_analysis_06

Many community-based organisations (CBO) can be categorised as small businesses. This study examines the Websites of different categories of CBOs. It was decided to review the content of the Websites of metropolitan and rural CBOs in Victoria, a southern State of Australia. Victoria provides an interesting mix of areas, with the second largest city in Australia (Melbourne), as well as rural and (some) remote regions in a relatively small State. In all, the Websites of 45 CBOs were analysed in late 2006. Details of the study can be found in Burgess and Bingley (2007).

Micro_analysis_06

This study is unique in that it examines the changes in Website content of micro businesses in Australia, Canada and the UK over a number of years. The study draws from the work of Alonso Mendo and Fitzgerald (2006) to examine changes in micro business Website features using their proposed multi-dimensional framework as a classification system. In mid 2006 the researchers re-evaluated 39 Websites that had been examined in previous studies. Details of the study can be found at Burgess, Bingley and Sellitto (2007).

Winery_analysis_02

This was another study that examined how the content of Websites changed over a period of time. In this instance, the Websites of 76 wineries (58 of which were

Copyright © 2009, IGI Global, distributing in print or electronic forms without written permission of IGI Global is prohibited.

small wineries) were examined in 2000 and again in 2002. Details of the study can be found in Burgess, Sellitto and Wenn (2005).

OTHER INTERNATIONAL STUDIES

As mentioned in the Preface, one of the possible limitations of the use of own research to provide practical examples of what we are describing in each chapter, as well as reinforcing the concepts we are presenting, is that although some of our studies have been international, they have mostly been based in Australia. To reduce the chance of a 'localised' view being the only view that we present, we have selected a number of international studies that we also highlight throughout the book to reinforce our arguments. These studies are sourced from a variety of countries, including Hong Kong, Mexico, New Zealand, South Africa, Switzerland, Taiwan, the United Kingdom and the United States.

CONCLUSION

This chapter has introduced the idea behind the development of this book. The chapter commenced with a discussion of the difficulties faced in even examining small business research as there are a number of different definitions of small business in the literature. After this there was an examination of some of the models that have been proposed for small business Website development, with the limitations of these models discussed. Different providers of small business advice were discussed to show that none of them really provide a total Web presence solution for small businesses. Finally, we introduced a brief description of our own small business research, as this provides the basis for many of the examples of small business Web presence that we provide in the book.

REFERENCES

Alonso Mendo, F. & Fitzgerald, G. (2006). A multidimensional framework for SME e-business progression. *Journal of Enterprise Information Management, 18*(6), 678-696.

Breen, J., Bergin-Seers, S., Burgess, S., Campbell, G., Mahmood, M., & Sims, R. (2004). Formulating Policy on E-Commerce and Trade for SMEs in the Asia Pacific Region: An APEC study. In N. Al-Qirim & B. Corbitt (Eds.), *e-Business, e-Govern-*

Copyright © 2009, IGI Global, distributing in print or electronic forms without written permission of IGI Global is prohibited.

ment & Small and Medium-Size Enterprises: Opportunities and Challenges (pp. 134-155). Hershey, PA: Idea Group Publishing.

Burgess, L. & Cooper, J. (2001). The Adoption of the Web as a Marketing Tool by Regional Tourism Associations (RTAs) in Australia. In G. Finnie, D. Cecez-Kecmanovic, & B. Lo (Eds.) *Proceedings of the Twelfth Australian Conference on Information Systems (ACIS)* (pp. 67-72) Coffs Harbour, NSW, Australia.

Burgess, S. (2003). *A Definition for Small Business?*, IRMA Special Research Cluster - Small Business and IT (Victoria University), Melbourne, Australia.

Burgess, S. (Ed.) (2002). *Managing Information Technology in Small Business: Challenges and Solutions.* Hershey, PA: Idea Group Publishing.

Burgess, S. & Bingley, S. (2007). One size does not fit all: Website Content of Australian Community Based Organisations. In F.B. Tan, J. Thong, & L.J. Janczewski. *Pacific Asia Conference on Information Systems (PACIS).* Auckland, New Zealand.

Burgess, S., Bingley, S. & Sellitto, C. (2007). A Model for Website Content Decisions in Micro Businesses. In D, Kantarelis (ed.), *Global Business & Economics Anthology, Volume 1* (pp. 474-487). Worcester, MA: B&ESI.

Burgess, S., Breen, J. & Quiazon, R. (2009). Business to Consumer E-Services: Australian Accounting Practices and their Websites. *International Journal of E-Services and Mobile Applications, 1*(1), 38-51.

Burgess, S., Sellitto, C. & Wenn, A. (2005). Maturity in the Websites of Australian wineries: a study of varying Website content. *International Journal of Electronic Business, 3*(5), 473-490.

Chaston, I. & Mangles, T. (2002). E-commerce in Small UK Manufacturing Firms: A Pilot Study on Internal Competencies. *Journal of Marketing Management, 18*(3/4), 341-360.

Davidson, A., Burgess, S. & Sellitto, C. (2006). An Investigation of SMTE Web Site Usage in Australia: Implications for E-Commerce Adoption and Planning Processes. In N. Al-Qirim (ed.), *Global Electronic Business Research: Opportunities and Directions* (pp. 88-113). Hershey, PA: Idea Group Publishing.

DCITA (2004). *e-businessguide: An Australian Business Guide for Doing Business online.* Canberra: Department of Communications, Information Technology and the Arts (DCITA).

DTI (2004). *Business in the Information Age – International Benchmarking Study, Department of Trade and Industry.* London: Department of Trade and Industry.

Copyright © 2009, IGI Global, distributing in print or electronic forms without written permission of IGI Global is prohibited.

Retrieved 12/11/2007 from http://www.businesslink.gov.uk/Growth_and_Innovation_files/ibs2004.pdf.

DTI (2002). *Business in the Information Age – International Benchmarking Study, Department of Trade and Industry.* London: Department of Trade and Industry.

English, J. (2006). *How to Organise & Operate a Small Business in Australia* (10th ed.). Crows Nest, NSW: Allen & Unwin.

Fillis, I., Johansson, U., & Wagner, B. (2004). Factors impacting on e-business adoption and development in the smaller firm. *International Journal of Entrepreneurial Behaviour & Research, 10*(3), 178-191.

Ghosh, S. (1998). Making Business Sense of the Internet. *Harvard Business Review, 76*(2), 126-135.

Industry Canada. (2007). *ebiz.enable - Where to Start.* Retrieved 12/11/2007 from http://www.ic.gc.ca/epic/site/ee-ef.nsf/en/home.

Karanasios, S., Sellitto, C., Burgess, S., Johanson, G., Schauder, D., & Denison, T. (2006). The role of the Internet in building capacity: small businesses and community based organisations in Australia. Paper presented at 7th Working for E-Business Conference, Victoria University, Melbourne, Australia.

Levy, M. & Powell, P. (2003). Exploring SME Internet Adoption: Towards a Contingent Model. *Electronic Markets, 13*(2).

Martin, L.M. & Matlay, H. (2001). "Blanket" approaches to promoting ICT in small firms: some lessons from the DTI ladder adoption model in the UK. *Internet Research, 11*(5), 399-410.

Rao, S.S., Metts, G. & Monge, C.A.M. (2003). Electronic commerce development in small and medium sized enterprises: A stage model and its implications, *Business Process Management Journal, 9*(1), 11-32.

Sellitto, C. (2007). Online Direct marketing: A study of the subscription stage associated with winery e-Brochures. In P. Shackleton (ed.), *Proceedings of the 8th International We-B (Working for e-Business) Conference (CD-ROM)* (pp. 1-12), ECRU, Victoria University, Australia.

Sellitto, C. (2006). E-Commerce Experiences of an Early Internet Adopting Australian Winery: A Case Study. In S. Krishnamurthy & P. Isaias (Eds.), *Proceedings of the International Association for Development of the Information Society (IADIS) e-commerce Conference 2006* (pp. 199-206). Barcelona: IADIS Press.

Copyright © 2009, IGI Global, distributing in print or electronic forms without written permission of IGI Global is prohibited.

Sellitto, C. (2005). A Study of Emerging Tourism Features Associated with Australian Winery Websites. *Journal of Information Technology and Tourism, 7*(3/4), 157-170.

Sellitto, C. (2004). *Innovation and Internet Adoption in SME Wineries: An e-Business Best Practice Model*, School of Information Technology, RMIT University.

Sellitto, C. (2004). Internet Adoption by Australian Wineries: Perceived Benefits and Direct Marketing Practices. *International Journal of Wine Marketing, 16*(3), 58-72.

WebCentral. (2007). Retrieved: 16/11/2007 from http://www.Webcentral.com.au/Websitehosting.php.

Copyright © 2009, IGI Global, distributing in print or electronic forms without written permission of IGI Global is prohibited.

Chapter II
Web Presence Lessons for Small Businesses

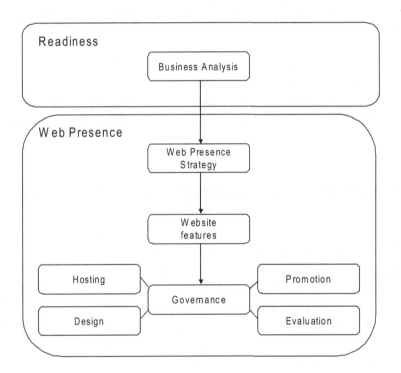

INTRODUCTION

Whilst writing this book it has become apparent to us that small businesses face numerous challenges and issues when they are considering their Web presence. In fact, although we thought we had the organisation of the book determined before we started, we found that it was necessary to not only increase the number of

Copyright © 2009, IGI Global, distributing in print or electronic forms without written permission of IGI Global is prohibited.

chapters, but also reorganise planned chapters. We believe this has allowed a more detailed explanation of the important issues that are investigated and explored in the book.

So, let's be honest with ourselves here. How many small business owner/managers are going to have the time to carefully sit down and work through all of the tenets that we have suggested in later chapters – whilst understanding the background (presented in this book) behind them? We believe that if they did they would benefit greatly from their investment of time. Alas, time is one resource that is limited in small businesses. In addition, in this chapter small business researchers are presented with a more concise summary of the lessons for setting up and maintaining a small business presence that have emerged during the writing of this book.

The purpose of this chapter, therefore, is to present the tenets from the book, as well as the lessons from ours and other studies, in a manner that might be more informative for small business owner/managers to consider - indeed, a Web presence primer for small business operators.

In the following sections we introduce the factors that small businesses should consider when setting up and maintaining their Web presence. Specific detail in relation to each of the areas is provided in the chapters in Parts Two and Three of the book. We will commence with a discussion of whether the small business is in a position to adopt a Web presence.

AT THE START: WEB PRESENCE READINESS

There are a number of reasons as to why a small business may not be ready to set up a Web presence. Small business owner/managers need to be aware of the various issues associated with organisational readiness for a Web presence. Performing a readiness assessment will assist businesses to address the barriers and opportunities relevant to adopting a Web presence and allow them to determine their most appropriate Web presence strategy. Armed with such knowledge, small businesses will be better positioned to engage in the process of analysing, developing and managing their Web presence.

Our own studies highlighted the importance of three major factors that can affect the e-readiness of a small business:

- *The outside environment.* This mainly revolves around whether there is suitable infrastructure available to set up a Web presence. It is not uncommon for there to be unreliable, slow or even no infrastructure in many developing countries or rural areas of developed countries.
- *The organisational environment.* Our studies showed the importance of organisational readiness, particularly in relation to having suitable technol-

Copyright © 2009, IGI Global, distributing in print or electronic forms without written permission of IGI Global is prohibited.

ogy already in place, but also the importance that the existing technology is compatible with any planned Web presence.

- *Characteristics of the owner/manager.* We revisit the importance of the owner/manager to the Web presence a number of times throughout the book. It is not uncommon for the drive of the owner/manager to be a key factor that leads to the eventual success of the Web presence initiative.

What the Small Business Needs to Think About

The following questions should be relatively easy for a small business to consider. Many of them provide a yes/ no type answer to support or inhibit the idea of the small business establishing a Web presence.

Factors External to the Business

Do Customers use the Internet?

If the answer here is no then a Web presence may not be relevant, unless the business wants to access new markets. If customers are using the Internet then the key question is what do they demand from a Web presence?

Do Competitors have a Web Presence?

If competitors do not have a Web presence then an opportunity exists to differentiate the business from them. Where competitors are online, it is important to understand what they are offering through their Web presence.

Do Suppliers and Trading Partners Demand a Web Presence?

Small business may need to interact with their existing and future trading partners through maintaining a Web presence. This issue of electronic engagement with industry partners and suppliers can be an obligatory requirement for many small business operators if they wish to maintain their existing/future relationships with these entities. Although not a focus of the book, it is still worth mentioning this here.

Are there government support policies and initiatives to assist in the development of a Web presence?

If the answer here is yes, then the key question is how can these help where a business is deficient in other areas?

Copyright © 2009, IGI Global, distributing in print or electronic forms without written permission of IGI Global is prohibited.

Is the Necessary Physical Infrastructure in Place?

In many locations this will not be a problem. However it is useful to be aware of the situation before adopting a Web presence. Even where it is a problem it is worth remembering that a business does not necessarily need to have access to the Internet from within the business to have a Web presence (although it does help!).

Factors internal to the business

Business Offerings

Are the product and services offered and overall strategy suited to the Web? If the answer is yes then the question is how can the Web presence be used to promote and/or sell products? If the answer is no, then changes to the businesses strategy may need to be made in order to facilitate a Web presence.

Skills Within the Business

Are there relevant skills and knowledge amongst employees to maintain the Web presence? If yes, the business is in a good position to develop and maintain the Web presence. If the answer is no then the business may need to offer training to employees or source expertise in other ways.

Capital

Is there sufficient capital to build and maintain the Web presence? If the answer here is yes, then again the business is in a relatively good position to adopt a Web presence. If the answer is no the business may need to consider developing a low cost Web presence, then once benefits materialize develop the Web presence accordingly

Top Level Support

Is the owner/manager prepared to provide the necessary investment of commitment, time and resources? This is the most important factor. If the answer here is yes then the business is in the best position to launch a Web presence

Existing Systems

Is there a need to integrate existing systems due to changed business processes? The Web presence should alter the dynamic workings of various small business activities

Copyright © 2009, IGI Global, distributing in print or electronic forms without written permission of IGI Global is prohibited.

(sales, ordering, marketing, and so forth). The small business operator needs to be aware that Web presence will most likely require some form of computer systems integration in order for the business to maximise its benefits.

After consideration of all of these factors and the decision that a Web presence is worth pursuing, the business needs to consider its business strategy (if it has not already done so).

BUSINESS STRATEGY AND PLANNING

In this book we highlight on numerous occasions the need for the small business to match its Web presence with its overall business aims and strategy. It is vital for a small business to be aware of where it is positioned in its particular industry before it embarks on a Web presence. To do this it needs to perform a thorough business analysis.

Our own research projects highlighted a range of different approaches by small businesses in varying types of industries and locations to many of the issues related to business strategy and planning. From a strategy viewpoint, simple approaches to having a Web presence, such as 'it is expected of us' or 'we need to have a presence' were reported. Other strategies used as a basis for enacting Web presence allowed cots/time savings, whilst a number of small businesses displayed quite sophisticated strategies, such as those involving co-operation (in developing countries) and co-opetition (or *co-operation with competitors* - in wineries). The importance of *linking* the Web presence strategy and the business strategy was mentioned by only a few small businesses. Consequently, there is a significant potential for many small businesses to improve this aspect of the development of their Web presence.

We also found that the resource constraints associated with small businesses was a common issue that limited the strategic potential opportunities of having a Web presence. For example, in considering the capacity needed to implement and maintain a Web presence within small businesses, our studies reported that many small businesses had employees that were self-taught, or they relied on building the firm's expertise from informal networks. Some businesses, accounting practices in particular, were quite prepared to source their professional Web requirements externally - if this expertise was not readily available within the business. In relation to limited finances, not enough small businesses considered the costs associated with setting up and maintaining the Web presence. In relation to considering external influences, the small businesses in our studies were more likely to consider what their customers wanted from their Web presence rather than examine what their competitors were doing.

Copyright © 2009, IGI Global, distributing in print or electronic forms without written permission of IGI Global is prohibited.

What the Small Business Needs to Think About

As with issues associated with e-readiness, the small business needs to consider both external and internal business factors when examining the inter-relationship between its Web presence and general business strategy. This means that the business needs to conduct a thorough business investigation – a SWOT (strengths; opportunities; threats; weaknesses) analysis is ideal in small the business environment—covering those internal and external factors that affect, or are affected by, the Web presence. Many of the factors listed in the next section do tend to overlap with the e-readiness area, however they still need to be considered also under the domain of business planning and strategy.

Factors Internal to the Business

Overall Business Strategy

The small business Web presence should be aligned with clearly defined business aims that may be embraced - low cost; differentiation of offerings; growth; alliance; co-opetition – or even lifestyle. A starting point is for the business to determine which strategies it wishes to adopt for its business. For instance, a business adopting a growth strategy might be keener to pursue aggressive Web presence strategies to access new markets. A business where lifestyle is an important focus might be more inclined to be more conservative.

Capital

What financial resources does the business have available to devote to the Web presence? Resources will be needed to cover set up costs and the ongoing maintenance of the Web presence.

Investment Appraisal

It is important to carry out an investment appraisal to determine if the project is worth pursuing. The appraisal needs to consider setup and ongoing costs and benefits and consider non-quantifiable factors as well. Benefits should be commensurate with the overall business and Web presence strategy.

Copyright © 2009, IGI Global, distributing in print or electronic forms without written permission of IGI Global is prohibited.

Capacity

What skills are available within the business? Are they relevant and accessible for building and maintaining the Web presence? The business may need to source ICT expertise externally. A balance will be required between levels of expenditure and ensuring that adequate expertise is sourced.

Products and Services

What types of goods does the business offer? Small businesses need to consider that although physical products can be ordered over the Internet they also have to be delivered. Certain types of goods, such as those having an *informational* component or those that can be *digitised* and downloaded may be more suited to the Internet.

Factors External to the Business

Competitors

Which competitors have a Website? What level of sophistication have they achieved? What is their target market? It is important to examine competitor Websites on a regular basis. The contents of their Websites can be quickly analysed by storing their features in a competitor comparison matrix. Table 1 documents an example of how the Websites of five competitors can be quickly examined.

Furthermore, a small business should think about tracking what its competitors are doing using an automated Website tracking service.

Customers

Do the small business' customers use the Internet? Are they requesting specific Web presence features? What particular features are they looking for?

Alliance

Are there opportunities to partner with other industry organisations to cross-promote products? Further opportunities in this area are examined when Web presence hosting and promotion are discussed.

By now the small business should have an idea of its business strategy and where it is positioned with respect to its available resources, industry-wide strength and how the external influences might impact on its operational environment. The

Copyright © 2009, IGI Global, distributing in print or electronic forms without written permission of IGI Global is prohibited.

Table 1. A Web presence competitor comparison matrix (adapted from Burgess and Schauder 1999)

FEATURE	Competitor					Total	%
	1	2	3	4	5		
BASIC PRODUCT DETAILS							
Product catalogue	1	1	1			3	60
Prices	1	1	1		1	4	80
TRANSACTION DETAILS							
Online Ordering	1		1			2	40
Online Payment	1					1	20
INFORMATION							
About the Business	1	1	1	1	1	5	100
About Trade Shows/ Coming Events	1		1			2	40
Product Support Features							
Frequently Asked Questions	1					1	20
Directions on how to use the product	1	1				2	40
OTHER LINKS							
Other websites of interest	1		1			2	40
Basic Internet Feature Sites	1		1			2	40
Search Engines	1					1	20
CONTACT DETAILS							
E-mail	1		1	1	1	4	80
By Form			1			1	20

next step is to determine its Web presence strategy and decide what Web presence content it needs.

WEB PRESENCE STRATEGY AND CONTENT

The Web presence strategy is considered after the overall business strategy has been determined. As was mentioned in the previous section, the Web presence strategy should reflect and support the business strategy.

What the Small Business Needs to Think About

Figure 1 shows how the business strategy can inform the Website strategy and then assist in the selection of Website features.

Copyright © 2009, IGI Global, distributing in print or electronic forms without written permission of IGI Global is prohibited.

Figure 1. Linking business strategy and the selection of Website features

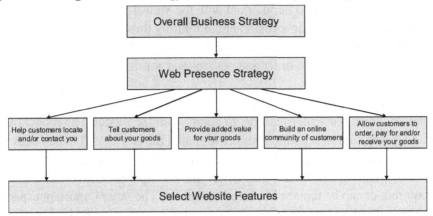

A small business will select different Website features according to the business strategy. Table 2 suggests how a particular Website strategy might be selected to match with a business strategy

In Table 2 we have identified the typical Web presence strategies that we have seen small businesses adopt. In most instances, the businesses adopting a conservative Web presence strategy will investigate ways to use their Web presence so as to improve their operational efficiencies. Typically, they will use the Website to help customers locate them, tell prospective clients about their products/services and in some instances, facilitate the purchase of goods.

The *Strategy/Feature model* (refer Figure 2), aims to ensure that small businesses consider the reasons for implementing particular Website features *at the content level*. Initially, a small business should consider which area of its Website implementation it wishes to enhance:

Table 2. Matching Web presence strategy to business strategy

Web Presence Strategy	Business Strategy		
	Improve Business Efficiency	Add Value to Your Goods	Help to Promote your Business
Help customers to locate and/or contact your business	X		
Tell customers about your goods	X		X
Provide added value for your goods	X	X	X
Build an online community of customers		X	X
Allow customers to order, pay for and/or receive your goods online	X		

Copyright © 2009, IGI Global, distributing in print or electronic forms without written permission of IGI Global is prohibited.

- **Contact:** Allowing customers to find or contact the business
- **Brand:** Attempting to build brand with the Website
- **Community:** Building a customer community through the Website
- **Goods:** Providing details about products and services, supporting them and/or allowing customers to order and perhaps pay for them.

Having determined the area and strategy that the business wishes to target, it can choose which particular features to adopt from the model. The model offers a (limited) selection of possible features to match the strategy - the business still needs to decide which will suit it. It is suggested that businesses review their Website features on a regular basis. They may determine that a particular Website feature is not required, or can be replaced by another feature. The other important aspect of the model is that businesses should choose strategies according to their needs. For instance, some businesses may just require a simple Web presence and not need to delve into the 'community' or 'goods' areas.

One important factor that small businesses need to be constantly aware of is that Website features need to be set up *and* maintained – and this should considered as there are distinct differences between different types of features. Many of these are described in the appendix to Chapter V.

Overall, we were not surprised that our studies showed that small businesses were conservative with their use of Website features. The prime objective of most small business Websites seemed to be to provide information – with features such as location or contact information and general information about the businesses being most prominent. Other features, such as product catalogues and frequently asked questions were also common on certain Websites. There were some examples of advanced features, such as interactive shopping carts, access to password protected areas and reasonably sophisticated membership or mailing lists, but these were not mainstream and were typically restricted to certain types of businesses (for instance, a few wineries and micro manufacturing businesses had interactive shopping features).

Having determined the content that it wants as part of its Web presence, the next decision for the small business to make is to determine how it wants this content hosted.

WEB PRESENCE HOSTING

We know from our own research projects that whilst most small businesses have their Website hosted externally, an increasing number are taking advantage of third

Copyright © 2009, IGI Global, distributing in print or electronic forms without written permission of IGI Global is prohibited.

Figure 2. The strategy/feature model (adapted from Burgess et al 2007)

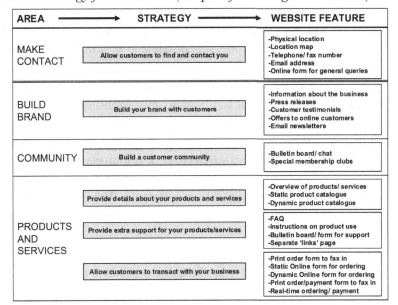

party Websites (such as portals) to supplement their Web presence. In this section we discuss the factors that a small business needs to think about in relation to where its Web presence is hosted.

What the Small Business Needs to Think About

General

Selection of Internet Service Provider

Before anything else, a small business wishing to have a Web presence will need to have an arrangement with an Internet Service Provider (ISP). This is to allow the business to surf the Internet, use e-mail for communication and possibly host their Website. The factors to be taken into account in the selection of ISPs are:

- Cost - be aware of additional traffic charges or charges for extra services
- Performance - speed, traffic limits and so forth.
- E-mail accounts - how many are needed? Can e-mail be accessed remotely?
- Support services/reliability/reputation

Copyright © 2009, IGI Global, distributing in print or electronic forms without written permission of IGI Global is prohibited.

Web Presence

Who will host the Web presence? The business will need to decide who will host its Website – if it decides to have one. It is possible to host the Website within the business (if the resources are available), but it is more common for it to be hosted externally. The business also needs to think about what, if any, features it would like to have hosted externally (that is, not on its own Website).

Who is responsible for content? It is vital to know who is responsible for updating content on the Website. There may be time delays and heavy costs associated with content being updated by an external party. It is important to think about this in advance of setting up the Web presence. Usually the small business will provide the content itself. They may even be able to update the Website themselves.

Small Business Website

There are a number of issues that a small business needs to consider if it decides to have its own Website.

Hosting

External hosting is suitable for most small businesses. This can sometimes be arranged through the selected ISP (and sometimes as part of the overall package). In some of our studies we have found that small businesses are using consultants that specialise in the industry area to host their Website and perhaps even contribute some generic, industry related content (such as online newsletters).

Hosting plans should be analysed in relation to cost, the amount of server space provided, traffic allowances and other services (such as the cost of updating content).

Building

The options available for building a Website are do-it-yourself, get someone else (such as a consultant) to do it or use a package or wizard (which are often provided to set up 'template' driven Websites by an ISP). It is important to keep track of cost, the skills needed to initially implement the site, how content is loaded onto the host server and the degree of difficulty associated with Website updates and modifications.

Copyright © 2009, IGI Global, distributing in print or electronic forms without written permission of IGI Global is prohibited.

The 'Extended' Web

There are an increasing number of small businesses that are having Website features hosted outside of their own Website.

Portals: Third-Party Support Services

External Websites, such as portals or regional directories, could be considered to extend the reach of the online presence further than the small business itself can typically achieve. This is to make the business more visible, or to obtain services that the business might not otherwise be able to adopt (such as online order/booking features and payment facilities).

By now, a small business has an idea of the types of features it wants on its Web presence and where these features will be hosted – on its own Website and/or as part of the 'extended' Web. In the next section we examine the design of the small business Website.

WEBSITE DESIGN

A small business will generally not have much control over the design of third party Websites that is uses to host Website features. In looking at Website design, this section therefore concentrates specifically on the small business' own Website.

What the Small Business Needs to Think About

The technical nature of much of the following discussion means that parts of it may not mean that much to small business operators, especially if they are using an external consultant to design the Website or are bound by a predesigned template. However, even small business operators in these situations can examine this section to see if there are recommendations about usability and accessibility that they can ask their consultants to implement on their Websites. Good practices for Website design for small business should consider the areas of usability, accessibility, markup encoding and the use of metadata. The following sections summarize good practices in each respective area.

Usability

For the small business operator, it is important to be aware of Website usability and the good practices that allow essential features to be incorporated when designing

Copyright © 2009, IGI Global, distributing in print or electronic forms without written permission of IGI Global is prohibited.

a Website. A small business incorporating these features can be confident that they have addressed an implementation issue that is simple to achieve and intrinsic to their Web presence. The features deemed to be essential in Website design when it comes to usability good practices include (Cox et al 2008; Nielsen et al 2000; 2002; 2006):

- Placing the company logo in the top left hand corner of all the Website's pages. The logo should be linked from all pages to return to the home page.
- The search feature is another fundamental Website design element that all users appreciate and expect to find on Websites.
- Search box placement should be positioned on the upper part of the homepage and be located on either the right or left hand side.
- Search box colour should always be white. Variations from white may confuse the user.
- Have an "About the company" page that allows the small business and the people that are responsible for publishing the Website's content to be identified. The feature addresses a trust and credibility element that is associated with online publishing.
- Consumers value their privacy and tend to divulge minimal personal information in the online environment. A privacy policy for any small business that may collect data via their Website is an expected design convention.
- By using relative sizing of text (that is, text sixe that adjust automatically) in the construction of the Website allows page layout to be easily adapted for different screen sizes and browser windows.
- Visited and unvisited links should be easily identifiable to aid Website navigation. The design recommendation associated with Website navigation is to use blue links for unvisited Web pages and a less saturated non-blue colour (historically and by default this has been purple) for unvisited links.
- The Web page 'download' time is still an important Website design issue even with the advent of broadband connectivity. Users tend to not want to wait more than 10 seconds for a page to load into their browser.
- Avoid using 'splash' pages. The Website splash page can be considered to be a visual design feature that aims at embellishing the look of the Website. The splash page contributes very little to the Website's information content.
- Avoid using frames. The advent of frames in the mid 1990s resulted in the breaking of many important user interface design conventions.

Copyright © 2009, IGI Global, distributing in print or electronic forms without written permission of IGI Global is prohibited.

Encoding, Accessibility and Metadata Features

Encoding Markup

A number of groups, such as the W3C (http://www.w3.org/), have been involved in initiatives to develop good practice guidelines for Website development. This includes responsibility for the development of specifications for the Hypertext Markup Language (HTML), which Web browsers use to access the Internet, and its extensions. These days, tools such as Microsoft FrontPage® create HTML code for a Web page as the designer builds the Web page onscreen – so little HTML 'coding' actually occurs.

However, the small business operator should be aware of good practice when it comes to proper use of code to markup the pages on their Websites. The small business manager should be aware of:

- Using XHTML 1.0 specifications as a minimum requirement that is associated with Website implementation.
- Some of the fundamental differences between XHTML and the versions of HTML. XHTML is highly recommended as the coding language of choice.
- The various checking tools that are available for validating Website code to see if it conforms with W3C proposed specifications.

At the very least, the small business should be able to approach its Website developers to determine if they are adhering to these recommendations.

Accessibility

In the interests of equal access to the Web for the disabled, small business owners need to be aware of adopting a Website that addresses accessibility by:

- Adherence to W3C recommended specifications for accessibility (some of these are listed in Chapter VI).
- Using a validation tool that analyses Web pages for their accessibility to people with disabilities (again, refer Chapter VI).
- Achieving the W3C's mandatory priority 1 rating for their Website and ideally aiming at achieving a pass for the W3C's three accessibility priority levels (refer Appendix Two of Chapter VI).

Copyright © 2009, IGI Global, distributing in print or electronic forms without written permission of IGI Global is prohibited.

Metadata

In Web terms, *Metadata* is text entered into the HTML code of a Webpage to help describe the purpose and function of the page. It assists in relation to providing information for ongoing maintenance of the page. It can also help in documenting intrinsic words or terms that may be discovered by search engines. Metadata has an integral function of documenting the important content published on the small business Website. The small business manager should be aware of these good practices:

- The importance of incorporating metadata at the time of creating Website pages. Retrospective incorporation is costly and sometimes difficult. This can be checked with Website design consultants before the Website is built.
- Using a basic level of Dublin Core (DC) element on each Web page of their site in an endeavour to not only record and document important business content, but to also optimise search engine returns (refer Appendix Three of Chapter VI).
- The incorporation of the basic level of DC elements as a minimum expectation for all Web pages with incorporation of the complete level of 15 DC element set being highly desirable.

Again, if its Website is being designed externally a small business should be able to approach its Website design consultant to determine if it adheres to these principles before the Website is built.

Now that the small business has decided how its Website, if it is to have one, will be designed it can start to think about how it can be promoted.

WEB PRESENCE PROMOTION

There are many approaches that small businesses can consider to help to promote their Web presence. We propose that the small business needs to select a variety of approaches to promotion and that it should develop a mix of strategies that will match its overall Web presence strategy – what the business is trying to achieve with its online presence.

One of the highlights of the research projects that we have conducted thus far is that they represent a quite diverse range of approaches used by small businesses to promote their Websites. There were examples of using traditional advertising media to promote the Internet address, direct marketing approaches using e-mail newsletters, intentional selection of domain names that match the business name

Copyright © 2009, IGI Global, distributing in print or electronic forms without written permission of IGI Global is prohibited.

and strategy, consideration of search engine ranking position and the role that third party portals (the 'extended Web') can play in promotion of the business.

What the Small Business Needs to Think About

In this section we list a number of strategies and suggest that the small business can select a range of these to suit.

Strategic

- Where possible, the small business should select appropriate domain name(s) for branding and recognition. These can help someone trying to find the Website to achieve their aim. Website addresses usually revolve around the company name or a well-known product brand name.
- Consider what is needed to rank high on general search engines. In this instance, the selection of appropriate metadata terms can assist with this – or the business can just pay search engines to rank higher in 'sponsored lists' when certain search terms are entered by users.
- Where appropriate, look to partner with third party Websites (such as portals) that have a greater reach or will expose the business to wider markets. Perhaps look to partner with specific third party Websites – by industry (such as accommodation portals) or region.
- Consider the use banner advertisements on other Websites that potential customers might visit to direct them to the business' Website.

Use Traditional Media

- Combine 'online' and 'offline' strategy - put the Website address on letterheads, brochures, packaging and in traditional media advertising.
- Consider running 'cross' promotions – advertising on traditional media, but potential customers enter competitions, or gain further information, online.

Targeted Promotion

- Think of using direct marketing approaches (such as e-newsletters)

Evaluation

On aspect of promotion that is most important is that the small business must be able to evaluate the success of promotional strategies. Thus, it is important to decide upon how each strategy will be assessed before it is implemented.

Copyright © 2009, IGI Global, distributing in print or electronic forms without written permission of IGI Global is prohibited.

Now, let's consider some important governance issues in relation to small business Web presence.

WEB PRESENCE GOVERNANCE

Corporate governance is concerned with improving the performance of a company allowing the commensurate benefits to flow to stakeholders, such as owners and employees. The particular characteristics of small businesses mean that the way they deal with corporate governance issues will be different from those associated with larger businesses. One or two people usually make major decisions in small business, primarily the owner and/or the managers(s) of the business. For them, governance is a combination of the views of the owner and the manner in which the business is run. It reflects the critical steps in the management of the business. We are particularly interested that small business operators view their ICT investments, and in this case their Web presence activities, as a *long term* investment and plan them as a key component of their other business activities.

Business continuity management (BCM) is a management discipline involving the plans that businesses can use to reduce the adverse effects of unexpected events that invariably can lead to business disasters. Such plans involve more than just backing up computer files and databases. They include the management and counseling of employees in the case of a system malfunction; advertising campaigns to inform important suppliers and customers of the implemented recovery protocols that deal with the potential failure of business computing systems. For our purpose, business continuity involves considering the continuation of ICT systems (particularly the Web presence) when unexpected events occur. This includes ensuring backups are in place, employees are not adversely affected and continuity of relationships with suppliers and customers is maintained.

A special part of good governance and business continuity from a Web presence viewpoint is that important and sensitive data is kept secure and private – and that businesses and their employees behave ethically and with cultural sensitivity in relation to dealing with their customers.

Some interesting aspects related these topics have come out of own research projects and those of others. Most small businesses that talked about securing data were aware of the need to develop strategies to manage this. These ranged from setting up secure systems themselves or using third party portals that had these checks and balances already in place. Another strategy was to avoid the *need* for credit card security by only allowing customers to fax credit card details to the business - something that we found to occur with many businesses throughout our studies. Most small businesses that discussed data security did show an awareness

Copyright © 2009, IGI Global, distributing in print or electronic forms without written permission of IGI Global is prohibited.

of the need to have suitable systems in place - with some admitting that they did not have the expertise to manage this. Although not specifically asked, there was some evidence that backing up of files did occur, but it was not seen as a high priority in some businesses. Certainly, there was no evidence of recognition of the role that business continuity planning or governance could play in the Web presence in relation to the use of those terms – but there was some evidence to indicate that a small number of businesses are thinking about some longer term implications of policies that would fit into these categories.

What the Small Business Needs to Think About

Security and Risk Management

Small businesses should assess the level of risk involved with different types of security breaches. Then, it can decide which strategy to adopt for each potential problem using a PDCMI approach - prevent it, detect and contain it, manage it or ignore it.

Prevention

The small business should do all it can to prevent a potential problem if there is a high risk of it occurring and it potentially has a high impact on the business. In these instances the business should:

- Put employee procedures in place – for instance, employees are not to open executable files received by e-mail - this is for the prevention of viruses and similar programs.
- Equipment should be protected - surge protectors, uninterruptible power supplies (UPS), restricted access (eg locks) - to ensure continuity of operations and to avoid malicious damage.
- Protective Software - firewalls need to be in place to protect the business from unexpected Internet intruders. Automated checkers should be used to prevent viruses from becoming operational.
- Check for encryption processes in transactions or secure communications.
- Put encryption processes in place where necessary.

Detect and Contain

Where a potential problem has a high risk of occurrence but will have a low impact on the business, these strategies should be considered:

Copyright © 2009, IGI Global, distributing in print or electronic forms without written permission of IGI Global is prohibited.

- **Put employee procedures in place:** Such as regular backups and the existence of offsite facilities that can be switched to (such as a 'backup' Website).
- **Software:** Virus protection, password protection
- **Check third party Website backup processes:** It is important to see what protections portal managers have in place for the data of their participating businesses.
- **Check for identity verification and put identify verification processes in place:** To ensure that access is only provided to those with appropriate authority.

Manage

These strategies should be considered where there is a low risk of occurrence of a problem, but could have a high impact. These would be instances such as a flood or earthquake.

- Consider implementing aspects of a business continuity plan
- Think of having an emergency backup Website to switch to.

Ignore

Where potential problems have a low risk of occurrence and a low impact if they do occur, it is suggested they are ignored.

General Issues

There are some other issues for small businesses to think about that fall under the heading of good governance.

Privacy

- *Implement a privacy policy.* It is important, especially for a Web presence, that a small business should have a privacy policy indicating how it handles sensitive customer data. In addition, this policy should be advertised on the Website.
- *Check third party Website privacy policies.* Where a business uses a third party Website, it is important that it examines the privacy policy of that business – especially in relation to how it handles data from the small business and its customers.

Copyright © 2009, IGI Global, distributing in print or electronic forms without written permission of IGI Global is prohibited.

Cultural Issues

- Small businesses should design Websites in a manner that is suitable for the diverse audiences it is targeting.

Copyright Law

- It is important to gain permission to use Website elements that are not owned by the business.
- Consider protecting Website material that has been created within the business with a patent or trademark – especially if it is made readily available on the Web presence.
- Seek information on the applicable laws and jurisdictions that apply in the countries that a business' target audience is located.

Import/Export Issues

- Be aware that Internet-based transactions and sales brings a new set of legal, cultural and logistical issues for the small business operator that should be investigated.
- Businesses may need to deal with geographically dispersed clients and will need to have a strategy in place for this.

Having examined some good governance issues, the final consideration for the business is to consider is how it evaluates the success of its Web presence.

EVALUATING WEB PRESENCE SUCCESS

Small businesses need to consider how they might evaluate the success of their Web presence. One of the interesting aspects of this topic that came out of our own research projects is that we noticed that a variety of techniques were used to judge the success of the Web presence. These ranged from quite sophisticated techniques to intuition (or a 'feel') about how successful the Web presence was. We found that there were a small number of businesses that judged the success of the Web presence against what they were trying to achieve with its existence – evidence that some businesses are considering their overall Web presence strategy. Another common theme was that it can be quite difficult to actually measure the success of the Web presence. Finally, there were a number if instances where small businesses were surprised by the effect of their Web presence – in some cases these were pleasant

Copyright © 2009, IGI Global, distributing in print or electronic forms without written permission of IGI Global is prohibited.

surprises (such as queries from markets they had not considered) and in some cases they were not so pleasant (when new customers did not 'flock' to the business).

What the Small Business Needs to Think About

Be Prepared

It is important for a small business to think about how the success of the Web presence investment will be determined as early as possible - something that should be done even before the Web presence is implemented and hopefully before any contracts for Website development are signed! Here are some hints as to what should be considered.

ICT Investments

Business aims: Think about how the Website will specifically address the aims of the business – and design the success measures around those aims

Quantify: Convert Web presence benefits and costs into dollars where possible. If not, try to measure the benefit or cost in some manner (for instance, in time saved).

Classifying ICT expenses: Consider the types of Web presence expenses that occur – are they fixed (do not vary according to the level of activity), variable (vary exactly according to the level of activity) or semi-variable? Can expenses be matched against sales revenue? If they are variable, do they vary according to sales or some other measure?

Type of ICT expense: Are the Web presence expenses being considered as ICT infrastructure and maintenance costs (which are costs associated with setting up the small business computer systems) or as ICT business project costs (or perhaps even a combination of these)? Chapter X has further detail about this.

Measuring Web Presence Success

There are a number of tolls that can be used to help measure Website performance:

- Website 'hit' counters. These are a crude measure, but perhaps useful in detecting surges in Website interest.

Copyright © 2009, IGI Global, distributing in print or electronic forms without written permission of IGI Global is prohibited.

- Log file analysis. These provide an analysis of traffic through the small business Website. An ISP or Website hosting service can usually provide these and associated reports to the business. A number of external services now offer these facilities.
- Search engine ranking.
- Treating Web presence expenses as ICT business expenses. This effectively means matching them against specific business revenue where possible (such as online sales).
- Employee time saved. If the business finds that its employees have more free time because of the Web presence – then this is an important benefit.
- Survey customers. This is something that should occur on a regular basis. Ask customers what they think about the Web presence.

CONCLUSION

This chapter should be viewed as a summary to understanding the important and necessary Web presence issues for the small business operator. The chapter has taken the various issues that have been described throughout the book and brought them together in the one location. Further detail on all of the issues (and others) is provided in the remainder of this book.

REFERENCES

Burgess, S., Bingley, S., & Sellitto, C. (2007). A Model for Website Content Decisions in Micro Businesses. *Global Business & Economics Anthology, 1*, 474-487.

Burgess, S., & Schauder, D. (1999). Assisting Small Businesses to Identify Internet Opportunities. *Millenial Challenges in Management Education, Cybertechnology and Leadership*, San Deigo, California, Association of Management and the International Association of Management, USA: (pp. 121-128).

Cox, C., Burgess, S., Sellitto, C., & Buultjens, J. (2008). *The Influence of User-Generated Content on Tourist Travel Behaviour.* Australian Regional Tourism Research Centre, Lismore, NSW, Australia.

Nielsen, J. (2000). *Designing Web Usability: The Practice of Simplicity.* New York: New Riders Publishing.

Copyright © 2009, IGI Global, distributing in print or electronic forms without written permission of IGI Global is prohibited.

Nielsen, J., & Loranger, H. (2006). *Prioritorizing Web Usability.* Berkeley, CA: New Riders Publishing.

Nielsen, J., & Tahir, M. (2002). *Homepage Usability.* Salem, VA: New Riders Publishing.

Copyright © 2009, IGI Global, distributing in print or electronic forms without written permission of IGI Global is prohibited.

Section II
Readiness, Business Aims and Planning

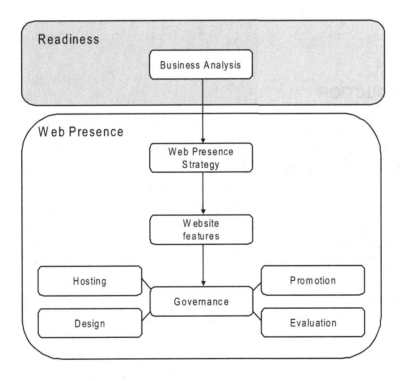

Chapter III
Readiness for a Web Presence

INTRODUCTION

The new global economy has resulted in the availability of unprecedented opportunities for small business. ICTs in particular have contributed to the underpinning of a revolutionary era of trade and commerce. The Internet in particular, and the ability to use the Web as a virtual shop front (having an online shop without physical premises) has not only allowed new forms of small businesses to emerge, but created an environment where they can compete with their larger counterparts. In what has been commonly become known as the new economy, one of the most fundamental tasks for small businesses is to investigate the usefulness and relevance of ICTs for their business. Furthermore, all small businesses need to assess their capacity to adopt ICTs allowing them to leverage the technology so that they are well positioned to expand their customer base, rationalize business processes and enter new markets. Porter (2001) observed at the height of the dot-com boom that it should be evident for many businesses that it was not whether to deploy ICTs, but how to use them as a competitive part of business strategy.

In this chapter we first look at some of the main barriers and drivers of ICT adoption. We then move on to examine the notion of the "readiness" of small businesses to set up a Web presence. We will also examine previous studies that have examined

Copyright © 2009, IGI Global, distributing in print or electronic forms without written permission of IGI Global is prohibited.

adoption of ICTs in small businesses, for the purpose of identifying those drivers and barriers that can affect small business wishing to go down that path.

What is a Web Presence?

Any small business operator who has used the Internet will have some notion of how of much information has been published on the Web. Even a business that has not taken steps towards building a Web presence may in fact have some kind of presence. For example, entering the name of a small business into the popular search engines such as Google™ or Yahoo® will in many cases result in dozens of 'hits' (search results) related to that business. These hits may include listings on industry related portals, directories, government associated Websites, blogs (Web logs – sites that capture user generated content through online conversations or postings), references on other business Websites and more. Even where a business has signed up with a third party directory such as the Yellow Pages™, the business may find that they now have some form of defacto Web presence. All these piecemeal listings and components of Web presence contribute to the image of a business. Hence, being aware of the consequences of having a Web presence becomes all the more important for small businesses.

A business' individual Web presence may be as simple as a home page business contact details. Conversely, the Website may be more intricate and include multiple pages with a catalogue of products, have an e-commerce facility for ordering products, and include interactive elements. Furthermore, the business may have as well as its own Website and a number of 'extended presences' that are either directly or indirectly related to the business. This 'extended presence' may not be controlled by the business. However, there are strategies that can be employed to promote a business beyond the individual Website presence. This may include affiliating with portals that sell similar products, listings with related interest groups, inclusion in local area Web-based directories of products and services and even active use of online auction facilities or trading Websites such as eBay™. Having a successful Web presence involves more than just having a well designed and engaging Website. The small business Website should not only actively centre and interact with customers through its own Website, but also take into consideration many of the other elements that contribute to the Web presence.

SMALL BUSINESS WEB PRESENCE

Despite the entrepreneurial and flexible nature of many small business operators, they have tended to lag behind their larger counterparts in terms of adopting a

Copyright © 2009, IGI Global, distributing in print or electronic forms without written permission of IGI Global is prohibited.

Web presence. The reasons are associated with resource limitations that are well documented in the small business literature and tend to be common across different technological adoptions. Overcoming the barriers to a Web presence allows the small business operator to avail themselves of a number of different benefits associated with the adoption of a Website. The extent of these benefits will largely depend on the context in which adoption takes place and what the business is trying to achieve. The next sections will explore the main barriers to, and benefits of, adopting a Web presence.

Barriers to Developing A Web Presence

One of the major reasons for small businesses not adopting a Web presence is a lack of awareness and knowledge amongst owner/managers of its business value. This is particularly true in small business where this person typically holds or is influential in the decision-making process. Many studies have revealed that the owner/manager is central to the successful adoption and continued utilization of a Web presence (we will discuss some of these later). The key issue for the owner/manager appears to be that there is a perceived need for the technology and an associated number of valuable benefits that result from using it. Similarly, a link has been found between businesses using advanced technologies and the education level of owner/managers, suggesting that adoption is more predominant amongst educated and more knowledgeable owner/managers (refer Chapter IV).

Another major obstacle associated with the successful adoption of a Web presence is the cost of equipment and software, consultants, maintaining a Web presence and various aspects of Website marketing. Furthermore, small businesses are often hindered by a lack of skilled employees. This issue affects the skills and knowledge requirements that are needed to implement new technologies and relate to the operational parameters of a Web presence. Typically, small businesses do not react quickly or adequately to skill deficiencies by encouraging the training of their employees. This issue is compounded because many small enterprises suffer from cultural obligations such as hiring family members and/or friends, which may lead to hiring people without the necessary skills. Many small businesses also indicate the lack of available time to explore new ideas or technology as a major inhibitor to adopting these new innovations. Even businesses that have recently adopted a Web presence may not realise that a Web presence can consume a large amount of time and by doing so can interfere with the daily operation of a business.

Small businesses also view as a barrier to the adoption of Web presence the issue of security - where owners tend to perceive that their computer, ICT activities and databases can be compromised. Security issues relating data protection, unauthorized intrusion, unsolicited e-mail, and viruses are a commonly cited reason as to

Copyright © 2009, IGI Global, distributing in print or electronic forms without written permission of IGI Global is prohibited.

why a small business will not adopt computer-based technology, and by inference a Web presence. The challenge here is that there is a general lack of awareness and knowledge concerning how to deal with these issues and their implications.

A number of other factors also pose problems for small businesses. In some cases factors such as expected lifestyle play a role in adoption. For instance, many operators that enter the tourism sector in an endeavour to achieve a more relaxed lifestyle, tend to view the Internet and the associated instantaneous communication mode as a threat that can impact on that lifestyle. Outside of the business there also factors that are worth mentioning. For instance, some regional and rural areas still do not have access to adequate and reliable ICT access, especially high capability broadband. There are also issues relating to government policies and the regulatory environment, especially concerning international trade. For example, certain products need government, taxation and customs clearance that are difficult to undertake when shipped after and being sold via the company Website - this can be a discouragement for the small business to adopt some of the more complex activities associated with a Web presence. How a business deals with these barriers to technology adoption is fundamental to not only the adoption of a Web presence but also its success. In summary the main barriers to Web presence adoption are (Karanasios 2008):

- Owner/managers do not see the value in a Web presence and/or lack understanding
- The cost involved
- Lack of internal skills and knowledge
- Lack of time to invest into a Web presence
- Security issues and a lack of understanding on how to deal with them
- Infrastructure issues.

One means of addressing these barriers and determining the position of a business to undertake an online initiative is to understand its *readiness* to do so. This is also referred to as organizational readiness and is discussed later. However, given the numerous barriers that are commonly documented to the adoption of Web presence, the associated benefits can be significant and add value to many small business activities. Indeed, there are a number of reasons for developing a Web presence. Although many studies have identified that one of the major benefits for small businesses is its use as an information and communication exchange, there are a number of other comprehensive benefits. They include the strengthening of customer relationships, the ability to reach new markets, more efficient business processes, reduction in expenses, improved business knowledge, the ability to attract investment, and even the creation of new products and services. Chapter IV

Copyright © 2009, IGI Global, distributing in print or electronic forms without written permission of IGI Global is prohibited.

discusses some of the drivers for Web adoption and the different strategies that can be employed to take advantage of them in greater detail.

IDENTIFYING FACTORS FOR READINESS

Having documented the various barriers that small businesses generally encounter in their adoption of ICTs, it is important to also consider some of the various factors that have been shown to enhance ICT uptake. Various governments around the world have not been blind to the limitations that small businesses face when it comes to new innovations and technology and have instigated encouragement programs - especially in the areas of e-business and the Web presence. These programs tend to have educational, guidance and support aspects and highlight for small business the benefits of ICT adoption. Such programs (one of which we discussed in Chapter I) tend to be delivered through the use of case studies, documented discussion forums and subsidized advice - allowing the small business to determine whether it is ready to move to Web presence. These programs also allow the small businesses to identify where any deficiencies may be - allowing the manager/operator to focus on improving and readying the business to overcome them.

Another tool or method in determining whether a small business may have deficiencies in its approach to the adoption of Web presence is through the use of various academic evaluation models. At the business level, a number of models that consider factors that affect the adoption of a Web presence have been proposed. These models are useful because they assist in the identification of factors that determine organisational readiness. The following section examines the use of academic models in identifying small business barriers and determining their readiness for adopting a Web presence. Two different works are discussed. The first focuses on Web adoption amongst European enterprises, whilst the second focuses on Website adoption and small businesses in Australia. They provide a useful lead-in to the discussion of business readiness for a Web presence.

Organisations and E-Commerce

Xu et al (2002) proposed a model that identified the facilitators and inhibitors of e-commerce allowing adoption behavior to be examined across different e-commerce environments. Data from 3,100 businesses and 7,500 consumers in eight European countries was collected to test the model. The model embraced six predictors of electronic adoption and proposed a framework that addressed issues that were *organizational, technological,* and *environmental* in context. A key finding from this study was that technology competence, business scope and size, consumer

Copyright © 2009, IGI Global, distributing in print or electronic forms without written permission of IGI Global is prohibited.

readiness and competitive pressure were found to be significant adoption facilitators for e-business, whilst a lack of trading partner readiness was a significant adoption inhibitor. The three contextual areas are now further expanded and documented.

Technological Context

Three factors should be considered regarding the technology context within the business. They are the existing ICT infrastructure, ICT expertise and ICT know-how (which refer to executives' knowledge of managing online selling and procurement). Again, in this context, factors concerning the technology itself and how it can be incorporated into the existing infrastructure and factors concerning human resources emerge as the most pertinent factors.

Organizational context

Within the organisational context, business scope and business size are two e-commerce adoption factors. The role of business scope as an adoption predictor can be explained from two perspectives. First, greater scope leads to higher internal coordination costs, higher search costs, and inventory holding costs. Since e-commerce can reduce internal coordination costs, lower search costs for both sellers and buyers, and improved inventory management, businesses with greater scope can be more motivated to adopt e-commerce. Second, businesses with greater scope have more potential to benefit from the relationship between e-commerce and traditional business processes. One factor that appears to be lacking in this contextual area is attention to the cost involved with actually adopting e-commerce. However, this issue may not have emerged as a relevant factor in the case of European enterprises.

Environmental Context

Three areas need consideration in this context: consumer readiness, competitor pressure/readiness, and trading partner readiness. Consumer readiness is an important factor for decision makers because it reflects the potential market volume, and thereby determines the extent to which e-commerce can be translated into profitability. It also reflects the extent to which consumers use the Internet. This study suggested that customer readiness can act as an adoption facilitator.

Competitive pressure refers to the level of pressure from competitors. This type of pressure can influence a business' decision to adopt new technology in order to avoid a competitive decline. Similarly the adoption status of a business' trading partners may influence technology adoption because as a precondition for electronic

Copyright © 2009, IGI Global, distributing in print or electronic forms without written permission of IGI Global is prohibited.

Figure 1. E-commerce, technology-organisation-environment framework (adapted from Xu et al 2002)

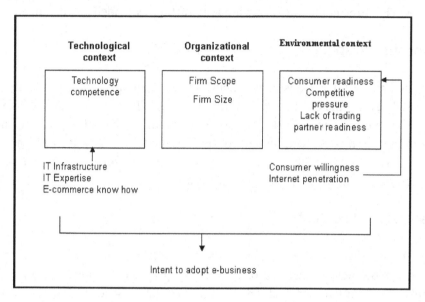

business to take place it is necessary that trading partners have similar systems to provide Internet-enabled services for each other.

Figure 1 depicts the framework and the associated relationships between these contextual areas. The combination of these three contextual areas can be used to assess the intent of a business to adopt e-commerce.

Small Business Website Adoption

From a small business perspective, one of the authors (Burgess 2002) proposed a Website adoption model that allowed a small business to make decisions concerning interacting with customers through a Website. In developing the model, the specific characteristics of small businesses were taken into consideration. The model was developed in the context of small businesses in Australia and can be thought as being generally applicable to any industry. The model, once fully enacted allows a small business to progress from the first stages of analysis and planning through to the actual implementation of the Website.

One component of the Burgess (2002) model related to the way that the small businesses investigated how prepared they were to adopt a Web presence, and focused on the internal business resources and their relationship with external entities or forces. The representation of the small business investigation aspect of the model is depicted in Figure 2.

Copyright © 2009, IGI Global, distributing in print or electronic forms without written permission of IGI Global is prohibited.

Figure 2. Business investigation phase of B2C website adoption model for small businesses

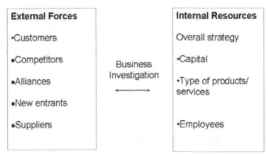

Similar to the organizational factors discussed so far, the business investigation phase of the Burgess (2002) model categorizes factors into contextual areas that represent the internal and external environment. In particular, within the external forces contextual area there is a focus on market entities such as competitors, new entrants, and customers. The model suggests that an analysis of the external environment includes an investigation of the following factors:

- **Suppliers:** Can an analysis of suppliers assist with customer interactions?
- **Competitors:** What are competitors currently doing?
- **Customers:** Is customer behavior different on the Internet? Is customer location important? Does it relate to the type of goods being offered?
- **New entrants:** The Internet is being seen as a great opportunity for many businesses to expand their market base. Is there a threat of new entrants to the industry?
- **Alliances:** Is there potential to collaborate with other businesses through the Internet?

An analysis of the internal environment includes an investigation of:

- **Overall strategy:** The overall business strategy and its alignment with the decision to develop a Website (for instance, does the business want to differentiate itself, reduce cost, grow or create alliances?).
- **Capital:** The resources (money and time) that can be devoted to the process. This is particularly a concern for small businesses.
- **Types of product/services:** Some products or services are seen as being more suited to being sold over the Internet. Can the product or service be tailored to suit the needs of individual customers?

Copyright © 2009, IGI Global, distributing in print or electronic forms without written permission of IGI Global is prohibited.

- **Employees:** The level of IT expertise within the business. This affects the ability of the business to implement the Website, the understanding of what can be achieved and/or the necessity to obtain external expertise.

The overlap of the issues that have been discussed is obvious. The next section incorporates much of the discussion in this section to introduce the notion of organisational readiness to adopt a Web presence.

ORGANISATIONAL READINESS

One of the crucial tasks involved in planning for the adoption of new technologies is to identify and understand the relevance of the forces that influence the business. In this section we discuss the different factors that contribute to the readiness of a business to adopt a Web presence. This section will assist small businesses to interpret the most relevant factors in their environment and determine the most appropriate response.

As suggested already, readiness factors can be categorized into two broad areas, internal factors (within the business), and external factors (outside the business). These can be categorised further. For instance, within the external environment there are factors related to the actual market (or industry forces), such as the influence of competitors and the needs of customers. How these factors affect the business will depend on the unique characteristics of the market sector that a particular small business participates in. There are also external factors that are related to the overall enabling environment, such as government policies geared towards small business and the availability, and quality of the telecommunications infrastructure that is needed to support a Web presence.

Before entering into a discussion of these factors, it is useful to gain an understanding of why a small business should assess its readiness for a Web presence. A good example of the need for assessing the business environment is the experience of a small hotel that developed a Website with the ability to accept customer credit card payments online (as a way of guaranteeing reservations). However, the business found that it and the bank were both unable to handle credit card details, making the investment into this feature a waste of business resources. Another important reason to assess the readiness of a business is that many of the tasks performed in doing this are similar to those involved in a comprehensive business analysis, which is an important step in the planning of a Web presence strategy and is introduced in the next chapter.

Copyright © 2009, IGI Global, distributing in print or electronic forms without written permission of IGI Global is prohibited.

External Factors

There are a number of external factors that can influence the adoption of a Web presence. Understanding how these factors influence the business will greatly support small businesses in their endeavor to cope with the development of a Web presence.

Two sets of readiness predictors are discussed here. The first refers to the enabling environment and includes government readiness and the telecommunications infrastructure. These two factors are crucial to the success of a Web presence and are an effective judge of the local e-business environment. The second group of factors refers to the market and includes an investigation of customers, competitors, partners and (to a lesser extent from the viewpoint of this book) suppliers. These factors will play a large role in determining the need for a Web presence

Government Readiness

One of the choices that have become increasingly unavoidable for governments worldwide is to support the small business sector to take full advantage of the range of opportunities offered by the Web and ICTs to remain competitive. Many governments understand the importance of supporting the adoption of ICTs in small business and have initiated policies and strategies to remove constraints and create a strong enabling environment. For example, as a result of government enthusiasm and commitment, Malaysia's ICT plan has been described as one of the most aggressive in the world (Ratnathicam, 2002).

Government readiness relates to issues such as reducing barriers and providing an overall conducive e-business environment. Through policy governments can also provide assistance for businesses through initiatives and support programs to assist with the diffusion of ICTs (Khan, 2002; Vatanasakdakul, Tibben, & Cooper, 2004). For small businesses this means there is help out there to assist in the development of a Web presence. Even a simple form of government support can provide greater visibility for the small business. For instance, Samoa, Purcell et al. (2004) found that for small tourism businesses that did not have their own individual Web presence it was important to have the business advertised on the Samoan Visitor Bureau Website.

A good starting point for investigating the types of support available for small businesses is the divisions of government that support small businesses. For instance, just some of the practical incentives and support initiatives provided to small businesses in some countries are presented in the Table 1.

The essential question here is how can these initiatives assist in the adoption of a Web presence? Most initiatives focus on reducing cost. Therefore, government

Copyright © 2009, IGI Global, distributing in print or electronic forms without written permission of IGI Global is prohibited.

Table 1. Government support initiatives for small businesses

Australia	Singapore	Canada	Malaysia
• Guidelines on setting up a web presence • Funding for IT and technical support • Internet optimization program	• Subsidies for computer training for employees • Secure e-payment services	• Electronic commerce guide for small business • Youth employment programs • ICT loans	• Loans to SMEs for the purchase of ICT equipment • Promote SMEs to have a website, and perform online transactions • Capacity building

support may actually contribute to the readiness of a business by helping to ease the financial burden associated with developing a Web presence and increasing capacity for them to tackle the barriers to creating a Web presence. In an example of how government strategies can help Karanasios and Burgess (2008) identified that some small Malaysian enterprises reported using government initiatives such as rebates on the cost incurred in developing a Website, no tax paid on ICT equipment and promotion on successful government tourism Websites.

Telecommunications Infrastructure

Gaining access to the necessary telecommunications infrastructure was once one of the main barriers to using the Internet. Whilst this issue still needs to be addressed in rural and regional areas, improvements over the last few years make this issue no longer a leading concern.

In many cases, small businesses will already be using telecommunications of some kind. Where this is not the case it is important to consider the type of Internet connection that the business requires, and what is actually available. For instance, in Australia recently a small business owner was under the impression that he would have a broadband connection when he would set up at a new Website, only to find out after setting up the business that broadband would not be available for anther five years. The most popular Internet connection options are dial-up (low-cost), broadband, cable and ISDN (which is a moderate to expensive option depending on the use). Fortunately, in many cases gaining access to the Internet should be relatively straightforward – but this is not the case everywhere. It is also important to consider the support system and technology that may be required to keep the technology functioning (such as router, second telephone line and so forth).

Customers

An investigation of the business target audience and existing customer behavior is likely to reveal the need to develop a Web presence. In countries such as Australia

Copyright © 2009, IGI Global, distributing in print or electronic forms without written permission of IGI Global is prohibited.

over 70 percent of the population use the Internet. Worldwide there are one billion Internet users. Younger, more technology savvy, markets in particular demand more information online and greater sophistication from a Web presence than older less technology enabled markets. When catering to a younger demographic group, small businesses may even need to adopt innovative approaches such as providing content not only for PC's but also for mobile (cellular) telephones and other portable devices.

A good reference point of customer readiness is to determine the level of Internet penetration amongst existing and potential customers. Next, a business should investigate the expectation of its customers. Are customers looking for information about products and services or communicating with the business? This question is central to developing an understanding of the readiness of the market and the success of the Web presence.

Here a business should also reflect upon the products and services it provides. Are they suitable to be sold over the Internet? Where are the customers situated? If the business plans on distributing physical products to customers they should consider the geographic dispersion of customers. The distribution of electronic products (such as software or reports) will require further technical and security considerations on both the business and consumer side. The role of customers as part of a small business Website strategy is revisited again in Chapter IV.

Suppliers and Trading Partners

Many small businesses rely heavily on larger suppliers and partners for survival. In fact, in many instances a move to an online mode of operation will be primarily to satisfy these entities. In tourism for example, travel agencies and other intermediaries in the tourism supply chain place pressure on smaller operators to adopt the Internet because they prefer to do business online to reduce costs. The same type of pressure applies to many small businesses that are part of a franchise group. For example, in an industry area were the majority of small businesses are franchises, there may be pressure on owners to adopt and conform to developing a Web presence as dictated by the franchise consortium. The central question here that a small business needs to ask is whether suppliers and partners use the Internet, and are there any benefits associated with interacting with these entities by having a Web presence? This will raise issues such as the compatibility of systems and the appropriateness of processes - issues that will require consideration and impact on the adoption decision-making. In some cases, a small business that is part of a franchise will already have a Web presence. Here a business needs to consider the value of adopting its own individual Web presence. From our point of view, if small businesses set up these Websites they may be more likely to use it for B2C purposes.

Copyright © 2009, IGI Global, distributing in print or electronic forms without written permission of IGI Global is prohibited.

Competitors

With a majority of small businesses online in developing countries and many of those having a Web presence, it is highly likely that a small business' competitors will already have a Web presence. Therefore, in some cases adopting a Web presence may be a reactive strategy to actions competitors have already taken. Within the business' competitive environment the central question is whether a competitor is marketing or selling similar products or services over the Internet? What are their strategies? Where there is little or no Web presence in an industry area, a business may have the opportunity to differentiate itself from others by being an early adopter of the technology. Conversely, where competitors are already online it is important to understand how they are using their Web presence, and react accordingly. Some businesses that have an unsuccessful presence have lost customers to competitors because their Web presence did not meet the expectations of customers. Therefore in some cases even businesses with an existing Web presence may need to make some organizational changes and restructure their Web presence.

Along these lines, the Internet has created the possibility of enabling new entrants into markets. Some of these businesses are technologically 'savvy' and use Web technologies to gain access to markets. Therefore, despite the challenges associated with the resource limitations that small businesses experience (cost, lack of employee skills and so forth) - for some businesses not adopting a Web presence may pose an even greater risk.

Other Factors

Chaffey et al (2003) identify a number of external factors that can influence business adoption of the Internet, these being economic conditions, legal constraints, cultural factors and ethical and moral constraints. We examine a number of these factors in later chapters of the book.

Internal Factors

Within a business there are many elements that may inhibit or support the adoption and implementation of new technologies. As noted earlier, government initiatives may support small businesses through financial stimuli and incentives to build capacity. Other factors will need to be addressed directly by the business.

Several factors are captured in this context. They refer to the characteristics of the business and the relevance of Web technologies for the business, as well as an investigation of financial and human capital. After performing an analysis

Copyright © 2009, IGI Global, distributing in print or electronic forms without written permission of IGI Global is prohibited.

of the internal factors, small businesses are in a better position to make decisions concerning their Web presence.

The Business: Structure, Strategy, and Activity

The dimensions of a business will largely determine the relevance of developing a Web presence. This is based on the products and services it offers, the structure of the business, its size and its strategy. Generally speaking, readiness is proportional to business size with larger firms being the most ready (reflected by the fact that almost all large businesses have a Web presence), while small businesses are the least ready. Small businesses can operate in a number of different ways. Some of them are independently owned, whilst others are part of a franchise or business group. This will impact the relevance of a Web presence. Concerning the types of services or products sold, many customers now rely on the Internet for researching and purchasing tourism products and digitised goods. While there is less online demand for purchasing items such as consumables, there is still demand for information about these goods. As an example, in a discussion by one of the authors with a health food-store owner it was found that customers used the Internet to find out more about products and then visited the store in person to make purchases. Therefore, it could be argued, as noted earlier that customers are driving the need for a Web presence.

The strategy of the business will also play a role in readiness. Businesses that want to grow, access new markets, reduce communication and advertising costs, and streamline processes will almost certainly require a Web presence to facilitate at least part of this change. Businesses wishing to grow must also be prepared to manage any increase in customer queries and even product orders generated by the Web presence. However, in most circumstances there will be a lag between a new (or improved) Web presence and increased interest in the business. Therefore a business should develop a plan to determine how long they are willing to wait to achieve acceptable results. The central question is: what is it that the business is trying to achieve through its Web presence and how does this reflect the overall business strategy?

Owner/Manager Readiness

Owner/manager readiness is the quintessential factor concerning the overall organizational readiness and the success of a Web presence. There are many different ingredients that contribute to an owner/manager being 'ready'. Factors such as enthusiasm, awareness and perceived value of the Web presence are all good indicators of readiness. The key is that owner/managers recognize the need for

Copyright © 2009, IGI Global, distributing in print or electronic forms without written permission of IGI Global is prohibited.

developing a Web presence and are supportive of its use for business purposes. In other words, the owner/manager is central to Web adoption and continued utilisation. Without serious investment of time and capital from the 'top' any initiative is likely to fail. Owner/managers should be aware that they are likely to play a major role in guiding the success of a Web presence. Since many small businesses are managed in a personalised manner, it is important that owner/managers reflect upon their own perceptions and expectations of the Web presence and their commitment to its success.

Mostafa et al (2004) suggest that a number of traits of the owner/manager can influence their commitment to a Web presence. These can include personal traits (such as their need for achievement and risk taking propensity), factors which are likely to stimulate entrepreneurial activity (such as their previous work experience, their educational level and their age) and their behaviour when having to make decisions in uncertain situations.

Financial Resources

One of the main reasons for the inertia amongst small businesses in adopting a Web presence is the financial burden involved. Paradoxically, many small businesses report that the potential to reduce costs is one of the leading drivers to adopt a Web presence. In many cases, the initial cost of adopting a Web presence may pose a problem. However, the benefits may be immediate and typically include the reduction in communication and advertising costs. As the Web presence grows, other costs will be incurred and it becomes essential to monitor these costs within the small business budget. There are also hidden imposts, such as training for employees and the potential cost of distributing products over long distances. Therefore it is useful to be aware of not only the initial expenditure associated with a Web presence, but also the ongoing costs involved - which is an issue often neglected by small businesses. A cost-benefit analysis of having a Web presence becomes an essential pre-requisite when contemplating this exercise.

Knowledgeable Staff

The lack of skilled employees presents one of the most crucial internal readiness factors that small businesses are likely to encounter. In some countries there is already a shortage of employees with appropriate skills, and small businesses do not usually react adequately to this situation by providing relevant training for their employees. For many small businesses this will result in the owner/manager being responsible for maintaining the Web presence, and being drawn away from the daily operation of the business.

Copyright © 2009, IGI Global, distributing in print or electronic forms without written permission of IGI Global is prohibited.

The notion of 'knowledgeable' staff refers to technical competence (such as computer and Internet literacy), but also skills relating to e-commerce know-how (such as processing online orders and payments), and the service skills needed to deal with customers online. Small businesses involved in international trade may also need to consider that employees will need an understanding of the culture and language of the client.

This factor also extends to the availability of skilled human capital in the local area (the external environment), which is a particular problem for rural and regional enterprises. Where this presents a challenge, small businesses could consider providing ongoing training employees, which will in turn impact on the overall cost. A key point that owner/managers should bear in mind is that any skill deficiency amongst employees is likely to result in them operating and maintaining the online presence themselves.

Compatibility of Existing Systems

The adoption of online technologies requires some change in how the business operates and how technology is used. Some businesses operate in technology stagnant conditions – where the industry has reached a stage of maturity, and therefore technology has changed very little over time. Introducing a Web presence in such an environment may require significant organisational changes. Therefore, it is important for the small business operator to consider the impacts of a Web presence on business processes due to the likely integration of existing computer systems. Arguably, even where there is minimal use of computerized systems, businesses will need to take into consideration factors such as how the Web presence will affect orders, internal and external communication and inventory management.

Fortunately, most small businesses are not hindered by cumbersome IT infrastructures and business processes and with some careful planning the integration of a Web presence should not be problematic. This is especially true if management has the motivation and a skill set that allows the small business to be 'ready' for the move to the Web.

Readiness also relates back to what the business is trying to achieve through its Web presence. In some cases, the amalgamation of the Web presence into the business will be smooth. For instance, it was reported by one small business owner to an author that incorporating the Internet and a basic Website was not a problem because it simply involved purchasing a computer connected to the Internet. On the other hand, where more sophisticated Web presences are developed, such as incorporating online sales and so forth, there are more issues that need to be considered (such as the systems and processes that need to be in place to support online sales). The compatibility of the Web presence also raises questions about

Copyright © 2009, IGI Global, distributing in print or electronic forms without written permission of IGI Global is prohibited.

Table 2. Summary of organisational readiness factors

External factors		Internal Factors	
Government:	Policies and incentives to support the adoption of a web presence	**Business:**	Suitability of the web to the business
Infrastructure:	The physical infrastructure that must be in place	**Knowledgeable employees:**	Human capacities to deliver and maintain the web presence
Customers:	Customer behavior and their expectations of the business	**Financial resources:**	Available financial assets to invest into a web presence
Competitors:	The use of the web by competitors	**Owner/manager:**	Investment of commitment and resources
Suppliers and partners:	The use of the web by suppliers and partners	**Compatibility of existing systems:**	Adaptability of the web presence to existing IT structures and processes

running and maintaining it. For instance, in some cases businesses will choose to run and maintain the Web presence from within the business. This is typically an expensive and technically complicated solution.

Thus far this section has examined the pertinent factors influencing small business organizational readiness. As noted, a number of internal and external forces tend to drive organizational readiness.

Table 2 summarizes the main points within each contextual area.

Now we move on to discuss the results of some of our own research and some other studies in the context of this chapter.

OUR PREVIOUS STUDIES

Develop_06

This study developed an e-readiness framework tailored to small tourism businesses. In developing the framework, field research was conducted in Malaysia and Ecuador with small tourism enterprises. The framework categorised the most pertinent ICT adoption factors into four interrelated contextual areas that included Market readiness, Organisational readiness, Owner/Manager readiness and the Macro environment. The framework is depicted in Figure 3 and shows how each contextual area that affects the business is dependant on the readiness of the small business owner/manager.

Copyright © 2009, IGI Global, distributing in print or electronic forms without written permission of IGI Global is prohibited.

Figure 3. E-readiness framework for small tourism enterprises

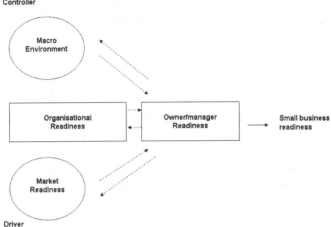

During the study, the importance of the owner/manager in overcoming certain obstacles emerged as one of the most important adoption factors. For example, the owners of a lodge explained that when they first settled in a remote mountainous region and established their business, there was no telephone line. To rectify this, when they used to drive to the nearest large town (roughly four hours away) they would stop by the local telephone company, and request in person for a telephone line to be setup in the village. A first line was installed a few years later, and more lines were added later.

At that point, the lodge began to use the Internet via a dial-up connection, which was extremely expensive (greater than US$100 per month including telephone calls) and unreliable. Furthermore, due to a lack of maintenance the quality and reliability of the local telecommunications infrastructure deteriorated rapidly over the last few years *"it was old technology and now it is ancient"*. At the time of the study, the owners could only connect via a telephone line about 60 percent of the time, and even then the connection was extremely poor. As a result, it was very difficult to conduct a conversation. The owners then told the story of how they acquired the idea of using a satellite-dish to access the Internet from a tourist who visited the lodge with one in his van. After performing a basic cost-benefit analysis they decided that a long-term solution would be to use a satellite-dish that provided an efficacious means of accessing the Internet. They then embarked on purchasing a second-hand satellite-dish from the USA, and had it transported to the nearest town. Without any prior experience in this area they managed to make it operational using trial and error. This innovative solution resulted in stable Internet access and decreased telecommunications expenses, and generally as a result of the Internet and their

Copyright © 2009, IGI Global, distributing in print or electronic forms without written permission of IGI Global is prohibited.

online presence they were able to attract more customers. Indeed, because of the deterioration of the existing infrastructure, the Internet became the only reliable means to receive a reservation, and communicate with customers.

Wineries_PhDsurvey_04

This research PhD investigated ICT adoption by small to medium size wineries and developed an e-business best practice model. One component of the e-business model unexpectedly identified aspects of small winery technological readiness. The important aspect of technological readiness for small wineries included the ICT infrastructure, regional availability and provision of Internet services and the integration of existing winery computer systems with the Internet. A summary of identified technological readiness issues follow.

ICT Infrastructure

Business response to consumer and supplier enquiries is greatly enhanced by the speed and reliability of the communication infrastructure. The Internet improves the overall level of communication responsiveness of an organisation, and by leveraging such ICT capabilities, a business can provide immediate and on-demand responses for important partners. Indeed, this higher responsiveness can allow differentiation between competitors.   Thus, one of the benefits for wineries of being connected to the Internet 24 hours a day, was having constant access to information and communication facilities, a feature that influenced the overall responsiveness of the wine business. One issue identified in the study associated with technological readiness was slow data speeds and regular drop out rates when connected to the communication infrastructure network. Many wineries interviewed in the study provided overwhelming evidence of regional ICT infrastructure being substandard and one that acted as a barrier to e-business best practice.

Regional Internet Service Providers (ISP)

The choice of ISP was found to be an important factor for wineries when it came to establishing their Web presence. In general, businesses that are located in regional and rural areas have been shown to have significantly less choice in the ISP they use. Moreover, the available ISP may not offer the cost effective 'un-timed' local call as a standard connection. This un-timed local call issue is important considering that the telephone system remains the main source of Internet connection for many regional and rural users. Consequently, an important winery e-business practice

Copyright © 2009, IGI Global, distributing in print or electronic forms without written permission of IGI Global is prohibited.

associated with readiness involved selecting an ISP that had a local communications hub that allowed un-timed call access - an issue that reduced business costs.

Compatibility of Existing Computer Systems

The use of existing ICT-integrated winery computer systems was found to be closely associated with any planned expansion of the winery. Small wineries were found to have basic computer system requirements that were accommodated within the small office/home office environment. The ability to expand the business tended to be associated with a significant use of information technology in capturing data and enhancing communications - one that was premised on the integration of existing computer systems with the Internet. The value of this integration allowed a winery to link its information rich back-end system(s) with the Internet communication infrastructure. Thus, for wineries, a readiness issue was associated with the ability to integrate their existing and future winery computer systems with Internet technologies - providing a winery with the flexibility to improve and streamline business information flow.

Other Studies

Internet Retailing Adoption by SMEs (Lee & Cheung 2004)

As underscored in this chapter, one of the most fundamental tasks for small businesses is preparing for Internet adoption and understanding organisation readiness. Providing the perspective of small businesses in Hong Kong, Lee and Cheung (2004) examined the organisational readiness of small businesses for Internet retailing. They focused their attention on three small businesses to understand what leads to adoption and the factors that determine organisational readiness. They found that the main determinants of organisation readiness were strong support for Internet retailing projects, management ICT knowledge and background and prior success with Internet related projects.

The participants (who were all top managers) shared several common characteristics. For instance, they all had extensive knowledge about their own business and industry. They appreciated the Internet retailing projects, and were inspired by the opportunities offered by the Internet. Furthermore, all the managers had insights on the Internet retailing projects, and importantly were willing to be the pioneers in their own industry. In fact, the prior successful experience of businesses with Internet-related projects had exhibited a strong impact on their confidence to adopt Internet retailing. In one case, the awareness of successful 'e-retailing' cases in the USA was an incentive one business to expand using the Internet. In other words,

Copyright © 2009, IGI Global, distributing in print or electronic forms without written permission of IGI Global is prohibited.

this study showed that previous encounters with the Internet had influenced the adoption of Internet retailing.

An interesting finding from this study was that the participants indicated that customer readiness did not impact the small businesses decision to adopt the Internet retailing project. In fact, all three businesses indicated that e-commerce adoption in Hong Kong and in most Asian countries was low. Trust, security and privacy concerns were given as the main reasons for the apparent inertia amongst Asian populations. This is despite the fact that Asia is home to most of the worlds Internet users and has showed the strongest growth in terms of numbers of users. Nevertheless, the low penetration rate of Internet shopping in Hong Kong and in most Asian countries did not affect the decisions of the three companies to adopt Internet retailing and developing a strong Web presence The authors attrobute this to the relatively small set-up cost of developing a Web presence and selling online as well as the perceived benefits of the Internet retailing projects.

E-Commerce Adoption in Developing Countries
(Molla & Licker 2005)

In the context of businesses in developing countries, Molla and Licker (2005) conducted a study to examine e-readiness amongst small, medium and large businesses in South Africa. Their study aimed to identify environmental challenges and the limitations that are different to those experienced in developed economies. The authors constructed and empirically tested an e-readiness model called the Perceived E-commerce Readiness Model (PERM). They identified relevant e-commerce, managerial, organisational, and contextual factors that could explain e-commerce adoption amongst South African businesses. Their model focussed on internal organisational capabilities and the characteristics of individual businesses as well as macro forces.

As can be observed in Figure 4, the model identifies two contextual areas (Perceived Organisational e-Readiness) and (Perceived External e-Readiness) that consist of a number of subsequent factors. The factors within the Perceived Organisational e-Readiness contextual area are consistent with the discussion so far in this chapter. They are manager awareness, commitment, and governance of e-commerce, and resources based factors such as technology and human resources. Within the Perceived External e-Readiness contextual area the factors relate to outside forces such as the government, the market, and the supporting industry. After an assessment of these factors the business then decides whether to adopt ecommerce or not (represented by the flows in the diagram). After the initial adoption is successful more widespread use of e-commerce is employed (the authors refer to this as institutionalisation). The model is one of very few in the context of

Copyright © 2009, IGI Global, distributing in print or electronic forms without written permission of IGI Global is prohibited.

developing countries that managers can apply to audit their organisational and the external environment. One limitation that the authors acknowledge is that it is not industry specific.

Summary of our Studies and Other Studies

These studies have highlighted the importance of three major factors that can affect the e-readiness of a small business:

- *The macro environment.* The examples provided here highlight some of the challenges faced by small businesses in developing countries and in rural areas in developed countries where there is a lack of suitable infrastructure available.
- *The organisational environment.* The examples showed the importance of organisational readiness, particularly in relation to having suitable technology already in place, but also the importance that the existing technology is compatible with any planned Web presence.
- *Characteristics of the owner/manager.* The reader will note that we revisit the importance of the owner/manager to the Web presence a number of times throughout the book. In one of these examples, the drive of the owner/manager was a key factor that lead to the eventual success of the Web presence initiative.

Figure 4. Perceived e-commerce readiness model (PERM) (adapted from Molla & Licker 2005, Figure 2: 883)

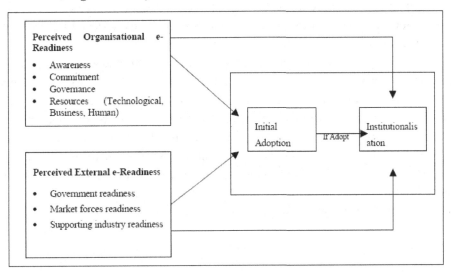

Copyright © 2009, IGI Global, distributing in print or electronic forms without written permission of IGI Global is prohibited.

TENETS – LESSONS FROM THE CHAPTER

The small business operator needs to be aware of the various issues associated with organisational readiness. Performing a readiness assessment will assist businesses to address the barriers and opportunities relevant to adopting a Web presence and allow them to determine the most appropriate action. Armed with such knowledge small businesses will be better positioned to engage in the process of analysing, developing and managing their Web presence. Table 3 summarises that main themes of this chapter and provides a useful guide for the small business operators.

CONCLUSION

This chapter began by discussing the barriers and drivers for a Web presence. Small businesses face a number of different challenges when developing a Web presence. Likewise there are numerous reasons for adopting a Web presence and this will depend on what a business is trying to achieve. Not all businesses face the same challenges or have the same opportunities, and they will be affected by their state of readiness. This chapter identified the notion of the small business *Web presence* and outlined some of the main factors that contribute to the *readiness* of a small business to adopt a Web presence. Readiness for some small businesses will be influenced by various external factors such as how their customers wish to engage them, and the availability of appropriate infrastructure and government assistance in establishing a Web presence. Internal factors will also regulate the degree of small business readiness when it comes to a Web presence - these factors deal with issues associated with the appropriate access to technological skills, management commitment to Web presence and the suitability of products/services to the Web environment. The internal factors that impact on small business readiness tend to be intrinsically related to resource available.

The discussion in this chapter indicates that different approaches can, and should be undertaken when considering adopting a Web presence. Furthermore, the small business will need to examine the identified issues that are internal and external to the business in order to gauge business readiness for a Web presence. Indeed, there is no 'one-size fits all' solution, and that a flexible approach to adoption is required that takes into consideration the business environment and organizational resources. The next chapter discusses the role that many of these factors play in business strategy and planning, leading to the development of a small business strategy for a small business Web presence.

Copyright © 2009, IGI Global, distributing in print or electronic forms without written permission of IGI Global is prohibited.

Table 3. Factors for small business to consider when assessing their e-readiness level

External Factors	Rationale
Do customers use the Internet?	If the answer here is no then a web presence may not be relevant, unless the business wants to access new markets. If customers are using the Internet then the key question is what do they demand from a web presence
Do competitors have a web presence?	If competitors do not have a web presence then an opportunity exists to differentiate from competitors. Where competitors are online, it is important to understand what they are offering through their web presence
Do suppliers and trading partners demand a web presence?	Small business may need to interact with their existing and future trading partners through maintaining a web presence. This issue of electronic engagement with industry partners and suppliers can be an obligatory requirement for many small business operators if they wish to maintain their existing/future relationships with these entities.
Are there government support policies and initiatives to assist in the development of a web presence?	If the answer here is yes, then the key question is how can these help where a business is deficient in other areas?
Is the necessary physical infrastructure in place?	In many cases this will not be a problem. However it is useful to be aware of the situation before adopting a web presence. Even where it is a problem it is worth remembering that a business does not necessarily need to have internal access to the Internet to have a web presence
Internal Factors	**Rationale**
Is the product and business suitable and overall strategy suited to the web?	Here if the answer is yes then the question is how can the web presence be used to promote and/or sell products? If the answer is no, then changes to the businesses strategy may need to be made in order to facilitate a web presence.
Are there relevant skills and knowledge amongst employees to maintain the web presence	If yes, the business is in a good position to develop and maintain the web presence. If the answer is no then the business may need to offer training to employees
Is there sufficient capital to build and maintain the web presence?	If the answer here is yes, then again the business is in a relatively good position to adopt a web presence. If the answer is no the business may need to consider developing a low cost web presence, then once benefits materialize develop the web presence accordingly
Is management prepared to provide the necessary investment of commitment, time and resources?	This is the most important factor. If the answer here is yes then the business is in the best position to launch a web presence
Is there a need to integrate existing systems due to changed business processes?	Web presence should alter the dynamic workings of various small business activities (sales, ordering, marketing, etc). The small business operator needs to be aware that web presence will most likely require some form of computer systems integration in order for the business to maximise benefits.

Copyright © 2009, IGI Global, distributing in print or electronic forms without written permission of IGI Global is prohibited.

REFERENCES

Australian Bureau of Statistics (2005). *Business Use of Information Technology 2003-04*, Commonwealth of Australia, Melbourne, Australia.

Burgess, S. (2002). *Business-to-Consumer Interactions on the Internet: A Model for Small Businesses.* School of Information Management and Systems, Monash University.

Chaffey, D., Ellis-Chadwick, F., Johnston, K., & Mayer, R. (2006). *Internet Marketing: Strategy, Implementation and Practice,* 3rd ed, Financial Times/ Prentice Hall, UK.

Chyau, C. (2005). *Why Should Countries Embed ICTs into SME Policy.* United Nations Asia-Pacific Development Information Programme, Bangkok, Thailand.

Grandon, E., & Pearson, J. M. (2004). Electronic commerce adoption: an empirical study of small and medium US businesses. *Information & Management, 42*(1), 197-216.

Ihlstr, C., Magnusson, M., Scupola, A., & Tuunainen, V. K. 2003. SME barriers to electronic commerce adoption: Nothing changes-everything is new. In G. Gingrich (Ed.), *Managing IT in government business & communities* (pp. 147-163). Hershey, PA: Idea Group Publishing.

Jones, M. V., & Dimitratos, P. (2004). *Emerging Paradigms in International Entrepreneurship.* Butterworth-Heinemann, MA.

Kamel, S., & Hussein, M. (2004). King Hotel goes online: The case of a medium enterprise in using e-commerce. *Journal of Electronic Commerce in Organisations, 2*(4), 101-115.

Karanasios, S. (2008). *An E-Commerce Framework for Small Tourism Enterprises in Developing Countries.* Victoria University.

Karanasios, S., & Burgess, S. (2008) Tourism and Internet adoption: a developing world perspective. *International Journal of Tourism Research, 10*(2), 169-182.

Khan, H. (2002) The best practices of e-commerce strategies for small and medium sized tourism enterprises in Singapore. *Proceedings of the Asia Pacific Economic forum (APEC) International Tourism Symposium*, Seoul, Korea.

Lee, A. K. C., & Cheung, S. C. (2004) Internet Retailing Adoption by Small-to-Medium Sized Enterprises (SMEs): A Multiple-Case Study. *Information Systems Frontiers, 6*(4), 385-397.

Copyright © 2009, IGI Global, distributing in print or electronic forms without written permission of IGI Global is prohibited.

Molla, A., & Licker, P. S. (2005) E-Commerce adoption in developing countries: A model and instrument. *Information & Management, 42*(6), 877-899.

Porter, M. E. (2001) Strategy and the Internet. *Harvard Business Review, 79*(3), 62-78.

Tornatzky, L.G., & Fleischer, M. (1990). *The processes of technological innovation.* Lexington, MA: Lexington Books.

Vatanasakdakul, S., Tibben, W., & Cooper, J. (2004) What prevents B2B eCommerce adoption in developing countries? *Proceedings of the 17th Bled eCommerce Conference*, Bled, Slovenia.

Xu, S., Zhu, K., & Kraemer, K. L. (2002) A cross-country study of electronic business adoption using the technology-organization-environment framework. *International Conference on Information Systems*, Barcelona, Spain.

Copyright © 2009, IGI Global, distributing in print or electronic forms without written permission of IGI Global is prohibited.

Chapter IV
Business Strategy and Planning

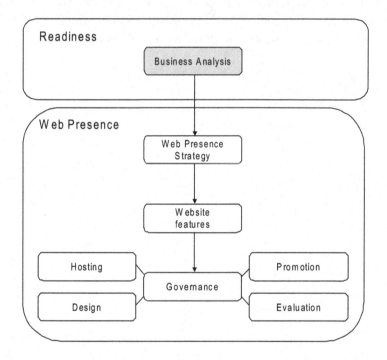

INTRODUCTION

In the previous chapter we highlighted the importance of planning for an effective Web presence. In fact, the existence of a disciplined planning approach is seen as an enabler for the effective use of ICTs and e-commerce in small businesses,

Copyright © 2009, IGI Global, distributing in print or electronic forms without written permission of IGI Global is prohibited.

whilst short-range management perspectives and lack of planning are viewed as barriers.

This chapter builds on the tenets identified in the previous chapter to examine how a small business might prepare itself for a Web presence. We believe that small business operators/ managers should know their strategic business direction before they consider establishing a Web presence. We will commence by investigating some basic business theory.

COMPETITIVE FORCES

It is necessary for a small business owner/manager to understand the environment in which the business operates and exists. More than twenty years ago, Porter and Millar (1985) proposed a model that related to competitive forces (refer Figure 1) in an endeavour to assist managers to identify strategic information and communication technology opportunities. Although this model was suggested in a time when ICT adoption was nascent, the basics of the model still tend to hold today. Indeed, Porter in 2001 updated the model in the *Harvard Business Review* to take into account the value of ICTs. He suggested that that it had become evident that for many businesses it was not whether to deploy ICT, but how to use the technology

Figure 1. The five competitive forces model (adapted from Porter & Millar 1985)

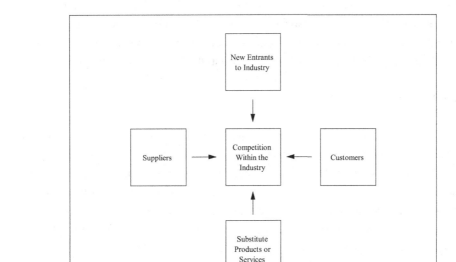

Copyright © 2009, IGI Global, distributing in print or electronic forms without written permission of IGI Global is prohibited.

as a competitive part of business strategy - a strategy that complemented some of the traditional ways that they went about their business (Porter 2001).

In planning for a Web presence, a small business should consider those aspects of the competitive forces model that relate to the business. As we are considering setting up the Web presence to deal with customers we will not discuss *suppliers* as a competitive force. However, they remain an important part of a business' supply chain. We will now briefly consider the different competitive forces.

Customers

For this book, customers are the target of our Web presence. Chapter VIII covers how a small business Web presence can be promoted to customers. However, it is also important to know whether customers are ready to do business online and, if they are, what they expect. This will be discussed later in this chapter. Arguably, the advent of ICTs has strengthened the bargaining power of customers due to the increased number of products and services that they can access. Previously, access to products and services was restricted by geographical region, whilst now buyers can potentially source their requirements from any business in the world that has a Web presence and the ability to distribute its products and/or services to them in a timely and cost effective manner.

Substitute Products/Service

A substitute product is used to replace an existing product. A recent example of this has been the introduction of 'digital' music, which can be downloaded online, competing with the compact disc (which replaced cassette tapes, and so on). It is important for small businesses to key an eye out for what might be happening in their industry, especially if it is an area of constant innovation or change.

New Entrants

This occurs when a new competitor enters the market. These new competitors or entrants to an industry can be a considerable threat because they bring a desire to gain market share, may undertake industry activities in new and innovative ways, and sometimes have a substantial amount of resources. It is beyond the scope of this book to discuss strategies to combat new entrants, however, these strategies can include building barriers to entering an industry sector and attempting to lock existing customers of the business into long term agreements.

Copyright © 2009, IGI Global, distributing in print or electronic forms without written permission of IGI Global is prohibited.

Competitors

An understanding of the competition within an industry area is important to small businesses. The advent of ICTs is significant in that it has widened the geographical market and resulted in a greater number of potential competitors - not just from businesses in the same region, but from logistically enabled entities in other parts of the world. A later section of this chapter is devoted to how to evaluate the Web presence of competitors.

BUSINESS STRATEGY

When established, the Web presence of a small business will also become part of its ICT profile. ICTs are increasingly being employed in businesses to assist them to gain competitive advantage. Competitive advantage occurs when a business gains a lead on its competitors in the marketplace. The pursuit of competitive advantage occurs when a business attempts to disturb, enhance or limit the competitive forces at work in its own industry sector. One manner in which businesses can do this is to add value to their products and/or services.

As we are particularly interested in Websites that are set up for the purposes of dealing with customers, it is appropriate to examine some of ways in which ICTs can help to provide value to the goods and services of a small business.

Porter and Millar (1985) stated that 'value' is measured by the amount that buyers are willing to pay for a product or service. They mention three ways that organisations can compete with their products or services (these are known as the three generic strategies for improving competitiveness):

- Be the low cost producer.
- Produce a unique or differentiated product.
- Provide a product or service that meets the requirements of a specialised market.

We will now examine each of these.

Low Cost Producer

The opportunity to be a low cost producer occurs when a business produces a product or service of similar quality to competitors, but at a lower cost. The price of a product or service generally contains three components (Benjamin and Wigand 1995):

Copyright © 2009, IGI Global, distributing in print or electronic forms without written permission of IGI Global is prohibited.

- *Production costs.* These costs represent the physical or other primary processes that are needed to create and distribute the goods or services.
- *Coordination costs.* These represent the costs of all of the information processing necessary to coordinate the work of people and machines that perform the primary processes.
- *Profit margin.*

Lowering any of these cost areas can provide a means for the organisation to lower the price of the product or service. One useful way to lower costs is for a business to produce its goods more efficiently than its competitors. In our particular instance we are interested in ways that small businesses may be able to use Internet technologies to help them do this.

Competing on Differentiation

This involves providing value in a product or service that is not provided by a competitor. Alter (1992) suggested a number of ways of differentiating product offerings by combining them with ICTs. Some of these will now be discussed.

Helping the Customer Purchase the Product

This operates on the basis that ICTs can be used to help the customer purchase the product by expediting transactions (perhaps by providing online payment facilities) or ensuring the product is delivered faster. One useful innovation adopted by freight companies over the last few years is to provide a service where customers are able to track the delivery of their products. Small businesses using these freight services for delivery are able to provide customers with an online Web address that allows them to track exactly where their product may be in the logistics cycle.

Assuring Fit to Customer Needs

The key to these types of systems is that they are flexible enough to be able to allow some type of personal customization to occur with minimal manual intervention by employees. Some examples include:

- **Matching to customer requirements:** For instance, ICTs allow the automatic storage and recall of the special needs of customers (such as vegetarian meals) for flight or accommodation bookings. Smaller businesses can take advantage of this feature by including questions that relate to purchase preferences on

Copyright © 2009, IGI Global, distributing in print or electronic forms without written permission of IGI Global is prohibited.

online order forms, or keep track of customer preferences through their purchases.

- **Customising information products:** An example of this is the use of desktop
publishing and database facilities to 'customise' local newspapers that span
several districts allowing a combination of local articles and advertisements.
This might be useful for businesses that provide regular online newsletters to
customers. Rather than provide a generic newsletter to all customers, different
newsletters (or specially customised newsletters) might be sent out according
to customer preferences the business has stored in its databases.

- **Customising physical products:** This can be done where the production system is linked in with a (perhaps online) ordering system. A customer orders a
product with individual specifications and the automated production process
takes over. Obviously such a system would require a significant investment
and would rely on having a critical mass of orders to justify that expense – so
it may be beyond the realm of many small businesses.

Enhancing the Product

Different techniques can be used to provide extra value for the customer by enhancing the product:

- *Incorporating ICT into the product to provide further information on its use.*
For instance, one easy way for a business that sells microwave ovens to do
this online would be to provide online recipes that are tailored specifically for
their products.

- *Providing product information or knowledge.* A simple way for small businesses to do this is by putting a Frequently Asked Questions (FAQ) section on
the Website, where the answers to typical questions a business receives about
a particular product can be published in a '24/7' (24 hours a day/ 7 days a
week) environment. This provides extra product support outside of the normal
hours a business may be open.

- *Providing cost control information.* These systems provide better information
for users on efficient use of a product or service. In other words, whenever a
business stores transactional information about its customers (for instance, when
a small catering business invoices its business customers on, say, a monthly
basis), it is able to provide quite detailed information to the customer - from
its database - as to the customers' purchases for that month. The providers
of services, such as gas and electricity, often do this. The customer is able to
compare usages and costs over different periods, as well as being informed of
the most cost effective and efficient times to use the service. Often, the busi-

Copyright © 2009, IGI Global, distributing in print or electronic forms without written permission of IGI Global
is prohibited.

ness can make this service available online to customers via a secure login feature. However, there should be a critical mass of transactions that occurs to justify the expense of setting up this feature.

Summary of Business Differentiation

Clearly, ICTs can be used in a number of ways to help differentiate an organisation's products and/or services. This section has provided a number of detailed suggestions as to how Internet technologies may be used by a business to differentiate products and/or services by:

- **Quality:** This relates to product or service traits (such as durability) that provide a degree of excellence when compared with the products or services of competitors.
- **Product Support:** The level of support provided for the product or service. This can include information on how to use the product, product replacement/return strategies, and so forth.
- **Time:** This works on the concept that buyers will pay more for a product that is provided/ delivered quickly, or will choose a product of similar price and quality if it is available *now* over a competitor's product that is not currently available.
- **Personalisation/ Customisation:** This is the process of customizing/tailoring a product or service to a purchaser's determined profile.

Filling the Needs of Specialised Markets

The third of the three generic strategies for improving competitiveness is where the organisation identifies a particular specialized or niche market for its products and/or services. The advantage of targeting such a market is that there may be less competition than in more general markets. It could be argued that the effort taken to prepare and market the products or services of a business for a specialised market is just another form of differentiation.

Other Strategies

In addition to Porter's suggested three generic strategies, various other business strategies are commonly encountered that organisations can adopt to assist them in dealing with elements of the five competitive forces model.

Copyright © 2009, IGI Global, distributing in print or electronic forms without written permission of IGI Global is prohibited.

Innovation

Innovation occurs when an organisation invents new ways of doing business. In some cases this may lead to differentiation of products. In other cases it may lead to new ways of doing business and may alter the fundamental structure of an industry. Innovation in a small business is not restricted to the use of ICTs, with many entrepreneurs looking for innovative ways to improve manufacturing processes or new ways to deliver services as a way to keep a step ahead of competitors. The idea behind being 'innovative' from the point of view of this book does not mean that a Website has to be used in a manner that has not been employed before. However, there may be, for instance, a Website feature that has not been employed in a particular context before. The ability to spot these opportunities (and subsequently take advantage of them) is often what can make the difference between a typical small business owner and an *entrepreneur* as individuals can often differ in their propensity to accept and act upon these ideas. The term *innovator* is used to describe those businesses that are first to adopt such a new idea. Those that see the potential soon afterwards and also adopt the idea are known *early adopters*. As the innovation becomes more commonplace in the industry it is adopted by the *early majority* and the *late majority*. Those that will never adopt the idea are known as *laggards* (Frenzel and Frenzel 2004). There is a reason why everybody is not an early adopter – although the potential rewards may be attractive, there is always a risk involved in implementing something new. Small business owners are often quite conservative and may be more comfortable with others taking the initial risk. However, as the idea becomes more commonplace its adoption is less likely to provide rewards as attractive as those for the initial adopters.

Growth

A growth strategy involves the expansion of an organisation's capacity to produce goods and services and/or expanding into new markets. This strategy would be suitable for a business looking to its Website to assist in getting access to new markets. By our previous description, an *entrepreneur* would adopt a growth strategy and would look to employ combinations of the three generic strategies, innovation, alliance and co-opetition to grow the market and thus the business. However, as we describe later in this book, not all small business owners are entrepreneurs and not all of them wish to grow their business.

Copyright © 2009, IGI Global, distributing in print or electronic forms without written permission of IGI Global is prohibited.

Alliance

An alliance strategy involves the establishment of a business linkages or alliances with any other element of the five competitive forces model. Typically, these types of linkages can include mergers, acquisitions, joint ventures or other marketing, manufacturing or distribution agreements between businesses. However, for a small business it is possible to set up much less formal alliances with business and other partners. These can involve directing business to each others' Websites. Another technique is to become involved with third parties via third party Websites, often known as portals (as already discussed). Many alliances occur on the *supply* side of the small business (Turban et al 2006), which is not the realm of this book. The next section discusses a special type of alliance strategy.

Co-Opetition and Complementors

Similar to alliance, co-opetition is a business strategy proposed by Bradenburger and Nalebuff (1996) that recognizes the business relationships with not just the suppliers, customers and competitors, but also complementors. Complementors can be defined as businesses within an industry sector that generate products that enhance the value of another firm's product in the eyes customers. Hence, one company's product has a synergistic action on another company's product - this action is commonly reciprocated. An example of this is the way that the increasing power of microprocessor chips has allowed software companies to develop more sophisticated and faster applications. The microchip manufacturers can be viewed as complementors because their product allows the software developers to enhanced and produce a better product. By creating more powerful applications the software developer provides an incentive for the microchip producer to further increase processing power. Hence, the businesses have major incentives to act as complementors for each other. A small business needs to be aware of potential complementors in their industry sector that can be facilitated by having a Web presence. This Web presence can be as simple as having links to another company's Website to promote mutually compatible products or services. Figure 2 depicts the value chain interaction of suppliers, customers, competitors and complementors that tend to be associated with co-opetition.

Summary of Business Strategies

In this section, a number of important concepts associated with business theory and strategy were introduced. The issue of 'value' was deemed to represent the amount that buyers are willing to pay for a product or service. The five competitive forces

Copyright © 2009, IGI Global, distributing in print or electronic forms without written permission of IGI Global is prohibited.

Figure 2. Co-opetition interaction (adapted from Bradenburger & Nalebuff, 1996)

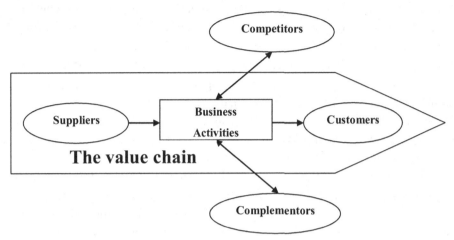

model suggests that any strategic approach that is used to add value to business products or services will directly affect, or be affected by, existing competitors, customers and suppliers. Furthermore, any new entrants to the industry or the advent of substitute products and/or services will also impact on a business's 'adding value' strategy when it comes to the five forces model. Three generic approaches for improving competitiveness were introduced and it was proposed that these strategies could be adopted by organisations in their pursuit and implementation of information technology. Moreover, other possible strategies such as innovation, growth, alliance and co-opetition were also highlighted as possible methods that an organisation can use to improve their competitiveness in an industry sector.

Now that we have examined the relationship between ICTs and business theory, we can go on to examine some techniques that allow a small business to determine its own business strategy.

ICT INVESTMENT APPRAISAL

One of the important aspects of adopting new innovations or technologies is to undertake an appraisal to determine if the investment is worthwhile. One of the challenges associated with investment appraisal of ICTs is that whilst it can be relatively easy to identify the costs associated with a project it is not always easy to identify the benefits. Benefits tend to be often intertwined with other business activities, such as changes in business processes or targetted marketing campaigns, hence, are difficult to clearly identify. In larger businesses, ICT investments can

Copyright © 2009, IGI Global, distributing in print or electronic forms without written permission of IGI Global is prohibited.

be extremely difficult to appraise, especially if they are for the *ICT infrastructure,* where this expenditure represents the networks of computers and electronic communications used to deliver business applications and services. These are usually seen as being core technologies that are used by the entire business and it is difficult to relate them to any specific revenue stream. To a lesser extent, small businesses face similar problems in that they usually have one or more computers, often networked, that support the sharing of data, shared computer peripherals (such as printers) and communications (such as e-mail). Again, these can be difficult to link to a particular revenue stream. In these instances, large businesses will often assess the ICT investments against expected improved performance from the systems, such as improved decision making capabilities, faster report generation and so forth. Sometimes the performance and cost of these systems is benchmarked against other, similar businesses or may be compared against a documented industry *best practice.*

However, there are some instances of ICT investments where quantitative benefits can be assessed. These usually occur where a particular project has been identified that can be clearly separated from other activities of the business. In the case of a Web presence, it might be possible to identify the incremental costs associated with setting up, implementing and maintaining the Website. If sales are set up on the Website it will be possible to identify the sales that originate from online orders. However, small businesses need to be aware that even at a basic level there will be some intertwining of online and 'regular' activities. For instance, what if a customer that would normally purchase a product decides to do so online, but would have made the purchase through regular channels anyway? It is arguable as to whether there is any benefit gained for the business. Also, the business needs to be aware that other features on the Website can also provide benefits. For instance, extra information provided about a product on the Website might convince a customer to buy it, or even product support information on the Website might mean that a business receives less labor-intensive telephone enquiries. The business should be aware of as many of the costs and potential benefits of the Web presence as it assesses its investment.

Keeping all of this in mind, it might still be possible to perform a simplistic cost benefit analysis of the quantifiable costs and benefits of adopting a Web presence. Typical approaches that can be used by small business are:

- **Payback period:** This is where the initial cost of setup of the ICT project is calculated as the amount that needs to be *paid back.* Then, for forthcoming years the annual surplus of the project is calculated by subtracting the annual costs from the annual revenue. The surplus is then added up each year and the time calculated to pay back the initial investment is called the payback period. Businesses will often have a benchmark payback period that they require for each project.

Copyright © 2009, IGI Global, distributing in print or electronic forms without written permission of IGI Global is prohibited.

- **Net Present Value (NPV):** This technique takes into account the *time value of money.* This works on the notion that a dollar invested today is worth more than a dollar in the future. For any potential project the initial outlay is totaled against the annual surplus over a period of years (often three to five years, but sometimes longer). The difference from the payback method is that the surplus in years 1, 2, 3, ... is *discounted* against a benchmark annual rate that the business sets, often a standard rate that it would achieve if it invested the initial outlay instead of commencing the project. If the *discounted* return from the project adds up to more than zero, then the project is performing better than the benchmark rate and would be seen as being worthy to invest in.
- **Internal Rate of Return (IRR):** The Internal Rate of Return is a calculation that offsets the projected annual surpluses over future years against the initial outlay of the ICT project and determines an annual *rate of return* for the project. The difference between this technique and NPV is that IRR does not start with a predetermined 'benchmark' rate. It is a calculated rate of return for a project that would return an NPV of 0.

The topic of ICT investment appraisal is revisited in Chapter X, where we look at evaluating the success of the small business Web presence.

DETERMINING BUSINESS STRATEGY

Before considering how small business owner/managers can determine their own business strategy, it is useful to briefly examine some well-known techniques for analysing the business position.

SWOT Analysis

The SWOT analysis has been traditionally used in the marketing or economics areas of the business. The term SWOT is an acronym for Strengths, Weaknesses, Opportunities and Threats. An analysis is performed on the various areas of the business to identify current or potential strengths and weaknesses when compared with other competitive forces (such as those identified in Porter's five forces model). From this analysis, the organisation identifies actual or potential opportunities to gain strategic advantage or threats to the organisation's well being. Actions taken by the organisation to take advantage of an opportunity are proactive. Actions taken by the organisation to combat a threat are reactive.

Copyright © 2009, IGI Global, distributing in print or electronic forms without written permission of IGI Global is prohibited.

The analysis of the strengths and weaknesses of the organisation and its competitors should include (Kotler et al, 1989):

- The relative size and scope of the business.
- The resources available.
- Skill levels within the business.
- Customer types and preferences.
- Customer loyalties and behaviour.
- Existing Company images and brand.
- Relative ability to serve the market.
- Relative ability to control distribution and resellers.

Once an actual or perceived opportunity or threat has been identified, the organisation can examine ways in which IT can be applied in a proactive or reactive manner. Indeed, one of the advantages of the SWOT analysis from the viewpoint of this book is that it requires an investigation of internal and external factors affecting the business that are very similar to those that we have already identified in this chapter and the previous one.

Critical Success Factors

John Rockart (1979) was the first to introduce the concept of critical success factors (CSFs). CSFs are used to identify factors that are critical to the success of a business operation. Critical success factors are the limited number of areas in which results, if they are satisfactory, will ensure successful competitive performance for the business. They are the few key areas where 'things must go right' for the business to flourish. If the results in these areas are not adequate, the efforts for the period will be less than desired. As a result, critical success factors reflect the areas of business activity that should receive constant and careful attention from management. The current status of performance in each area should be continually monitored, and that information should be made available to decision makers (Rockart, 1979). CSFs can be used to identify areas of the organisation where the effective use of IT could help to ensure its 'successful competitive performance'. The method encourages executives to identify what is important to them in their business, and outlines a number of steps to be followed in the identification of CSFs (Alter, 1992):

1. Identify the primary mission of the organisation and the objectives that define satisfactory overall performance for the organisation.
2. Identify critical success factors.

Copyright © 2009, IGI Global, distributing in print or electronic forms without written permission of IGI Global is prohibited.

3. For each CSF, identify pertinent indicators or measures of performance that can be tracked. These are often known and key performance indicators, or KPIs.
4. Develop systems for collecting and using this information.

Although CSFs are historically a tool used by larger businesses, it is useful for a small business owner/manager to think about *what must go right* within the business as the direction of the business is being charted. It is especially useful to do this immediately after a SWOT analysis has been carried out and in deciding what factors are most important when setting up the Web presence.

KNOWING HOW THE BUSINESS IS PLACED

This section examines how a small business might use a SWOT analysis and target areas of Porter's Five Competitive Forces model to assist with analysing where they are situated competitively in their industry.

A number of factors have been highlighted as being important in the exploitation of ICT in small business. **Many of these factors were described in the previous chapter as contributing to the 'e-readiness' of a small business to adopt Internet technologies.** These factors, classified as internal and external factors in the previous chapter, include available resources (money and time), owner/manager involvement, training of user-managers, the level of internal ICT expertise, the use (or absence of use) of planning methodologies, involvement of end users and the impact of the external environment (use of consultants and vendors). **In fact, much of the analysis carried out as part of the e-readiness toolkit in the previous chapter complements what follows here.**

The areas covered in the following analysis are those typical of a SWOT analysis investigating the business aims and resources available within the business (internal factors) and external forces that affect the business.

Internal Factors

It is important for small business owner/managers to understand the level of commitment required to have an effective Web presence. Mostafa et al (2004) suggest that the allocation of resources such as adequate human, technological and financial resources can reflect the level of commitment to the Internet presence – recognising of course that a lack of skilled staff and limited resources are typical barriers facing small businesses in this arena.

Copyright © 2009, IGI Global, distributing in print or electronic forms without written permission of IGI Global is prohibited.

Overall Business Aims

It is vital that those involved with developing a Web presence have an understanding of not only the technical issues, but also the overall aims of the business. It is important that the Web presence initiatives are aligned with the business aims and strategy. Is the Website going to be an extension of the existing business, or a new initiative? Is the business looking to gain new customers or are lower costs the primary aim? Are there opportunities for alliances or chances to be involved in co-opetition? These can all impact on the type of Website being developed.

One important factor that will affect the direction of the business is the reason for its existence in the first place. Earlier in this chapter we addressed the idea of the typical small business owner versus the entrepreneur. The typical small business owner might be looking to have a business that provides for his or her family and be content to have a clientele that provides for a comfortable living. Other small businesses are operated for lifestyle reasons. For instance, many small accommodation providers start businesses in rural or seaside areas because of the lifestyle – and may not necessarily even be concerned if their business returns a small loss! Of course, the contrast is the entrepreneur who is looking for all opportunities to grow the business and will look to the Website as one of the means that this can occur. The simple fact of the matter is that business aims differ and the strategies employed in the business (including the Website strategy) should reflect these aims.

As mentioned earlier in the chapter, typical strategies that can be adopted by a small business are a (low) cost strategy, a differentiation strategy, a growth strategy, an alliance strategy or strategy involving co-opetition. It is important that the Web presence strategy of the business complements its overall business strategy.

A low cost strategy is self-explanatory – a business tries to deliver its products or services at the lowest cost possible. Fundamental to this strategy is the effort to gain efficiencies from using ICTs to reduce operating costs. A differentiation strategy means that a business tries to differentiate itself within an industry sector by providing products or services that consumers perceive as being different to a competitor - perhaps by using some of the online strategies mentioned earlier in the chapter. With a growth strategy, a business is looking to expand its market. Such a strategy should match the aims of the business. For instance, a business that serves a local market (such as a gardening service) with no growth aspirations should carefully consider whether or not they need a Web presence. They may be able to provide other, added value, services that are important to existing customers.

An alliance or co-opetition strategy allows a business to form a partnership with external partners, such as customers, suppliers or even competitors, for mutual

Copyright © 2009, IGI Global, distributing in print or electronic forms without written permission of IGI Global is prohibited.

advantage. It will be seen later in this book that Internet technologies provide a means to facilitate such collaborations.

An important thing about these strategies is that they can be combined – for instance, a small business may have a differentiation strategy, but also be looking to grow (growth strategy) and one way they might decide this is by setting up an alliance with other businesses (alliance strategy).

Capital and Investment Appraisal

One of the major differences between small businesses and their larger counterparts is that small businesses typically do not have the financial (or even liquid) resources available to experiment with untested Web applications. Thus, small businesses are often conservative in their use of ICTs (including the Internet), choosing *safer* strategies that will enable them to obtain efficiencies and perhaps save costs – but not necessarily providing them with a level of *differentiation* that will encourage customers to switch to their products or services. The lack of ready capital, combined with the typically conservative nature of small businesses, means that the majority of them make a fairly low-cost entry into developing their Web presence. This also means that small businesses should be assessing the cost of setting up and maintaining their Web presence early on.

The important aspect to assessing the value of the potential investment is to try to quantify as many benefits and costs (both setup and ongoing) as possible for a pre-defined length of time (three to five years). This will allow the business to carry out some form of investment appraisal (such as payback, NPV and/or IRR). Where benefits are not quantifiable, the small business operator should at least try to apportion some value to them, so that they can be considered as part of the overall analysis when deciding whether or not to continue with the investment. When assessing the quantifiable and non-quantifiable outcomes, it is important to remember is that the most important thing is that the benefits match the business and Web presence strategy. The next chapter discusses the notion of setup and ongoing costs of individual Website features in more detail.

Capacity

Employees may be required to provide some technical skills or knowledge to implement and/or assist in the maintenance of the organisation's Web presence. Where the technical skills required to implement and maintain an organisation's Website are unavailable, it is necessary to use expertise external to the organisation. Often small businesses rely on informal networks to source this advice, such as family members or friends, although increasingly small businesses are starting to take

Copyright © 2009, IGI Global, distributing in print or electronic forms without written permission of IGI Global is prohibited.

advantage of the services of external consultants and vendors. It is important to look beyond the cost of external advice and be aware of the level of expertise that these sources can provide. For instance, friends or family members might have proficient technical skills and may be able to build an inexpensive Website, but do they understand Website design best practice or how to make the content of the Website match the business Website strategy? It is important that small businesses get the balance right – they often look for the most inexpensive sources of expertise (capacity), but these may not always be suitable.

Type of Products and/or Services Offered

The type of products and/or services offered by a small business will influence the Web presence they may have. For example various products and services will differ according to the (Peterson et al 1997):

- *Cost and frequency of purchase.* Goods vary along this dimension from low cost, frequently purchased goods (such as milk) to higher cost, infrequently purchased goods (such as a television).
- *Value proposition.* Goods vary along this dimension between being 'tangible and physical' and 'intangible and service related'.
- *Degree of differentiation.* This is determined by the extent to which a seller is able to create a competitive advantage by differentiation.

There are a number of different considerations to be taken into account with online versus traditional shopping. Online purchases that involve physical products will need to be delivered. This may take some time and may involve paying an additional logistics and freight cost. Physical shopping can take some time if the location of the purchase is some distance away – and there may be a cost involved in getting to that location.

Peterson et al (1997) suggest that consumers are unlikely to engage in prolonged Internet searches for low valued and frequently purchased goods. They are still likely to buy tangible or physical goods such as bread or milk in a retail store. This is more likely to be because of the speed in which they can get the goods. However, highly priced and less frequently purchased goods embrace a different set of business marketing and sales parameters. As the consumer generally allocates more time to seek information about these types of goods, purchases may be made in either the retail arena or online. There are some exceptions. With tangible or physical products where there is a high degree of differentiation (such as with used cars), the need for personal inspections may cause the consumer to purchase from a retail outlet. Although, with intangible or informational products where there is a high degree of

Copyright © 2009, IGI Global, distributing in print or electronic forms without written permission of IGI Global is prohibited.

differentiation (such as with software packages), the swiftness of delivery by direct download may encourage consumers to purchase over the Internet.

In the end, a small business needs to be aware of the type of customers that are being targetted for its particular goods and develop its Web presence strategy accordingly.

External Factors

Competitors

It is important for small businesses to be aware of how and why their competitors are employing their Web presence. An appropriate way of achieving this is for the small business operator to examine competitor Websites on a regular basis and determine if they themselves need to review or update their own Web strategy. Using this competitor Website evaluation can be easily undertaken by asking salient questions such as:

- Which of our competitors have a Website?
- What level of sophistication have they achieved?
- What features do they have that might be effective for our business?
- What do customers think about their Website?
- What are their goals?
- Who are they trying to attract (target market)?

An analysis of competitor Websites can be an indicator for a small business of the stage that they are at in relation to an online presence within their industry. Indeed, a matrix analysis can be used to document the main features of, say, a company's five major competitors, to determine where the company stands amongst its competitors in the scale ranging between early adopter and late adopter. This can be set up fairly easily using a spreadsheet. An example can be seen in Table 1. In this table, typical Website features are listed in the first column. The next few columns represent each major competitor of the business (in this case, there are five – realistically, the names of the competitors would be placed here rather than the numbers 1-5). Where a competitor already has a particular feature fully implemented on their Website, a score of one is given. Different features can be added to the spreadsheet as they are observed on competitor Websites. The last two columns represent the total number of businesses that have a particular feature and the percentage of competitors that have the feature (in this case, the total as a proportion of the five competitors that were identified).

Copyright © 2009, IGI Global, distributing in print or electronic forms without written permission of IGI Global is prohibited.

As further features become commonplace amongst competitors or on the Internet, extra rows can be added to the spreadsheet. If the business has no Internet presence at all, a comparison table such as this can show the features that may be necessary when building the site initially. It also shows what features that may be introduced that have not been adopted by competitors where it may be possible to gain a short-term competitive advantage. This basic technique was used in the studies referred to in this book that were conducted by the authors and involve the analysis of small business Websites.

However, small businesses might also be interested in when their competitors make changes to their Websites or third party Web presence. Instead of having to monitor competitor Websites on a regular basis, small businesses can register the Website address with one of these services and be notified when there are any changes made to the Website. There are different types of services available. Some are free and some charge a fee to use them. They can monitor occurrences such as

Table 1. A Web presence competitor comparison matrix (adapted from Burgess & Schauder 1999)

FEATURE	Competitor					Total	%
	1	2	3	4	5		
BASIC PRODUCT DETAILS							
Product catalogue	1	1	1			3	60
Prices	1	1	1		1	4	80
TRANSACTION DETAILS							
Online Ordering	1		1			2	40
Online Payment	1					1	20
INFORMATION							
About the Business	1	1	1	1	1	5	100
About Trade Shows/ Coming Events	1		1			2	40
Product Support Features							
Frequently Asked Questions	1					1	20
Directions on how to use the product	1	1				2	40
OTHER LINKS							
Other websites of interest	1		1			2	40
Basic Internet Feature Sites	1		1			2	40
Search Engines	1					1	20
CONTACT DETAILS							
Email	1		1	1	1	4	80
By Form			1			1	20

Copyright © 2009, IGI Global, distributing in print or electronic forms without written permission of IGI Global is prohibited.

changes in content, addition or removal of Website features, changes in bulletin boards or forums and even changes to graphics or videos on the Websites. Some of the different tools that are available can be found by entering in 'Website changes' into a search engine.

Customers

Organisations will need to be aware of the increasing empowerment of consumers as they gain improved access to the Internet and become more skillful and sophisticated in using this technology. The Internet has empowered customers with easy access to relevant information allowing them to more easily make decisions based upon price, quality, product suitability and after sales service than when they had to physically travel to each vendor.

However, not all potential customers are Internet savvy. There are still areas in the world where Internet connections are not readily available (we referred to this in the previous chapter) and even where high speed connections are available and affordable it is important to realise that many people may not be high powered users. A typical example of such a group are the elderly, many for whom the Internet, and even computers, are a mystery. Hence, it is important for the business to know which of the categories of Internet users, if any, that its target market falls into.

Alliances

The easiest way to set up alliances in the online environment is to provide links to the Websites of partner businesses. For instance, an organisation that sells fishing supplies over the Internet may provide a link to a local business where customers can book fishing trips, or perhaps even fishing books or videos (from an online bookstore). These types of arrangements often occur as 'affiliate' or 'associate' programs, where the organisation receives a commission for directing a sale to the organisation that receives the sale of the complementary product.

Another popular way to foster alliances over the Internet is to participate in a portal. A portal is a special type of Website that provides links to (and sometimes information about) other Websites, usually around a particular theme – such as an industry or a particular region. A small business participating in a portal generally hopes to attract customers that will be drawn to the theme of the portal. Also, portals may provide features or services that the business can take advantage of, such as online purchasing. These features might be difficult to set up for a small business on its own Website. Portals feature prominently in Chapters VI and VIII.

Copyright © 2009, IGI Global, distributing in print or electronic forms without written permission of IGI Global is prohibited.

Summary of Determining Business Strategies and Factors

In general this last section examined aspects relating to the business ICTs, investment appraisal and the determination of an appropriate business strategy. Aspects of the SWOT analysis and Porter's five competitive forces model have been discussed as a means for performing a business investigation. These have classified into internal factors and external forces. Furthermore, the internal factors include an examination of the overall strategy of the business, the capital available to the business, the availability of skills of existing employees and the characteristics of products and services. The external forces analysed include competitors and customers, together with an examination of the benefits of forming alliances with external forces.

OUR PREVIOUS STUDIES

Accountant_07

This study involved interviews with 20 managers of accounting practices, predominantly in small and medium sized businesses. In relation to Web presence strategy, all of the small practices stated the somewhat generic *need to have a Web presence* or that *the market expected it* as their primary Website strategy. A higher proportion of medium sized practices identified that their Websites were *a resource for clients*. Two factors that did emerge from the larger practices were that many of them viewed their Website as being a *resource for employees to use* as well as a *means for recruiting new staff.*

A number of the smaller practices actually highlighted the fact that they were small, and that this limited the options that they had to create their Websites and, more importantly, update it on a regular basis.

In relation to providing the relevant ICT skills, this issue was typically managed by one or two partners (in addition to their normal duties). This was usually in conjunction with an external consultant. This was also the case with some medium sized businesses, but they were more likely to have dedicated ICT staff in their employ. Both small and medium sized practices were prepared to supplement their shortage of skills with the use of external consultants where appropriate.

Turning to factors that are external to the practices, one strong theme that emerged from almost all of the practices was that they were very client-focussed. This focus defined their ICT strategies as they examined ways to deliver a better, more efficient service and even determined how far they pushed their ICT applications. When asked what was planned in the future, a number of interviewees responded that they would be driven by what their clients demanded.

Copyright © 2009, IGI Global, distributing in print or electronic forms without written permission of IGI Global is prohibited.

A small number of practices actually examined what competitors were doing on their Websites. Of these, many employed the same consultants as their competitors to help with the design of similar Websites. Interestingly, some practices were specifically involved in the design of their Websites themselves, for the specific purpose of making their Website look different to these other Websites.

Outer_06

This study involved interviews with 18 small businesses in outer suburban Melbourne (Australia). This study primarily concentrated upon capacity building issues. The researchers were interested in how the businesses build capacity for the use of ICTs and what formal and informal networks they might use for these. Some of the businesses indicated that they used more than one source for this purpose. A large proportion of interviewees (59%) indicated they were 'self taught', and almost a third had turned to a partner or family member for support. Only two indicated that had they attended a university level short course. The general theme, as expected, was for small business owners/managers to turn to informal networks (such as family members or friends) for assistance and instruction. An interesting finding in relation to sourcing support was that most specialised software packages (such as MYOB) had useful call centres that provide step-by-step instructions in the use of these packages.

The small businesses were also specifically asked if they were interested in engaging with universities or local government. There was some interest (five businesses overall) in taking short courses if they were available, across a range of skill sets in the business and ICT areas.

The main use of the Internet amongst the businesses was to research products and events occurring in their particular industry. Generally, no business indicated that they had received any direct sales through the Internet. The main benefit of the Internet came from indirect promotion online. For instance a health food storeowner indicated that since her suppliers had listed her on their Website as a distributor of their product she had seen an increase in sales.

The use of a Website, although common, has not resulted in any great benefit for the businesses. It seemed that businesses are developing Websites simply *because it is the trend* without any strategic planning. Even a small business that was a Website developer suggested that customers rarely visit the Website first. Usually customers call the small business and then the owner points them to the Website for more information.

Copyright © 2009, IGI Global, distributing in print or electronic forms without written permission of IGI Global is prohibited.

Develop_06

As noted earlier, an alliance strategy involves the establishment of business linkages or alliances with any other element of the five competitive forces model. The Internet creates opportunities for businesses to establish alliances that include joint ventures or other marketing links between businesses. During this study in Malaysia and Ecuador it was found that even though these types of relationships were difficult to initially establish, once in place, significant benefits resulted. For example, several lodge-tour operators collaborated with other similar tourism operators to develop a common Website promoting 'eco-lodges'. These small businesses were able pool their resources and develop a more sophisticated Website to represent the entire group. This allowed the tourist destination to be promoted to a greater degree than it may have been if each operator had solely used their own business-maintained Website. It also allowed tourists to plan trips by using the services of more than one of the operators. Another benefit that emerged from collaborating together in such a manner was that the group was able to promote themselves on a popular American based tourism portal. Individually, each tourism operator would not have had the resources to undertake this type of promotional activity.

Wineries_PhDsurvey_04

This research PhD investigated ICT adoption by small to medium size wineries and developed an e-business best practice model. The study found important evidence of co-opetition strategy operating in this industry sector that involved both complementors and competitors. In examining small winery Web presence, some 35% of wineries were found to have links that directed their Website visitors to other winery Websites. The study proposed that winery Web presence and these competitor-to-competitor links were an act of reciprocity between the wineries. In view of the extremely competitive environment in which wineries operated, especially with respect to wine sales, it might appear surprising that a relatively large number of wineries would redirect visitors on their own Website to a competitor's site. This paradox may be explained by co-opetition and suggests that a winery Web presence is one that focuses on using the Website as a promotional tool to foster a regional balance between groups of wineries for tourism purposes. Because tourism is integral to winery profitability, enticing visitors to an area is a challenge for all wineries. The linking to the competitor winery Website can be viewed as providing a service to a winery's customers as they explore and plan their next trip to the wine region. Wineries can thus use links from their Website to neighboring winery Websites to promote mutually beneficial aspects of tourism. Hence, these small wineries can participate as autonomous entities both online and in the physical world (this type

Copyright © 2009, IGI Global, distributing in print or electronic forms without written permission of IGI Global is prohibited.

of interactivity also occurs at the personal level amongst winery owners) where a group of competitors can be seen to work together for mutual benefits.

Another finding reported in the study that can also be examined from the context of co-opetition is that a notable group of small wineries provided links to the distributors and/or retailers of their wines. Maintaining good relationships with distributors is an important and essential marketing strategy for wineries - hence incorporating distributor and retailer links on their Website can promote important partners who are selling their wine. The winery can be viewed as a complementor to the third party retailers and distributors by providing a click-through link to their Websites. Conversely, the retailers and distributors add value to the winery product by broadening the scope of consumer access to wines via their retail outlets. Not reported in the study and a feature that can appear on various retailer and distributor Websites are links to individual winery Websites - a feature that reinforcing the value of Web presence for the smaller wine-maker. Furthermore, some wineries, in order to foster tourism, have linked to accommodation, cafes and restaurants in their surrounding region. Clearly, these tourism service industries act as third party complementors to the wineries, whilst they themselves benefit through wineries attracting visitors to the general area.

The study also identified small winery e-business strategies associated with four ICT areas infrastructure, e-mail, Web presence, and business-to-business to activities. The relevant aspect of the study that relate to Web presence included:

- Placing all relevant wine, winemaking and winery information on the Website with a view to achieving time and cost savings - savings gained by directing the plethora of winery enquiries to the Website (Internal factor - capital).
- The wine region as a tourist destination. By publishing tourism related information on the Website, the winery contributes to tourism activities and visitors tend to have a holistic experience when they decide to go to a region. The Australian wine industry has been a recent global success story and wineries appear to have adopted Web presence as part of an integral relationship with tourism (External factor - alliances).
- Management of the winery Website where a specific individual should take responsibility for the Website (Internal factor - skills).
- The registration of popular winery label names as domain names that contribute to the intellectual value or property associated with the winery (Internal factor - capital).
- Adherence to the various government regulatory requirements, whereby all wineries selling via the Internet need to prominently display legal warnings as an obligation associated with their Web presence (External factor - customer

Copyright © 2009, IGI Global, distributing in print or electronic forms without written permission of IGI Global is prohibited.

focus. This issue is a consequence of the regulatory environment that governs business activities).

- The practice of reciprocal hypertext linkages on the winery Website - or in some instances a listing may be sufficient - to the Websites of important industry partners and even competitor wineries (External factor - alliances and/or complementors).
- Offering a *secure, encrypted* sales service on a winery's Website that is essential for building consumer trust (Internal factor - skills associated with infrastructure).
- Utilize e-mail permission marketing to link the promotional newsletters (opt in) and Website wine ordering. Winery sales need to employ e-mail for contact with customers, whilst the winery Website ordering facility captures client details. Importantly, the Website on its own is neither an operative or successful business function, and thus a tandem operation of Website and e-mail is required (External factor - customer focus).

Tourism_04

In interviews with 59 small and medium sized tourism enterprises (SMTEs), the researchers examined a number of areas that were covered in this chapter. Overall, businesses generally performed better than would have been expected from a business investigation viewpoint. Most of the businesses seemed to adopt a fairly conservative strategy for their Web presence, which is consistent with previously documented small businesses behavior.

Some typical comments received about Web presence strategy were:

- "The main purpose is to get in touch with more people locally and internationally."
- "To provide information for international customers."
- "So people could get into contact with us."
- "I think a Website is cheap advertising compared to traditional means like TV ads."

Not many businesses considered internal factors, such as cost and employee skill level. Of the businesses that did look for external expertise, most of them relied on outside businesses for advice rather than informal networks. Only a small proportion of the businesses considered the overall investment they would need to make in creating and maintaining their Website:

Copyright © 2009, IGI Global, distributing in print or electronic forms without written permission of IGI Global is prohibited.

- "The package quote included everything."
- "The consultant provided me with package cost."
- "It cost only a few hundred of dollars to maintain it, that's not that much".
- "A friend constructed the whole Website and then gave me a price."
- "The cost of developing ranged from $5,000 to $12,000."
- "Initially I had not considered labour hours needed to maintain site."
- "I did it after a cost analysis decided it was feasible."
- "I was careful with the hosting company; I was concerned the cheaper they are they less service you receive."
- "The cost of developing site and maintaining it, and the other things, is not an issue – it is done during work hours."
- "The cost blew out beyond expectation. I had no idea how demanding it would be. I went for the middle quote."

From an external point of view, many businesses considered what their customers wanted from the Website. However, fewer businesses examined how competitors were using their Websites:

- "My customers are mostly professional people and they would have access to computers and want to work through a Website".
- "Initially I did not consider customers, but I do now."
- "I believe customers want a Website that is basic and easy to use."
- "We constantly perform 'active research' through feedback to improve the Website based on customer needs."
- "Yes, customers want the site in German and Spanish."
- "Of course we consider what customers want."

APEC_02

This study involved interviews with six successful small business in the APEC region: three small businesses and three micro businesses. These businesses either already used the Internet to great effect or were in the process of introducing online strategies. All of the businesses were looking to expand their activities. One key finding that came though in the interviews was the *entrepreneurial* nature of the owner/managers. They were all interested in examining ways to find resources to support their Internet use, either through accessing government support to improve their capital situation or through training to build capacity for the use of the Internet for themselves and their employees. Quite interestingly, a strong theme that came through was the need to integrate their online activities with their business strategy.

Copyright © 2009, IGI Global, distributing in print or electronic forms without written permission of IGI Global is prohibited.

Businesses from developing countries in particular did indicate that access to a reliable ISP was an issue (which is an e-readiness factor).

Other Studies

A Study into E-Commerce Adoption in New Zealand Small Businesses (Al-Qirim 2007)

Al-Qirim (2007) was particularly interested in those factors that lead to electronic commerce (EC) adoption in SMEs in New Zealand. From the literature, he identified a number of factors that may influence the adoption of EC:

- Characteristics of the innovation (technological factors), such as the relative advantage it would provide, its compatibility with existing systems and its cost.
- The environment in which the business operated, such as the level of competition in the industry, external pressure from suppliers or buyers and external support from vendors.
- The characteristics of the CEOs (what we would probably refer to as the owner/ managers) of small businesses – their innovativeness and their level of involvement.
- Organisational characteristics, such as the information intensity level of products and/or services.

The study involved a survey of New Zealand SMEs, followed by two focus groups. Al-Qirim divided EC adopters into two groups – 'low level' and 'advanced level' EC adopters. 'Low level' adopters tended to just browse the Internet and use e-mail, but they might also have a static Web page. 'Advanced' level EC adopters were more likely to have more than a Web page and perhaps use the Website to sell goods and collect payments online – with possibly intranet or extranet usage as well.

In relation to technological factors, low level adopters did not report many advantages of their Internet uses. The higher level adopters reported barriers like cost, time, and compatibility as being factors that could impede adoption of higher level features. However, factors such as the relative advantage that the features could offer, the level of information intensity in products, the level of competition and pressure from buyers and suppliers could encourage adoption. This highlights the importance of taking note of the internal and external factors mentioned in this chapter that can come into play when considering more advanced EC uses.

Copyright © 2009, IGI Global, distributing in print or electronic forms without written permission of IGI Global is prohibited.

Al-Qirim also found that the larger the business the better the position they were in to adopt advanced levels of EC. This was not a surprising finding. In relation to environmental factors, few SMEs considered the role of competitors or suggested that they adopted specific EC technologies because of the marketplace. It was interesting that technology vendors were seen as a negative influence to EC adoption! The level of innovativeness of the CEO was seen as a key to adopting EC

Internet Technology and the Performance of SMEs in Mexico (Amoros, Planellas and Batista-Foguet 2007)

In this study the authors identified four sets of factors from the literature that may be linked with business growth. As with other parts of this chapter, these factors can be divided into internal and external factors. Internal factors include *activity factors* (the type of activities [such as commercial, manufacturing and service activities]) and *managerial factors* (such as the perception that the Internet can help the business, who influences on adoption and previous experience in using the Internet). External factors relate to the *competitive environment* and include the influence of customers and suppliers, level of integration with the sector and the level of integration with the Internet. *Controlling factors* relate to the organisation and relate to the number of computers, how many of them are connected to the Internet, the number of e-mail accounts and the size of the business.

Amoros et al (2007) conducted a survey of 102 small businesses in Mexico at the end of 2005, investigating their ICT infrastructure, their use of the Internet and distinct characteristics of this use and related this to various performance factors. Their most important finding was that those businesses that used the Internet to a greater extent were those that had greater and sustained growth. Manufacturing and service based businesses were receiving greater benefits than retail businesses.

As with the Al-Qirim (2007) study, the motivation of CEOs (or owner/ manager as we would call them) was an important influence in the level of Internet use.

Another important finding was that it was important for small businesses to be involved in Internet use when other businesses in the same sector were employing the technology.

Factors Influencing Website Comprehensiveness in Taiwan (Chan and Lin 2007)

Chan and Lin (2007) surveyed 72 SMEs in Taiwan to determine how factors such as communication requirements, the level of competition in the industry and support and incentive factors affected how comprehensive the Websites of SMEs were.

Copyright © 2009, IGI Global, distributing in print or electronic forms without written permission of IGI Global is prohibited.

As with other studies, they found that the level of intensity of competition within an industry was likely to (positively) affect the level of Website comprehensiveness, as was the size of the business.

Also, the older the business was the more comprehensive its Website was likely to be.

Two external factors provided interesting results:

- As the need to communicate with customers increased, so did the level of comprehensiveness of the Website
- Support and incentives from government sources also positively affected the level of Website comprehensiveness.

However, there was no link found between the level of Website comprehensiveness and the performance of small businesses.

Summary of our Studies and Other Studies

These studies highlighted a range of different approaches by small businesses in varying types of industries and locations to many of the issues discussed in this chapter. They highlight the importance of understanding business aims and the wide variety of factors that should be considered before setting up the Web presence.

From a strategy viewpoint, simple strategies for having a Web presence (such as 'it is expected of us' or 'we need to have a presence') were reported, through strategies that used the Web presence to save costs or time, to a number of small businesses that displayed quite sophisticated strategies, such as those involving co-operation (in developing countries) and co-opetition (in wineries). The importance of linking the Web presence strategy and the business strategy was mentioned by a few (but not many) small businesses.

One strong point that came out from the other studies we reported was the influence of owner/ managers in levels of electronic commerce and Website adoption. From our point of view this is to be expected as they set the direction of the business.

A number of the studies reported the limited resources of small businesses as being something that limits the strategic potential of the Web presence. For instance, in relation to building capacity to implement and maintain the Web presence within small businesses, the studies reported findings that were not dissimilar to what we would have expected. Many small businesses had employees that were self taught, or they relied on building their expertise from informal networks. Some businesses (the accounting practices in particular) were quite prepared to source their professional external expertise if it was not available within the business.

Copyright © 2009, IGI Global, distributing in print or electronic forms without written permission of IGI Global is prohibited.

It was quite common for small businesses to consider some, but not all, of the costs associated with setting up and maintaining the Web presence.

In relation to considering external influences, the small businesses in our studies were more likely to consider what their customers wanted from their Web presence rather than examine what their competitors were doing.

TENETS – LESSONS FROM THE CHAPTER

It is vital for a small business to be aware of where it is situated in its particular industry before it embarks on a Web presence. To do this it needs to perform a thorough business investigation. The areas for analysis in this investigation are listed in Table 2.

CONCLUSION

The chapter highlighted a number of important concepts associated with business theory and strategy. The issue of 'value' was deemed to represent the amount that buyers are willing to pay for a product or service. The five competitive forces model suggests that any strategic approach that is used to add value to business products or services will directly affect existing competitors, customers and suppliers. Furthermore, any new entrants to the industry or the advent of substitute products and/or services will also impact on business adding value strategy when it comes to the five forces model. Three generic approaches for improving competitiveness were introduced and it was proposed that these strategies could be adopted by organisations in their pursuit and implementation of information technology. Moreover, other possible strategies such as innovation, growth, alliance and co-opetition were also highlighted as possible methods that an organisation can use to improve their competitiveness in an industry sector. Furthermore, a small business needs to examine and identify its business strategy, ensuring that there is a match between strategy and adoption of a Web presence. This chapter has provided a number of detailed suggestions as to how a small business could use its Web presence to differentiate products and/or services. Clearly, ICTs can be used in a number of ways to help differentiate an organisation's products and/or services. It was suggested that Internet technologies might assist the small business by enhancing product and/or service quality, provide product support, enable efficient and timely deliveries and allow customization of products and/or services to a purchaser's determined profile.

Also introduced in the chapter was a series of steps that a small business could follow when performing a business investigation, which involved an assessment of

Copyright © 2009, IGI Global, distributing in print or electronic forms without written permission of IGI Global is prohibited.

internal and external factors. The internal factor analysis involves documenting the overall business strategy, investigating available resources (capital and capacity) and consideration of the types of products and/or services offered by the small business. The external factors analysis involves an examination of how competitors are using their Websites, customer expectations of business Web presence and consideration of possible alliances. Aspects of the SWOT analysis and Porter's five competitive forces model were discussed as a means for performing a business investigation.

Table 2. Business investigation factors

Type of Factor	Factor	Method of Investigation
Internal	Overall business strategy	Small business web presence should be aligned with clearly defined business aims that may embrace - Low cost ; Differentiation; Growth; Alliance; Co-opetition. A starting point is for the business to determine which strategies it wishes to adopt.
	Capital	What financial resources does the business have available to devote to the web presence? Resources will needed to cover set up costs and the ongoing maintenance of the web presence.
	Investment Appraisal	It is important to carry out an investment appraisal to determine if the project is worth pursuing. The appraisal needs to consider setup and ongoing costs and benefits and consider non-quantifiable factors as well. Benefits should be commensurate with the overall business and web presence strategy.
	Capacity	What skills are available within the business? Are they relevant and accessible for building and maintaining the web presence? The business may need to source ICT expertise from outside the business. A balance will be required between expenditure and ensuring that suitable expertise is sourced.
	Products and Services	What types of goods does the business offer? Small businesses need to consider that although physical products can be ordered over the Internet they also have to be delivered. Certain types of goods, such as those having an *informational* component or those that can be digitised and downloaded may be more suited to the Internet.
External	Competitors	Which competitors have a website? What level of sophistication have they achieved? What is their target market? It is important to examine competitor websites on a regular basis. The contents of their websites can be quickly analysed by storing their features in a competitor comparison matrix. A small business should think about tracking what its competitors are doing using an automated website tracking service.
	Customers	Do the small business' customers use the Internet? Are they requesting web presence features? What particular features are they looking for?
	Alliance	Are there opportunities for gains to be made by partnering with other organisations to cross-promote products? Further opportunities in this area will be discussed when web presence hosting and promotion are discussed.

Copyright © 2009, IGI Global, distributing in print or electronic forms without written permission of IGI Global is prohibited.

The next chapter discusses the next phase of the process, how the results of the business investigation can be matched to a Web presence strategy and, more particularly, how particular Web presence features can be selected.

REFERENCES

Al-Qirim, N. (2007). A Research Trilogy into E-Commerce Adoption in Small Businesses in New Zealand. *Electronic Markets, 17*(4), 263-285.

Alter, S. (1992). *Information Systems: A Management Perspective.* California: Benjamin/Cummings.

Amorós, J. E., Planellas, M., & Batista-Foguet, J. M. (2007). Does Internet technology improve performance in small and medium enterprises? Evidence from selected Mexican firms. *Academia: Revista Latinoamericana de Administración,* (39), 71-91.

Bayne, K. M. (2000). *The Internet Marketing Plan: The complete guide to instant Web presence.* 2nd edn, New York: Wiley.

Benjamin, R., & Wigand, R. (1995). Electronic markets and virtual value chains on the information superhighway. *Sloan management review, 36*(2), 62-72.

Booth, A. (1999). *Making the Internet Work for Your Business.* New South Wales, Australia: Allen-Unwin.

Bradenburger, A., & Nalebuff, B. (1996). *Co-Opetition : A Revolution Mindset That Combines Competition and Cooperation.* New York: Doubleday.

Burgess, S. (2002). Information Technology in Small Business: Issues and Challenges. In S. Burgess (Ed.), *Information Technology in Small Business: Challenges and Solutions* (pp. 1-17). Hershey, PA: Idea Group Publishing.

Burgess, S., & Schauder, D. (1999). Assisting Small Businesses to Identify Internet Opportunities. *Millenial Challenges in Management Education, Cybertechnology and Leadership* (pp. 121-128). San Deigo, California, Association of Management and the International Association of Management.

Duan, Y., Mullins, R., & Hamblin, D. (2000). Making Successful E-Commerce: An Analysis of SMEs Training and Support Needs. *1ˢᵗ. World Congress on the Management of Electronic Commerce*, Ontario, Canada.

Frenzel, C. W., & Frenzel, J. C. (2006). *Management of Information Technology.* 4th edn, Thomson Course Technology, Canada.

Copyright © 2009, IGI Global, distributing in print or electronic forms without written permission of IGI Global is prohibited.

Jones, M. V., & Dimitratos, P. (2004). *Emerging Paradigms in International Entrepreneurship.* Butterworth-Heinemann, MA.

O'Brien, T. (2000). *E-Commerce Handbook: A Practical Guide to Developing a Successful E-Business Strategy.* State Government of Victoria, Tri-Obi Productions, Melbourne, Australia.

O'Brien, J.A. (1999). *Management Information Systems: Managing Information Technology in the Internetworked Enterprise,* 4th edn, Irwin/ McGraw-Hill, USA.

Pearlson, K., & Saunders, C. (2006). *Managing and Using Information Systems: A Strategic Approach,* 3rd edn, Wiley, New York.

Peterson, R. A., Balasubramanian, S., & Bronnengerg, B. J. (1997). Exploring the Implications of the Internet for Consumer Marketing. *Journal of the Academy of Marketing Science, 25*(4), 329-346.

Porter, M. E. (2001) Strategy and the Internet. *Harvard business review, 79*(3), 62-78.

Porter, M. E. (1979). How competitive forces shape strategy. *Harvard business review, 57*(2), 137-145.

Porter, M. E., & Millar, V. E. (1985). How information gives you competitive advantage. *Harvard Business Review, 63*(4), 149.

Rockart, J. (1979). Chief Executives Define their own Data Needs. *Harvard Business Review, 57*(2), 81-93.

Schlenker, L., & Crocker, N. (2003). Building an e-business scenario for small business: The IBM SME Gateway project. *Qualitative Market Research: An International Journal, 6*(1), 7-17.

Shu-Ching, C., & Jin-Ying, L. (2007). Factors Influencing the Website Comprehensiveness of Small to Medium-sized Enterprises: An Empirical Study. *International Journal of Management, 24*(2), 203-215.

Turban, E., King, D., Viehland, D., & Lee, J. (2006). *Electronic Commerce 2006: A Managerial Perspective.* Pearson Education, USA.

Turban, E., Leidner, D., Mclean, E., & Wetherbe, J. (2006). *Information Technology Management: Transforming Organisations in the Digital Economy.* 5th edn, New York: John Wiley & Sons.

Copyright © 2009, IGI Global, distributing in print or electronic forms without written permission of IGI Global is prohibited.

Viehland, D. (1999). New Business Models for Electronic Commerce. *Millenial Challenges in Management Education, Cybertechnology and Leadership* (pp. 141-143). Association of Management and the International Association of Management 17th Annual International Conference, San Diego, California.

Copyright © 2009, IGI Global, distributing in print or electronic forms without written permission of IGI Global is prohibited.

Section III
Web Presence Implementation and Evaluation

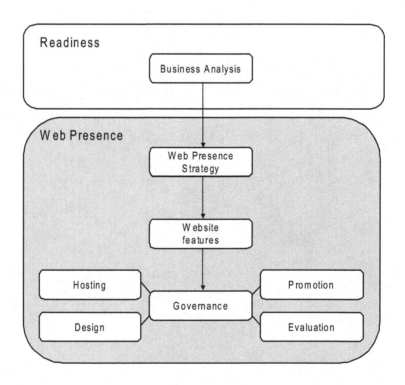

Chapter V
Web Presence Strategy and Content

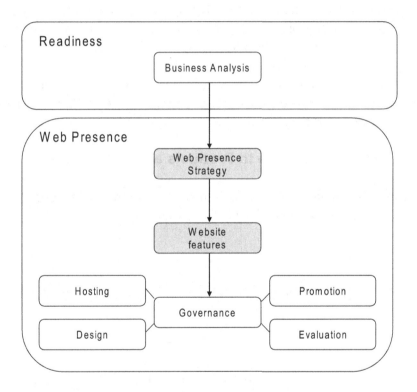

INTRODUCTION

The purpose of this chapter is to discuss how a small business decides upon its Web presence strategy and then determines what features will make up the content of its Web presence. The Web presence strategy is considered after the overall busi-

Copyright © 2009, IGI Global, distributing in print or electronic forms without written permission of IGI Global is prohibited.

ness strategy has been determined and a SWOT analysis performed (refer previous chapter). First we will examine the Web presence strategy.

WEB PRESENCE STRATEGY

The Web presence strategy will differ according to the factors that were considered in the previous chapter. For instance, if a small business is following a growth strategy it might be more inclined to be proactive in developing its Web presence, or perhaps if it is in a competitive industry it might look to its Web presence as a way to get an edge over competitors (Burgess 2002). Figure 1 shows how this chapter will link the material from previous chapters into the selection of Website features. The overall business strategy (identified through the business analysis) will be used to select matching Web presence strategies (such as those listed in Figure 1). The Web presence strategies will then be used to select particular Website features to be employed as part of the overall Web presence.

However, before discussing these it is necessary to provide a little more background. The next section provides some examples of how ICTs and in particular the Internet can assist the business to achieve its aims.

How can ICTs Add Value to Products and/or Services?

Ahituv and Neumann (1990) have identified three factors that influence the likelihood of strategic ICTs potential in an organisation:

Figure 1. The link between business strategy and selection of Website features

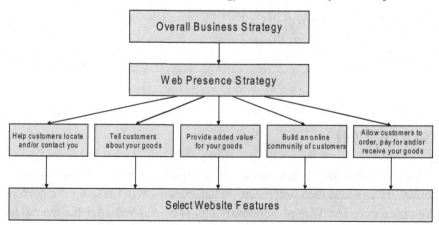

Copyright © 2009, IGI Global, distributing in print or electronic forms without written permission of IGI Global is prohibited.

- *The presence of significant information content in key relationships between buyers and sellers.* ICTs, and especially the Internet, are obviously suited to the transferal of information. ICTs can provide benefits in the areas of cost (cheaper transmission of information), speed of data transfer (faster transmission) and reduction in data entry errors (less mistakes). A typical example of this is the tourism industry, which is information intensive. These days, customers make key decisions in relation to where and how they travel based upon the information they can access about different destinations and how to get there. The vast majority of small businesses that have a Web presence, irrespective of their industry, tend to use it to pass some type of information onto customers. Where it is information that does not change very often, such as the business address or telephone number, it is very cost effective to add it to the Web presence. Other information, such as evolving marketing campaigns, could change more often and require some type of monitoring on a regular basis to keep the information up-to-date. This notion of the cost of keeping information *current* will be examined a little later in this chapter.

- *The presence of competitive pressures in the industry* (such as deregulation, ICT innovation, or competition intensity). This forces industry participants to look for creative ways to gain competitive advantage by closely examining the potential of ICTs as a part of their constant investigations of all parts of their business to try to gain an edge on competitors. In this instance, the business is looking to its Web presence to help it add value to its products or services. As indicated in the previous chapter, this can occur by using the Web presence to assist in ensuring that its goods fits the needs of customers, enhances their products or services or helps customers to purchase them.

- *Businesses whose main offerings, products or service, have a limited life* (such as unsold airline seats or vacant hotel rooms). In these instances, it is useful to have flexible ICT systems to manage these effectively – for instance, allowing goods to be offered at cheaper prices at short notice (typically as their 'life' or ability to be sold is about to expire). Such systems generally offer the opportunity to package the price of 'limited life' goods in different ways, depending upon different circumstances (such as high and low seasons or special sales). There are now many online booking engines that allow this to occur. In this instance, competition generally occurs on price and not added value.

Porter and Millar (1985) suggest that ICTs change the way that companies operate by altering the process that they use to create their products, as well as altering the actual products themselves. A process they describe as 'transforming the value chain' can do this. Each business process (which they call a 'value activity') has

Copyright © 2009, IGI Global, distributing in print or electronic forms without written permission of IGI Global is prohibited.

a physical and an information component. The physical component is the actual physical action that occurs with the process. Traditionally, this has been the major area targetted to add value to a product. New technologies allow an emphasis to be placed upon the information component. The information component can be a combination of the data that needs to be recorded about the occurrence of a value activity (for instance, recording that a certain amount of raw materials have been used in a production batch) or information for a customer about how to use a product, which can easily be provided on a Website).

DETERMINING WEBSITE CONTENT

One of the key tenets of this book is that the Web presence of a business can be broken down into a number of Website elements. The Web presence content of a small business therefore consists of a number of Website 'features' that are an important element that can impart functionality to a site (Fisher et al 2007). These features generally allow a small business to do one or more of the following things (Burgess 2002):

- Provide information to current or potential customers.
- Facilitate communication between the business and its customers, or even between customers themselves.
- Allow customers to buy products or services online.

The important thing is that each Website feature can be traced back to the particular business strategies that have been discussed. In particular, the two strategies that we will highlight now are:

- *Improved business efficiency.* This is similar to Porter's strategy: *be the low cost producer.*
- *Add Value to Products or Services.* This is, of course, similar to Porter's strategy: *produce a unique or differentiated product.*

There is also one other business benefit that particular Website features can provide. This is:

- *Help to Promote the Business.*

There is an entire chapter later in this book (Chapter VIII) that discusses promotion of the Web presence, so we will concentrate upon the first two strategies now.

Copyright © 2009, IGI Global, distributing in print or electronic forms without written permission of IGI Global is prohibited.

Table 1. Matching Web presence strategy to business strategy

Web Presence Strategy	Business Strategy		
	Improve Business Efficiency	Add Value to Your Goods	Help to Promote your Business
Help customers to locate and/or contact your business	X		
Tell customers about your goods	X		X
Provide added value for your goods	X	X	X
Build an online community of customers		X	X
Allow customers to order, pay for and/or receive your goods online	X		

A small business will select different Website features according to its business strategy. Table 1 suggests how a particular Website strategy might be selected to match with a business strategy.

In Table 1 we have identified the typical Web presence strategies that we have seen small businesses adopt. In most instances, businesses adopting a conservative Web presence strategy will look to ways to use their Web presence to improve their business efficiencies. Typically they will use the Website to help customers locate them, tell customers about their offerings and, in some instances, perhaps facilitate the purchase of goods by customers.

We suggest that one of the differences between what we propose in this book and much of the other advice currently availably for small businesses is that we are fine with this. If a small business has a conservative strategy and is not looking to expand, then is it not obvious that they should have a Website that matches their business strategy? A Website that helps to improve their efficiencies might be just what is needed. However, if a small business is looking to expand, then perhaps its Website strategy needs to be more adventurous.

In Table 2 we link the typical Websites features that we have found on small business Websites in our studies with the Web presence strategies that we introduced in Table 1 (Burgess et al 2007). Please note that this list of Website features is not comprehensive, it is *typical* of many small businesses. The key here is that once a small business has decided upon its Web presence strategy then Table 2 can assist them to determine *specific* Website features that can help them to match this strategy.

To make this all a little easier for small businesses to absorb, we draw from some of our own work (Burgess et al 2007), the *Strategy/Feature model* (refer Figure 2), which aims to ensure that these businesses consider the reasons for implementing

Copyright © 2009, IGI Global, distributing in print or electronic forms without written permission of IGI Global is prohibited.

Table 2. Linking Web presence strategy to website features (Source: Burgess et al 2007)

Web Presence Strategy	Website Feature
Help customers to locate and/or contact your business	Physical location
	A location map
	Telephone/ Fax number
	Your Email address
	Online form for customers to fill in to contact you
Tell customers about your goods	General product/ service details
	Product catalogue
Promote your business (by building your brand with customers)**	Information about the business
	Press releases
	Customer testimonials
	Special offers to online customers
	Online form to fill in to receive newsletters
Provide added value for your goods	Frequently asked questions (FAQ)
	Instructions on how to use your product
	A separate 'links' page
Build an online community of customers	Bulletin board/ chat facilities/ Weblogs
	Special membership clubs
Allow customers to order, pay for and/or receive your goods online	Allow customers to print orders to then fax in
	Allow customers to order via Online forms
	Customers can print a credit card payment form to fax in (combined with order form?)
	Real-time order and payment

** Refer Chapter VIII Web Presence Promotion

particular Website features *at the content level.* Initially, a small business should consider which area of its Website implementation it wishes to enhance:

- **Contact:** Allowing customers to find or contact the business
- **Brand:** Attempting to build brand with the Website
- **Community:** Building a customer community through the Website
- **Goods:** Providing details about products and services, supporting them and/or allowing customers to order and perhaps pay for them.

Copyright © 2009, IGI Global, distributing in print or electronic forms without written permission of IGI Global is prohibited.

Figure 2. The strategy/feature model (adapted from Burgess et al 2007)

AREA ⟶	STRATEGY ⟶	WEBSITE FEATURE
MAKE CONTACT	Allow customers to find and contact you	-Physical location -Location map -Telephone/ fax number -Email address -Online form for general queries
BUILD BRAND	Build your brand with customers	-Information about the business -Press releases -Customer testimonials -Offers to online customers -Email newsletters
COMMUNITY	Build a customer community	-Bulletin board/ chat -Special membership clubs
PRODUCTS AND SERVICES	Provide details about your products and services	-Overview of products/ services -Static product catalogue -Dynamic product catalogue
	Provide extra support for your products/services	-FAQ -Instructions on product use -Bulletin board/ form for support -Separate 'links' page
	Allow customers to transact with your business	-Print order form to fax in -Static Online form for ordering -Dynamic Online form for ordering -Print order/payment form to fax in -Real-time ordering/ payment

Having determined the area and strategy that the business wishes to target, it can choose which particular features to adopt from the model. The model offers a (limited) selection of possible features to match the strategy – the business still needs to decide which will suit it. For instance, it is quite logical for a business offering accommodation to place its physical location and a location map on its Website. A home-based business dealing in mail-order type goods might wish to just interact with its customers on a virtual basis and not reveal the location of their home! It is suggested that businesses review their Website features on a regular basis. They may determine that a particular Website feature is not required, or can be replaced by another feature. For instance, we have noticed some volatility in relation to features that businesses adopt to encourage customers to purchase orders through their Website. Some businesses have switched from the 'simpler' option of allowing customers to print out an order form and fax it into them, to a more complex, real-time order/ payment system. What is just as interesting is that some businesses that have had the more complex feature have de-evolved back to the simpler one! The other important aspect of the model is that businesses should choose strategies according to their needs. For instance, some businesses may just require a simple Web presence and not need to delve into the 'community' or 'goods' areas.

Copyright © 2009, IGI Global, distributing in print or electronic forms without written permission of IGI Global is prohibited.

We believe that the Strategy/Features model allows the small business to relate decisions about Website content to simplified business strategies. Individual small business owner/managers will be able to decide upon their strategy and then relate this to particular Website features depending upon their individual business requirements. The model promotes a conservative Web presence strategy where the business strategy is cautious. Alternatively, a business may decide to trial a more complex feature (such as real-time ordering and payment) and then, in its next Website features review, revert back to an easier to operate (and more conservative) option such as allowing customers to print out an order form and fax it in. Arguably, this is one of the first small business models to focus on business strategy and operational perspectives as a primary point of reference rather than conceptualising the theoretical value of Website content.

MAINTAINING WEB PRESENCE CONTENT

One important thing that a small business needs to do is to consider how up-to-date its Website features are on a regular basis. In other words, in many instances it is not good enough for a small business to just add a Website feature to its Web presence – the feature often needs to be maintained (Burgess 2002; Fisher et al 2007). There are two things that a small business needs to know about each Web presence feature that it chooses to implement:

- Website features can range from being really 'easy' to **set up** (quick, inexpensive and requiring only basic skills) to quite 'complex' (time consuming, expensive and requiring technical skills).
- Some features can be really easy to **maintain** over time, some may be quite difficult – perhaps taking up valuable labour hours to keep them up to date.

So, when a small business is considering what features to have as part of its Web presence, it should think about how much effort it will take to implement the feature and how much effort will be needed to maintain them. In some cases a feature that is easier to set up may be harder to maintain. Here are some examples of different Website features and how they might differ in relation to setup and maintenance:

- **Business contact details:** It is really easy to put these up on a Website and, since the business location and contact telephone numbers rarely change, they also require little maintenance.
- **Product catalogue:** On the surface it appears that this is quite easy to put on a Website. You can just enter the product details and price as plain 'text' – which

Copyright © 2009, IGI Global, distributing in print or electronic forms without written permission of IGI Global is prohibited.

is quite simple to do. The problem occurs if the products and/or their details change regularly, such as prices. Each time they change the small business will need to manually change them on the Website. However, if the business keeps a separate product database it is possible to link this with their Website. Whilst this can be quite costly and complex to set up, the benefit is that any changes that are made are automatically reflected on the Website. So – one option is easier to set up but harder to maintain. The other is more difficult to set up but easier to maintain!

Table 3. Ease of setup and maintenance of Website features (adapted from Burgess 2008)

Type of feature	Website feature	Ease of setup	Ease of maintenance		
Help customers to locate you and/or contact your business	Physical location (address)	E	E		
	A location map	E	E		
	Telephone/ Fax number	E	E		
	Your Email address	E	E		
	Online Form for customers to fill in to contact you	E	E	M	
Inform customers about your goods	General product/ service details	E	E		
	Static product catalogue **OR**	E	E	M	C
	Dynamic product catalogue	C	E		
Provide added value for your goods	A separate 'links' page	E	E		
	List local community events	E	E	M	
	Online form to fill in to receive newsletters	M	M		
	Frequently asked questions (FAQ)	E	E	M	
	Instructions on how to use your product	E	E	M	
Build an online community of customers	Online bulletin board (moderated?) for queries and customer discussion	C	M	C	
		C	M	C	
	Set up special membership group	M	M		
Allow customers to order, pay for and/or receive your goods online	Allow customers to print orders to then fax in **OR**	E	M		
	Allow customers to order via Online forms **OR**	M	M		
	Orders placed via a form and linked to a database of purchase orders **OR**	C	E		
	Customers can print a credit card payment form to fax in (combined with order form?) **OR**	E	M		
	Automated payment	C	E		
	Direct download (of digital goods)	C	E		

Copyright © 2009, IGI Global, distributing in print or electronic forms without written permission of IGI Global is prohibited.

To assist small businesses to determine how easy particular Website features are to setup and maintain, Table 3 provides a guide as to how easy, moderate or complex a particular Website may be to set up and maintain.

The classifications are: **EASY (E)   MODERATE (M)   COMPLEX (C)**

Sometimes these classifications may vary depending upon the business situation – in these instances there may be two classifications together - for example, MC suggests that the feature may be moderate to complex to implement.

There is an appendix at the end of this chapter that examines the Website features discussed here in greater detail. In addition, the classification of the ease of setup and maintenance of individual Website features is discussed.

OUR PREVIOUS STUDIES

Accountant_07

This analysis of the Websites of 100 accounting practices and subsequent interviews with 20 partners provided some revealing insights into the Website content of an industry that provides professional services.

In relation to basic information provision features, all accounting practice Websites included a telephone number, e-mail address, and fax number. All but one had their physical location on their Website. One in four accounting businesses included a location map on their Website. Almost all of the businesses provided information about the business. A little under two-thirds of the businesses provided information about partners' qualifications – which was obviously seen as an important way to project the professional image of those businesses. An important feature of accounting practice Websites was the inclusion of these qualifications in two-thirds of the Websites. Some 95% of the accounting practice Websites we examined included information about the services offered by the practices. Also, nearly half of the accounting practice Websites listed the types of clients they catered towards. It is interesting to note, however, that only 7% of Websites provided a specific contact name.

It was found that a large majority of the accounting practice Websites also have some type of news information (52%) and/or newsletter (61%) available on their Websites. Testimonials from clients were not a prominent feature (5%). Unlike other types of businesses, hardly any accounting practices provided a Frequently Asked Questions (FAQ) feature on their Websites. Just over half of the practices provided links to other Websites that may be of interest to visitors. Again, this would

Copyright © 2009, IGI Global, distributing in print or electronic forms without written permission of IGI Global is prohibited.

be lower than the proportion expected for other industries, where most businesses provide such links.

One in five practices had calculators on their Websites to assist clients to model their superannuation situation, model their financial investment future performance and/or perform several types of taxation calculations. The Website analysis showed that approximately one quarter of the Websites analysed had a restricted access or 'log-in' feature, which allowed access to restricted areas of the Website via a password. These 27 businesses were contacted to determine:

- Who had restricted access (clients and/or staff),
- The types of features that could be accessed via the login, and
- Whether there were any services provided through the restricted pages.

Of the 23 firms that responded, it was found that the restricted pages are mainly provided for clients and interested parties. Two firms stated that the restricted pages are for employees' use. Five practices indicated that their log-in pages included a file-transfer protocol (FTP) facility through which clients can securely upload and transfer files to the practice. One firm stated that their log-in facility allowed clients to view their portfolio accounts. Another firm also provided internal correspondence, management reports and other business activity statements via the log-in page.

The provision of interactive forms (32%), either firm-generated (11%) or from external organisations (21%), is also a feature of the one hundred Websites that were analysed. The forms provided on the Websites (for example, financial checklists) were generally in a PDF format and available for downloading. The interactive forms are firm-specific and require the client or interested party to complete an enquiry or subscription form on-line which is then sent electronically to the firm.

There was **no** evidence of online order or payment facilities on any of the accounting practice Websites.

CBO_analysis_06

This analysis of the content of 45 community-based organisations (CBOs) revealed some interesting differences in Website content between different types of CBOs. The different types of CBO Websites that were analysed were those of neighbourhood houses (otherwise known as 'drop-in' centres), sporting clubs, youth services, public libraries and charities.

The first category of features that were examined related to information provision features. These features provide the Web surfer with information about how to contact or find the organisations and some basic information about the organisations. Most of the CBOs had an e-mail address and telephone number on their

Copyright © 2009, IGI Global, distributing in print or electronic forms without written permission of IGI Global is prohibited.

Website. Fewer sporting clubs and youth services Websites had a single physical address – this could be indicative that the activities associated with these CBOs are spread over different locations. Note that hardly any sporting clubs saw a need to put a fax number on their Website. Neighbourhood houses were more likely to have a location map (perhaps indicating their single location) and a 'policy' statement (outlining their goals). However, only metropolitan neighbourhood houses had a location map. It was interesting that none of the youth services Websites had policy statements. Typically, these Websites were 'flashier' and were obviously attempting to grab the attention of their target group. However, the majority of the two types of CBOs that we identified as being community/welfare (neighbourhood houses and charities) did see a need to present their policies and/or mission statements on their Websites.

Neighbourhood houses and youth services Websites had information for potential enrolees about courses and programs that they offered on their Websites, whilst sporting clubs tended to have information for potential members about how to participate at the club. Whilst most public libraries had information about the services offered on their Websites, no library had information about how use the library's services (perhaps this is seen as being common knowledge). Libraries, charities and sporting clubs were also more likely to have news features (the latter usually highlighting the recent achievements of an individual or team). Libraries were the only Websites to offer their Websites in multiple languages. Not surprisingly, sporting clubs were the only CBOs to have a calender of events or a fixture on the Website (a feature we added into the study after examining the Websites)!

Most of the CBOs had links to other useful Websites. Only libraries included comments from their users as to the standard of their service (perhaps they were trying to attract new users?). Note that only sporting clubs had results or statistics on their Website. Libraries, sporting clubs and a small proportion of charities had a membership login facility. For the sporting clubs this was usually to access or record results or statistics. Many libraries also had a feature where clients could join online as well. One quarter of the youth services Websites had a discussion group or forum. This could again reflect the nature of the group that they are targetting – more likely to be comfortable with operating in this medium. An interesting point is that only rural youth services Websites had this feature and this may reflect the physical distance between forum participants. None of the CBOs examined had features where the Website would be customised differently for separate users (a feature sometimes used for differentiation purposes by larger businesses).

There was little evidence of online ordering or payment features in the CBO Websites, apart from libraries, who allowed clients to reserve books online and access their online catalogue (again, two features we added after examining the

Copyright © 2009, IGI Global, distributing in print or electronic forms without written permission of IGI Global is prohibited.

Websites in this study). Charities had facilities for the printing and faxing in of donation forms, or donating directly via their Websites. Of the others, larger sporting clubs were more likely to have a booking/ payment feature – a rural golf club had a facility to book accommodation packages and a rural triathlon club had an interactive order/payment facility to order sports clothing and to book into events. The youth services Websites had an interactive facility for fundraising donations and a separate site had a downloadable form (for faxing in) to order a referral guide. The one neighbourhood house with such a feature had online forms for enrolment in services or as a volunteer.

Micro_Analysis_06

This analysis of 39 micro business Websites occurred across three geographical areas (Australia, Canada and the UK) and five business groups (Bed and Breakfasts (B&Bs), art galleries, manufacturing businesses, business services and other businesses).

The analysis indicated that the most prominent type of feature was, not surprisingly, that of information provision, with all businesses having at least one of these features. Closely following this was the presence of features related to promotion of the business, with all but two of the businesses having at least one such feature. Only three of the businesses (8%) had a membership or mailing list feature. However, some 38% of the businesses had a feature for online ordering and/or payment. The most popular manifestations of this were businesses with interactive online sales and payment features (seven businesses), those that allowed their customers to send orders by online form for later processing (six businesses) and a smaller number of businesses (two) that allowed their customers to print off an order form and fax it in to the business for later processing. The *business type* did appear to influence whether the business had some type of ordering/ payment feature, with a very high proportion of B&Bs (67%) and manufacturing businesses (75%) having this feature. However, there was also one other finding of note. It appears that the type of business can even affect the type of transactional interactivity feature. All six of the B&Bs had a *Web form* on their Website that potential customers could fill in to make a booking. This meant that payment for the booking had to be dealt with manually by the B&Bs at some later time. In the case of the manufacturing businesses, five of the six businesses with ordering/ payment features had *online interactive sales* that allowed their customers to order and pay for their products in the one effort. This is an important finding in relation to the types of features that different types of businesses have on their Websites.

Copyright © 2009, IGI Global, distributing in print or electronic forms without written permission of IGI Global is prohibited.

Figure 3. Identified features of winery websites in the study's identified focus areas (adapted from Sellitto 2005)

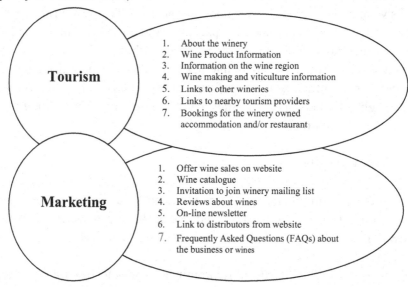

Wineries_survey_05

This research identified an emergent tourism focus associated with winery Websites. The Australian wine industry has been a recent global success story and wineries appear to have adopted the Website as part of an integral strategy surrounding tourism. The study identified that winery Websites had a high degree of features associated with tourism and direct marketing - two areas that correlated well with and highlighted the important operational areas of the small wine business. The wine tourism information published on Websites allowed the visitor to be informed about the winery and wine products. The other form of information reflected the commercial aspects of the winery and dealt with direct customer marketing information that focuses on product promotion and sales. Figure 3 summarizes the identified features of winery Websites in the study's identified focus areas of tourism and direct marketing.

Tourism_04

In this study we interviewed 59 small tourism businesses (consisting of 23 businesses in rural Victoria and 36 businesses, split between the two major cities in Australia, Melbourne and Sydney). The businesses that were interviewed were divided into

Copyright © 2009, IGI Global, distributing in print or electronic forms without written permission of IGI Global is prohibited.

accommodation (bed and breakfasts and hostel/ backpacker establishments) and attractions (local tour operators and museums/ galleries).

An interesting aspect of this study is that we specifically investigated aspects of Website adoption that related specifically to the topic of this chapter, the development of a Website strategy and specific Website features. Whilst we did not ask the businesses when they formulated their Website, we did ask them to tell us if they had a strategy and what it was. Our expectation was that most of the businesses would have a brochure type Website with perhaps some interaction with outside parties (such as customers). The results were not surprising. The majority of the business used the Website as a basic brochure site – to provide information. A slightly lesser number (but still a majority) had set up the Website as part of their promotional strategy. A few businesses used the Website for direct online payments from customers. Most of the businesses seemed to adopt a fairly conservative strategy for their Website, which is consistent with the literature on Website development and most common for small businesses.

Winery_Analysis_02

This study examined the Websites of 76 Australian wineries (58 of which were small wineries) over a two year period (ending in 2002). At that time, a number of Website features were identified that could be regarded as 'standard' on the Websites of Australian wineries. These features are:

- Information about the business
- Information about the wines
- Business contact information, including e-mail address, physical address, telephone and fax numbers.

However, at the time there were also a number of features that we considered may eventually become 'standard'. The features that we identified to fit this category were:

- A location map on the Website
- The option to print out order forms and fax them when wishing to place an order
- Membership and/or mailing lists
- Information about the local region.

Hindsight now tells us that location maps and information about the local region now play a more prominent role on Websites. Wineries are still moving between

Copyright © 2009, IGI Global, distributing in print or electronic forms without written permission of IGI Global is prohibited.

different types of ordering/ payment online models (varying from the *print out an order form and fax it in* option to *online interactive sales*). Interestingly, it is still the smaller wineries that are more likely to have online sales than their larger counterparts, who often have deals limiting the distribution of their wines through their distributors. Another possible explanation for this relates to the small winery having a high reliance on direct marketing to the consumer for profitability. The direct marketing approach not only allows the winery to develop wine brand recognition but also to gain substantial taxation rebates on all their direct customer sales. The Australian Federal and State governments have recognized the importance of the small winery to the development of regional and rural areas and have introduced taxation rebates on wine sales to foster this. Hence, in an endeavour to improved regional economic outcomes, wineries have been entitled to a form of compensatory subsidies and enjoy a taxation rebate of 29% on any direct sales. One of the pathways for the small winery - either new or established - is to leverage the taxation rebate on direct sales via mail order, cellar door or by having a Web presence. For larger wineries, direct consumer sales tended to be minimal when compared to their retail income.

During the period of the study, the Websites of wineries showed some evidence of maturing. More wineries added simple features to their Websites than deleted them, but overall there was a continued degree of conservatism associated with the Website features. The main area of volatility occurred when wineries experimented with different models of online sales over the two-year period.

Other Studies

A Study of Strategy and Small Business Web Presence (Fisher, Craig, & Bentley 2007)

Many small business operators tend to overlook the need for a relevant strategy when it comes to implementing a Website - an issue that results in many business operators not realising the full potential of online presence. Fisher and colleagues (2007) examine the nexus between strategy and small business Website adoption suggesting that the Website tends to be viewed as merely an extension of marketing practices. The authors highlight four Website implementation areas that small business owners can use to manage their Website and Web-business strategy. These areas include:

*   Articulating the business and Website strategy. The small business owner needs to acknowledge and recognise the value of having a Website as a contributing element to an overall business strategy. This acknowledgement tends to confirm

Copyright © 2009, IGI Global, distributing in print or electronic forms without written permission of IGI Global is prohibited.

a certain commitment by the small business operator that the Internet is an important element in achieving some of the business's strategic objectives.

- Website quality. This area includes aspects of Website adoption and Web presence that addresses issues associated with usability, Website design and information quality.
- Website features and functionality. The authors link Website maturity with an increased degree of functionality through features that can be viewed as adding value to the small business' online presence.
- Maintenance and monitoring of the Website. Relates to the small business owner having an interest in the maintenance activities associated with the upkeep of their Website. Changes in Website activities over time tend to reflect the evolution of the small business' Internet strategy.

The study examined factors associated with these areas using both Website analysis and small business operator interviews to propose a simple classification model for strategy-Web maturity. The model categorises owners with respect to the manner they relate and value their Web presence and business strategy - a categorisation range that defines mature business types at the advanced end, whilst lagging types are grouped at the lower end of the spectrum. The characteristics associated with these two business categories are summarised as:

- Mature. These businesses have a well designed and maintained Website with a relatively high degree of functionality. The owners recognised the clear link between Web presence and business strategy, with many businesses being e-commerce ready.
- Lagging. This group of business owners tended to have a limited understanding of the role their Website has in the overall business strategy. Their Websites tend to be poorly designed and maintained with minimal or no functionality.

Fisher et al (2007) further indicated that small business Website features could reflect different degrees of the Web, allowing small businesses to grouped as intermediate between the mature and lagging types.

E-Business Strategy: A study of North West England SMEs (Meckel, Walters, Greenwood, & Baugh 2004)

Research undertaken by Meckel et al (2004) sought to identify the strategies that small and medium size businesses used with respect to electronic business. The researchers examined the decision-making behaviour of small business operators,

Copyright © 2009, IGI Global, distributing in print or electronic forms without written permission of IGI Global is prohibited.

collecting empirical data using the survey instrument. One of the outcomes of the study was to document the different formal approaches that SMEs had used that reflected a strategy that could be applied to e-business adoption. Many of the approaches embraced existing and well document models with SWOT (Strengths, Weaknesses, Opportunities and Threats) and critical success factor (CSF) being the most popular. PEST factors (Political Economic, Socio-cultural and Technological forces) also rated as an important approach for enacting strategy, whilst other contemporary models such as Porter's Value Chain and Five Forces were not widely used. Notably, product portfolio analysis and the balanced score card approach were seldom used. The study also identified similar SME types based on their attitudes toward formal business strategy, the use of e-business and adoption of technology that could be used to engage in e-business. The five groups identified were:

- The e-business strategy leaders. Theses businesses were the only ones to have a specific e-business strategy. They tended to have a greater exposure to technology that allowed them to use e-business at a high standard.
- The old-fashioned SMEs. These companies did not have a formal business strategy, nor did they have a strategy specific to e-business. Such firms engaged their local constituency more so than those at the national or international level.
- The blind e-business user. These businesses use e-business technologies, but have no strategies associated with their normal operations (including any specific to e-business).
- The e-adoption leaders. The SMEs classed in this group have a high level of e-business adoption, but paradoxically do not have any e-business strategy in place.
- The formal strategy leaders. Have adopted formal business strategies and have low levels of e-adoption. Generally have the lowest use of technology.

The authors went on to identify different methods associated with the creation of Web presence. They found that a high proportion of SMEs that had adopted e-business tended to keep this separate from their normal business activities. Indeed, a high proportion of SMEs were found to have outsourced their Web presence, with internally available staff members being the next option associated with maintaining and managing the Web presence.

Summary of our Studies and Other Studies

Our studies showed that small businesses were conservative when it came to implementing Website features. The prime objective of most Websites seemed to

Copyright © 2009, IGI Global, distributing in print or electronic forms without written permission of IGI Global is prohibited.

be to provide information - with features such as geographical location, contact details and general information about the businesses being most prominent. Other features, such as product catalogues and frequently asked questions were also common on certain Websites. There were some examples of advanced features, such as interactive shopping carts, access to password protected areas and reasonably sophisticated membership or mailing lists, but these were not mainstream and were typically restricted to certain types of businesses (for instance, a few wineries and micro sized manufacturing businesses had interactive shopping features).

Two other studies were described in this chapter that were based on the work of Fisher et al (2007) and Meckel and colleagues (2004). Fisher and colleagues (2007) suggested that the Website tends to be viewed as merely an extension of marketing practices by many small business operators and highlight several Website implementation areas that small business owners could focus on to potentially better manage their Website and Web-business strategy. These focus areas included the articulation of the Website strategy, Website features and quality, and the practical issue of Website maintenance and monitoring. The study reported findings that allowed small businesses to be mapped to different categories with respect to their Web strategy. Meckel et al (2004) on the other hand examined the decision-making behaviour of small business operators and document the different formal strategies used that could be applied to e-business adoption. Many small operators embraced existing and well documented evaluation models, with SWOT and the critical success factor approach being most popular. The study also identified similar business types based on their attitudes toward formal business strategy, the use of e-business, and the adoption of e-business related technology.

Table 4. Determining Web presence strategy and features

Chapter topic	Factor	Consideration
Website Strategy	Link to business aims	Select website strategies that will match business aims: • Help customers to locate and/or contact your business • Tell customers about your goods • Provide added value for your goods • Build an online community of customers • Allow customers to order, pay for and/or receive your goods online
Website features	Match to website strategy and identify how they assist the business	• Improve efficiencies • Add value to products or services • Help to promote the business
Web presence maintenance	Consider both website feature setup and maintenance	Remember that website content needs to be setup *and* maintained and that both have a cost associated with them.

Copyright © 2009, IGI Global, distributing in print or electronic forms without written permission of IGI Global is prohibited.

TENETS – LESSONS FROM THE CHAPTER

There are a number of lessons from this chapter that can be applied by small businesses when considering how they should measure their Web presence success. These are listed in Table 4.

CONCLUSION

This is one of the most important chapters of this book as it introduces many concepts that are not necessarily familiar to the small business owner/ manager. Building on the identification of business aims and strategy in the previous chapter, the small business owner is encouraged to ensure that the Web presence strategy matches the overall aims of the business. The various features in the Web presence can offer a combination of helping customers to locate and/or contact the business, informing customers about products and services, providing added value for your products and services, helping to build an online community of customers and allowing customers to order, pay for and/or receive your goods online. Website features can be selected which match the Web presence strategy (and thus the overall business aims). However, each Website feature needs to be maintained as well as set up. The cost of maintenance of some Website features can be considerable, so it is important that this is considered as part of the decision as to what Website features to include as part of the Web presence. The next chapter examines some of the hosting options for the selected Website features.

REFERENCES

Ahituv, N., & Neumann, S. (1990). *Principles of Information Systems in Management,* 3rd edn, Wm C Brown, USA.

Burgess, S. (2008). Determining Website Content for Small Businesses: Assisting the Planning of Owner/Managers. *International Journal of Knowledge Management Studies, 2*(1), 143-161.

Burgess, S. (Ed.) (2002). *Managing Information Technology in Small Business: Challenges and Solutions.* Hershey, PA: Idea Group Publishing.

Burgess, S., Bingley, S., & Sellitto, C. (2007). A Model for Website Content Decisions in Micro Businesses. *Global Business & Economics Anthology, 1,* 474-487.

Copyright © 2009, IGI Global, distributing in print or electronic forms without written permission of IGI Global is prohibited.

Fisher, J., Anamieke, C., & John, B. (2007). Moving from Web presence to e-commerce: The Importance of a Business-Web strategy for small-business owners. *Electronic Markets, 17*(4), 253-262.

Meckel, M., Walters, D., Greenwood, A., & Baugh, P. (2004). A taxonomy of e-business adoption and strategies in small and medium sized enterprises. *Strategic Change, 13*(5), 259-269.

Porter, M. E., & Millar, V. E. (1985). How information gives you competitive advantage. *Harvard Business Review, 63*(4), 149.

Sellitto, C. (2005). A Study of Emerging Tourism Features Associated with Australian Winery Websites. *Journal of Information Technology and Tourism, 7*(3/4), 157-170.

Copyright © 2009, IGI Global, distributing in print or electronic forms without written permission of IGI Global is prohibited.

APPENDIX: MORE ON WEBSITE FEATURES

The following pages provide more detail about the Website features introduced earlier in this chapter. They are listed under the headings of typical strategies that the Web presence might perform. These are:

- Help consumers to locate and/or contact your business
- Tell consumers about your goods
- Provide extra online support for your goods
- Build an online community of customers
- Allow customers to order, pay for and/or receive your goods online

Every feature is classified twice: as easy, moderate or complex to **set up** and **maintain.** Examples are given as to whether different types of small businesses (a bed and breakfast [B&B], an art gallery, a manufacturing business and a professional business services operation) may or may not find the feature useful.

Note the comments at the end of each series of features. They can provide some insights into the types of decisions that small businesses may need to make about use of the features.

Table 1A.

What does the business want to do?	Website feature	Ease of setup	Ease of maintenance	Recommendation			
				B&B	Gallery	Manufacturing	Business Services
Make people aware of your physical location	Physical location	Easy	Easy	Yes	Yes	Yes	Yes
	A location map	Easy	Easy	Yes	Yes	Possibly	Possibly
Make people aware of your telephone/ fax numbers	Telephone/ Fax number	Easy	Easy	Yes	Yes	Yes	Yes
Let people contact you online	Your Email address	Easy	Easy	Yes	Yes	Yes	Yes
	Online form for customers to fill in to contact you	Moderate	Easy to Moderate (depends upon number of queries)	Possibly	Possibly	Possibly	Possibly

Copyright © 2009, IGI Global, distributing in print or electronic forms without written permission of IGI Global is prohibited.

Table 2A.

What does the business want to do?	Website feature	Ease of setup	Ease of maintenance	Recommendation				
				B&B	Gallery	Manufacturing	Business Services	
Provide a general description of what you offer	General product/ service details	Easy	Easy	Yes	Yes	Yes	Yes	
Provide a product catalogue or details of your offerings	Static	Easy	Moderate to Complex (depends upon number of changes that occur)	No. Unless the B&B sells 'other' products (eg home made goods)	Either of these types of catalogues might be an option, but the gallery should consider the number of art works and the level of turnover before adoption	A catalogue may be a good idea. The more products, the more attractive a dynamic catalogue is.	Probably not. Perhaps just provide some details on the types of services provided and perhaps some simple costings.	
	Dynamic	Complex	Easy (as the catalogue is linked to the business database the website changes whenever the business website changes)					

Copyright © 2009, IGI Global, distributing in print or electronic forms without written permission of IGI Global is prohibited.

Help Consumers to Locate and/or Contact Your Business

Comments: It is usually fairly easy to provide contact details as part of business Web presence. Businesses for whom it is vital that people know how to find them (such as B&Bs and galleries) should consider putting a location map on the Website to help people find them. In relation to letting people contact the business– the easiest way is to make sure the e-mail address is easy to find. Consider having different e-mail addresses for different purposes, such as:

sales@yourbusinessname.com.au or *support@yourbusinessname.com.au*

There may be some cases the business might not want to put a physical location on the Website – there are a number of reasons for this. One might be that the business operates solely online. Another could be that it is a home-based business and really does not want customers coming to visit at home. In these cases the business might wish to include a postal office box address on the Website. However, most businesses will probably indicate a physical location on the Website.

Website forms provide an option for customers to fill in, perhaps with a particular query. After filling out the form, consumers click on the 'submit' button and the contents of the form are automatically e-mailed to the business. Such forms are relatively easy to set up for someone with Website experience, but not as easy as entering simple text (such as your business telephone number) onto the Website.

Tell Consumers About Your Goods

Comments: Most businesses should consider putting a general outline of the types of products or services that they offer on their Websites. It is easy to enter and maintain because these general business characteristics do not usually alter significantly over time.

Product catalogues are a different prospect. These are usually reserved for businesses that have a number of clearly identifiable products. As mentioned in the chapter, the more products there are the better it may be to consider the (complex) task of connecting the business Web page to the product catalogue. Again, if the business product details do not change very much it might be suitable to have a 'static' catalogue that can be updated manually.

Provide Extra Online Support for Your Goods

Comments: There are various ways to add extra support for business products or services on the Website. The easiest way is to set up links to other Websites that

Copyright © 2009, IGI Global, distributing in print or electronic forms without written permission of IGI Global is prohibited.

Table 3A.

What does the business want to do?	Website feature	Ease of setup	Ease of maintenance	Recommendation			
				B&B	**Gallery**	**Manufacturing**	**Business Services**
Provide links to other websites	A separate 'links' page	Easy	Easy - but regularly check to ensure the links are all working	Yes. This can be a great feature for supporting goods – where other sites have information of interest to customers.			
Provide a list of local events	A separate 'events' page	Easy	Easy to moderate (depends upon how often changes need to be made)	These can be useful if the business is interested in attracting visitors to its location, so might be more suited to tourism businesses. It is a way of listing other things that customers can do when they visit you. Providing a link to a regional portal may keep these events up to date (then you don't have to!).			
Provide answers to typical questions	Frequently asked questions (FAQ)	Easy	Easy to Moderate (depends upon how often changes need to be made)	Probably not	Possibly. Depends upon the types of questions asked and how regularly they are asked.		
Provide support on product use	Instructions on how to use your product	Easy	Easy to Moderate	No	No	Possibly. Depends upon the products being sold.	
Provide personal product support	Provide a specific email address or form for direct contact	Easy	Moderate to Complex (requires regular monitoring by an employee)	No	No	Possibly – but this may be very time consuming if customers are to be dealt with individually	
Support customers interacting with each other	Provide an online bulletin board (moderated?)	Complex	Moderate to Complex (staff may need to monitor discussion)	Possibly. There would have to be enough customers involved and the business would want the service to be there to increase the discussion about products or services.			

Copyright © 2009, IGI Global, distributing in print or electronic forms without written permission of IGI Global is prohibited.

provide support business goods and services. For example, a small rental car business might provide a link to a Website that provides online directions. A winery might provide links to regional events that are occurring to allow a potential visitor to plan a visit to the winery to coincide with a major tourism event. Another way is to set up an FAQ area. If there are a number of questions that are asked regularly it can save you a lot of time by adding in this feature. Another useful feature that can add is to provide customers with hints on how to use your products or apply your service effectively. For instance, a business selling cooking appliances might put recipes designed for their products on their Websites. The option to provide customers with the ability to contact you directly can be quite time consuming if you receive many queries. Remember that each of these will need to be dealt with personally by an employee. However, it may just turn out to be a replacement for existing telephone or face-to-face support. It is quite complex to set up a bulletin board or similar facility where customers can interact with each other. It may require constant monitoring by business staff in relation to the content of the discussions and the level of 'support' provided. However, such a feature may promote a customer community online (see next section).

Build an Online Community of Customers

Comments: The idea of building a customer community through the small business Website is to provide customers with extra support, information on special deals and sometimes even a social experience that they may not be able to get with competitors. These types of features can also make customers feel that they are part of a special group, receiving treatment that other (perhaps less regular?) customers may not receive.

Table 4A.

What does the business want to do?	Website feature	Ease of setup	Ease of maintenance	Recommendation			
				B&B	Gallery	Manufacturing	Business Services
Set up a forum for customers to discuss your products/ services	Provide an online bulletin board (moderated?) [see above – can also be used for product support]	Complex	Moderate to Complex (if a staff member is needed to monitor the discussion)	See earlier discussion on bulletin boards. These are complex to set up. A business may need to moderate the discussion, which could be time consuming. It does provide a forum for customers to discuss your goods.			

Copyright © 2009, IGI Global, distributing in print or electronic forms without written permission of IGI Global is prohibited.

One of the easiest ways to do this is to set up a bulletin board (as discussed earlier for product support). It can provide a forum for customers to discuss aspects of your products. Again, a business will need to decide if the reward to the business is worth the effort needed to set up and maintain it.

There is also a possibility of setting up a 'secure' area of the Website for customers (perhaps loyal ones?) to enter if consumers are given a special user ID and password. This is a little more complex and probably not the realm of this discussion.

Emerging alternatives to the bulletin board are Web 2.0 (or social networking) Websites (discussed in Chapter XI).

Allow Customers to Order, Pay for and/or Receive your Goods Online

Comments: This section addresses the area of moving to 'e-commerce'. A primary reason for having a Website might be to encourage customers to physically visit the business and purchase products and/or services. A simple alternative for a conservative small business that is popular is to provide a form online that can be printed by customers - allowing them to order products, book services or even add their credit card details. These forms are then faxed to the business. Businesses that are still concerned about online security or do not want to set up online credit card payment systems may wish to do this. It should be remembered, however, that these fax orders will need to be dealt with manually. If businesses are confident that they may receive a substantial number of online orders, they may wish to consider an automated online ordering and payment system. However, these businesses should investigate fully the various fees associated with establishing these automated and secure systems that process credit card transactions online. Many small businesses now look to external Websites (such as portals) to sell their goods - as many portals often have the infrastructure set up already to deal with such transactions. At the extreme level, businesses that sell digital goods or services may wish to set up a system whereby customers can automatically order, pay for and download the goods in one transaction, without the need for intervention by an employee of the business.

Copyright © 2009, IGI Global, distributing in print or electronic forms without written permission of IGI Global is prohibited.

Table 5A.

What does the business want to do?	What goes on the website	Ease of setup	Ease of maintenance	Recommendation			
				B&B	Gallery	Manufacturing	Business Services
	Allow customers to print orders to then fax in	Easy	Moderate (orders/ bookings not entered into the orders/bookings database automatically)	Both of these techniques are conservative ways to take orders or bookings. They are relatively easy to set up, but will require some effort to manually process the orders once they are in. Also, the customer will have to wait for the business to respond to see if the product is in stock or the booking successful. If a business is unsure about how many orders might be received, this may be a good way to start off.			
Place orders or make bookings	Allow customers to order via Online forms	Moderate					
	Orders placed via a form and linked to a database of purchase orders	Complex	Easy (orders/bookings are automatically entered into the orders/ bookings database)	This automates the ordering/ booking process as it is linked to the relevant database. The business should be sure that there are enough online orders to ensure the investment is worthwhile.			
	Customers can print a credit card payment form to fax in (combined with order form?)	Easy	Moderate (payments will have to be processed manually)	If this is done it is usually a part of the order or booking form (see above)			
Pay online	Automated payment	Complex	Easy (payments are processed automatically)	This is quite complex to set up and the business should assess the setup and transaction costs. In addition, if physical products are involved then, although the payment process is automated, employee intervention will still be required to ship the product.			
Set up automatic download of goods	Customers receive digital goods online	Complex	Easy	Again, this is quite complex to set up. There will be a limited number of businesses that offer customers a service that involves downloading goods – a typical example of this is the music industry. In these cases, it may be possible to completely automate the order, payment and 'digital' (online) delivery of these goods so that the customer is able to perform all of these tasks without intervention from an employee of the business. For the small number of businesses where this is possible it would be worth investigating this option.			

Copyright © 2009, IGI Global, distributing in print or electronic forms without written permission of IGI Global is prohibited.

Chapter VI
Web Presence Hosting

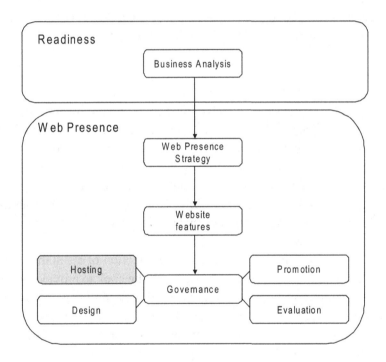

INTRODUCTION

In earlier chapters we discussed the need to link Web presence strategy with anticipated small business direction and motivations - where this strategy would invariably be reflected in the business's Website activities. In this chapter we examine and elaborate on the diversity of options available to the small business operator

Copyright © 2009, IGI Global, distributing in print or electronic forms without written permission of IGI Global is prohibited.

when hosting their Web presence - hosting options that can impact on Websites features. Arguably, the appropriate use of Web hosting services have evolved to the point were they are an integral part of the Web presence experience for the small business operator.

WEB PRESENCE OPTIONS

Previously we discussed the notion of a small business **Web presence** as opposed to its own **Website**. In reality, it is typical for a small business to have its own Website, but then perhaps also have some sort of presence on other Websites, such as Web portals (which are discussed later in this chapter). In order to discuss the different options that are available to small businesses, it is necessary to first examine the different aspects that are involved in Web presence hosting.

ISP Selection

We have already described and alluded to Internet Service Providers (ISPs), whose basic function is to provide Internet access for businesses and individuals. Hence, for a small business operator, the ISP is typically the entity through which they arrange their Internet connection, allowing them to *surf* the Internet for information and use *e-mail* to communicate with others. The ISP can usually also *host* a Website for the small business. Indeed, there are numerous specialist ISPs that host Websites for particular industry groups that a small businesses might wish to use. We will revisit this later.

It is not the aim of this book to discuss the selection of a suitable ISP in any depth. Furthermore, it is also beyond the scope of the book to provide a list of ISPs given the vast numbers of services found in modern and technologically developed countries. What we *do* examine are some of the integral factors that should be taken into consideration when a small business operator selects an ISP. These factors are discussed in relation to surfing the Internet and communicating using e-mail, and then will move on to other services and features they may offer. The small businesses need be aware of several factors associated with the selection of an ISP. These include:

- **Cost:** The cost of purchasing ISP activities and services may be more than the regular basic fee that is generally charged on a monthly basis. Is there a separate fee for downloading/uploading data after certain limits are reached?

Copyright © 2009, IGI Global, distributing in print or electronic forms without written permission of IGI Global is prohibited.

Are there costs associated with support? As communication infrastructure over time becomes cheaper for the ISP to maintain, will these savings be passed on? Is there provision to move to a less expensive bundle of services without penalty?

- **Performance:** This refers to the download/upload speed associated with communication and data transfer. How fast is the connection? Is it the traditional twisted-pair copper dial-up connection? Is it cable, broadband or satellite? Does it slow down after certain traffic limits are reached? Indeed, this may actually be a preferred option for a small business, in that it may be prepared to have a slower connection for a period if it means that costs can be controlled.

- **E-mail:** How many e-mail accounts can be established with each service account? Can they be customised to the different areas of the business, thus optimising internal business communication? [For instance, support@*businessname*.com or sales@*businessname*.com]. Is there a Web-based e-mail client that can be accessed if business staff are travelling and are away from the business? Is this client adaptable to the small screens associated with hand held mobile devices increasingly encountered amongst small business operators and staff.

- **Support/Reliability:** Is support available 24/7? Is there a telephone number to call? Be wary of unlimited online support, for if the connection is down – this equates to no support. Is there a limit on the number of support calls that can be made before charges are incurred? How long has the ISP been in business? Have they stood the test of time and established industry credentials and reputation? Arguably, industry service awards can reflect high performance or customer service satisfaction - have they won any awards?

- **Installation:** Once an ISP has been engaged and contracts purchased - how are services physically provided? Does the ISP have support or contracted staff to visit the business premises and assist with installation? Are there detailed instructions provided to install the service on the business' computers? Is there a support CD with automatic installation?

The selection of an ISP can be even more complicated in instances where its services are bundled with other goods, such as the purchase of a new PC, the subscription to the services of a telecommunications provider or the provision of a cable or pay-television service. Hence, the small business operator would be well served to seek out the views of others that use, or may have used, the ISP to gauge existing customer opinions of what can be expected of the service. Another issue that needs to be considered is if the ISP offers free (or inexpensive) hosting of a Website, which we will consider in the next section.

Copyright © 2009, IGI Global, distributing in print or electronic forms without written permission of IGI Global is prohibited.

Things to Consider in the Web Presence

There are a number of technical matters a small business needs to consider when setting up a Web presence.

- **Who will *host* the Web presence?** This refers to physical location of the Website, with its composite files and appropriate business content. A **host** computer is just a computer that stores applications or information that can be accessed by other computers. If a business decides to have its own Website, it will need to decide where it is to be hosted. Many large businesses host their own Websites on their own equipment and premises, but most small business Websites are hosted externally. This external hosting of the small business Website is primarily due to the technical skills need to set up and maintain a host, as well as the restrictive costs that may be involved. If a business decides to use the services of other Websites (such as portals), then these are hosted externally. Hosting can also be related to the type of Website performance that is required and is closely allied to Website functionality. For example, if the small business requires a search or credit card purchasing facility, then the selection of a hosting service is limited to those that are technically capable of being able to provide these types of services.

- **Who is responsible for *putting content* on the Web presence?** If a small business hosts its own Website, then it will need to take full responsibility for producing Website content. If the Website is hosted on a third-party provider or service, then different arrangements for content publication are possible. Generally, but not always, the small business will be responsible for providing the Website content. How this is then loaded onto the Website depends upon the agreement between the business and Website host. Sometimes the small business will be able to add the material directly to the Website - this assumes that it has employees with the skills to do this. Sometimes, the small business is able to send new content directly to the Website hosting service, who takes the responsibly for publishing it on the Website. There are also issues in relation to how the Website is designed - these issues will be discussed in Chapter VII. Suffice to indicate at this point that some hosting services do provide basic templates that allow the small business to establish a relatively sophisticated looking Web presence. Similar issues occur when the small business uses the services of other Websites, such as portals. Sometimes they will be able to load content directly and other times they will need to rely on these third-party administrators to do it for them. It is important to understand the differences in cost and flexibility with respect to the control of the Website features in the Web environment that arise in these different situations.

Copyright © 2009, IGI Global, distributing in print or electronic forms without written permission of IGI Global is prohibited.

- **Who is responsible for *maintaining the content* on the Web presence?** An important issue to consider when implementing the small business Website is the on-going resources required - embracing time, skills and cost attributes - to keep the content of the Website up to date. All information published on the Website should be current. This is where the control of the process of updating the Web presence is vital. Does the business have to rely on an external party to update the content when it is needed, or can it do it itself? If the external party is needed, do they charge for each update, or for each Web page altered or created? How quickly do they respond to requests to change the content? This is why the business really needs to be aware of how its Web presence features will be initially established and subsequently maintained. In having a Web presence, the small business information needs to be current - hence, there needs to be an awareness that timely Website updates and maintenance are paramount. This applies to whether the small business has created a Website on its own server or whether the Website has been established by a third-party provider on a shared server. These questions need to be considered *before* signing up with any type of hosting service that facilitates of Web presence.

We will now examine some of the specific issues involved in a small business setting up its own Website.

HOSTING, BUILDING, AND MAINTAINING A WEBSITE

As mentioned earlier, a small business has a number of options in relation to where its own Website can be hosted. A few of these options will now be discussed.

Hosting

Before a Website is activated and goes live it must be physically located or 'hosted' on a Web server. A Web server is a computer permanently connected to the Internet through a dedicated line that display Websites on the World Wide Web. Web servers need permanent technical attention. Fortunately, small businesses do not need to own and operate their own server within the business premises, but may use the services of a third-party that specialize in providing this service. This involves renting space on their servers and is the preferred option for most small businesses. Small businesses may also elect to own their own server but to have it on the premises of the Web host. Another option available to small businesses is to develop a server with a dedicated line within the business premises. This is a sophisticated and an expensive option that might be appreciated by technology

Copyright © 2009, IGI Global, distributing in print or electronic forms without written permission of IGI Global is prohibited.

enthusiasts. However, as a word of caution, this approach can only be justified in rare cases. For example, in a study of tourism enterprises that the authors were involved in, one technically minded owner hosted the business Website within the premises that not only involved maintaining a dedicated Web server, but also running a backup one.

In general, small business operators will most likely need to consider some form of hosting service to facilitate their Web presence. Web hosting has become affordable in recent times and numerous third-party operators provide reliable, cost effective hosting activities that are underpinned by high-powered technical systems. Some Web hosting services have specialised in the small to medium size business sector and provide relevant Web plans that reflect their expertise in this sector (for example, WebCentral is a high profile company in Australia that offers a selection of such Web hosting options and services depending on small business requirements). These types of services allow the small business to engage a third party to deal with the technical and governance complexities of being online. Indeed, many ISPs that previously only dealt with Internet connectivity have diversified to offer a myriad of Web services. An option for many small businesses in the early days of the Internet was to use a free Website hosting service. These free hosting opportunities still exist, and provide different levels of activities (some even provide e-commerce order and payment facilities), but there are usually sections of the site where the ISP puts their own advertising material that the business has no control over. These can be popular for the resource poor small businesses and provide a cost effective first step to getting the business online. For instance, to mitigate some of the cost of developing a Web presence, Karanasios & Burgess (2008) found that some small businesses chose to host their Website for free at first, and later moved onto paid hosting once benefits had materialized. The small businesses that used the free hosting services had a Website address that had a sub-name of top-level domain associated with the provider - for example www.ISP_provider.com/*your business/*). Arguably, these small businesses would not be easily found on a search engine because their distinct particulars may be ancillary to the characteristics associated with the more dominant name of the free provider. There will be more on Website domain names in Chapter VIII.

With respect to Web hosting activities, there are different levels of Website implementation plans that are available for small businesses. Clearly, the small business operator needs to be aware of these various options when engaging a hosting service - an awareness that allows them to make an informed decision on which plan best suits their needs. As a general rule, the greater the sophistication and complexity required in hosting a Website the higher the pricing. Most Web hosting services provide a variable number of differently priced and scaled plans to accommodate the requirements of most small business. An example of this hosting

Copyright © 2009, IGI Global, distributing in print or electronic forms without written permission of IGI Global is prohibited.

Table 1. Comparison Web hosting plans for small business

Features offered	Economy level hosting plan	Business level hosting plan
Server space	200MB	500MB
Monthly data transfer (traffic)	10GB	20GB
Mailboxes	Unlimited	Unlimited
Support for a domain name	√	√
SiteBuilder Basic (Web Design Tool)	√	√
Statistics Program (Tool for analysing web presence performance)	√	√
Database support*	√	√
Dynamic web pages	√	√

* The database allows customer and sales data to be captured and stored. (Plans summarized from WebCentral 2007)

plan variability can be seen in the service provided by WebCentral. WebCentral is one of Australia's largest Web hosting providers, and has an economy level plan that allows a small business to have a basic and static Website. This *entry-level* hosting plan allows the small business to use a freely available design tool to build and maintain their Web presence. The company reports that this is one of the most popular small business Web hosting services that they sell (WebCentral 2007). Another type of Web hosting plan offered by WebCentral allows the small business Website to be dynamically created as well as automating the collection of customer information and online sales. This business level plan also provides access to a database (for, perhaps, an online product catalogue). The types of services that WebCentral provides the small business operator are commonly encountered and offered by various other hosting services in different countries. Table 1 compares these different types of plans and the variety of features offered.

Part of the process of selecting a Web hosting service also involves considering where hosting occurs, the ancillary support services provided by the company, aspects of the computer systems being used and also the hosting company's reputation. These important areas are now expanded on.

Where to Host

One important decision for small businesses is the location of the Website host. For instance, for many small businesses in developing countries the utilisation of a hosting service in another country can result in considerable cost savings. For

Copyright © 2009, IGI Global, distributing in print or electronic forms without written permission of IGI Global is prohibited.

instance, during a study by one of the authors in Ecuador (Develop_06) it was found that small businesses that hosted their Website in the USA paid as little US$9.80 per month, while a business that chose a local hosting service paid a monthly equivalent of US$120. In addition to this cost saving, hosting a Website in another country is preferable when the majority of the business' customers reside in that country - connectivity is more reliable and file download times can be noticeably faster. Lake (2000) suggests that for small businesses in developing countries an international host (such as one that might be located in the USA) can improve the perceived credibility of the business, and may alleviate the fears that customers may have concerning purchasing from a business in a developing country.

Support

The support facilities are the most critical aspect of engaging a third-party to manage and maintain the small business Website. For the small business operator, who may be resource-poor, Website hosting support will entail timely access to technical advice within a narrow window of reporting any Website issues. This service should be of relative high quality and be available 24/7. Support should also entail the use of user-friendly and freely available Web hosting tools that allow the small business to manage not only the Website, but also their e-mail accounts and associated Website database facilities (where they have the skills to do this).

Technical Performance

Computer technology may be a potentially complex area for the small business operator to comprehend. However, it is important that they understand that the hosting company's servers need to be robust and reliable - a feature that enables business Website presence to be perceived as operating in a stable and high performance environment. Furthermore, the hosting service should have technically able systems that provided quality outcomes with respect to ICT stability and security. Hosting providers also need to demonstrate that they have an appropriate infrastructure that allows for higher-than-expected visitor traffic to be easily accommodated. This infrastructure needs to also address issues associated with guaranteeing Website and database backup, as well as having standby servers to be used in emergency situations. This aspect of the hosting service has important implications for small business performance continuity - poor technical capabilities by the hosting service can leave the business without an e-mail service or loss of important data captured via Website operations. More on this in Chapter IX.

Copyright © 2009, IGI Global, distributing in print or electronic forms without written permission of IGI Global is prohibited.

Reputation

The reputation of a hosting business can be a good indicator of the quality associ-ated with the service that a small business operator can expect when considering a hosting plan. Reputations are generally developed over time through the provision of highly regarded service, support and technical expertise. Hence, the reputation of a hosting service may involve examining the company's capacity with respect to the number of staff it employs, the centres it operates, and latest systems in place. Reputation may also be gauged by the relationships a host service may have with prominent industry groups. Host service industry awards can also be an important indicator of a company's performance in building its reputation - one that distinguishes it from other hosting companies. Also, word-of-mouth via official and/or informal networks can be an important source for determining host service reputation.

Government Sponsored Web Hosting

A Web presence can be facilitated by government support. This can be especially relevant for the home based business operator that has not only limited resources, but also suffers from a lack of social business networking opportunities because of their isolated situation. Breen et al (2005) identified that innovative local munici-pal or civic governments can provide a free (or heavily discounted) Web hosting

Figure 1. E-government activity (adapted from Breen et al., 2005)

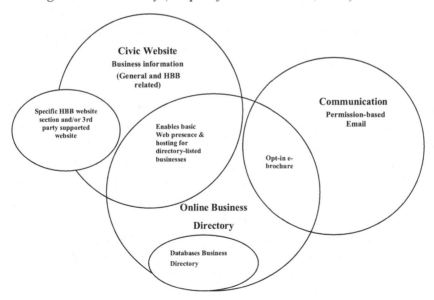

Copyright © 2009, IGI Global, distributing in print or electronic forms without written permission of IGI Global is prohibited.

service on their own larger Websites for many small businesses. This hosting is easy to implement and also has a synergistic value for civic government, allowing them to engage and promote various services to these isolated businesses. Indeed, under the guise of e-government service provision, a series of important Website hosting features can be used to assist the small business operator. This e-government model is depicted in Figure 1 and highlights the spheres in which ICTs can be used by civic governments for small business engagement. Website hosting is positioned at the centre of the model with related ICT features associated with database consolidation and e-brochure marketing activities.

The e-government model proposes that the civic government Website is the main tool being used to publish and disseminate business related information. The business database directory allows the capture and listing of local business details - a form of defacto Yellow Pages® directory. Within the guise of this online directory listing, civic government can provide a business with the opportunity to have a Web presence without the associated overheads of owning a Website - in effect they freely provide the Web space and hosting service. The small business operator should be well informed of any civic or local government promotion and support for Web presence - a service that allows them to engage their customers both professionally and without drawing significantly on their limit resources.

Building

Having decided who will host its Website, a small business is faced with a decision as to how to actually build and implement the Website. It is not the intention of this book to provide direction in relation to how to build a Website, beyond the issues addressed in Chapter VII on some of the important aspects of Website design. However, it is appropriate to discuss the different options available to the business.

Do it Yourself (DIY)

Many ISPs will host a small business Website, but will not provide tools nor support for the development and design of the site. The ISPs can interpret their role as a third-party provider as purely one of being a *hosting* service. If this is the case, then the Website needs to be developed and organised by the people within the small business - this may be the operator, a family member or in some instances an employee with the requisite set of technical skills. Sometimes, the small business may need to make an investment in skilling appropriate personnel to design, create, implement and update the Website. These investment costs may be significant. However, the small business does gain greater flexibility and control over its Website to make changes easily and in a timely manner. In turn, this allows the Website to publish

Copyright © 2009, IGI Global, distributing in print or electronic forms without written permission of IGI Global is prohibited.

the small business's information and material in a current, relevant and accurate manner - information features that tend contribute to perceptions that a business is professional in dealing with the public. Indeed, it is not necessary for a small business to understand the complexities of the Web formatting code such as HTML or an interactive language such as javascript (some issues associated with HTML are discussed in Chapter VII). Simpler, less expensive options are available to the small business in the guise of applications packages, such as Microsoft FrontPage® or Adobe's Dreamweaver®, that have been developed for the design and creation of Websites and pages. These applications allow the design of simple Web pages quickly and inexpensively, but have the capability to do much more in the hands of the technically skilled user. If a small business is not in a position to build its own Website, either through lack of personnel or lack of time, then this option should not be considered. It should be noted that the Website is usually developed on the personal computers of the small business and then 'uploaded' to the host server.

Get Someone Else to Do It

This option may be chosen if the small business requires a Website to have a unique design and specific business-affiliated features. In other words, they want a special look or some special functionality on the Website. In these instances, a small business will need to engage an appropriate Web design or ICT consultant and consequently this option can be relatively more expensive when compared to other Website creation opportunities. Indeed, Website design consultants have today evolved to the point were they are often seen to have expertise in a selected industry area, providing pertinent advice for businesses in that sector. For example, a number of specialist Web presence consultants have been identified as providing relevant services to small accounting practices. These consultants will not only design, create and sometimes host an accounting business Website, but will also identify and maintain appropriate accounting content - for instance, regular online news bulletins discussing the latest accounting news in the region that a practice is located.

Use a Package or Wizard

'Off-the-shelf' packages are available to assist the small business establish a Website. These Website wizards allow the small business operator to create a simple, basic Website, through to sites that are more complex with a high degree of functionality. The common feature associated with these off-the-shelf design packages is that they provide the user with an understandable and easily usable step-by-step process that allows a Website to be created. Some hosting services provide tools to design

Copyright © 2009, IGI Global, distributing in print or electronic forms without written permission of IGI Global is prohibited.

Websites according to a number of available templates and then implement the site on their server for a regular fee. Some of these tools include interactive *wizards* that the small business can use for Website development. Although, these solutions are particularly advantageous for resource poor small businesses, a major limitation is that their Website becomes difficult to differentiate amongst all the other businesses with similar looking sites. A number of operators in an Australian tourism study used a template to develop their Web presence, mainly because of a lack of technical expertise and financial resources. However, one business owner became frustrated because the Web presence was underpinned by design limitations and any changes attracted significant additional fees. In fact, in some of our studies we have come across businesses that have specifically designed Websites themselves, or had them customised by external consultants, to *differentiate* themselves from their competitors who have use packaged solutions.

Depending upon the tool or wizard being used, sometimes the small business may build the Website on its own computers and then upload it to the host server. In other instances, the tool or wizard is located on the host server and the small business accesses it remotely (usually via the Internet) to build and amend the Website directly on the server.

THE 'EXTENDED' WEB

One of the areas covered in this chapter that has resulted from our small business studies and observations of Website trends, is this section on what we term the extended Web. The extended Web refers to the opportunities available to the small business to use the services of other Websites. These other Websites can include the Yellow Pages®, civic government sites, regional online directories and Web portals, which not only allow the small business to disseminate important promotional information, but also can increase the business' operations in the Web environment. The most overt example of this type of extended Web opportunities is where a small business operator is able to offer online sales facilities that are sourced from another Website, but appear to be seamlessly available on their own site.

The Web Portal

Arguably, Web portals have become an exemplary avenue for many small businesses to increase their Web presence and exposure. A Web portal can be described as:

... an infrastructure providing secure, integrated access to dynamic content from a variety of sources, in a variety of source formats, wherever it is needed. Value is

Copyright © 2009, IGI Global, distributing in print or electronic forms without written permission of IGI Global is prohibited.

added to the information by filtering it according to the purpose of the portal and shortening user search costs by the provision or directory or other search services. Value may also be added for the user by the addition of customisable and personalisable options and extra or bundled services. (Burgess, Bingley and Tatnall 2005)

Although there is no clear and definitive categorisation of the different types of Web portals that exist, Tatnall et al (2006) has suggested several groupings or categories. Here are some that are relevant to the small business environment:

- **General portals:** These Websites aim to provide links to other sites that can be either closely related or quite diverse in the topics or material they cover. General portals provide links to all sorts of different sites of the user's choosing, for instance, search engines (such as Google™), ISPs, and e-mail services (such as Hotmail).
- **Vertical Industry portals:** These Websites are usually based around specific industries and aggregate information relevant to particular groups in those industries. They aim to facilitate the exchange of goods and services in a particular market as part of a value chain.
- **Community portals:** Such Websites are often set up by community groups, or are based around special interest groups. The sites attempt to foster virtual communities where users share a common location or interest, and provide many different services. Sometimes community portals represent specific regional areas - hence, are referred to as regional portals.
- **Personal/Mobile portals:** These portals represent Websites that embody the trend towards mobile or what is termed pervasive computing. These personal/mobile portals are increasingly associated with mobile (cellular) phones, PDAs and the evolving trend to wireless devices.
- **Information portals:** These Websites can be viewed as a category in their own right in that they provide highly valuable and in depth information on a specific topic.

Clearly, there are now many more options available to a small business when establishing their Web presence. Many of these are associated with Web portals. Portals are intended to be Websites that users will keep returning to as a point of access based on their own interests - they often are used as a starting point for specific groups of users when accessing the Internet. What is useful about portals is the way that these special sites are now being used to facilitate access to other sites that may be closely related, something that is evident in the case of special purpose portals, or even with some general portals. The evolution of the Web portal is such

Copyright © 2009, IGI Global, distributing in print or electronic forms without written permission of IGI Global is prohibited.

that these Websites now offer a range of functional services to the small business user that can include real-time order and payment processing facilities.

Another category of Website that is available to small business is those that offer online marketplaces, such as eBay™, for businesses to transact their goods. Although initially set up as a vehicle for consumers to transact their goods with other consumers, sites such as eBay™ have a number of small businesses (and some larger ones) taking advantage of the services offered. Such sites have almost become a form of pseudo-Website hosting and building service, given that the commonly available 'store' features allows a business to include information about itself and its products, as well as provide a mechanism by which those products can be sold.

Web 2.0 Sites

In recent years as complex technologies have become easier to use a new type of Website has emerged, known as Web 2.0. These Websites have embraced different presentation formats, allowing the user to store videos online (such as YouTube), store and update information (such as Wikipedia) and provide comments (on things such as news stories) via Web logs (or 'blogs'). The fundamental nature of these Web 2.0 sites is that an individual can post different types of content (depending upon the Website) and other individuals can respond - hence, sometimes the term *social networking* Websites is used by some people when they refer to Web 2.0 sites.

These types of sites currently have limited use in a commercial sense, but there is anecdotal evidence that suggests this is changing. For example, YouTube has been used to post notices and comments by American and Australian political parties - an activity that forms a part of their re-election advertising strategy. Travel Websites (such as Yahoo® Travel) include a 'blogs and comments' feature that allow users to add their opinions about hotels and other destinations - importantly, travel consumers have started to take notice of what these users are saying as their comments are perceived to be impartial. On some Web 2.0 sites like TripAdvisor® (http://www.tripadvisor.com/), several accommodation providers are taking the opportunity to respond to negative customer reviews with a conciliatory approach in attempts to manage any poor customer experiences. This observation of accommodation provider behaviour might be suggestive of the perceived influence that such user-generated content sites can have on business activities associated with customer relationship management.

Benefits of the Extended Web to Small Business

So, what benefits can the "extended' Web provide for small businesses? Portals perform many different functions, but their core elements embrace activities that

Copyright © 2009, IGI Global, distributing in print or electronic forms without written permission of IGI Global is prohibited.

include Website or Web page search, publishing relevant content, community building, and providing online commerce features (Eisenmann et al 2002). The key question for any small business is whether these Websites are going to provide these services on a more cost effective or efficient basis than they could themselves? Furthermore, does the Web portal allow the small business to progressive extend the business' reach beyond what their own standalone Website could possibly achieve? Does the portal provide services not available or too costly for the small business to reasonably implement via their own Website? Some of the advantages that portal Websites offer to small businesses include (Tatnall et al 2006):

- **A secure environment:** The capital and ongoing outlay for real-time ordering and payment facilities can be significant for a small business. Also, it can be quite complex to integrate these facilities with a business' Website - especially with respect to security. Indeed, the cost and integration challenge for small businesses is reduced by being able to source these activities from a portal or similar Website. Portals often have a secure payment infrastructure that enables small businesses to integrate their accounts receivables with the portal payment facility.
- **Search and directory services:** There is a greater likelihood that search engines will return listings of the popular portals at a higher level than for an individual small business Website. By listing with these portals, small businesses increase the likelihood of being identified and sourced by users that search for businesses via portal Websites.
- **Community and relationship building:** Portal Website features such as chat rooms, message boards, instant-messaging services, online greeting cards, and other interactive Web services are fundamental elements of portal infrastructure. Collectively, these features contribute to fostering community building and relationship establishment activities that are commonly encountered in the Web portal environment. The small business entity can utilise these relationship-building activities to formally or informally develop closer ties with businesses that may also have portal presence. It is envisaged that many of the social networking activities associated with Web 2.0 sites may also become commonplace on portal sites.
- **Regional relationship building:** Portal Websites can also facilitate and enhance regional relationship building amongst small business groups. In addition to all of the community building benefits noted, regional portals provide the advantage that participating small businesses can feel that they are contributing to the identifiable local community. There are also cost and efficiency benefits through dealing with businesses in the local area, especially where

Copyright © 2009, IGI Global, distributing in print or electronic forms without written permission of IGI Global is prohibited.

physical products are being transacted. This is in addition to the goodwill that can eventuate through dealing in the local area.

Clearly, small businesses now have various options beyond just implementing their own Websites in order to consolidate their Web presence. For example, a small accommodation business may wish to use the booking service offered by a specialised accommodation portal. By using this portal service, the accommodation provider not only can reach a wider geographical market, but also dispense with the need to know about the complex technology associated with the booking system. Thus, the small business can increase its potential booking rates with minimal overheads associated with directly implementing this facility on their own Website. One drawback can be that the portal booking service is typically not linked to the business's own booking database - often requiring manual checking. Another example of appropriate use of portal features may involve small manufacturing firms, such as wineries. The winery can have good reasons for using the online shopping cart facility that may be available as part of a regional or industry portal. Again, this may provide access to more customers and lead to extra turnover without having to be concerned about implementing shopping cart technology. A disadvantage of this is that a link needs to be set up with the business' inventory database, which may be costly and inconvenient. A simpler example of an extended Web presence is when a small business provides basic contact information that is published on a regional or industry portal. This can be quite inexpensive and because the information does not change readily, is relatively easy to maintain. A more specialised example is where a business may wish to attract potential customers to a region, and realises that a regional portal has a listing of numerous tourist attractions and regional events. Why should they repeat this information on their own Website? They could rely on customers seeing this information as they link to the business through the regional portal, or perhaps more realistically provide a link back to the specific page on the portal. Let someone else worry about updating the information! (Burgess 2006).

OUR PREVIOUS STUDIES

Accountant_07

Interviews with accounting practices revealed some interesting outcomes in relation to Website hosting, building and content management. After classifying the businesses into micro, small and medium sized practices the study identified the following Website management characteristics:

Copyright © 2009, IGI Global, distributing in print or electronic forms without written permission of IGI Global is prohibited.

- The majority of practices had their Websites *hosted* externally (the exceptions were one micro and one medium sized practice, who hosted their own Websites). External hosting occurred either through an ISP or a specialist Website consultant.
- Only seven of the businesses had some control over the *initial building* of the Website. Notably, four were micro practices.
- All of the businesses had some control over *Website content.* However, eight of the practices relied on an external consultant (generally accounting Website specialists, as described earlier in the chapter) to provide some content, such as up-to-date accounting profession news.
- The Websites were maintained with varying degrees of regularity:
  o Weekly/ Fortnightly (3 Websites)
  o Monthly (5)
  o Bi-monthly/ Quarterly (3)
  o Yearly (1)
  o Ad hoc or 'as needed' (6)

Wineries_PhDsurvey_04

This research PhD investigated Internet adoption by small to medium size (SME) wineries and developed an e-business best practice model based on the experiences and perceptions of a group of early Internet adopting wineries.

When considering the technical practices associated with e-business implementation, the study identified that ISP hosting features associated with security and encryption of online sales was a significant consideration for smaller wineries. Moreover, the hosting service used by one of the investigated wineries was found to be good value for money and provided excellent service in the small business' regional area. The winery alluded to the local service centre established by the ISP hosting service as assisting the business to limit its telecommunications cost.

Another aspect of the study identified a winery portal that was established by a group of small wineries allowing them to collectively market themselves from one central Web point. Significantly, some small wineries did not have their own Websites before the portal was developed and this was their first form of Web exposure. The portal provided benefits such as enhancing wine sales, allowed marketing of individual wineries, facilitated the promotion of the region as a tourism area and generally fostered an environment for electronic information dissemination. One of the most important aspects of the portal's function was the provision of security infrastructure similar to what a commercial Web hosting service would provide. The wineries found that they did not have to be concerned about the technical and

Copyright © 2009, IGI Global, distributing in print or electronic forms without written permission of IGI Global is prohibited.

transactional processes associated with online ordering. Moreover, this infrastructure aspect of portal hosting dispensed with the need for each winery to duplicate this secure ordering feature on their Websites. An examination of the backend functionality of online purchasing for wineries revealed that a partial automation of the transactional process were in place - even though customers order online, there is no automatic redirecting of funds from purchaser account to winery account.

Other Studies

The Security Risks Associated with Web Hosting (Jones 2001)

Jones (2001) provides a comprehensive guide to security and Website hosting. He argues, as we have in this book, that a businesses Website can be crucial to the business, and as such needs to be functional, quick to load and available 24/7. Failure to do so can result in losing potential as well as existing customers. This presents a daunting task for many small businesses and as has been suggested in this book that outsourcing Web hosting operations provides an effective and efficient solution.

In light of this, Jones (2001) suggests any benefits offered by hosting externally must be balanced increased security risks. This is because sensitive information is often held on servers including bank details, which may be accessed by undesirable persons. Overselling is common in the ICT industry and likewise for hosting firms promising high levels of security. Jones (2001) warns against being wooed by sales pitches surrounding security. He goes so far to warn that often new hosting firms are aware of problems even before customers complain. To combat some of these concerns, Jones (2001) provides the following suggestions below and suggests that secure Web hosting will never be fail proof. However, by following the relatively simple guidelines businesses drastically reduce the chances of security problems.

- A business should ask a hosting firm whether they can test the security of their hosted Website. Along these lines, develop a testing contract to ensure ongoing testing and protect both the business and the hosting firm. Jones (2001) cautions that refusal to do this may be in indication that the hosting firm may have something to hide.
- A business should examine whether there are safeguards in place to control access to sensitive information. Also, ensure that the hosting firm has a secure firewall in place. Providing it is set up correctly firewalls provide a much higher level of security.
- Another important issue to examine is the approach the hosting company takes to the customer's systems. A business should determine if the hosting firm sets up each system on a standardised basis. This is because if each site is set

Copyright © 2009, IGI Global, distributing in print or electronic forms without written permission of IGI Global is prohibited.

up uniquely, this may result in them not being set up with the latest security patches for the operating system and server software.

- A vital concern for small business is how they will actually access their information on the server. Jones (2001) warns that secure firewalls can be compromised by allowing clients to remotely access their systems using insecure means (such as FTP, telnet and PCanywhere).

The Effects Of Website 'Downtime' (Graham, 2001)

Like many other authors and consultants, Graham (2001) suggests it makes sense to host a business Website with an external provider. He also provides some useful criteria that can be used by small businesses to make informed decisions concerning selecting the right hosting firm. He posits that *"Today, 99% availability may not be good enough. The top providers ought to be advancing toward 100%, with plenty of nines after 99%"* (Graham, 2001: 12).

As a first step, he suggests that businesses search for a firm that can provide the following:

- **High availability:** Involves making sure that the Website is never down. This means procedures to recover from a system and Website crash.
- **Security:** Is a complex task in the arena of e-business and is especially true concerning hosting. Therefore, Web hosting firms must be aware of the latest trends in the field. As a check, firms should have secure log-on procedures, firewalls, and intrusion detection systems, and continuous testing (see Chapter IX).
- **Customer service:** Is an important factor because it will determine the relationship between the two parties and therefore needs consideration. Graham (2001) warns that not every firm will have the necessary people skills.
- **Capacity on demand:** Means an efficient way to deal with how big a support system to build. Some firms are adept at providing tailored solutions while others may have a standard 'one size fits all' approach.
- **Rapid recovery:** Is linked to the issue of high availability businesses should insure that a Web hosting firm has disaster recovery plans in place.

Graham (2001) continues to say that key to the success of Web hosting and managing the relationship with the hosting firm is creating a service level agreement so that both parties are clear on what is expected.

Copyright © 2009, IGI Global, distributing in print or electronic forms without written permission of IGI Global is prohibited.

Summary of our Studies and Other Studies

There are only two studies mentioned here as we had already mentioned some of the considerations of this chapter in earlier chapters of the book. What we do know is that most small businesses have their Website hosted externally, a number do take advantage of third party Websites (such as portals), not enough of them consider the cost of setting up their Web presence and even fewer the effort needed to maintain it. Many small businesses in developing countries and rural areas of developed countries still find accessing suitable and cost effective connection to the Internet to be an issue that effects what they are able to achieve.

TENETS – LESSONS FROM THE CHAPTER

There are a number of lessons from this chapter that can be applied by small businesses when considering the most appropriate means of hosting their Web presence. These are listed in Table 2.

Table 2. Web presence hosting factors

Type of Web Presence	Factor	Consideration
General	ISP selection	Factors to be taken into account: • Cost • Performance • Number of email accounts • Support services/ reliability/ reputation
	Web presence	• Who will host the web presence? • Who is responsible for content?
Small business website	Hosting	• External hosting is suitable for most small businesses • Be aware of hosting plans available in relation to server space, traffic allowances and other services.
	Building	The options are do-it-yourself, get someone else (such as a consultant) to do it, or use a package or wizard. It is important to keep track of cost, the skills needed to adopt your preferred option, how content is loaded onto the host server and how easy it is to modify.
The 'Extended' Web	Portals: Third-party support services Web 2.0: Valuable user generated content	External websites, such as portals or regional directories, could be considered to extend the reach of the online presence, to make the business more visible, or to obtain services that the business might not otherwise be able to adopt (such as online order and payment facilities). With respect to Web 2.0 sites there is a view that they have limited use in a commercial sense, but there is anecdotal evidence that suggests this is changing.

Copyright © 2009, IGI Global, distributing in print or electronic forms without written permission of IGI Global is prohibited.

CONCLUSION

Although this chapter is labelled 'Web Presence Hosting', it has actually covered much more than that. The hosting of the Web presence is associated with the selection of an appropriate ISP, and raises questions about available finances and skills within the small business structure. In general, small business operators will most likely need to consider some form of hosting service to facilitate their Web presence. Web hosting has become affordable in many areas in recent times and numerous third-party operators provide reliable, cost effective hosting activities that are underpinned by high-powered technical systems. When considering hosting options it is also necessary to think about the type of Website a small business will need to implement and more importantly, maintain over time. The consideration even extends to thoughts as to whether the business needs a Website at all.

Small business operators need to also consider external avenues for enhancing their Web presence. Will the small business be able to have an online presence by using just a Web portal? The more common alternative is for the small business to have its own Website, but to additionally use the services of a number of external Websites allowing them to extend their geographical reach, improve their online visibility through enhanced search returns or increase functionality, especially with respect to online sales. For those businesses that are intending to create and implement their own Website, the next chapter discusses Website design.

REFERENCES

Bajaj, K. K., & Nag, D. (1999). *E-Commerce: The cutting edge of business.* New Delhi: McGraw-Hill.

Breen, J., Sellitto, C., Ali, S., & Paguio, R. (2005). E-Government Services Provided for Home Based Business Operators: A Study of Victorian Local Councils. *Proceedings of the 6th International We-B (Working for e-business) Conference. E-links: Community, Business and University (CD-ROM)*, (pp. 92-99). Melbourne, Australia, ed. P. Shackleton, , E-Commerce Research Unit, Victoria University.

Burgess, S. (2006). A Model for B2C Customer Interactions on the Web by Small Businesses: Adjustments for the Extended Web. In K. Dhanda & M. G. Hunter (Eds.), *Grand Challenges in Technology Management: Proceedings of ISOneWorld 2006*, Las Vegas, Nevada. The Information Institute, Washington DC.

Burgess, S., Bingley, S., & Tatnall, A. (2005). Matching the Revenue Model and Content of Horizontal Portals. *Proceedings of The Second International Conference on Innovations in Information Technology*, Dubai, UAE, UAE University.

Copyright © 2009, IGI Global, distributing in print or electronic forms without written permission of IGI Global is prohibited.

Burgess, S., & Schauder, D. (2001). Web Site Development Options for Australian Small Businesses. In M. Khosrow-Pour (Ed.), *Managing Information Technology in a Global Economy: Proceedings of the 2001 Information Resources Management Association Conference*, Toronto, Canada, ed., Idea Group Publishing, Hershey, PA.

Eisenmann, T. R., Hallowell, R., & Tripsas, M. (2002). *Internet business models: text and cases*. McGraw-Hill Education-Europe, UK.

Goodman, S., Kelly, T., Minges, M., & Press, L. (2000). International perspectives: compuitong at the top of the world. *Communications of the ACM, 43*(11), 23-27.

Graham, A. (2001). Don't Let Downtime Be the Downfall of Your Web Site. *Journal of Business Strategy, 22*(2), 10.

James, J. (2003). Sustainable Internet access for the rural poor? Elements of an emerging Indian model. *Futures, 35*(5), 461-472.

Jones, D. (2001). Web Hosting — The Security Risks. *Network Security, *(12), 14-15.

Karanasios, S. (2008). *An E-Commerce Framework for Small Tourism Enterprises in Developing Countries*. Victoria University.

Karanasios, S., & Burgess, S. (2008). Tourism and Internet adoption: a developing world perspective. *International Journal of Tourism Research, 10*(2), 169-182.

Lake, S. (2000). E-Commerce and LDCs: Challenges for enterprises and governments. *E-Commerce and LDCs Roundtable, United Nations Conference on Trade and Development*, Kathmandu, Nepal.

Patel, N. V. (2003). E-commerce technology. In L. Harris, P.J. Jackson & P.M. Eckersley (Eds.), *E-Business fundamentals* (pp. 43-63). New York: Routledge.

Payne, J. E. (2002). *E-Commerce Readiness for SMEs in Developing Countries: A Guide for Development Professionals*. Academy for Educational Development/ LearnLink, Washington, DC.

Sellitto, C., & Burgess, S. (2007). A Study of a Wine Industry Internet Portal. In A. Tatnall (Ed.), *Encyclopedia of Portal Technologies and Applications* (pp. 979-984). London: Information Science Reference. UK.

Tatnall, A., Burgess, S., & Singh, M. (2006). Small Business and Regional Portals in Australia. In M. Khosrow-Pour (Ed.), *Encyclopaedia of E-Commerce, E-Government and Mobile Commerce* (1016-1021). Hershey, PA: Idea Group Reference.

Copyright © 2009, IGI Global, distributing in print or electronic forms without written permission of IGI Global is prohibited.

WebCentral. (2007). [http://www.Webcentral.com.au/Websitehosting.php], Retrieved: 16/11/2007.

Wicklein, R. C. (1998). Designing for appropriate technology in developing countries. *The Australian (IT Section), 20*(3), 371-375.

Copyright © 2009, IGI Global, distributing in print or electronic forms without written permission of IGI Global is prohibited.

APPENDIX: DIFFERENT TYPES OF INTERNET CONNECTIONS

In this section we discuss the major options available to small businesses to connect to the Internet. No matter the Internet needs of a business it is important to consider the technical dimensions of how the Internet will be used. For instance, a business hosting a Website internally must consider that the Website should generally be available to customers 24 hours per day, seven days per week. Even businesses planning only to use e-mail communication to receive bookings online will need access to a reliable connection. This may pose a problem for some rural and regional businesses where even basic telephone connections are a luxury and telecommunication costs are high.

Obviously the type of Internet connection selected by a business depends on what is available as well as what the Internet will be used for. For simple uses of the Internet only a slow Internet connection is required. However, for a business to move to more integrated activities access to a computer with a medium to fast Internet speed is required. Table 1 provides a useful guide on how an Internet connection may be used. The table is instructive because it provides not only a guide

Table 1. A guide to how the Internet may be used

E-commerce technique	Internet access		Instrument for access		
	Slow	Medium to fast	Computer (PC)	Mobile Phone	PDA*
Email (simple)	OK	OK	OK	OK	OK
Email (complex)	-	OK	OK	-	Maybe
Newsgroups, bulletin boards, chat rooms	OK	OK	OK	Maybe	OK
Information database (stand-alone or simple updates)	OK	OK	OK	Maybe if adapted	Maybe if adapted
Software applications (stand-alone or simple updates)	OK	OK	OK	Unlikely	Unlikely but possible
Website (brochure ware, simple)	OK	OK	OK	Maybe if adapted	Maybe
Web-based applications (e.g. product ordering/ tracking)	-	OK	OK	Maybe if adapted	Maybe
Voice over Internet (VoIP)	-	OK	OK	Maybe	Maybe

* *Personal digital assistant*
Source: *Adapted from Payne (2002), Figure 4, p.23*

Copyright © 2009, IGI Global, distributing in print or electronic forms without written permission of IGI Global is prohibited.

for how the Internet may be used, but also the possibility of accessing different aspects of the Internet from various different devices.

Before a business decides to adopt new technology it should consider the types of technology that are available in its location as well as possible alternatives. There are three main types of Internet access and these are discussed below (Karanasios 2008).

Dial-Up Connections

Dial-up connections are the most common type of Internet connection available, particularly for home users. A dial-up connection allows users to connect to the Internet via a local server using a standard 56k modem, which converts data from analogue to digital format. Although dial-up connections are widely available, they suffer from a number of limitations. The speed of a dial-up connection is problematic for most users and will pose an issue for small businesses hoping to exploit the Web. Furthermore, when connected to the Internet through a dial-up connection the same telephone line cannot be used for telephone calls. This means that if a customer attempts to call the business they will receive a busy signal or even disconnect the connection. Both results are equally irritating for the business and customer.

Although dial-up connections may be economical for low use users, a major cost is that a user must pay the cost of a telephone call each time a connection is made. A connection can take up to a few minutes to establish, which is an additional burden. It is obvious from the discussion that a dial-up connection is best suited to low level users of the Internet and not for businesses aiming to absorb maximum benefits from the Internet.

ADSL Connections

ADSL (Asymmetric Digital Subscribers Line) connections are becoming more popular because of the advantages they provide users. Unlike dial-up connections, ADSL connections work by 'splitting' the telephone line, which means users can talk on the telephone and be connected to the Internet at the same time. This is a large benefit for small businesses, which need to be available on the telephone all the time – or at least during business hours. Furthermore, ADSL connections are always connected, which eliminates the need to spend time creating an Internet connection. Depending on the plan and Internet Service Provider ADSL connections have different speeds ranging from 256Kbps to 1Mbps download speed to 128 to 256Kbps upload speed. Another major benefit of ADSL is that a wireless connection can be established. This eliminates the needs for telephone cables and provides extra flexibility to small business.

Copyright © 2009, IGI Global, distributing in print or electronic forms without written permission of IGI Global is prohibited.

The major frustration of ADSL is that it is not available to all locations. Small businesses in rural and regional areas in particular may find that they do not have access to an ADSL connection. However, as described ADSL offers many significant advantages over dial-up and is a sound economic choice for most small businesses.

Cable Connections

Cable Internet connections are considered one of the most efficient types of Internet connection offering high speed and reliable Internet access. As the name suggests cable Internet connections are completely dependant of the telephony infrastructure and therefore a business is not affect by problems such as 'hogging' the telephone line. This is important because often there is a limitation to the number of telecommunication devices that can share a single telephone line – as most business will have Internet, telephone, fax and EFTPOS, it makes sense to use a separate line for Internet access. Generally speaking the speed of cable is faster than ADSL and is especially useful for businesses with large information and communication requirements. Like ADSL, cable Internet connections are not available in all locations. Again, businesses outside of major urban centers are likely to find that they are out of reach of many ISPs.

Other Options

As there has been some discussion provided on the limitations of small businesses in rural and regional areas to access the Internet, it is useful to provide some examples of alternatives. For example, VSATs (Very Small Aperture Terminal) have been used in remote areas, where the quality of the telephone lines are poor, as a reliable means of communication and an alternative to traditional fixed line connections (Bajaj & Nag, 1999; Goodman, Kelly, Minges, & Press, 2000). Wireless Loop Protocol is another alternative. This is a system that connects users to the public network with radio signals. The technology is claimed to bring down the cost of 'per line' telephone connection from $US 910 to $US 210 and facilitates both voice and data transmission (James, 2003). Although promising, these alternative models of Internet adoption require careful consideration in the context of small business. Two factors that need consideration are (Wicklein, 1998):

- The way in which the technology will fit with traditional business practices and the local telecommunications system. Will it work under local conditions? Is it adaptive?

Copyright © 2009, IGI Global, distributing in print or electronic forms without written permission of IGI Global is prohibited.

- Is a support system required to keep the technology functioning? To what degree can the technology operate on its own, to do its job with few or no other supporting facilities or devices to aid in its function. Businesses should consider if the cost of the technology rises because of the need for supporting devices

At the time of writing, many telecommunications providers around the world are providing relatively low cost wireless broadband access. This may have a dramatic effect on the types of connections available to small businesses.

When making a decision on the type of Internet connection it is also useful to consider the ISP that will provide the Internet connection. There are literally thousands of ISPs available and most offer basic service such as access, domain name services, and electronic mail (Patel, 2003). Concerning access to the Internet, a technical consideration that requires attention by small businesses is the number of ISPs that they will subscribe to. There is evidence to suggest that for some small businesses that more than one ISP is appropriate. Why? When one connection fails the business can use the second as a backup. This approach is more common in countries where the telecommunications infrastructure is considered very unreliable. For instance, evidence from the Asia Foundation (2005) studies showed that 18 percent of businesses surveyed in Indonesia used two ISPs in order to ensure better access and continuous connection. Some 21 percent of businesses surveyed (that were Internet users) in Thailand had two ISPs, while seven percent had three ISPs. Even small business in major capital cities might like to consider subscribing to a low cost or even prepaid dial up plan, which can be used as a backup in the event that the primary Internet connection is unavailable.

Copyright © 2009, IGI Global, distributing in print or electronic forms without written permission of IGI Global is prohibited.

Chapter VII
Website Design

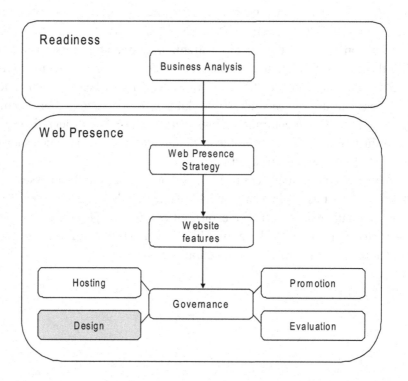

INTRODUCTION

This is the most technical of the chapters in this book. It is centred on Website design and is the only chapter in the book where we exclusively refer to *Website* rather than *Web presence.* In the previous chapter we discussed how a small business, once it decides to have a Website, needs to decide where it will be hosted, how it will be built and how its content will be initially loaded and then maintained. Website

Copyright © 2009, IGI Global, distributing in print or electronic forms without written permission of IGI Global is prohibited.

design is considered at the time of implementing the Website and then again at any major redesign of the Website.

BACKGROUND

The Website has generally become an expected operational tool in the small business environment and should evolve over time to reflect its needs and the demands of prospective and existing customers. Arguably, the small business Website that has been designed appropriately will have a certain element of fundamental functionality - allowing the business to easily address future implementation and new technology issues. Moreover, a small business that has adopted various Website design conventions tends to be well-positioned, in not only in attracting new users to its site, but also increasing its opportunities for e-commerce activity and online marketing. The design of the small business Website does not need to be complex and there are some that advocate that the simpler the site, the easier it will be to use (Nielsen 2000).

The Website can be viewed as a publishing medium and there is a commonly held belief that good design should aim at making information visible and manageable (Sellitto and Wenn 2005). Appropriate Website design should utilise information effectively, with each Webpage interface being a vehicle for conveying that information. Furthermore, evidence suggests that design can be the differentiator between a successful and unsuccessful Website - where the adoption of good practices in Website implementation can alleviate some of the drawbacks of unexpected maintenance associated with more complex and costly sites. Some of the good practice aspects of Website implementation need to encompass aspects of design that are associated with usability, proper coding of pages, accessibility and metadata (discussed later). In an environment where ICTs are constantly evolving and changing with respect to interactivity and customer expectations, the need to adopt good practice conventions or guidelines becomes a necessary requirement. Within the general ICT community there are various groups that have provided an open forum for discussion on development of Website design conventions. Groups such as the World Wide Web Consortium (W3C), the Web Accessibility Initiative (WAI) and the Dublin Core Metadata Initiative (DCMI) all have been instrumental in formulating a set of self-regulating guidelines. Notable authors such as Jakob Nielsen, (http://www.useit.com/) have strongly advocated the mantra of Website usability as an essential good practice when it comes to Website implementation. For the small business there should be an awareness of the various development and Website approaches that allow for the improvement of site maintenance and

Copyright © 2009, IGI Global, distributing in print or electronic forms without written permission of IGI Global is prohibited.

content integrity - developments that invariably lead to enhanced satisfaction for the online customer.

Hence, this section of the book is not about how *cool* the small business Website can be portrayed. Nor is this section about what *content* should be included on the Website - content is invariably associated with small business strategy and the demands of the business's target audience and is discussed in previous chapters. The discussion in this chapter focuses on issues that have resulted from commonly recognized design problems that indicate that small business Websites must appropriately address encoding conventions, accessibility and usability factors. As such, this chapter uses a good practice approach to document and detail aspects of Website implementation that small businesses can use to initiate or enhance their Internet presence. For the small business manager an awareness of such practices is important. Given that many small businesses will themselves manage and implement their own Website, exposure and awareness of these good practices potentially encourages them to adopt certain expected conventions. In the event of a small business outsourcing their Website design, they are in an informed position to deal with design consultant queries and demands.

Usability

Website usability is associated with features that allow Websites to be easy to learn and remember, reliable and efficient to use, and impart audience satisfaction. Although many definitions of Website usability have been proposed, the approach used here draws from the works of usability expert Jakob Nielsen (Nielsen 2000; Nielsen and Tahir 2002; Nielsen and Loranger 2006) - works that tend to be based on behavioural research and observational studies of Website users. For the small business owner, the adoption and maintenance of a Website that embraces usability values can be easily achieved with benefits that are associated with improved visitor experience. This can translate into increased customer enquiries, higher e-commerce transactions and successful direct marketing activities.

An important component of Website success for the small business is the way that the Website home page (the opening page) presents and functions from a usability perspective. Many of the usability principles and conventions that apply to the home page can be used for designing other aspects of the Website. The importance of the home page as a virtual showcase for people when they visit a Website should be recognised. An appropriately designed and usable home page allows prospective customers and users to gain an initial positive impression of the organisation, as well as being able to effectively access published information. Hence, certain usability protocols are based on the design elements that have been deemed as essential when it comes to Website design.

Copyright © 2009, IGI Global, distributing in print or electronic forms without written permission of IGI Global is prohibited.

Essential Usability Design Features

Usability design features that are considered to be essential address areas associated with Website searching, data collection and privacy, avoiding the use of deleterious and non-functional features, and an acceptable Web page download time. These essential features have, or are becoming, design conventions and should be incorporated by all Website implementation projects (Cox et al 2008). We will now discuss these essential usability design features, which should be viewed as a set of good practice guidelines for addressing Website usability. These features are a selective summary derived from the work of Nielsen and colleagues (2000;2002;2006).

Logo Placement. Most businesses will have a trade mark or representative emblem that can be used as a corporate logo on their Website. Logos are two-dimensional images and the design recommendation is that they should occupy the top left hand corner of the Website's pages. Furthermore, the logo should be linked from all Website pages to return to the home page. By 'linked' we mean that if someone clicks on the logo they are returned to the home page of the Website. By using this design convention, Website users are reassured as they move through the site with the logo acting as a:

- Road sign allowing them to know that they have not left the site
- Navigational aid that allows people to return to the familiar home page should they get confused as to where they are.

Indeed, the corporate logo as a form of identity (branding) may serve as a sub-conscience navigational aid for users by providing them with a sense of location which allows them to confirm where they are. This feature can be considered one of the fundamental design elements that most Website users look for.

Search facility. The search feature is another fundamental Website design element that users appreciate and expect to find on Websites. Searching the Internet for information about a particular product, service or topic has become an intrinsic aspect of user behaviour - words or phrases are 'Googled' to find high ranking and appropriate sites. This general concept of searching for particular information is now also an expectation when individuals visit an organisation's Website. People expect a search facility allowing them to find specific information relevant to the organisation. In terms of Website design the organisational search facility should have two aspects - the facility should be located on the home page and it usually is represented as an entry box. For the business that has a relatively small number of pages that compose their Website the search facility can be overlooked. However, the omission of this feature from the larger small business or medium size business Websites is poor design.

Copyright © 2009, IGI Global, distributing in print or electronic forms without written permission of IGI Global is prohibited.

Search box placement. The convention for positioning a Website's search facility is to place it within the upper part of the homepage. The search box should be located on either the right or left hand side of the page. Placing the search box on the upper part of the page makes it easily identifiable and visible for the Website visitor. The search box should also have a single button labelled 'Search' adjacent to it and should allow the entry of at least 25-30 characters. Other button labels such as 'Go' or 'Find' are not as intuitive as the word 'Search' in representing the functionality behind this Website design element.

Search box colour. The search box entry area should always be colored white. This feature is associated with the expected layout and design convention that is used when implementing input forms and screens. Variations from white may confuse the user.

About the company. This design feature allows the organisation and the people that are responsible for publishing the Website's content to be identified. The feature addresses a trust and credibility element that is associated with online publishing. This Website design feature should be used by all organisations regardless of size. This feature is a fundamental design element, like including a logo and search function on a Website.

Privacy Policy. When organisations collect data via their Website it has become an expected design convention to include a privacy policy. This policy should be easily identifiable and accessible from the organisation's homepage. Consumers tend to value their privacy and tend to divulge minimal personal information in the online environment. With Websites that engage in data collection - be it associated with client sales, e-newsletter subscription or interactive social participation (as evident on many Web 2.0 sites) - an explicit statement of what the organisation does with the data should be stated.

Body text size is frozen. The use of specific text size that does not adapt to a user's browser is problematical with displays staying the same regardless of window size. This frozen-type of text display results in Web pages:

- Adopting a unsightly and unexpected page scroll mode on smaller displays, and
- Depicting a conspicuous amount of white space when viewed on larger screens.

Good Website design should use relative sizing of text in the construction of the Website, allowing each page layout to be easily adapted for different screen sizes and browser windows.

Copyright © 2009, IGI Global, distributing in print or electronic forms without written permission of IGI Global is prohibited.

Differentiate visited and unvisited links. Website navigation can sometimes be confusing. Visitors tend to arrive at a business Website through numerous entry points that can include a re-directed link from an external site or a 'click through' from a search engine listing. As a general rule, users tend to intuitively think about some key navigational issues such as: where am I? Where can I go to next? Have I been to this Web page before?

The design recommendation associated with Website navigation is to use blue links for unvisited Web pages and a less distinct non-blue colour (historically and by default this has been purple) for unvisited links.

Download time. The Web page download time is still an important Website design issue even with the advent of broadband connectivity. Early work suggested that fast Web page download was a definitive design feature and that users would not wait more than 10 seconds for a page to download. Even with the advent of broadband there has been a commensurate increase in the inclusion of images and graphics, and arguably this 10 second rule still holds. Clearly the small business' target audience and any limitations in their ICT access needs careful consideration when designing the Website. For example, if a small business had groups of customers, or potential customers, that live in rural and regional areas where Internet connectivity tends to be associated with slow and variable download times, this usability design element becomes an important implementation issue (Download times can be calculated using a free services such as Web Page Analyzer™. This service is available online at http://www.Websiteoptimization.com/services/analyze/).

Avoid using splash pages. The Website 'splash' page can be considered to be a visual design feature that aims at embellishing the look of the site. The splash page typically provides an enlarged company logo or a small animation on a Website, devoid of any other detail, before transferring the user to the home page of the Website. The splash page contributes very little to the Website's information content. Website visitors generally decide within a short period of time if they will stay or leave a site depending on whether they find appropriate content. Hence, the inclusion of splash pages tends to impede rather than enhance the location of relevant information. The splash page is analogous to the traditional magazine cover and is arguably not relevant in the online environment. A magazine cover's function is one of visually attracting prospective readers to pick up the publication, browse and then hopefully purchase the magazine. The splash page feature tends to mimic the magazine cover's function, and is associated with trying to entice people to enter and view/visit the body of the Website - a functional feature that does not really apply given that people have already made a decision to visit the site. Some businesses - particularly small ones - may be dazzled by the visual effects of the splash page and be misled into assuming that this is a useful design element.

Avoid using frames. The advent of frames in the mid 1990s resulted in the

Copyright © 2009, IGI Global, distributing in print or electronic forms without written permission of IGI Global is prohibited.

breaking of many user interface design conventions - conventions that included being able to bookmark pages, having a unique Web address (URL) associated with each different Web page and disrupting the browser print function. Although the use of frames has become less prevalent, their use still persists and is a feature that contributes to poor Website design.

Good Practice and Usability

For the small business operator, it is important to be aware of Website usability and the detailed good practice guidelines that allow essential features to be incorporated when designing a Website. A small business by incorporating these features can be confident that they have undertaken an important strategy that is simple to achieve and intrinsic to their Web presence.

Encoding Conventions

Website implementers have historically tended to overlook the selection of appropriate coding conventions when developing Websites (Sellitto and Wenn 2005). In an environment of high-powered Website development software, the initiatives undertaken by international groups that include the W3C (http://www.w3.org/) to formulate and direct proper Website encoding conventions has increased an awareness and acceptance of good practice guidelines. As the umbrella group for Website protocol development, the W3C provides a united and directing body that addresses, as part of its objectives, the development of relevant coding specifications that can be used for Website development (W3C 2003). This section of the chapter is somewhat technical, but is required to provide an explanation for where things currently stand in relation to Website design.

The W3C undertakes a responsibility for updating and renewing the specifications for Hypertext Markup Language (HTML) - the publishing language of the World Wide Web, which is that part of the Internet we access with our Web browsers (such as Internet Explorer). HTML performs a special role in the World Wide Web. When users type in a Web address (URL), a request is sent to the host computer where the Website is housed. If the request is for the home page of the Website, a file representing this home page is sent to the Web user making the request. This file is typically formatted in HMTL – which contains the content (such as text) contained on the Web page, as well as instructions as to how that content should be formatted and the location of images on the page. These instructions include the location of graphics, the colour of text and background and so forth. When the user's computer receives the file, it is the job of the Web browser to interpret the

Copyright © 2009, IGI Global, distributing in print or electronic forms without written permission of IGI Global is prohibited.

HTML file and present it on the screen according to the HTML formatting instructions (Power 2002; 2003).

Early on, Websites were typically developed by typing in HTML code into an editor and saving it as an .htm file. Nowadays, it is common to use a page editor, such as Microsoft FrontPage, that allows Web documents to be formatted with tools similar to those available in Microsoft Word or Microsoft PowerPoint. FrontPage simultaneously builds the HTML code for the page as the user formats it using these familiar tools. It has specialised tools to create links to other pages and Websites on the Internet. Indeed, early versions of HTML were adequate to meet the needs of Website developers. However, there was general agreement that a more precise and flexible option was required for Website development - this was termed eXtensible hypertext markup language (XHTML). XHTML can be viewed as a reformulation of HTML that imparts a certain amount of coding strictness when creating Websites. XHTML extends and replaces the last version of HTML as a specification bridge to the more complex eXtensible Markup Language (XML). XML is another more powerful language that allows users to define their own types of presentation elements and structural components that can be applied to the myriad of different types of Web document (Sellitto and Wenn 2005). The use of XHTML was viewed as a convergence bridge between XML and HTML. The current specification for Website development is for XHTML version 1.0 with an updated and stricter version of XHTML 2.0 proposed in future. The move to this stricter specification in future will not only support mobile devices, but will ostensibly negate the need to support much of the poorly constructed Websites that have been founded on old HTML code.

The use of XHTML has gained industry wide recognition since January 2000, when the W3C recommended the format as the preferred specification. One of the main features of XHTML is that it enforces stricter and neater markup coding (W3C 2003). This allows Website implementation to adhere to a convention that assists with general understanding of markup technical issues, which in turn can alleviate the need for frequent cost-intensive maintenance of Websites. There are subtle but important differences between HTML and XHTML coding that necessitates an adherence to coding rules when preparing each individual Webpage. Some of the important XHTML features can be found in Appendix One.

Encoding Tools

When creating and editing Website pages various errors in markup coding can, and undoubtedly do, occur. In an attempt to promote the use and fidelity of aspects of its markup specifications, the WC3 has introduced open source tools that are freely available and allow for proper checking of hypertext coding conventions. For the

Copyright © 2009, IGI Global, distributing in print or electronic forms without written permission of IGI Global is prohibited.

small business Website that is developed in-house by an employee or family member, these tools are an important resource that allows the business to address some of the expected coding practices. Some of the more reputable and widely supported tools include the following:

- *Markup Validator.* This is one of the free and open source validation tools recommended by the W3C. Also known as HTML Validator, this tool gives Website creators an appropriate indication of how a Web page conforms to the W3C recommended encoding practices. The release of an updated version of this validation tool in August 2007, allowed three types of Webpage checking. If the Website has already been implemented, then the address of individual Web pages can be submitted for checking with an appropriate report generated. If, on the other hand, Website pages are completed but are not active in the Web environment, individual files can be submitted for validation. Lastly, any Webpage in the production phase can have the raw code pasted into a multi-lined input form for code validation before being completed as a file. In addition, Markup Validator can be used to check for conformity against previous versions of HTML, as well as the W3C recommendations for XHTML. This is a free service with regular updated versions released periodically by the W3C. Markup Validator is available online at http://validator.w3.org/.
- *Link Checker.* The W3C's Link Checker can be used to test to see if a Website has any *broken links.* A broken link occurs where the Website has a link that does not lead to another Website. This may be for reasons such as the Website no longer exists, or the Website address has been entered incorrectly. The business Website that has obvious broken links is likely to dissuade potential customers from exploring the Website's content. Non-active links that lead to the dreaded "*error 404. The page cannot be displayed*" message can tend to be a consequence of poor Website maintenance and should be removed to reduce user frustration. Link Checker is a free service maintained by the W3C and is available online at http://validator.w3.org/checklink.

Good Practice and Encoding Markup

For small business operators, there should be an awareness of good practice when it comes to proper use of code to markup the pages on their Websites. The small business manager should be aware of:

- Using XHTML 1.0 specifications as a minimum requirement that is associated with Website implementation.

Copyright © 2009, IGI Global, distributing in print or electronic forms without written permission of IGI Global is prohibited.

- Some of the fundamental differences between XHTML and the versions of HTML. XHTML is highly recommended as the coding language of choice.
- The various checking tools that are available for validating Website code to see if they conforms with W3C proposed specifications.

An adoption of markup conventions will tend to be commensurate with reduced Website maintenance and the associated costs. Even when the business uses a tool such as Microsoft FrontPage to create its Website, it should ensure that the markup code that is automatically generated conforms within these specifications. The small business is also well positioned with respect to other businesses that have overlooked this aspect of their Website development.

Accessibility

Access to the Internet is often taken for granted, even by those people with physical and cognitive limitations. There is a common assumption by many Website implementers that visitors will be relatively youthful, technologically savvy and cognitively enabled (Sellitto and Wenn 2005). Arguably, Website access for many individuals is not problematic. However, Website access can be restrictive for numerous individuals who may have a disability, limited functional capacity or others who may simply be members of the aging population. For the small business operator there needs to be a special awareness that individuals with various limitations will, and do, visit their Websites. Furthermore, the design of the small business Website can, and should, be implemented so as to address certain accessibility conventions that foster, improve and enhance Web use by all groups.

There are some designers that may argue a Pareto principle (80:20 rule) when it comes to Web presence and relegate features associated with Website accessibility to the optional category. However, the implementation of accessible Websites should be examined in context, especially when one considers the broad range and number of people that have some form of disability (Ridge 2000). Indeed, the number of individuals who visit Websites that are deemed to be disabled can be considerable - some estimates suggests that up to 10% of the global population will have some disability limitation (Krunic and Ruzic-Dimitrijevic 2007). Moreover, the global income of people that are classified with various forms of disabilities has been reported as being circa $US700 billion (Sellitto and Wenn 2005). Several reasons exist as to why the small business needs to address accessibility when considering Web presence. One reason is the existence of legislative laws that promote the proper construction of accessible sites. Another reason as to why a small business needs to make its Website site accessible is that paradoxically, the inclusion of ac-

Copyright © 2009, IGI Global, distributing in print or electronic forms without written permission of IGI Global is prohibited.

cessibility features tends to also improve the Web experience for people who are non-disabled (Powell 2002).

The promotion of universal Internet access for individuals with limitations has been embodied in various government legislations around the world. The USA has legislation that makes it a requirement that all government agencies make their electronic information accessible to individuals with disabilities (Powell 2002). This legislation comes in the form of the Section 508 regulation (http://www.section508.gov/) that accommodates the use of assistive technologies in the Internet environment and has evolved to become a Website accessibility convention. Other countries such as Canada, Australia and the UK have various forms of legislation that deal with the discrimination towards the disabled that extends to the information services and communication sphere - the domains that are predominantly delivered today via ICTs such as e-mail and the Web. Arguably, businesses in general, and (given their predominance) small businesses in particular, are not exempt from these types of rules and regulations.

As mentioned earlier, the incorporation of Website accessibility features, when implemented to meet the needs of the disabled, tend to also improve the experience for all Website visitors. As a general rule, the creation of systems that are accessible to individuals with limited capacities tends to result in benefits for all users of those systems (Powell 2002). Consider the introduction of building access ramps to aid wheelchair users - a feature that made walking and building access easier for all individuals. Similarly in the Web environment, Websites that address accessibility issues tend to have the unplanned consequence of also improving the experience for users. Clearly, the small business operator with an accessible site can potentially benefit from all visitors having a more informed and cohesive experience. Furthermore, by addressing Website accessibility requirements the small business enacts a form of protective policy that may avoid potential litigation, costly settlements and unfavourable publicity that may stem from a poorly designed Website.

Websites that are poorly designed from an accessibility perspective tend to be particularly unfriendly for various disabled groups or people with limited abilities. Different groups will encounter various challenges when visiting such Websites. Consider the following pertinent examples of how different groups can be affected (Sellitto & Wenn 2005):

- For the vision impaired that include the blind, people with low vision and/or people with decreased colour perceptions, poorly designed sites will render assistive technologies such as screen-readers and screen magnifiers inoperable.
- Users that have minor cognitive disabilities can feel lost or disorientated when using the Website due to absent navigational elements. Websites that

Copyright © 2009, IGI Global, distributing in print or electronic forms without written permission of IGI Global is prohibited.

have overtly text-intense information can also cause difficulties in both the reading of this text, and also in allowing the information to be interpreted in a relevant context.

- Individuals with a hearing impediment do not have the ability to perceive or interpret information that may be conveyed by sound. Hence, these people will have information gaps if captioning (or an alternative) is not provided with Website elements that include video clips or audio streaming.
- The elderly as a group are generally afflicted by reduced visual acuity and poor co-ordination. Websites with few or no accessibility features can result in this group having difficulties with small text displays and loss of orientation if Website navigation is complex.

The W3C advocates the proper design of Websites to address accessibility - an advocacy that is promoted through the organisation's long running Web Accessibility Initiative (http://www.w3.org/WAI/). Part of this initiative has been the documentation of various guidelines, open-access software tools and ongoing policy formulation. In the late 1990s, the W3C approved a reference version of the Web Content Accessibility Guidelines (WCAG) 1.0 that contained a set of fourteen general principles that promote accessible Website design (W3C 2007). These guidelines, should be viewed as an evolving set of conventions that have been agreed upon to promote easier accessibility for the disabled in the Web environment (W3C 2000). A future set of guidelines (WCAG 2.0) is being developed by the W3C and will apply to different technologies. However, these guidelines are not anticipated to be implemented in the foreseeable future. The guidelines cover a diverse range of implementation features that are associated with (W3C 2007):

- Websites that incorporate non-text elements such as images, animations, audio, video, and so forth, should provide some form of text equivalents for these elements.
- Information content that uses colour to convey meaning should also have some alternative form of explanatory information on the Website.
- Content should be organised clearly and in a logical manner so information context is maintained
- Content that serves as an alternative for non-browser supported features. These may include applications associated with applets or plug-ins ('mini programs' that operate in conjunction with the Website).
- Website information content that provides a summary of any graphs and charts that are depicted on the site.

The process of evaluating Websites against accessibility guidelines uses a set of both automatic and user evaluated definitions that address different levels of

Copyright © 2009, IGI Global, distributing in print or electronic forms without written permission of IGI Global is prohibited.

compliance. Three priority levels for implementing Website features that impact on accessibility have been proposed in the WCAG 1.0 document. High accessibility adherence across all three levels would be ideal. However, in reality different Website conformance occurs. A conformance level for addressing the different priority levels can be viewed in Appendix Two.

AccessibilityTools

Part of the process associated with generating appropriately accessible Web pages is having the relevant tools to evaluate Web page accessibility. For the small business Website that is developed in-house, these tools are invaluable for gauging Website accessibility design. Moreover, the small business owner can easily use such tools to check the accessibility of their commercially designed site.

Several freely available online tools for checking Website accessibility are available. These tools are maintained by the general Web community in an endeavour to encourage and implement Website accessibly. These sites include:

- **WebXACT:** This free online service allows people to test Web pages for content that conforms to the commonly proposed conventions and features associated with accessibility. A report is generated for each submitted Web page highlighting any inconsistencies with the automatic and manual checkpoints of the W3C proposed guidelines. WebXACT is located at http://it.toolbox.com/wiki/index.php/WebXACT.
- **Truwex:** This Website validation service is comprehensive and can be used to monitor the accessibility compliance status of Websites. The online tool supports Website conventions that are associated with Section 508 (USA) and WCAG 1. Truwex is located at http://checkWebsite.erigami.com/accessibility.html.
- **WAVE accessibility tool:** This service reports Web page accessibility compliance that addresses the Section 508 (USA) and WCAG 1 guidelines. This Website evaluation service allows files to be uploaded. The WAVE Accessibility Tool is located at http://wave.Webaim.org/index.jsp.

Good Practice and Accessibility

In the interests of promoting equal access to the Web for people who may have a disability, limited functional capacity or others who may simply be members of the aging population, small business owners need to be aware of Website accessibility issues. Good practice when it comes to accessibility conformance for the small business is one of:

Copyright © 2009, IGI Global, distributing in print or electronic forms without written permission of IGI Global is prohibited.

- Having an awareness of the W3C recommended specifications for accessibility
- Achieving the W3C's mandatory priority 1 accessibility rating for their Website
- Using a validation tool that analyses Web pages for accessibility
- Ideally aiming at achieving the W3C's priority 3 accessibility level.

Metadata

In the Web environment there is a need to use some form of ordered documentation system that can be applied to the content of Web pages - a process that can be considered to be similar to using an inventory or library cataloguing system (Sellitto and Wenn 2005).

A system or process that records the characteristics of content is termed *metadata*. In this instance, metadata is typically placed early in the HTML code of a Web page.

In effect, metadata is data about other data - allowing a document to be interpreted with some form of meaning and structure. Accurate and reliable metadata can be conveniently incorporated into Websites and their component pages when they are created. Indeed, the retrospective inclusion of metadata in Websites or other forms of electronic documents is expensive, can be time consuming and inaccurate, and invariably may be impossible due to the loss or disappearance of descriptive data sources (Sellitto and Wenn 2005). Hence, the appropriate incorporation of metadata by a small business at the time of Website implementation:

- Is an important process that is associated with the electronic description of business documents and information.
- Allows the small business to easily identify and re-use information through powerful nuance-based and intelligent search tools. Easy access and discovery by intra-business search tools can assist with data-warehousing implementation to return more relevant returns after user enquiries.
- Contributes to the documentation of the small business knowledge base that allows for future review, audits and understanding of past document genesis.

In the context of Website content, three types of metadata have been suggested as being appropriate (Summers and Summers 2005):

- **Descriptive:** This type of metadata will include information that is specific to a particular content element published on the Website. Content elements may either be text, images, sounds, video, and so forth, and will have their

Copyright © 2009, IGI Global, distributing in print or electronic forms without written permission of IGI Global is prohibited.

own descriptive identity. For example, if a picture of, say, someone named Adam were to be published on a Website then it should include metadata that describes the content page and image. Descriptive metadata invariably allow some or all components of Website content to be discovered and will usually involve the use of elements such as title, description and keywords that can be embedded in the Web page. For the page that contains Adam's image the following could be used (in the following, DC refers to Dublin core, which we will discuss later):

<meta name="DC.title" lang="eng" content = "Picture of Adam">
<meta name="DC.description" lang="eng" content="This is a image of Adam that I took on vacation last year in New York.">
<meta name="DC.subject" content="image, Adam Doe, New York, Vacation"/>

- **Intrinsic:** This type of metadata records the compositional nature of Website elements, their physical size and/or origins. This information tends to be technical in nature and may relate to a file size, form or type. It may also list the software application that has been used to generate the data element. For example, an image may be described as being of 36k in size, of gif file type, and was derived using an imaging application. Examples of intrinsic metadata can be embedded in Web pages using two format elements as such:

<meta name="DC.format" content="36k"/>
<meta name="DC.format" content="image.gif"/>

- **Administrative:** This type of metadata is associated with Website content creation and can include the name of the creator, date and place of creation, etc. For example, a Website image may have been produced the photographer John Doe, on February 5, 2008 in New York. The metadata could be incorporated into the Web page in the following manner:

<meta name="DC.creator" lang="eng" content = "John Doe">
<meta name="DC.date" content="February 5, 2008, New York" />

These three types of metadata provide information about each distinct element published on the Website (an image in the example given) that can assist with content classification and identity.

As can be seen from the above examples, each of the above metadata types can have certain elements or grouping themes that are integral descriptors when

Copyright © 2009, IGI Global, distributing in print or electronic forms without written permission of IGI Global is prohibited.

it comes to Website content. Indeed, using metadata in the Internet environment is reliant on a framework that can be used to document the various aspects of each Web page and their inclusions. Like accessibility and encoding conventions associated with Website development, the W3C advocates the use of a Resource Description Framework (RDF) as a language that is specifically set up to describe and subsequently allow documentation of the content published on Websites (W3C 2004). The W3C's framework also alludes to formulating and using various RDF descriptive vocabularies that can be applicable to Website content. (There is on-going discussion with respect to which content descriptions should be used - one new proposed standard that addresses all digital types of media is called Resource Description and Access (RDA), due for publication after 2008).

Descriptive vocabularies used within the concept of an RDF schema allow Website content properties and relationships to be recorded. One vocabulary of metadata elements that has gained widespread use in Website design is the *Dublin Core* (DC). The original workshop for establishing the DC metadata elements was held in Dublin, Ohio, hence, the term 'Dublin Core'. There have been subsequent annual workshops resulting in a number of DC updates and recommendations that have resulted in the DC set of metadata elements being viewed as an appropriate convention that is accepted by many in the global information community (DCMI 2007). These are further described in Appendix Three.

Metadata Tools

An aim of the various information communities around the world is to encourage Website designers and creators to embed metadata elements into Web pages (Sellitto and Wenn 2005). Many commercially available Website design and development applications have this incorporated as a functional feature. However, numerous organisations such as the Dublin Core Metadata Initiative (DCMI) and the W3C have endorsed metadata generating tools, making them freely and readily available online so as to be able to check and/or create appropriate metadata elements that can be used on a Web page. For the small business there are several easy and simple to use tools that can be used to optimize and prime their Websites with metadata formats. These include:

- **Meta-maker:** This is an online metadata tool that allows DC compliant data elements to be generated. The service is provided by the United Nation's Food and Agricultural Organisation (FAO) and has a high degree of flexibility. The tool allows a user to generate nascent metadata by using a simple input form that can be saved to a variety of diverse encoding formats (eg HTML, XHTML). The newly created metadata elements can then be simply cut and

Copyright © 2009, IGI Global, distributing in print or electronic forms without written permission of IGI Global is prohibited.

pasted into the appropriate section of a Web page that is being design or implemented. For people that already have a Website in place, the tool can extract important metadata elements from existing Web pages and generate a set of DC elements. The extracted metadata can then be simply reintroduced into the page the next time Website maintenance is undertaken. Meta-maker is available online at http://www.fao.org/aims/tools/metamaker.jsp.

- **DC-dot:** This tool is a metadata editor that extracts and validates metadata from existing Web pages. DC-dot is maintained by the University of Bath in the UK, and provides a service that allows a Web page to be retrieved and metadata to be automatically generated. The metadata can be subsequently edited, or added to, via a simple interactive form that allows a user to output the elements in different formats. DC-dot is available online at http://www.ukoln.ac.uk/metadata/dcdot/.

Good Practice and Metadata

For the small business operator there should be an awareness of good practice when it comes to recognising the importance of incorporating appropriate metadata on their Websites. Hence, with respect to Website design and metadata the small business manager should be aware of:

- The importance of incorporating metadata at the time of creating Website pages. Retrospective incorporation is costly and sometimes difficult.
- Using a basic level of DC element on each Web page of their site in an endeavour to not only record and document important business content, but to also optimise search engine returns.
- The incorporation of the basic level of DC elements as a minimum expectation for all Web pages. The complete level of 15 DC elements set is recommended.

Metadata has an integral function of documenting the important content published on the small business Website. Metadata incorporation can not only assist with Website maintenance by acting as a form of procedural narrative of Web page changes, but also assist in the preservation of content. Moreover, metadata has historically been associated with assisting businesses to achieve elevated search engine listings of its Website - a function that may provide a definitive advantage over a competitor that does not.

Copyright © 2009, IGI Global, distributing in print or electronic forms without written permission of IGI Global is prohibited.

OTHER STUDIES

A Study of Website Design Associated with US Small Hotels (Stephens, 2004)

Stephens (2004) investigated Website design elements that are important in facilitating trust between buyers and sellers that engage in electronic commerce. The research was based the investigation of small hotels located in the United Stares of America. Stephens highlighted that small hotel operators need to exploit consumer trust in the Internet environment in order to compete with larger accommodation chains - trust being an important element that can be conveyed using a Website's visual design and information content. Using differently designed small hotel Websites, the proposition that trust between online entities can be influenced by Website design features was examined. Several Website design features were proposed as part of Stephen's trust-enablement framework (TEB). These design features or components include:

- **Page layout:** The attributes of this Website design feature included the background colour and white space of each page, the font size of published text, scrolling and the interplay of different colours.
- **Navigation:** Website visitors should be able to a judge that navigation should be easy to learn and use, consistently portrayed and provide visual feedback for users.
- **Profession style:** The profession style of the Website needs to objectively promote visual, functional and design consistency - allowing the business brand to be positively promoted.
- **Graphics:** Graphics and images are an important aspect of Website design allowing content to be depicted in context. As such, enhanced image-based sites invariable outperform text-based equivalents. The indiscriminate incorporation of Website graphics needs to also be counterbalanced against the impact on download performance.
- **Information content:** Content forms the basis of any Website visit. Information published on a site can embrace attributes such as being timely and accurate - allowing the reader to be better informed about hotel services and promotions. Website content should be well structured, easy to find through a search facility, and incorporate details about products or services that are relevant to the typical visitor.

Stephens' (2004:313) work is interesting in that it undertakes a comparative evaluation of Websites with a range of trust-building design elements to conclude

Copyright © 2009, IGI Global, distributing in print or electronic forms without written permission of IGI Global is prohibited.

that " .. page length, navigation, professional style, graphics and information content are significantly related to trust in the small hotel industry". Furthermore, the
research found that vast majority of Websites examined scored low on many of
the trust design features - leading to the suggestion that small business operators
implementing the design elements described would be a standout and potentially
be able to increase market share.

A Simple Approach for Small Business to Test Website Usability (Nielson 2000:2003)

An important component of Website success for the small business is the way that
the Website home page presents and functions from a usability perspective. The
concept of usability embodied in these works tends to be premised on the notion
that Website usability is associated with features that allow Websites to be easy to
learn and remember, reliable and efficient to use, and impart audience satisfaction.
Nielsen (2000) as the contributor of many articles to the Website design literature
over the last fifteen years indicates that only five users are required to test a site for
its usability. Indeed, with only five users some 80% of all usability issues can be
identified, whilst, testing with 15 users allows most problems to be documented.
Significantly, with no testing, there are no insights into the how the Website performs with respect to usability. Nielsen (2003) proposes a small firm's Website can
benefit from using four simple usability practices at the design stage - committing
the operator to minimal financial outlay. Assuming a simple brochure site that many
small operators will have, the a four-step approach suggested includes:

- Determine the customers' questions. Existing clients or customers are a primary information source for the business and operators need to determine
what customers want to know about the business as well as details about their
shopping trip. This type of information can be collected on the small business
premises and the answers to these questions are primary sources directing
Website content as they tend to reflect customers' information needs.
- Review initial design according to usability guidelines. Use an existing set of
usability guidelines to review the existing small business Website for some of
the fundamental issues associated with usability. This can be achieved via an
experienced usability design agency or through a system of well documented
and proven usability checklists. Based on the review of the existing site, the
worst of the usability issues identified should be corrected in a redesign of the
Website.
- Test a paper prototype in-store. The newly redesigned site allows the small
business operator to use page printouts - a form of paper prototype - within

Copyright © 2009, IGI Global, distributing in print or electronic forms without written permission of IGI Global
is prohibited.

the store to gauge existing customer perceptions of the new design. At least five users (10 minutes per session) should be approached for this evaluation process - potentially allowing a significant proportion of usability design issues to be highlighted. These can then be corrected or implemented in a second design iteration of the site.

- Improve Search Engine Visibility. This step is aligned with usability in that it caters to the way that people are most likely to arrive at the small business Website - either through the direct promotion of the site by the business, or most likely via listing on a search engine. Consequently, search engine optimisation can be enhanced with some Website design features. One design feature that allows some search engine optimisation is to ensure that Website titles - particularly those on the home page - are relevant and representative of the business site. The home page should also include a set of the most anticipate and salient query terms.

Nielsen (2003) in proposing the steps for improving Website design in the small business environment acknowledges that some understanding of usability issues is required by operators. However, he also indicates that most projects will have a budget much bigger than the one he has proposed - allowing a deeper evaluation of the Website design. Given, the importance of usability some evaluation is better than none at all.

Summary of Other Studies

The two studies described provide pertinent and relevant examples of some of the design issue that potentially confronts the small business owner. Stephens' (2004) investigations of small hotel Websites highlighted the issue of trust as an important factor that could be conveyed using a Website's visual design and information content. The research concluded that design elements such as Web page length, navigational features, the style, inclusion of graphics and information content are significant as a Website trust-building design features. In contrast to Stephens (2004), the proposals of Nielsen (2000; 2003) provide a practical four-stage approach for small business entities to test, refine and subsequently improve their Web presence through a usability approach - committing the operator to minimal financial outlay. Nielsen further highlights that testing a Website's usability is relatively simple, and with just five typical users providing design feedback, some 80% of the usability issues can be identified. Significantly, with no testing, there are no insights into how the Website performs with respect to usability.

Copyright © 2009, IGI Global, distributing in print or electronic forms without written permission of IGI Global is prohibited.

TENETS – LESSONS FROM THE CHAPTER

Good practices Website design for small business should consider the areas of usability, accessibility, markup encoding and the use of metadata. Tables 1 and 2 summarize these important good practices in each respective area.

CONCLUSION

This chapter focused on issues that have resulted from commonly acknowledged Website design challenges that small business operators and managers must ap-

Table 1. Usability features in good practice in website design

Usability	Good practice usability features
Usability overview - For the small business operator, it is important to be aware of website usability and the detailed good practices that allow essential features to be incorporated when designing a website. A small business incorporating these features can be confident that they have undertaken an important strategy that is simple to achieve and intrinsic to their web presence. The features deemed to be essential in website design when it comes to usability good practices include:	Placing the company logo in the top left hand corner of all the website's pages. The logo should be hyper linked from all pages to return to the home page.
	The search feature is another fundamental website design element that all users appreciate and expect to find on websites.
	Search box placement should be positioned on the upper part of the homepage and be located on either the right or left hand side.
	Search box colour should always be white. Variations from white may confuse the user.
	Have an "About the company" page that allows the small business and the people that are responsible for publishing the website's content to be identified. The feature addresses a trust and credibility element that is associated with online publishing.
	Consumers value their privacy and tend to divulge minimal personal information in the online environment. A privacy policy for any small business that may collect data via their website is an expected design convention.
	By using relative sizing of text in the construction of the website allows page layout to be easily adapted for different screen sizes and browser windows.
	Visited and unvisited links should be easily identifiable to aid website navigation. The design recommendation associated with website navigation is to use blue links for unvisited web pages and a less saturated non-blue colour (historically and by default this has been purple) for unvisited links.
	The web page download time is still an important website design issue even with the advent of broadband connectivity. Users tend to not want to wait more than 10 seconds for a page to load into their browser.
	Avoid using splash pages. The website splash page can be considered to be a visual design feature that aims at embellishing the look of the site. The splash page contributes very little to the site's information content.
	Avoid using frames. The advent of frames in the mid 1990s resulted in the breaking of many important user interface design conventions.

Copyright © 2009, IGI Global, distributing in print or electronic forms without written permission of IGI Global is prohibited.

Table 2. Encoding, accessibility and metadata features in good practice website design

Encoding, Accessibility and Metadata	Features
Encoding markup - For the small business operator there should be an awareness of good practice when it comes to proper use of code to markup the pages on their websites. The small business manager should be aware of:	Using XHTML 1.0 specifications as a minimum requirement that is associated with website implementation. Some of the fundamental differences between XHTML and the versions of HTML. XHTML is highly recommended as the coding language of choice. The various checking tools that are available for validating website code to see if web pages conform with W3C proposed specifications.
Accessibility - In the interests of equal access to the web for the disabled, small business owners need to be aware of adopting a website that addresses accessibility by:	Adherence to W3C recommended specifications for accessibility. Using a validation tool that analyses web pages for their accessibility to people with disabilities. Achieving the W3C's mandatory priority 1 rating for their website. Ideally aiming at achieving a pass for the W3C's three accessibility priority levels.
Metadata - Metadata has an integral function of documenting the important content published on the small business website. The small business manager should be aware of these good practices:	The importance of incorporating metadata at the time of creating website pages. Retrospective incorporation is costly and sometimes difficult. Using a basic level of DC element on each web page of their site in an endeavour to not only record and document important business content, but to also optimise search engine returns. The incorporation of the basic level of DC elements as a minimum expectation for all web pages with incorporation of the complete level of 15 DC element set being highly desirable.

propriately address. The Website design issues included encoding conventions, accessibility priority levels, essential factors that enhance usability and the incorporation of descriptive metadata. A good practice approach in these Website design areas was documented - these practices allowing the small business to enhance their Web presence. In effect small business managers should have an awareness of these good design practices given that they will commonly themselves manage - either personally, through an employee or even a family member - and implement their own Websites. Furthermore, in the event of a small business outsourcing their Website work, they are in an informed position to deal with consultant queries and demands.

Copyright © 2009, IGI Global, distributing in print or electronic forms without written permission of IGI Global is prohibited.

REFERENCES

Bingley, S., & Sellitto, C. (2005). Web Features for Wine Tourism. In C. Sellitto & A. Wenn (Eds.), *Proceedings of the 6th International We-B (Working for E-Business) Conference. E-links: Community, Business and University (CD-ROM)* (pp. 118-125), Melbourne, Australia. ECRU, Victoria University.

Brody, F. (1996). Interactive Design: State of the Art and Future Developments: An Argument for Information Design. in Multimedia Graphics, eds. W. Velthoven, J. Seijdel & N. Brody, Thames & Hudson, London: 16-19.

Chapman, N., & Chapman, J. (2006). *Web Design: A Complete Introduction*. Chichester: John Wiley & Sons, Ltd.

Cox, C., Burgess, S., Sellitto, C., & Buultjens, J. (2008). *The Influence of User-Generated Content on Tourist Travel Behaviour.* Australian Regional Tourism Research Centre, Lismore, NSW, Australia.

Davidson, A., Burgess, S., & Sellitto, C. (2006). An Investigation of SMTE Web Site Usage in Australia: Implications for E-Commerce Adoption and Planning Processes. In N. Al-Qirim (Ed.), Global Electronic Business Research: Opportunities and Directions (pp. 88-113). Hershey, PA: Idea Group Publishing.

DCMI 2007, Dublin Core Metadata Element Set, Version 1.1: Reference Description, DCMI Group, [http://dublincore.org/documents/dces/], Retrieved: 21/8/2007.

English, J. (2002). Going Solo: In Your Own Small Business. 8th Ed edn, Allen and Unwin, Sydney.

Gammack, J., Hobbs, V., & Pigott, D. (2007). *The Book of Informatics.* South Melbourne, Australia.

Grassian, E. (2000). *Thinking Critically About World Wide Web Resources.* UCLA College Library, Retrieved: 13/7/2004.

Hillier, M. (2003) The Role of Cultural Context in Multilingual Website Usability. Electronic Commerce Research and Applications, *2*(2003), 2–14.

Huang, X., & Leong, E. K. F. (2006). The Development of Web Sites. In N. Al-Qirim (Ed.), Global Electronic Business Research: Opportunities and Directions (pp. 42-62). , Hershey, PA: Idea Group Publishing.

Ihlstrom, C., & Nilsson, M. (2001). Size Does Matter: SMEs Special Barriers in Adoping E-Business. In J. Cooper, L. Burgess & C. Alcock (Eds.), *Proceedings of the 6th Collaborative Electronic Commerce Technology and Research (CollECTeR)*

Copyright © 2009, IGI Global, distributing in print or electronic forms without written permission of IGI Global is prohibited.

Conference (pp. 171-178). Coffs Harbour, NSW. The Faculty of Informatics University of Wollongong.

Krunic, T., & Ruzic-Dimitrijevic, L. (2007). Condition of Web Accessibility in Practice and Suggestions for its Improvement. *Informing Science Journal, 100*(2007), 71-86.

Lawson, R., Alcock, C., & Cooper, J. (2001). Diffusion of Electronic Commerce in Small and Medium Enterprises.In J. Cooper, L. Burgess & C. Alcock (Eds.), *Proceedings of the 6th Collaborative Electronic Commerce Technology and Research (CollECTeR) Conference*, Coffs Harbour, NSW, eds., , The Faculty of Informatics University of Wollongong.

Lazar, J., Jones, A., & Greenidge, K. (2005). Web-STAR: Development of Survey Tools for Use with Requirements Gathering in Web Site Development. In A. Sarmento (Ed.), Issues of Human Computer Interaction (pp. 37-48). Hershey, PA: IRM Press.

Nielsen, J. (2002). *E-mail Newsletters Pick Up Where Websites Leave Off.* [http://www.useit.com/alertbox/20020930.html], Retrieved: 21/08/2007.

Nielsen, J. (2000). *Designing Web Usability: The Practice of Simplicity.* New York: New Riders Publishing.

Nielsen, J. (2000). *When Bad Design Elements Become the Standard.* [http://www.useit.com/alertbox/991114.html], Retrieved: 31/3/2002.

Nielsen, J., & Loranger, H. (2006). *Prioritorizing Web Usability.* Berkeley, CA: New Riders Publishing.

Nielsen, J., & Tahir, M. (2002). *Homepage Usability.* Salem, VA: New Riders Publishing.

Nielsen, J. (2003). *Usability for $200.* [http://www.useit.com/alertbox/20030602.html], Retrieved: 8/7/2008.

Nielsen, J. (2000). *Why You Only Need to Test With 5 Users.* [http://www.useit.com/alertbox/20000319.html], Retrieved: 8/7/2008.

Powell, T. (2003). *HTML & XHTML: The Complete Reference.* 4th edn, Berkeley: Osborne/McGrawHill.

Powell, T. (2002). *Web Design: the complete reference.* 2nd edition edn, Berkeley: Osborne/McGrawHill.

Copyright © 2009, IGI Global, distributing in print or electronic forms without written permission of IGI Global is prohibited.

Ridge, J. (2000). *Web Design for Access Opens Doors to World.* Melbourne.

Schneider, G. P. (2007). *Electronic Commerce.* 7th edn, Course Technology, Boston, MA.

Schneider, G. P. (2002). *Electronic Commerce.* 3rd edition edn, Course Technology, Boston, MA.

Schneidermann, B. (1999). *Readings in Information Visualisation: Using Vision to Think.* New York: Morgan Kaufmann.

Sellitto, C. (2006). E-Commerce Experiences of an Early Internet Adopting Australian Winery: A Case Study. In S. Krishnamurthy & P. Isaias (Eds.), *Proceedings of the International Association for Development of the Information Society Conference 2006* (pp. 199-206). Spain: IADIS Press.

Sellitto, C. (2005). A Study of Emerging Tourism Features Associated with Australian Winery Websites. *Journal of Information Technology and Tourism, 7*(3/4), 157-170.

Sellitto, C., & Wenn, A. (2005). Emerging Practices and Standards for Designing Business Websites: Recommendations for Developers. In A. Sarmento (Eds.), Issues of Human Computer Interaction (pp. 85-109). Hershey, PA: IRM Press.

Stephens, T. R. (2004). A Frame Work for Identification of Electronic Commerce Design Elements That Enable Trust Within the Small Hotel Industry. *Proceedings of the 42nd Annual Southeast Regional Conference* (pp. 309-314). Huntsville, Alabama, USA, Association for Computing Machinery.

Summers, K., & Summers, M. (2005). *Creating Websites that Work.* Boston: Houghton Mifflin.

Turban, E., Leidner, D., Mclean, E., & Wetherbe, J. (2008). *Information Technology Management: Transforming Organisations in the Digital Economy*, 6th edition ed. New York: John Wiley & Sons.

Turban, E., Leidner, D., Mclean, E., & Wetherbe, J. (2006). Information Technology Management: Transforming Organisations in the Digital Economy, 5th ed. New York: John Wiley & Sons.

W3C (2007). *Web Content Accessibility Guidelines (WCAG) Overview,* W3C. [http://www.w3.org/WAI/intro/wcag.php], Retrieved: 16/8/2007.

W3C (2004). *RDF Vocabulary Description Language 1.0: RDF Schema.* W3C. [http://www.w3.org/TR/2004/REC-rdf-schema-20040210/], Retrieved: 22/8/2007.

Copyright © 2009, IGI Global, distributing in print or electronic forms without written permission of IGI Global is prohibited.

W3C (2003). *HyperText Markup Language (HTML) Home Page.* [http://www.w3.org/MarkUp/], Retrieved: 1/6/2003.

W3C (2000). *Techniques for Web Content Accessibility Guidelines 1.0.* W3C. [http://www.w3.org/WAI/GL/WCAG10-TECHS/], Retrieved: 16/8/2007.

Watchfire (2007). *Site Quality & Accessibility.* Watchfire Corporation, Retrieved: 22/08/2007.

Wienman, L. (2000). *Designing Web Graphics.3.* New Riders Publishing. Indianapolis, USA.

Copyright © 2009, IGI Global, distributing in print or electronic forms without written permission of IGI Global is prohibited.

APPENDIX A: FEATURES OF XHTML

Some of the important features of XHMTL are:

- **DOCTYPE declaration.** The basic structure of a Web page when coded in HTML has required the html, head and body elements. When conforming to XHTML coding conventions there must also always be a top-of-page DOC-TYPE declaration that denotes the version of code that is being used.
- **Concept of well-formed documents.** XHTML is 'well formed' where the specification encourages the specific nesting and closing of tag elements.
- **Case sensitivity.** XHTML is lower case specific. Consequently all XHTML documents must use lower case coding when marking up Webpage elements and attributes. For example the use of <li> and <LI> would constitute different tags. HTML allows a breach of this convention.
- **Tag closure.** Previous versions of HTML do not enforce the closing of some tags. The XHTML protocol guidelines are to have all element tags closed. For example:

This is correct coding (the paragraph element is terminated):

<p>This is a paragraph that includes descriptions of material content associated with markup languages.</p>

This is incorrect coding (the paragraph element is not terminated):

<p> This is a paragraph that includes descriptions of material content associated with markup languages.

It can be seen that certain coding practices that are perfectly legal in HTML need to be altered for them to be acceptable in the XHTML specification. They are subtle but different. (A full description of the differences between HTML and XHTML is available on-line at the W3C Website (http://www.w3.org/TR/xhtml1/#diffs).

APPENDIX B: WEB CONTENT ACCESSIBILITY GUIDELINES

The *Techniques for Web Content Accessibility Guidelines 1.0* can be viewed at the W3C Website (http://www.w3.org/WAI/GL/WCAG10-TECHS/). Fourteen guidelines are suggested, and these are then split into further sub-guidelines that

Copyright © 2009, IGI Global, distributing in print or electronic forms without written permission of IGI Global is prohibited.

are each assigned a priority according to how mandatory the requirement is. The priority levels are:

- **Priority 1:** This is a mandatory requirement. Failure to meet the accessibility guidelines at this level results in one or more groups being unable to access information satisfactorily on the Website.
- **Priority 2:** Website creators should aim at addressing this accessibility level. Addressing this level will remove significant barriers to accessing most Web documents.
- **Priority 3:** Ideally this should be the level of accessibility that is always aimed for when implementing a Website. An attempt at satisfying this level will enhance information access on all published Website pages.

A simple summary of the 14 guidelines (as described on the WC3 Website) are:

- Provide equivalent alternatives to auditory and visual content.
- Do not rely on color alone.
- Use markup and style sheets and do so properly.
- Clarify natural language usage
- Create tables that transform gracefully.
- Ensure that pages featuring new technologies transform gracefully.
- Ensure user control of time-sensitive content changes.
- Ensure direct accessibility of embedded user interfaces.
- Design for device-independence.
- Use interim solutions.
- Use W3C technologies and guidelines.
- Provide context and orientation information.
- Provide clear navigation mechanisms.
- Ensure that documents are clear and simple.

Further details of the different levels of Website evaluation within each priority area are available in more detail at the WC3 Website.

APPENDIX C: DUBLIN CORE METADATA ELEMENTS

The international standards organisation (ISO) has formally endorsed the basic DC set of elements through the ISO Standard 15836-2003 and NISO Standard Z39.85-2007 statements. The DC makes use of standard formats and descriptive elements that can be applied to all different Website technologies. The DC metadata set of

Copyright © 2009, IGI Global, distributing in print or electronic forms without written permission of IGI Global is prohibited.

descriptors assists in providing long-term access to digital resources - allowing designers of Website to go a long way to effectively preserving the information content that is published. The process of preserving Website content through using metadata inadvertently makes the content more accessible and searchable. Indeed, the adoption of a descriptive vocabulary such as the DC by Website designers will contribute to supporting advanced searches - an issue that is important in lifting a business Website listing on search engines.

The strength of using the DC is based on its simplicity. The simple nature of creating a basic set of descriptors is a relatively cost effective way of promoting content discovery on Websites. Indeed, the functional characteristics of the DC vocabulary are that they provide the foundation for semantic interoperability - a foundation that can assist with the move to what is being termed the Semantic Web. As a descriptive vocabulary, the DC data element set contains 15 standard formats for documenting the contents of each Website page. From a practical perspective, metadata elements can be incorporated into Website pages using the <meta> tag, with the different DC descriptors embedded usually within the head tag of each page.

The importance of incorporating metadata that describes Website content may be obscure for the small business. However, the DC set of elements are easy to embed in pages at their point of creation and will assist with any search activity that is carried out on the Website. The incorporation of Website metadata elements is proposed at two levels:

- **Basic level:** This basic metadata inclusion should address elements such as Title, Creator, Subject, Description and Date. This is a minimum and mandatory set of descriptive elements that effectively represents the functional descriptors that can have an impact on search engine returns.
- **Full level:** At the full level, all 15 DC elements should be used to describe Website content. These elements include the basic level descriptions as well as the remaining 10 elements that include Publisher, Contributor, Type, Format, Identifier, Source, Language, Relation, Coverage, and Rights. The use of the full set of DC metadata elements is encouraged.

Copyright © 2009, IGI Global, distributing in print or electronic forms without written permission of IGI Global is prohibited.

Chapter VIII
Web Presence Promotion

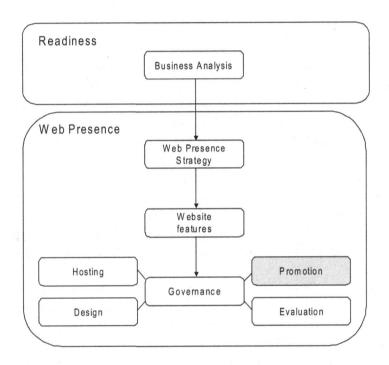

INTRODUCTION

There are literally millions of businesses with a Web presence on the Web and more and more being added every day, all competing to attract customers. Building a Website without any promotion is likely to result in little traffic. Therefore a Web

Copyright © 2009, IGI Global, distributing in print or electronic forms without written permission of IGI Global is prohibited.

Figure 1. Promoting the web presence and the business (adapted from Karanasios, 2008)

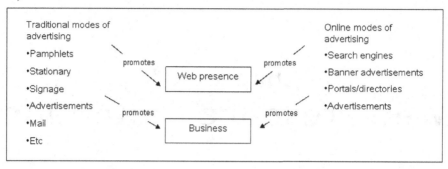

presence must be well positioned to maximize its potential. The most sophisticated and captivating Website is ineffective if it cannot be found by customers. A Web presence that is effectively promoted can also provide competitive advantage. From this perspective the promotion of a Web presence is one of the most critical steps involved in its development. Despite this, this step is often one of the most neglected tasks by small businesses.

The Web itself provides a number of different promotional channels for small businesses. Outside of the Web the use of traditional media can also play a vital role in promotion of a Web presence. In this chapter we suggest that online and offline methods should complement one another and by using both approaches a business is better placed to reap the maximum benefits from an investment into a Web presence.

Although the purpose of this chapter is to discuss the promotion of the Web presence, the overarching objective of any Web presence and marketing plan of course is successful promotion of the business. In other words, by promoting the Web presence the business is also being promoted at the same time. Figure 1 illustrates the independencies between the offline and online promotion methods of marketing the Web presence and the business.

APPROACHES TO WEB PRESENCE PROMOTION

The Web presents a number of useful channels to promote a Web presence. As a first step, a business should update existing forms of Web promotion to include the business e-mail and URL. This means updating online directories such as the Yellow Pages® and any other reference to the business.

Copyright © 2009, IGI Global, distributing in print or electronic forms without written permission of IGI Global is prohibited.

One phenomenon that most businesses are probably aware of is the popularity amongst Internet users to search for information, business details and products using search engines. Search engines are a popular way to find a Website, with other popular means being links from other (third party) Websites and promotion of the Website through traditional media (such as television, radio, newspapers and billboards).

This means that being listed in search engines should generally be a priority for small business. However, it also emphasizes that a business should not 'place all their eggs in one basket' as a mixture of online and offline approaches are typically ideal. Understanding this, this chapter will discuss a range of Web presence promotional techniques.

Before choosing any medium for promotion, whether it is a search engine, portal, a directory or small advertisements, as a basic precedent the following points must be considered. When considering these points it is useful to reflect upon the original goals of the Web presence, which will aid a business to measure the advantages and drawbacks of each approach.

- The initial and ongoing cost of the promotion
- The reputation of the promotion provider
- The effect the medium may have on the image of the business
- The potential to engage new and existing markets
- The presence of competitors.

This section begins by describing the most imperative task of promotion through search engines. It will describe and discuss various other levels of Web promotion. The final section of this chapter is devoted to e-mail newsletters as a Web means of promoting the Web presence and marketing the business to existing and potential customers.

Search Engines

Simply put, a search engine is an online application that searches the Web for information related to a search term entered by a user. After searching the Web, the search engine returns a ranked list of relevant Websites usually named 'hits'. Two of the most popular search engines are Yahoo!® and Google™. Therefore it makes sense for small businesses to attempt to rank well with these two search engines, especially Google™.

From a small business point of view, search engines offer two major benefits, they are free to register for and they are the closest things on the Internet to a telephone directory. There are a number of ways to register with the major search engines.

Copyright © 2009, IGI Global, distributing in print or electronic forms without written permission of IGI Global is prohibited.

These should be investigated because not all search engines work in the same manner and may require different levels of investment. A strategy should be adopted to ensure that the business is registered so that it appears as high on the list of search hits as possible when particular key words are entered. The reason it is important to list high on such a listing is because customers are unlikely to view much more than one search engine page when looking for a business. In fact, some search engines do not return more than three pages of hits. This means that if a Website does not rank well it is essentially worthless, from this perspective anyway.

Generally speaking, it is likely that search engines will eventually find and automatically index the business' Website (at the same time the Websites indexed on all the major search engines only account for a portion of the Websites actually available on the Web), but the process can generally be sped up by submitting the URL of the home page of the Website to the search engines concerned. This does not necessarily guarantee a high ranking. This section will discuss approaches to assisting a business to rank well with a search engine.

Ranking well with search engines requires an understanding of the way that the major search engines operate. Some search engines use 'crawlers' or 'spiders', which search the Internet for new addresses to include in their indexes. They search and index the Meta Tags of Websites. Other search engines, like Google™, work by ranking URLs by the number of links a Website links to, basically working on the number of time a URL appears on the Web. In fact, search engines generally rank Websites higher if they are cross-linked with other Websites (Chaston, 2004). Therefore, in the case of Google™, building links is extremely important. A business could concentrate on building incoming links, as search engines typically search for these. To achieve this, a business can submit the Website to portals, directories or other Websites to build links and subsequently the number of times the URL appears on the Web. The key is that links should be 'quality links' rather than high in number. Quality links are those from popular directories and portals. To develop quality links a first step could be for a small business to contact trade groups, local government associations or other trade societies that they belong to, in order to build reciprocal links. As a benchmark, a business should also review what its competitors' sites link to and from. As a warning a business should avoid using software programs to build links, because this approach is sometimes penalized by search engines. As an alternative, a small business may opt to use a promotional company that specialises in developing quality links. There are many these businesses available offering a range of different services along these lines.

Beyond registering with a search engine and building links, search engine marketing can be very complicated. However, it can be an effective method of attracting targeted visitors. Whilst some small businesses may choose to use the services of a business to promote the new Web presence, they may also choose to pay a search

Copyright © 2009, IGI Global, distributing in print or electronic forms without written permission of IGI Global is prohibited.

engine to be indexed faster and/or be ranked higher. For others, there are a number of fundamental search engine operational matters that should be understood. One particular term that a business will need to become familiar with is 'search engine optimisation'. This is an expression used to describe the process of obtaining a high position for a Website. As noted, this is as important as developing a successful Website. As a first step a small business should gain an understanding of the search words (or keywords) that Internet users are likely to use when searching for similar products and services. A good indicator is to determine under which search terms competitor Websites appear in search engine results. A number of Internet tools exist that can assist a small business to understand the keywords that are being used by users searching for related products and services. Word Tracker® (www.wordtracker. com) is such a tool. It works by listing the keywords people are using to search for a particular item. A downside of such tools is that they usually incur a fee. Once the keywords have been established they should be included in the metadata for the Website.

After establishing the most popular search terms, the next step is to make changes to the Website to make it friendlier to the search engine indexing and search techniques. This is a key to effective search engine optimization. Even though design and content issues were discussed in Chapter VI, it is important to at least be aware of the following basic tenets and reflect upon the design and content of a Website.

Title Tag and Meta Description Tags

In the first lines of code for a Webpage lie the Title Tag and Meta Tags, which should look something similar to:

```
<title> keywords  <title>
<meta name=" description " content=" description ">
```

Search engines use these two important tags to generate their indexes of Websites. The Title Tag should include a succinct description of the Website of around five to ten words of 60 or so characters. As a rule a business should avoid using generic words that use up space such as 'the', 'and', 'we' and not necessarily the business name (unless the business name is one that is popular and easily recognizable). This description will appear hyperlinked on the search engines when the Website is found.

Although each Web page has many Meta Tags, businesses should only concern themselves with the Meta Description. The Meta Description Tag is equally as important as the Title Tag. The Meta Description Tag should include the keywords

Copyright © 2009, IGI Global, distributing in print or electronic forms without written permission of IGI Global is prohibited.

and a short description of up to 250 characters of what each Web page contains.

Content

The first few paragraphs on any Web page are typically the most important as this is what is considered by typical search engines. Therefore it is imperative that the text is relevant to the intended audience. As some search engines also check whether the key words appear in the first few paragraphs of text it is worth including the key words in the text.

Images

Some search engines only look at text and skip over any images, pictures and special effects. From this point of view, it is then important to at least have some text on the home page. Where pictures are used a small business should attach an ALT tag to it, which is a brief description of the image.

Site Map

A site map allows search engines to more efficiently navigate a Website and index all the pages. Therefore a site map should be including in the design of a Website. This is also a basic tenet of Website design and was discussed in Chapter VI.

Banner Advertisements

A Web banner or banner advertisement (' banner ad') is a form of advertising that involves embedding an advertisement into a Web page. It is intended to attract traffic to a Website by linking Internet users to the Website of the advertiser. Many large organisations use banner ads as they work in a similar manner to television advertisements in their ability to increase brand awareness. However, from the point of view of a small business there may be little real benefit in *buying* advertising space on another small business Website (Chaston, 2004). A potential negative of using banner ads is that more and more Web users regard them as annoying and newer versions of Internet browsers are allowing users options to disable such 'pop-ups' or block images from selected Websites. Where banner advetisements are used it is important that they are well placed on relevant Websites to maximise their effectiveness. As an alternative to banner advertisements, businesses should consider the relatively more targeted approach of Adword advertisements or content matches (see Targeted Adverstising section).

Copyright © 2009, IGI Global, distributing in print or electronic forms without written permission of IGI Global is prohibited.

Figure 2. Example of Google™ advertisements

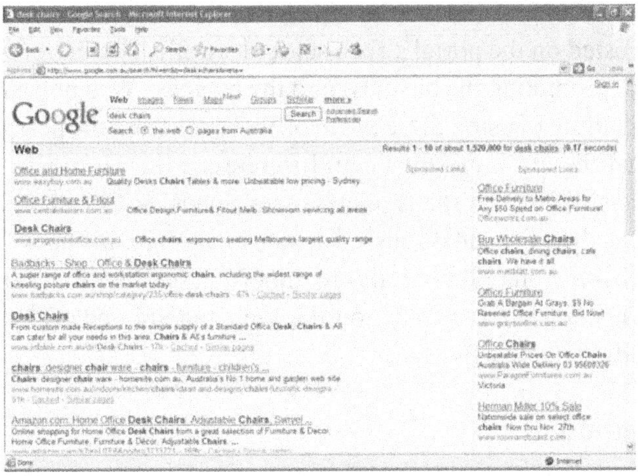

Targeted Advertising

Search engines also offer small businesses the opportunity to target small advertisements so that they appear whenever a user enters a particular set of keywords. For instance, Google™ provides a tool named Google™ Adwords, which allows small businesses to target Internet users when they are searching for information about related products and services. Other search engines and social networking sites offer similar tools. Search engines and other Internet companies use a similar model to offer 'content matches', whereby feature ads are displayed on relevant Websites, use a similar model. These models have become extremely popular in recent years and are more effective than traditional banner advertisements. This model of advertising operates on a 'charge per click' fee, whereby the business pays each time a user clinks on the advertisement. Depending on the popularity of the keywords the charge will range from a few cents to more than a dollar. This will create an extra cost, however the benefit is potentially a significant increase in traffic.

Portals

Portals can provide customers with much that they need to plan for the purchase of a product. For instance, some tourism portals are setup so that visitors can easily set up their own personalized tours from one Website. They are typically in a position to provide in-depth destination information and offer a whole range of products that a consumer may seek on a destination (WTO 2002). Some examples of these sites are www.travelocity.com, www.expedia.com, and www.wildasia.com. These

Copyright © 2009, IGI Global, distributing in print or electronic forms without written permission of IGI Global is prohibited.

portals are often critical in the promotion of a Web presence as many customers will access the portal first and then be directed to the small business Website (which may be also hosted on the portal's Web server as well). Therefore, portals can play the dual role of promoting the business and the business Web presence. However, a general shortcoming of using these types of Websites from the perspective of small business is that the only way they can differentiate themselves is when a user is directed to their Website (if it has one) (Gupta, Jones, & Coleman, 2004).

Portals have already been discussed at some length in this book. From the point of view of Website promotion portals are important because they boost the amount of times a businesses URL appears on the Web and are one of the most effective means of building quality links.

Domain Names

The address of a Web page is given by its URL (Uniform Resource Locator). The URL is the standard means of locating Web pages no matter where they are stored on the Internet. A typical URL takes the form:

http://www.businessname.com/index.html

A URL is made up of a series of different parts:

- The *protocol* (the type of resource being retrieved: in this case hypertext transfer protocol)
- The *Internet address of the server computer*, in this instance *www.business-name.com*
  Note the designation at the end, which is used to indicate the type of organization. Common designations are:
  .com or .co – commercial
  .org – organisation
  .edu – educational
- The *country*, for instance...
  .au – Australia
  .cn – China
  .jp – Japan
  .sg – Singapore
  .uk – United Kingdom

Copyright © 2009, IGI Global, distributing in print or electronic forms without written permission of IGI Global is prohibited.

If there is no country then it has traditionally been assumed that the business is based in the United States. So, a business setting up in Australia might use the Website address....

http://www.businessname.com.au/index.html

- The *path* of the Web resource being retrieved. In the previous example this is *index.html* which is often used as the name for the home page of a business.

Typically, typing in the URL without the protocol or path will still lead the user to the home page, so a user will only have to type in:

www.businessname.com.au

...to access the home page of the business.

Businesses may not always use their business name as their sole URL. If they have a well-known product or brand (or are perhaps trying to establish one), then perhaps they might also set up a domain name as follows:

www.brandname.com.au

Typically, this will be set up in such a way that, on typing this address in, the user will be redirected to the business Website.

This means that users are often able to *guess* the URL of a business by typing in 'www.', then the business or brand name, combine it with '.com' or '.co' and perhaps add a country designation.

Often, internet service providers will provide a business with some space for a Website on their server as part of a package deal. This may sometimes include the (often free) use of a *sub domain* name. Typically, the format of this URL will be:

www.ISPprovider.com/businessname/index.html

Although inexpensive, which may make it a popular option with some small businesses, it takes longer for a user to type this type of sub domain name in and also makes it virtually impossible for them to *guess* the URL of the business.

The URL or domain name that a business chooses is important in terms of promotion. Although it is important to have a memorable domain name it is not necessarily important to include keywords or relevant phrases in the domain name. It is also worth noting that some search engines may penalise Websites if they have more than one domain name (Davison, Burgess, & Tatnall 2008).

Copyright © 2009, IGI Global, distributing in print or electronic forms without written permission of IGI Global is prohibited.

E-mail Advertising

E-mail advertising presents a valuable opportunity for small businesses to promote the business and the Web presence. However, if used incorrectly e-mail newsletters may impact negatively on the image of a business. Here we only refer to targeted e-mail advertising as opposed to mass unsolicited e-mail, often referred to as spam. Spam has received significant negative attention because it can congest e-mail Inboxes, mail servers and Web traffic and frustrates users. Moreover, the response rate for unsolicited e-mail is particularly low. A well-designed subscription e-mail newsletter, however, can be very effective. By providing visitors with useful and pertinent content, a business can create a long-lasting relationship that will grow. In terms of Web presence promotion a business can use the e-mail newsletter to inform customers about the new Web presence or even about specials, offers and so forth. The e-mail newsletter as a promotional technique is described in more detail as a marketing tool later in this chapter.

A Note on Blogs and Social Networking Sites

In addition to the online promotion strategies mentioned in the foregoing discussion there are various second generation Web based (Web 2.0) services such as blogs, social networking sites and so forth that can be used to promote a Web presence. A blog is simply a Website where a particular person or business can store and share thoughts, comments, product descriptions and so forth through text and images on virtually any topic imaginable. Readers of the blog may also leave comments. Blogs have increased with popularity in recent years because they are an effective means of displaying personal and business viewpoints. Scott (2007) suggests that a significant amount of people are successfully 'blogging' for marketing puposes. He also argues that blogs are powerful and have allowed smaller companies to compete against larger players. A major benefit of a blog is that it requires very little skill to set up and allows readers to leave feedback. They are therefore an effective way to monitor what people are saying about the business. Blogs can be used to promote a business, its products and its Web presence because they allow businesses to participate in discussions of products and services and even write reviews of their products. Therefore they are a potentially rich emerging source to reach existing and new customers as well as the media (Scott, 2007).

Social networking sites such as Facebook, MySpace and Bebo operate by building communities of people who share interests and activities, or are interested in exploring the interests and activities of others. Early on Birch et al. (2000) suggested a business may promote itself by establishing a presence in Internet communities.

Copyright © 2009, IGI Global, distributing in print or electronic forms without written permission of IGI Global is prohibited.

These sites offer a collection of various ways for users to interact through e-mail, file sharing, discussions and so forth. From this perspective they are a potential rich source of promotion that taps into the online social space and word-of-mouth. Although this is a relatively new area especially in terms of exploitation by small business, there is evidence that there are some benefits from using these sites. This is an area that is likely to grow in potential for small business as more and more Internet users sign up to social networking sites and services. As such, it is important that small businesses pay attention to trends in this area. More on this in Chapter XI.

Promotion Outside the Internet

To maximize advertisement costs businesses should take advantage of existing advertisement endeavors to promote the Web presence. There are dozens of ways to promote the Web presence in traditional media. This includes printing the business URL in local newspaper advertisements, pamphlets, business cards, signage, radio and television advertising and even shopping bags. All these 'bits and pieces' contribute to increasing the awareness of a Web presence. If a business distributes letters and invoices through traditional mail the new URL should be printed on the stationary. In other words, anywhere a potential or existing customer may view the business name should be seen as an opportunity to promote the new Web presence. These strategies are particularly important because most small businesses target local customers. In support of the usefulness of traditional promotional techniques and online promotion, the authors of a report produced by UNCTAD (2004) titled *'Use of the Internet for efficient international trade: guide for SME managers'* recommended that a small business take advantage of traditional marketing techniques. The authors provide the example of a Bhutanese tour operator that in 2003 received 15 percent of orders through its Website, allowing the business to bypass its foreign agents. This was largely thanks to the fact that the *Lonely Planet* guidebook (a popular travel guidebook) about Bhutan recommends a selection of Bhutanese tour operators (and lists their Website URLs).

Notwithstanding the various forms of online and offline promotion discussed so far, one of the most important form of promotion for a small business is likely to be word-of-mouth, which remains as one of the most reliable and effective modes of promotion. Given that advertising is expensive a business must harness the power of word-of-mouth. The most effective method of generating word-of-mouth and interest is developing a Web presence that visitors would be likely to recommend!

Copyright © 2009, IGI Global, distributing in print or electronic forms without written permission of IGI Global is prohibited.

Which Promotion Channel Works?

Tracking how a people find their way to the business Web presence is essential to gaining an understanding of which promotion channels work well. This is relatively simple as each Website captures information concerning how visitors are finding the Website, the keywords they are using in search engines, and the Website they arrived from and even leave to. A business can also include a question on a booking or query form on the actual Website asking how the customer found the business. This will help to identify promotional methods that are underperforming and those that are most successful. We discuss this further in Chapter X.

Online Promotion Checklist

The following checklist summarizes the main points discussed so far concerning the promotion of a Web presence. It is a useful guide than can be followed when developing a varied promotion strategy.

- Update all existing online references to the business to include the URL and e-mail address.
- Promote on popular portals and directories.
- Create quality incoming and outbound links with popular portals and directories.
- Register with popular search engines.
- Determine keywords that the target market uses to search for similar products are services.
- Make sure the Website has been optimized to rank well with popular search engines.
- Use tools such as Adwords and content matches on search engine result pages for similar products and services.
- Use an e-mail newsletter to inform customers of the Web presence.
- Continuously monitor the progress of the Website ranking in the major search engines and new developments in second-generation Web based services.
- Include the Web presence details on *all* traditional media. As a rule, the Web presence should be listed wherever the business name appears.

A CASE IN HAND: THE E-NEWSLETTER

In the previous discussion the e-mail newsletter was discussed as an effective means promoting a Web presence. This section builds on the earlier discussion of e-mail

Copyright © 2009, IGI Global, distributing in print or electronic forms without written permission of IGI Global is prohibited.

newsletters and describes its use as a marketing tool that can be used to attract new customers as well as build relationships with existing customers.

Website adoption and e-mail communication have become standard information medium that have been adopted by most modern day businesses. Indeed, e-mail as a technology has matured to the point where it is now the preferred and expected communication form amongst individuals and between organisations. Just as e-mail has evolved as the preferred communication form, the Website is now regarded as an essential publishing medium. Arguably, the potent communication features associated with these technologies is no more evident than in the numerous theories and frameworks that permeate the information systems and marketing literature - addressing aspects of Web advertising, e-commerce, Web-enabled business systems and Web integrated supply chains.

The use of e-mail as a communication form has also been used in direct marketing allowing a business to send people marketing material in an effective and low cost manner. This form of direct marketing strategy is conditional on people opting-in or allocating permission to an organisation to send them information. The use of this online permission-based marketing tends to have several aspects - one of initially acquiring consumers and the other of retaining and engaging them. Online permission-based marketing, direct online marketing, permission marketing and e-mail marketing have been used as interchangeable terms throughout this section. These terms tend to be commonly encountered in academic and general publications Retention of customers is important and is generally associated with providing promotional material that is relevant and informative - allowing the business to maintain the client relationship. Regardless of the nuance or context of the promotional material, it is the electronic newsletter (e-newsletter) that allows the incorporation of marketing elements such as general product or corporate information, product recommendations and loyalty offerings that endeavour to facilitate repeat customer purchases. A third aspect of online permission marketing seldom alluded to is the concept of being able to unsubscribe - where a recipient can eas-

Figure 3. Three phases of online permission marketing

Copyright © 2009, IGI Global, distributing in print or electronic forms without written permission of IGI Global is prohibited.

ily and unconditionally opt-out of receiving marketing information. The phases of online permission marketing are represented in Figure 3.

Within the context of a business having a Web presence, the subscription phase is intrinsically linked to appropriately designed Website features. Arguably, many smaller-type businesses tend to be reliant on their direct marketing activities to sustain profitability with the ongoing client relationship being critical for their survival. Hence, the small business needs to be aware of the importance of the subscription phase and address pertinent aspects of their Website design to successfully engage in direct online marketing.

The Importance of Permission

Permission marketing was a concept coined and developed by Godin (1999) and takes into account the inordinate power of the Internet to quickly and inexpensively reach customers. Permission marketing in the Internet age is similar to the traditional direct marketing that has been historically practiced by businesses - both types of marketing being recognized for efficiently engaging potential or existing consumers. It has been suggested that permission marketing is the evolution of the direct marketing phenomenon to an electronic environment providing an effective means of influencing consumer interest and behaviour. Godin indicates that the traditional way of informing people about a product or service was based on interruption - stop what you are doing and listen to my message. The advent of the Internet has extended this interruption concept to the e-mail medium, where the use of unsolicited e-mail (spam) can be a form of direct marketing that has become the bane of many recipients. Clearly, when using e-mail for online marketing, it is essential to seek permission of the recipient to send them messages - something that dramatically improves the chances of the message being read. As such, this type of direct marketing information tends to have characteristics that the receiver anticipates and is of high relevance. Furthermore, the opt-in reader can be more responsive and receptive to the marketing messages. However, they may tend to be temper this responsiveness if it starts to intrude on their activities.

Functional Perspectives of the E-Newsletter

The vehicle predominately used for online permission marketing activities is the electronic newsletter, which can be easily produced and delivered to subscribers. When it comes to the examination of features that enhance online permission marketing and e-newsletter functionality, there appears to be a limited, but growing amount of published research that deals with this form of customer interaction. E-newsletter functionality has been found to relate to characteristics such as

Copyright © 2009, IGI Global, distributing in print or electronic forms without written permission of IGI Global is prohibited.

a relatively short e-mail subject line length, a clear indication of the sender, the newsletter's information, and characteristics of any special offer that are part of the e-newsletter offer. Other important functional features of e-newsletters include minimal scroll or length, inclusion of images, different content formats such as HTML or plain text, frequency of delivery and being able to easily unsubscribe from receiving the newsletter.

Implicit in the successful implementation of a permission marketing strategy for small businesses are a number of Website features that are relevant to the e-newsletter subscription processes. Pertinent e-newsletter subscription features associated with Website design should entice prospective customers to request marketing from the organisation. Features that assisted the subscription process involved a clear offer or invitation to receive a marketing newsletter - hence, an invitation that is appropriately highlighted using either the newsletter or signup wording has become a standard method of enhancing reader subscription. Other types of practices that are associated with the subscription process is a declaration of the frequency of newsletter dispatches, the minimal collection of personal data at signup and the ability to offer different newsletter formats (HTML/text). Furthermore, the e-newsletter offer should not pre-select newsletter options for readers, and should declare the company privacy policy with respect to collecting consumer/reader e-mail data. Paradoxically the subscription stage should also highlight the ability to unsubscribe from receiving the newsletter at a later date.

Clearly, opting-in to receive e-mail marketing is an important component in the customer engagement process and can be viewed as part of the 80:20 rule in marketing - 80% of a business's resources and efforts are used in capturing new customers, compared to only 20% of resources needed to promote to existing customers. Hence, the ability to initially capture consumer details is a crucial step in the online permission marketing process for the small business entity. Furthermore, there are appropriate good practices associated with obtaining such customer details when it comes to Website design—practices that increase the likelihood of the direct marketing strategy being successful. Various Website design components identified as important in the sign-up or subscribe process are now discussed.

Website Features and E-Newsletters Subscription

There tend to be a core set of Website features that can allow a small business to appropriately instigate and offer an e-newsletter. These features are directly associated with the information content of the small business Website and assist people with the subscription decision-making process - an issue that is at times not explicitly obvious to designers and implementers. The selection of these features can be viewed as being subjective, however, the selection of features is based on one

Copyright © 2009, IGI Global, distributing in print or electronic forms without written permission of IGI Global is prohibited.

of the author's experience as a researcher and educator in the Website development and design sphere. The implementation of the following e-newsletter subscription features are proposed as a good practice approach to Website design for the small business operator.

- *Invitation.* A small business needs to extend an invitation to Website visitors to read and receive their marketing publications - normally via an e-newsletter. The concept of extending an invitation to people is one of engaging and subsequently identifying the interested target audience - a form of customer segmentation. Segmentation allows a marketing message to be formulated and potentially personalised and can be a valuable strategy that assists with customer retention. Furthermore, the Website should make it clear that the e-newsletter is free, whilst the invitation to subscribe should be offered on the home page of the business Website.

- *Semantics.* The semantics of using specific types of words in the e-mail subscription process are important. The expression *newsletter* or *signup* is found to be the most commonly used, and anticipated wording that people look for on a Website when they wish to subscribe to receive company information. Seemingly, the use of these words is a form of visual cue that directs the visitor to the appropriate e-mail marketing section of the Website.

- *How often?* The declaration of e-newsletter frequency is an important aspect of the subscription process. Declaring e-newsletter frequency tends to alleviate the perception a business may be enticing a potential subscriber to sign up for an unlimited and/or uncontrolled amount of contact. The Website should explicitly indicate the frequency of e-newsletter distribution when people subscribe to receive marketing material.

- *Data collection.* Implicit in any marketing campaign is the issue of protecting consumer privacy, hence, the Website subscription process should engage in a limited, but workable collection of data elements. This minimalist approach to data collection only needs to realistically ask for a subscriber's name and e-mail address.

- *Format.* Consumers will have a preference for different newsletter formats that may have a more visual basis (HTML-derived), or be a simpler form (notepad-text type) that has advantages associated with small file sizes and reduced download times. These two formats should be offered at subscription time, with the default being the simpler text option.

- *Option buttons.* Not pre-selecting any of the signup options can be considered to have a business-client trust building dimension. Hence, Website design should avoid the pre-selection of any option buttons associated with the e-newsletter subscription process.

Copyright © 2009, IGI Global, distributing in print or electronic forms without written permission of IGI Global is prohibited.

- *Un-subscribing.* An essential requirement that can instil confidence in potential clients and customers when they subscribe to an e-newsletter is to let them know of how they can unsubscribe. Hence, the e-newsletter subscription stage needs to also provide information on the Website about being able to un-subscribe from the newsletter.
- *Privacy.* Consumers tend to value their privacy and a good e-newsletter subscription practice is to declare the small business data privacy policy. The privacy policy should be readily accessible on the subscription page - a feature that can be easily incorporated with hypertext linking.

Good Practice and E-Newsletters

Many small businesses have traditionally engaged their clients directly, either through a postal mail out, or in a one-to-one encounter in the store. Arguably, it is the small business that has much to benefit from adopting an electronic marketing strategy as an extension of their historical direct marketing activities. However, the important caveat for the small business in the Web environment is to seek permission from Website visitors to engage them electronically through the e-mail communication medium.

Small business owners need to be aware of Website features that can be good practice when it comes to addressing this important the customer acquisition phase. Moreover, the features proposed embrace a simple design approach - incorporating a psychologically adept number of between five to nine features - a design that can serve as a guide for a small business that wishes to engage its constituency using permission marketing.

SUMMARY THUS FAR

If we have managed to get one message through so far – it is that it is better to adopt a variety of approaches to promoting a Web presence.

In fact, some businesses may have already indirectly promoted their Website by implementing Website features that add value to their goods in the eyes of their customers or will attract them to their Web presence in other ways. Although a small business might have some if its features hosted on a third party Website for functionality (for instance, a small accommodation that lists with an accommodation portal because they have a booking engine) they may even attract a greater market because of their existence on that Website.

It is also important to remember that the business can combine its offline and online promotions. For instance, it may actually be easier for the business to run

Copyright © 2009, IGI Global, distributing in print or electronic forms without written permission of IGI Global is prohibited.

promotions where online entry occurs, such as when potential customers enter their details into a database for the chance to win a prize.

Whatever promotion strategies are selected, the business should try to think of ways that they can determine whether they are successful or not. We will talk about this in Chapter X.

OUR PREVIOUS STUDIES

Accountant_07

In this series of interviews with Australian accounting practices we did not specifically ask about promotion of the business Website – but the topic was raised in general discussion by a number of interviewees.

Mention was made in a number of instances of the use of the Website as a promotional tool, specifically in relation to advertising the qualifications of partners and other employees as a *branding* tool. However, a small number of practices mentioned that they had subsequently *removed* the names of employees from their Websites as it made them easier to be 'poached' by other businesses! In a similar manner, some businesses hoped that the professional look of their Website might help them to recruit employees.

Interestingly, two practices commented that they appeared to be ranked higher on search engines after they relocated from suburban to 'city-based' premises.

One fascinating outcome of the study was that the Website was seen by a small number of practices as a means to *filter* certain client enquiries. Some practices made comments along the following lines:

"Clients wishing to have their individual tax returns done would look at our Website and see that we are not the business for them…"

Outer_06

A number of the small business owner/managers that we interviewed in this study of Australian small businesses suggested that a primary benefit of their Internet usage came from indirect promotion online. For instance, a health food store owner indicated that since suppliers had listed her on their Website as a distributor of their product she had seen a increase in sales. Also, it was indicated that now customers research products online and then come into the store to purchase. Similarly, two small businesses in the motor industry stated that they do not directly advertise online, but they have set up affiliations with professional automotive bodies and that these groups advertise online for them. One of these businesses communicates

Copyright © 2009, IGI Global, distributing in print or electronic forms without written permission of IGI Global is prohibited.

online frequently with these groups - especially when they are looking for spare parts, specifications, or how to deal with rare issues.

Develop_06

The Importance of Traditional Media in Promoting a Web Presence

Previous research (leading to this study) showed that traditional means of advertising impacts on the success of a Web presence and that in fact offline and online modes of promotion are linked. The study of small tourism businesses in Malaysia and Ecuador that had a Web presence found that nearly half suggested that including the business e-mail address and URL along with the business details in travel guide books significantly added to the amount of Website traffic, e-mails received and interest in the business. In fact, customers first discovered the business Web presence through the guidebook. One tour operator even indicated that this simple form of promotion had made the business 'famous'. In the case of this particular operator the promotion of the Web presence in the travel book was important because the business Website was difficult to locate through a search engine search and the owner lacked resources to devote to developing a specific online marketing strategy. In another case a lodge that did not have a Website but used e-mail to communicate with customers and receive bookings reported that since the business e-mail address was published in a guidebook the business experienced a significant growth in customers. This lends support to the critical task of making sure that a business includes its Web presence details wherever business details are published.

Winery Case Studies - Using Direct E-Newsletters

Extensive research by one of the authors concerning the relevant design issues associated with the e-newsletter has been undertaken in recent times. This direct marketing approach has received renewed interest from various firms and is one that is premised on potential customers opting to receive a marketing newsletter usually after they have signed up via the Website. The three studies that shed light on this approach relate to the research previous published in Wineries_survey_05, Winery_case_06 and Wineries_analysis_07.

One study (Wineries_survey_05) proposed that wineries tended to use a direct marketing strategy that involved gaining permission to send clients newsletters and marketing material. This practice appeared to be widespread and an inherent extension of the historical manner in which these small business entities engaged their customers. This study also reported that winery Website features had a quasi-tourism theme and that e-newsletter content might involve aspects of regional tour-

Copyright © 2009, IGI Global, distributing in print or electronic forms without written permission of IGI Global is prohibited.

Figure 4. Four dimensions of e-newsletter subscription

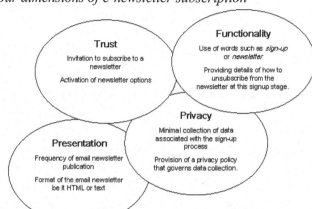

ism. Another winery-based study (Wineries_analysis_07) examined the customer acquisition phase associated e-newsletter subscription - segmenting the subscription Website features into various dimensions - trust, presentation, privacy and functionality. These dimensions effectively represented a broader or common set of themes that were used to shape and present a generally Website design framework for online permission marketing. The four dimensions and composite features are depicted in Figure 4.

The trust dimension dealt with engaging and capturing prospective consumer details that hopefully alleviated the perception that they would not inundate them with 'spam'. Website features that are affiliated with this dimension of the subscription process deal with the initial invitation on the Website to receive a newsletter and the appropriate issues associated with the activation of newsletter options. The presentation dimension related to the format of the e-newsletter and the frequency of receiving e-mail newsletters. Newsletter format should be either based on the HTML or text style allowing a diversity of content, whilst the frequency that a business engages prospective customer is directly associated with the newsletter being delivered to the readers inbox. Subscriber privacy deals with the consumer data collection process that necessitates the collection of minimal information at signup and a reference to the business privacy policy. Finally, the functionality dimension associated with Website design addressed the use of specific wording in the subscription process as well as the inclusion of an unsubscribe option.

Furthermore, the four dimensions were proposed as an evaluation framework that can be used to examine the e-mail-marketing subscription procedure. The framework was argued as being applicable as an effective Website evaluation tool that could be used by researchers to examine aspects of the subscription phase of permission marketing either generally or within specific industries. The framework

Copyright © 2009, IGI Global, distributing in print or electronic forms without written permission of IGI Global is prohibited.

was used to explore a set of Australian winery Websites - an industry group that has traditionally used direct marketing as their primary sales channel - to determine how these wineries have conformed with what can be deemed to be a necessary implementation feature associated with online direct marketing. Results of this exploratory study found that individually and collectively many wineries scored poorly across the four proposed dimensions. Arguably, the study results are ominous, and highlights how this important aspect of online permission marketing is not being appropriately or successfully addressed by small businesses - given that wineries are highly reliant on the direct sales method for profitability.

Another study (Winery_case_06) highlighted a stark contrast with this general finding to report the highly successful use of online permission marketing. The case study method was used to detail how a micro business was able to sell 70% of its product via direct online sales by using online permission marketing in tandem with Website ordering. The business has over the years built a reputation of producing a limited amount of high quality wine - consequently, it experiences high demand for its product, usually selling out with several weeks of a vintage's release. The only way that people can purchase this wine is directly from the winery - that up until several years ago involved being on the wineries mailing list.

The business was able to convert over a period of years its traditional paper-based customer lists to the electronic equivalent with the commensurate cost savings - a notable substitution of the traditional newsletter for an electronic one. Moreover, the only way that the business now communicates with clients is via the e-newsletter that can only be subscribed to on the winery Website. Clearly, the business has utilized e-mail as the primary communication tool for acquiring, contacting and subsequently engaging customers that had given permission to send them an e-newsletter. With a 70% online sales rate - the case may provide a method that could be viewed as being exemplary for other businesses that may also experience high product demand.

The winery Website design embraces many of the good practices associated with e-newsletter subscription - the home page extends an invitation to join the winery mailing list, minimal information is collected, no options are pre-selected and being able to unsubscribe is alluded to. The business only e-mails one or two e-newsletters to list customers a year advising them of their opportunity to purchase wine. The format of the e-newsletter is simple, personalized (it includes the name of the recipient) and concise - notifying winery clients of the latest releases that can be ordered on the Website. In switching to this new form of permission e-newsletter medium, the winery has experienced an increase in the number of people that have registered to receive the business newsletter. A consequence of this expanding electronic mailing list was that the winery has had to use an e-mail management service to oversee this aspect of its operation.

Copyright © 2009, IGI Global, distributing in print or electronic forms without written permission of IGI Global is prohibited.

Tourism_04

In this project, involving interviews with 59 small tourism businesses in country and rural areas of Australia, we asked the businesses how they promoted their Websites. Most businesses listed a range of techniques. Generally the most popular ones were putting the business URL on letterhead or in company brochures. Some businesses made a point of having dedicated URLS (such as www.companyname. com.au) rather than ones with a sub domain name. Some businesses used search engines, but many commented that search engine were now too general – this was especially noted by the accommodation businesses. They tended to rely more on regional portals or dedicated accommodation search portals rather than general search engines.

Other Studies

A Tool for Electronic Channels of Distribution in Hotels (O'Connor & Frew 2004)

As underscored in this chapter, small businesses have a range on options when it comes to promoting online. They are therefore confronted with the question of

Figure 5. Distribution decision matrix (adapted from O'Connor & Frew 2004, Figure 1: 195)

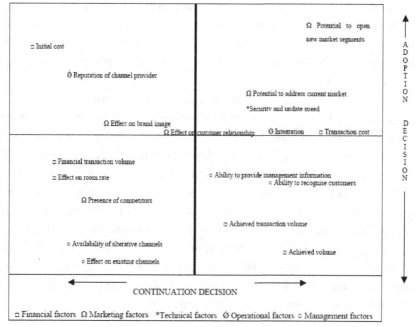

Copyright © 2009, IGI Global, distributing in print or electronic forms without written permission of IGI Global is prohibited.

which channel to use for promotion, providing information and also their services. O'Connor and Frew (2004) developed a tool that could be used by tourism businesses to allow them to make choices concerning marketing channels. Electronic channels play an increasingly important role in tourism promotion as well as the distribution of services, with most companies utilising a range of avenues to reach customers (O'Connor & Frew 2004). The matrix works by presenting the different factors that a business must contend with in both the decision to adopt and the decision to continue using the channel. The matrix (refer Figure 5) suggests that businesses need to consider technical, financial, promotional value and various other factors before implementing the use of a specific channel and provides a useful set of criteria for consideration in the channel evaluation process.

The matrix is interesting in the context of this chapter because it demonstrates the importance of different factors when making the decision on a channel to use and therefore is of practical use to a small business. The main adoption factors are operational and technical issues, such as ease of use, transaction speed, update speed, traffic levels, integration and security. The initial cost also needs to be considered, as does the channel's ability to service both existing and additional market segments. In contrast, the continuation decision appears to be more complex. Factors such as the transaction volume and the data that the channel provides back to the business to assist decision making and the ability to recognise customers are the most important factors.

The Accessibility of Small Business Websites
(Fry, Tyrall, Pugh, & Wyld 2004)

Fry et al. (2006) surveyed independent breweries in the UK to gain an understanding of how they use Websites and the accessibility of the Websites (how they are located on the Web). This is an interesting study in the context of this chapter because it provides some concrete examples of how small businesses are promoting their Websites. Most of the brewery Websites had easily recognisable Web addresses and were readily accessible via brewery directories, however they were difficult to locate using popular search engines. The Websites also tended to be information based Websites rather than marketing or selling tools.

An interesting, although not particularly surprising finding from this study is that larger breweries outperformed smaller breweries in respect to the accessibility of Websites. Even amongst different degrees of small businesses, those greater in size were found to have an advantage. This advantage was in the form of increased awareness of an Internet presence as well as a willingness to experiment with types of Internet presence. Small businesses greater in size also tended to be better re-

Copyright © 2009, IGI Global, distributing in print or electronic forms without written permission of IGI Global is prohibited.

sourced and as such were more able to obtain the expertise needed to effectively contest for the attention of customers on the Internet.

The authors also provide a useful set of non-technical criteria that can easily be followed to increase the potential of successfully promoting a Website. These suggestions echo those provided in this chapter.

- Select a meaningful URL that is easy to remember based directly on the company name.
- Promote the URL on all online literature so that it is directly available to potential customers online.
- Register with all major search engines.
- Follow the steps necessary to meet the criteria to be accessible to major search engines (discussed in this chapter).
- Promote URL on online and printed directories.
- Continuously examine the popularity and status of search engines and directories to ensure the Website meets the criteria to be accessible and that customers are using the medium.

Summary of Our Studies and Other Studies

One of the highlights of the set of studies we have mentioned here is that they represent the variety of approaches used by small businesses to promote their Websites. There were examples of using traditional advertising media to promote the Website address, direct marketing approaches using e-mail newsletters, intentional selection of domain names that match the business name and strategy, consideration of search

Table 1. A sample of promotional approaches

Type of Approach	Approach
Strategic	• Select appropriate domain name(s) for branding and recognition • Consider what is needed to rank high on general search engines • Partner with third party websites (portals) that have a greater reach or will expose the business to wider markets - look to partner with specific third party websites – by industry (such as accommodation portals) or region • Consider banner advertisements on websites that customers might visit
Use traditional media	• Combine 'online' and 'offline' strategy - put URL on letterheads, brochures, packaging and in traditional media advertising • Consider running 'cross' promotions – advertise on traditional media, but potential customers enter online.
Targeted	• Think of using direct marketing approaches (such as e-newsletters)
Evaluation	• Ensure that the success of promotional strategies can be evaluated.

Copyright © 2009, IGI Global, distributing in print or electronic forms without written permission of IGI Global is prohibited.

engine ranking position and the role that third party portals (the 'Web presence') can play in promotion of the business.

TENETS – LESSONS FROM THE CHAPTER

There are many approaches that small businesses can consider to help to promote their Web presence. **The key tenet that we are suggesting here is that the business needs to select a variety of approaches to promotion and develop a mix of strategies that will match the overall Web presence strategy – what the business is trying to achieve with its online presence.**

CONCLUSION

This chapter discussed various the promotion of a Web presence and outlined a number of ways that a business can undertake successful online promotion. Although this is an area that is continuously evolving, it is important that small businesses develop a variety of approaches to promotion of their Web presence and ensure that these work well with their 'offline' promotional strategies. The next chapter discusses the role that business governance plays in the Web presence.

REFERENCES

Birch, A., Gerbert, P., & Schneider, D. (2000). *The age of E-Tail.* Capstone Publishing, UK.

Chaston, I. (2004). *Small Business E-Commerce Management.* Palgrave MacMillan, USA.

Davison, A., Burgess, S., & Tatnall, A. (2008). *Internet Technologies and Business.* 3rd edn, Data Publishing and Arramlu Publications, Melbourne, Australia.

Fry, J., Tyrrall, D., Pugh, G., & Wyld, J. (2004). The provision and accessibility of small business Websites: A survey of independent UK breweries. *Journal of Small Business and Enterprise Development, 11*(3), 302-314.

Godin, S. (1999). *Permission Marketing: Turning Strangers Into Friends, and Friends Into Customers.* New York: Simon & Schuster.

Gupta, H., Jones, E., & Coleman, P. (2004). How do Welsh tourism-SME Websites approach customer relationship management? In A. J. Frew (Ed.), *Information and*

Copyright © 2009, IGI Global, distributing in print or electronic forms without written permission of IGI Global is prohibited.

communications technologies in tourism 2004 (pp. 424-433). Vienna: Springer. Austraia.

Karanasios, S. (2008). *An E-Commerce Framework for Small Tourism Enterprises in Developing Countries.* Victoria University.

O'Connor, P., & Frew, A. J. (2004). An evaluation methodology for hotel electronic channels of distribution. *Hospitality Management, 23,* 179-199.

Scott, D. M. (2007). *The New rules of Marketing and PR.* Hoboken, New Jersey: John Wiley & Sons.

UNCTAD (2004). *Use of the Internet for efficient international trade: Guide for SME managers.* New York, USA and Geneva, Switzerland edn, United Nations.

World Tourism Organisation (2002). *Information technology in tourism : the Asia-Pacific perspective: A report on WTO Asia-Pacific Conference on Information Technology in Tourism, Kunming, Yunnan Province, China, 8-9 April, 2002,* World Tourism Organisation, Madrid, Spain.

Copyright © 2009, IGI Global, distributing in print or electronic forms without written permission of IGI Global is prohibited.

Chapter IX
Web Presence Governance

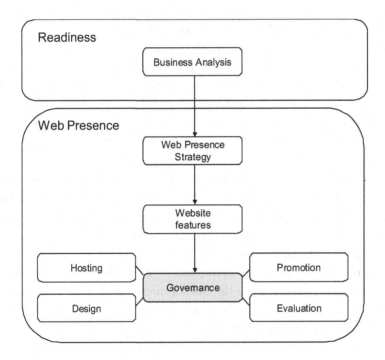

INTRODUCTION

The initial idea behind this chapter was to expand on the issue of security, predominantly in relation to ensuring that a small business operator would be confident that not only its own information was protected, but that customer information

Copyright © 2009, IGI Global, distributing in print or electronic forms without written permission of IGI Global is prohibited.

derived via its Web presence was also safe and secure. However, it seemed more appropriate to expand the discussion in the chapter to how the security associated with a small business Website might fit into an overall business continuity plan and the general governance of a small business, including a discussion of ethical and cultural issues. The purpose of this chapter is not to be a primer on corporate governance and business continuity. However, the chapter does introduce various concepts associated with these areas for the purpose of identifying their importance to the running of the business.

CORPORATE GOVERNANCE

Corporate governance is concerned with improving the performance of a company, allowing the commensurate benefits to flow to stakeholders, such as owners and employees. The particular characteristics of small businesses mean that the way they deal with corporate governance issues will be different from those associated with larger businesses. As previously stated in the book, many small businesses might not interested in focusing on business growth, tending to concern themselves more with maintaining a lifestyle. These businesses tend to be satisfied as long as they survive on a day-to-day basis and can provide themselves and perhaps their employees a comfortable living.

One or two people usually make major decisions in small business, primarily the owner(s) and/or the managers(s) of the business. For them, governance is a combination of the views of the owner and the manner in which the business is run. It reflects the critical steps in the management of the business.

How does a small businesses access the knowledge and/or skills it requires to meet its regulatory or legislative requirements? These skills are often not available within the business, especially in the case of micro businesses. Our own research has found that it is common for the small business to engage an accountant as a primary source to provide appropriate guidance and assistance for the business with respect to compliance and regulatory requirements. On some occasions, accountants will also be asked for advice that might be seen as being outside their normal briefing activities - such as providing recommendations on aspects of computer systems and related Internet issues. In these situations, the small business operator should be directed to appropriate consultants that have relevant expertise with information technology. Clearly, there is a key message here. Often accountants are seen as a 'trusted' source for many aspects of business advice and it may be questionable to seek advice or engage them in areas where their expertise does not necessarily exist.

Copyright © 2009, IGI Global, distributing in print or electronic forms without written permission of IGI Global is prohibited.

A common challenge faced by small businesses is the amount of time and effort they put into planning the direction of the business. Small business planning can include an examination and positioning of the business in the longer-term, may relate to assessing the market share of various goods and/or services, accounting practices associated with employees, budget forecasting and revenue predications, as well as the all important aspect of business cash flow. Of course, we are particularly interested that small business operators also view their ICT investments, and in this case their Web presence activities particularly, as a *long term* investment and plan them as a key component, along with their other business activities.

One of the areas where it is possible to make a case to small business operators that good governance practices can assist in the longer-term viability of their firms is by highlighting the benefits of business continuity management (BCM). Collectively, small businesses tend to be located in one common community with their employees, customers and suppliers all originating from that community (Haksever 1996). Consequently, small business stakeholders are more likely to be in a common geographical area, often forming part of a larger local community, with their viability as a business entity being reliant on the local economy. It is therefore as important for smaller businesses to ensure that there are strategies in place to deal with different types of business interruptions - an issue that is addressed by the concept of business continuity management (BCM).

Business Ethics

An important aspect of business operations and activities, including setting up and maintaining the small business Website, is an understanding that they are governed by rules of conduct – known as *ethics* – which help us to determine which activities are good, bad and obligatory. They need to be aware of ethics as they assist in setting up the direction of the business and help to frame its rules of conduct. Owner/ managers should ensure that employees, whose individual ethical standards are likely to differ from one to another, perform in a manner that is consistent with the business' ethical standards. Ethical standards are influenced by cultural, legal, religious national and other factors (Frenzel and Frenzel 2006). When setting up and maintaining the small business Website, businesses need to be aware of who will viewing the Website and who employees might be interacting with as a direct result of the Website. In the next section we discuss some of the cultural issues related to the small business Website. In the remainder of this chapter we discuss good practice in relation the prevention of potential Web presence problems and dealing with employees and customers when something goes amiss. We also discuss the protection and security of people's personal information (privacy).

Copyright © 2009, IGI Global, distributing in print or electronic forms without written permission of IGI Global is prohibited.

CULTURAL DIVERSITY AND WEB PRESENCE

This section examines some of the cultural issues that are applicable to the development of the business Website and Web presence in general. It is unlikely that the small business operator will have considered this issue as an important aspect of their Web presence.

Businesses that have a Web presence, as well as enjoying the potential benefits of increased audience reach and increased sales, may also face increased administrative complexity due to operating in different geographies. Indeed, once geographical boundaries could delineate the specific rules, regulations, laws and behaviour that shaped business trading. Schneider (2007) indicates that by having a Web presence, a business inadvertently operates across national borders, and that the environment that shapes trading behaviour tends to be related to the business laws and ethical standards that are reflected by that region's culture. Hence, the background and culture of Website visitors will impact on business related issues that may be associated with the regulations governing direct on-line sales, legal jurisdiction of any disputes that may arise from Website presence and the enforcement of any agreements (see Schneider 2007 for a discussion of these issues). Arguably, different Website visitors will have a different interpretation and perception of Website content - behaviour that the business operator needs to be aware of and all due to the trans-national activity that results from having Web presence.

In general, the notion of regional tendencies and cultural diversity have been demonstrated amongst different nations, with different cultural values found not only to influence the behaviour of the nation's society, but also their organisational structures (Hofstede 2001). Hofstede, showed that characteristics associated with national values explained why certain behaviour was more appropriate and likely in some cultures than in others. He proposed a five dimensional framework for assessing cultural tendencies and differences that embraced:

- **Individualism verses collectivism:** This dimension deals with cultural values associated with people working in a group situation compared to the situation where people may be expected to work solo and/or stand up for themselves.
- **Femininity verses masculinity:** A dimension that is seen to deal with the diverse roles and treatments of men and women in certain cultures.
- **Uncertainty avoidance:** Addresses the tendencies of some societies and cultural groups to reduce workplace uncertainty.
- **Small verses large power distance:** This dimension deals with the organisational power issues and interdependence encountered between organisational leaders and their workers.

Copyright © 2009, IGI Global, distributing in print or electronic forms without written permission of IGI Global is prohibited.

- **Long and short term orientation:** This dimension takes into account the historical context of societal values and examines the degree of importance that that past, present and future activities may hold for people.

An awareness of the diversity encountered in different cultures, can be viewed as a pre-condition to being successful as a global businesses entity. The concept of developing and distributing traditional manufactured product or services has always required internationalisation - what may have been successfully marketed in one country, may not be applicable to another country. Turban et al (2008) gives an example of how a General Motors car call the Nova whose name translated into 'no go' in Spanish affected sales in Spanish-speaking countries. Consequently, the understanding of a nation's traditional culture - in this example, the appropriate meaning associated with the translation of a linguistic expression - when introducing a new product or service should be an important business consideration. Furthermore, the international firm - large or small - that exhibits an awareness of the different cultural issues its target markets will tend to be well positioned in understanding how to undertake a successful marketing and sales program.

Marcus and Gould (2000; 2000a) used Hofstede's framework of cultural dimensions to explain the potential design issues that should be associated with the Website's user-interface. Furthermore, the internationalisation of the Website needs to also consider the cultural orientation of the target audience - not just local customised design, for it to be successful (Marcus, 2001). As Websites in general are developed, implemented and maintained, the creators of these sites would do well to understand their own cultural influences in the visual portrayal, content and communication value of the site. Moreover, these creators should consider how people from another cultural backgrounds perceive and relate to these Websites - there would invariably be a divergent interpretation of content based on their different backgrounds. Some of the different ways in which cultural influences are reflected in Website development include:

- Turban et al (2008) propose that the Website needs to address cultural, legal and language factors in order to engage a global audience. To successfully undertake online business activities will involve the localisation of the Website and must include translating languages and the adapting of Website content to the different cultural groups.
- User-interface design when it comes to Western and Asian cultural groups exhibits significant differences across a spectrum of communication features that include an appropriate and/or tailored use of presentation, interaction, metaphors, navigation type and appearance (Marcus, 2003).

Copyright © 2009, IGI Global, distributing in print or electronic forms without written permission of IGI Global is prohibited.

- Cultural diversity encountered around the world is such that many of the larger corporations have adopted different Website visuals and content that is published for audiences in different countries. Kaufman (2005) discusses some of the cultural issues associated with different Websites developed by the Honda Corporation for Sweden, India, Japan and the USA.
- Website design has been explored from a cross-cultural perspective and examined how different groups might prefer certain visual effects to be embodied in the Website (Würtz 2005).
- An examination of a variety of national Web portals across different countries identified differences that could be attributed to the diversity of cultural variations - variations that were based on that Hofstede's cultural dimensions (Zahir et al. 2003).
- The Website will attract international visitors and the perceptions and meanings associated with using different colours on the Website can be subjective and open to interpretation. For example, Powell (2002) indicates that the colour black in Western culture has been typically associated with death and sombre feelings - whilst in a country such as Japan, white is usually the colour associated with death. The pertinent point of this simple example is that it cannot be assumed that Website colours, and the manner in which they may be used to communicate a message to the visitor will be equally perceived.

Challenges/Opportunities for Small Businesses

Clearly, an understanding and awareness of the cultural diversity of a business's target audience should be considered in the context of Web presence. Many large organisations have developed their Websites with culturally appealing features that have been adapted to cater to different markets. Smaller businesses may follow this trend as soon as Web services emerge that offer advice on how best to implement cultural features on a Website. Indeed, it was Marcus and Gould (2000a) that suggested that the future direction of user-interface design and by implication Website development, will need cross-cultural theory as an accepted element of implementation. They proposed that certain cost-effective tools, or templates, would evolve that would allow multiple versions of the same Website to be used for different cultural groups.

Although possibly expensive to set up and maintain, small businesses dealing in export markets or across different, identifiable communities may consider setting up different Websites for different constituents, matched to different URLs (as we suggested in Chapter VIII. This may allow them to provide targeted, culturally sensitive content.

Copyright © 2009, IGI Global, distributing in print or electronic forms without written permission of IGI Global is prohibited.

Small businesses should be aware that their Websites might be viewed by anyone with access to a Web browser. Even if they only consider their offerings to be to the national market, they should be aware of the diversities of population that exist within that market.

BUSINESS CONTINUITY MANAGEMENT

Business continuity management (BCM) is a management discipline that was initially introduced (under another name) as an important mainframe related operation. In the early days of mainframe computers, businesses realised that it was necessary to have some type of data backup system in the event their computers failed - which was often a more than occasional occurrence. Over subsequent years, the concept of backing up computer applications and important data became commonly known as disaster recovery, where strategies were developed by businesses to manage the recovery of their systems when various deleterious and unexpected situations arose. Indeed, situations such as floods, fire, earthquakes, power outages or operator sabotage are some of the potential activities that can lead to organisational compromise, and ones that a disaster recovery plan can address. More recently, the term business continuity has emerged to describe the plans that businesses can use to reduce the adverse effects of unexpected events that invariably can lead to business disasters. Such plans involve more than just backing up computer files and databases. They include employee management and counseling and advertising campaigns to inform important suppliers and customers of protocols in place to deal with the failure of business computing systems.

Several notable events have brought increased focus the activities associated with BCM. The welcoming of the new millennium, when there was much concern and angst about the potential problems associated with the 'Year 2000 bug' (Y2K) highlighted the importance of continuity for all firms. Y2K was where computer programs, typically written in the 1960s and 1970s, stored the year component of a date as a two-digit number - for instance, the year 1969 would have been stored as '69'. To take into account the move to 1970, the computer would add one to the two digit stored year to make it '70'. In a crude example of how a calculation might occur - to calculate how many years a loan taken out in 1970 had been in operation in 1975, the number '70' would be taken from '75'. The major concern was what would happen at the turn of the century, when the year 1999 became 2000, and the two digit stored code ticked over from '99' to 00'. To calculate how old a loan taken out in 1970 would be in the year 2000 using the 'old' system, the number '70' would be subtracted from the number '00' - resulting in a figure of -70! There was great deal of investment and time put into resolving the Y2K bug by business

Copyright © 2009, IGI Global, distributing in print or electronic forms without written permission of IGI Global is prohibited.

and government - given the resultant scenarios, particularly in relation to how the world's financial systems might perform. In the end, it seems the investment was worthwhile as there were few reported instances of problems. However, some argue that the lack of problems meant that the problem was overstated and that far too many resources were devoted to it. In a way, this argument highlights one of the key dilemmas of BCM – how much should a business invest in a situation that may never occur?

Another important event to highlight the importance of BCM was the terrorist attack on the World Trade Center in New York in 2001 (9/11). During the aftermath of that attack many businesses realised that the business continuity plans that they had in place were inadequate. For instance, many employees were traumatized and could not put business continuity plans into effect. Communication infrastructure was inoperable or damaged within the immediate and broader geographical area of the attack, preventing businesses from communicating their requirements to invoke business continuity plans in offsite areas (Hill & Burgess, 2003).

More recently, there has been an increased emphasis on corporate governance activities and increased accountability and transparency in the manner in which organisations conduct business. Well-prepared and implemented business continuity plans can add to the level of confidence that business stakeholders can have in an organisation. Consequently, there are some important aspects of BCM that should be noted (Hill and Burgess 2003):

- Business continuity plans are typically developed to manage unexpected situations. A computer 'crashing' or similar occurrence should be something that is seen as an expected occurrence and would be supported by a regular backup process, perhaps with offsite storage. This type of occurrence will be discussed later in this chapter.
- BCM is about planning for something that may never happen. Obviously, a business will have some understanding of the typical problems that are more likely to occur through the prudent undertaking of regular risk analysis - this being one of the keys to determining how much of investment needs to be dedicated to various components of the business continuity plan.
- Continuity planning is not necessarily about having business insurance (in the short term, anyway). Whilst insurance is about compensation and replacement costs, these are usually paid after a period of evaluation and assessment of damage. For a small business, if its customers have gone elsewhere during this time, any insurance payment may come too late.

Although they are not able to invest at the same level that larger businesses can in continuity planning, various aspects of BCM can be adopted by small business

Copyright © 2009, IGI Global, distributing in print or electronic forms without written permission of IGI Global is prohibited.

operators, allowing them to continue providing goods, services and local employ-ment, as well as contributing to the maintenance of both business and societal cohe-sion. As we have mentioned a number of times in this book, small businesses are disadvantaged in comparison with larger businesses because of their small size and lack of resources. This severely limits the types of investments that they can make in BCM. Thus, we will consider the relevant aspects of business continuity planning that can be possibly be applied in regards to a small business Web presence.

Business Continuity Management and Small Business

The notion behind BCM is fairly new (especially for small businesses) and, as we have seen, it typically involves more than just backing up computer files and im-portant data. Some types of businesses (for instance, some financial institutions) are required by law to have sound BCM practices. Most small businesses are typically not amongst these businesses. However, there are some aspects of BCM that can be applied to small businesses (Burgess & Hill, 2004) and include ICT recovery and continuity, planning acceptance by employees and the importance of involving senior management in continuity issues. We will now discuss some of these.

Information Technology Continuity

This is probably the most relevant area of BCM in relation to Web presence and small business. Many business continuity plans have the restoration of ICT systems as a central part of the overall recovery plan. This may be because BCM as a discipline emerged from 'disaster recovery', when the aim of the businesses continuity process was simply to recover data when the mainframe computer failed. Indeed, in many organizations the ICT recovery processes are still considered in isolation from the rest of the business processes. The focus of the ICT recovery may therefore be on building enough redundancy into the system to replace elements that may fail - re-gardless of whether each component is essential to get the business up and running again in the event of an interruption. Small businesses generally will be found to be at divergent ends of the adoption spectrum when considering back up planning strategies with respect to their ICT systems. For instance, our own research sug-gests it is too common for a small business that has not had some type of computer failure to not back up their files at all! This, of course, will court disaster. Given that events associated with computer or database failures still occur, although seemingly less common than say five years ago, they can have compromising consequences for a business. On the other hand, small businesses that have lost important data or files often go too far in making sure that there are multiple copies of all files on different computers. This type of computer back up activity might also be sup-

Copyright © 2009, IGI Global, distributing in print or electronic forms without written permission of IGI Global is prohibited.

ported by operators also printing copies of business documents - allowing them to have hard copies of working documents as a precaution to everything 'going down'. The problem here is that the amount of time being devoted to perform all of the backups, plus the resources (paper, ink and physical space) needed to print a hard copy of everything actually diminishes some of the efficiencies that the ICT adoption provides in the first place. What is needed is a common sense attitude to backing up ICTs - an issue that is discussed later in this chapter.

When considering the Web presence, one important business continuity aspect to think about is continuity of business with suppliers and customers. Even if a small business has a problem that does not specifically relate to the Website, the Website can be used to help keep valuable business partners informed of what is happening. One way to do this is to have one or more *emergency* home pages that can be switched to in the event of a problem. For instance, in a rural area subject to bushfires, the business might have a temporary Web page that can be switched to at short notice that lets customers know it is still in business. This page will then redirect the visitor to the regular Web page. Indeed, if a customer were to be informed about the bushfire through the mass media, a quick visit to the Website might reassure them. This might be especially useful if other forms of communication infrastructure such as telephone lines were to be inoperative.

Organisational Employee Issues

Many business continuity plans are based on the assumption that all employees will be available after a business interruption occurs. There is also an implicit view that many of the tasks that need to be undertaken in the event of such an interruption are allocated in the stable environment that existed previously. The reality is that all employees may not be in a position to carry out these tasks, especially if they are injured or traumatized in some way. Now, it is likely to be beyond the scope of business continuity planning in small businesses to be prepared at any great level for these types of eventualities. However, we do know that the smaller the business, the greater the likelihood that its employees will perform multiple tasks. It may be appropriate in these instances to provide a number of employees with some simple duties to perform in the case of business interruptions – and to plan that if one person cannot carry out a task then another can. What about a sole proprietor? Perhaps plans need to be put in place for a consultant or even a competitor to take over the business as a result of events that may disable business operations.

Copyright © 2009, IGI Global, distributing in print or electronic forms without written permission of IGI Global is prohibited.

Importance of Involving Senior Management

It is important that senior managers be convinced that business continuity planning is necessary. This is certainly the case with small businesses, where small business owner/managers need to be convinced that resources should be used on *something that may not occur*. Perhaps this chapter in some way is helping to play that role, as could external consultants. Of course, the other major reason that motivates businesses to adopt some type of business continuity plan is that they have already experienced some type of business interruption. It is about being aware of what ICT discontinuity means for the business - with the associated consequences. Arguably, the resources allocated to such a plan should be commensurate with the risk of the interruption occurring and the possible losses that may occur if not action is taken.

In many organisations that are not subject to regulation and/or legislation in relation to BCM there may be several reasons why it may be difficult to get support from top management. Mitroff (2001) notes a number of defense arguments that are used to deny or under-estimate business vulnerability in the case of an ICT interruptions - arguments that can be persuasive in convincing management that business continuity is not necessary. Some of these are:

- **Denial:** Only others have this type of crisis.
- **Disavowal:** A crisis can happen, but the impact on us will be small
- **Idealisation:** Crisis do not happen to good organisations
- **Projection:** If a crisis happens it must be because someone else is trying to harm us.

As we have already mentioned, it can be difficult to convince owner/managers of small businesses to spend money to protect the business against an event that may or may not happen. Now, this discussion may seem a little *heavy* for a book that discusses small businesses and Web presence - but the simple fact of the matter is that we believe that a small business Web presence is an important part of the overall business activities, and the chances of a small business surviving a business interruption are more likely if it has a well thought out, simple, business continuity plan that reflects the relative size of the business. This book is not about governance (although we feel that we do espouse some good governance practices in it), nor is it about business continuity. However, we do believe that the value of the small business Web presence is enhanced by considering the implementation of a Website as a part of the overall ICT strategy, as well as a key component of the business. Operating the entire business whilst being guided by good governance practices and, where appropriate, protecting its future by consideration of how

Copyright © 2009, IGI Global, distributing in print or electronic forms without written permission of IGI Global is prohibited.

business continuity management may fit in, can only help to strengthen its position into the future.

SECURITY AND CONTROL

As we mentioned earlier on in the chapter, security is important for any business. Typically, small business owner/managers understand the types of security associated with physical security, such as the use of locks to restrict physical entry, but struggle when confronted with how to secure their own computerised files or deal with the challenges of doing business on the Internet.

The use of Internet technology is a pervasive activity that brings with it a set of security challenges. This book cannot hope to provide technical detail as to what specifically is 'out there'. What we can do is to hope to raise awareness of certain issues and outline some strategies for managing them. In this section, we discuss security and control in relation to ICTs as a whole - issues that impinge on the Web presence in a number of ways - and then move specifically onto the Web presence.

So, what types of things can cause problems with computers files?

- They can be corrupted, altered in some way, lost or even stolen.
- They can be stored on computers that may have a hard disk crash
- They can be stored on media (such as disks or USB sticks) and something happens to the media so that it is unreadable, or the media is lost.
- Someone might enter incorrect data into a system that is then stored as part of a data file and then used to make other (subsequently incorrect) calculations.
- Software that is used may have 'bugs', that leads to incorrect data being stored, perhaps through incorrect calculations or assumptions that are built into the software.
- Someone might intentionally damage equipment, media or data files. This can occur a number of ways – such as through physical intrusion or computer viruses.
- Someone without authorization might access data files.

As we mentioned earlier, these days the Internet provides a number of extra challenges:

- Someone might try to get access to a small business' sensitive information – either by accessing their computer files through the Internet or by attempting

Copyright © 2009, IGI Global, distributing in print or electronic forms without written permission of IGI Global is prohibited.

to trick them to enter their details over the Internet by posing to be someone else.

- Of course, the Internet has now become the primary means of delivery of malicious software, so businesses need to be aware of this. For instance, they should not click onto suspicious looking links in e-mails or run programs received using this medium. Sometimes it can appear that e-mails are sent from legitimate sources, as some malicious programs can access the e-mail address books of businesses and send destructive e-mails to the list of contacts.

Some business computers typically have a number of programs running in the 'background', while the computer is switched on, to act as gatekeepers to help to keep these programs out and/ or to minimise their effect if they take hold.

It is obvious that the possibilities of computerised data being compromised in some way are relatively high and cannot be ignored by business operators. So, what are some of the causes of these problems?

- **Human Error:** This can occur in a number of ways. For instance, the wrong data may be entered into a system, or a disk may be 'wiped' accidentally, and then the blank disk is copied onto the backup disks! There might also be problems in relation to human error in bug-ridden software.
- **Environmental problems:** As mentioned earlier, these can cause major interruptions to a business. They might be serious disasters (such as floods), power outages or voltage surges, or simply computer equipment failure.
- **Crime:** This can manifest in a number of ways. Someone can try to access the confidential data files of a business (using techniques such as 'hacking'). Others write software (such as viruses) to attack systems in general, without any specific targets. Another approach is when someone poses as a legitimate business in order to extract sensitive information about people.

One particular problem that is commonly encountered with micro businesses (especially home based ones) is that there is one computer in the business and it is also shared with the rest of the family. Thus, business activities are shared with computer games, casual Internet surfing and homework! It is **very** important in these circumstances to ensure that the activities do not overlap and that the business files remain secure.

What to Do?

It is important to understand the different types of problems that occur and to consider ways in which security problems can be minimised. There are a number

Copyright © 2009, IGI Global, distributing in print or electronic forms without written permission of IGI Global is prohibited.

of approaches to security that can be taken (such as those outlined in Frenzel and Frenzel 2004; Holtsnider and Jaffe 2001), but basically they revolve around the basic notions of *preventing* a problem, *detecting* it if it does occur, *limiting* its effect if it does occur, *recovering* from it and *rectifying* the situation so that it does not occur again. We will now discuss aspects of each of these.

Prevention

In the initial instance, this can be achieved by using some form of physical mechanism to protect the different types of computer systems that a business has - this even applyies to ancillary areas such as computer manuals, software disks and CDs and data storage devices. In the case of computers, **passwords** can provide a useful means of controlling access to business documents and files. Of course, there is no point in having passwords that are written on a note attached to the computer monitor, or are easy to guess, such as the name of a spouse or child.

For small businesses with a Web presence, passwords can provide a convenient way for them to access their Website or other online activities when they are away from the business, perhaps even to keep an eye on things whilst on holidays.

We have already discussed BCM, but a simple application of these principles is to **back up data files regularly** in the case of data being corrupted or lost completely. How often? A good rule of thumb is to backup as often as you are prepared to have to rebuild the system from the last backup! It is also a good idea to regularly store important data at a different physical site, and/or in a fire proof safe. For instance, there is little consolation for a small office or home-based business if all of the business data is stored in the premises (even in a different room) if all of the premises are destroyed. Moreover, there are third-party providers that specialise in continuity and backup services that can allow a business to maintain a set of data files in another geographical location via the Internet.

A small business hosting its own Web presence should think about what happens if its server goes down. Does it have alternatives that can be switched to? Similarly, if it has a Website hosted externally, what systems does the hosting service have in place if its systems go down? Does it have an off-site backup? How often does the host service back up important business files? Similar questions should be asked of any third party service that the small business considers using. There is little point in being listed on a service that is unreliable.

Many larger businesses, and to a certain extent smaller businesses, have an *intranet*, which is a private network, internal to the business and accessible only by employees. Intranets are very useful as a means of providing a single point of access to many business systems and to source up-to-date business information.

Copyright © 2009, IGI Global, distributing in print or electronic forms without written permission of IGI Global is prohibited.

This type of network technology application becomes important as the number of employees in a business grows, to facilitate organisational collaboration and information sharing. It is not the focus of this book to discuss intranets in depth, however it is important to briefly examine the main form of protection that is used to maintain them secure from intruders - by using a *firewall*. A firewall is a combination of hardware and software that only allows access to users with a certain Internet address - usually declared in an electronic computer listing or directory. By having a number of addresses that the business lists in its directory, a firewall provides access that is limited to business employees, even though they may be dispersed across different locations. These days, intranet access is often extended to certain external business partners, such as large suppliers or customers, who are provided with limited access to relevant business prevention systems. In these instances, protection against access to other areas is also managed by the firewall. When access to the intranet is provided to some external partners, it is known as an *extranet*.

Firewalls tend to be a composite part of the latest versions of many popular operating systems packages, such as Microsoft Windows, and have become a valuable tool for small businesses. When set up effectively, they can notify the user when an internally located computer-based program is attempting to transmit a message to the outside world (the Internet) or, perhaps more importantly, when a program from the outside world is attempting to gain access to a local computer. In many instances, this may be for quite legitimate reasons, such a virus protection software update, but at least users have the *option* to allow this traffic through their firewall or not.

Another type of control that can help to prevent outsiders from accessing data is known as **encryption**. Encryption is usually necessary when a message is sent over some type of network, such as a small office network, a wireless network and even the Internet. Sending a simple message over the Internet is perhaps like sending an open letter via the postal system - if the letter is intercepted then there is chance that it could be read by an unintended recipient. The idea behind encryption is to have a message coded (or *encrypted*) before it is transmitted - so that only the *intended* recipient has the ability to decode (*decrypt*) the message. That way if the message is intercepted along the way, it will not be possible to be read by the user.

Again, this book does not intend to outline the various techniques associated with encryption or decryption. However, from the point of view of having a Web presence it is vital to know what is happening in relation to the processing of online payments, both from a business and customer protection viewpoint. Many small businesses and their customers are wary of online credit card payments. For this reason (and sometimes because of the cost and difficulty of processing payments online), some small businesses provide an order form for their goods on their Website,

Copyright © 2009, IGI Global, distributing in print or electronic forms without written permission of IGI Global is prohibited.

to be printed by customers and *faxed* to the business – which is for most businesses (and many customers) a trusted method of paying 'remotely' for goods.

Some small businesses have an online 'form' that can be filled out by customers, which they fill out and then typically click onto a 'submit' button at the bottom of the form. Basically, this should be discouraged as it means the details of the form will be e-mailed to the business. E-mail is *not* the most secure means by which credit card details can be sent!

It is also important to have **guidelines** established with all employees of the business as to the proper processes involved in the security of the computer files of businesses. There should be written instructions outlining the processes involved in backing up files, ensuring that access restrictions (such as physical locks) are in place at the appropriate times. From the Web presence viewpoint, it is important that increased activity due to the online presence does not bring with it undesirable consequences, such as computer viruses. Employees should be aware of the risks of opening program (or any other types) of files received via e-mail that do not come from a trusted source.

Although this is less under the control of small businesses, another form of security is through the programming logic built into software applications. Many errors or problems with the data stored by software programs can be traced back to errors in data entry. These can occur in a number of ways, such as pressing an incorrect key on the keyboard or pressing it more than once. Well-designed software can include limit controls on any data that is input. For instance, let us assume that a program asks for someone's age, and the person entering the data, meaning to enter '33', accidentally types in '333'. This could have hazardous results in some calculations. Indeed, in preparing this program, developers should put limitations in place that allow for automatic checking at data entry - checking that would ensure:

- Only numbers are entered. If someone enters a letter or other character, the system notifies the data entry person about the error.
- A variable such as 'age' fell within certain limits – such as between 0 and 130. That way it would recognise that '333' was not a valid age. Note that this cannot pick up all such errors in number entry – for instance, if '43' were entered instead of '33' then it would likely go undetected.
- Variables such as age are often expressed in whole numbers (or integers). This is because they represent a number of years of life. As such, it is common to restrict the entry of numbers involving age to only whole numbers.

With online payment systems, this type of check is typically done with credit card numbers, where a particular algorithm is used to check to see if an incorrect digit has been entered as part of the credit card number.

Copyright © 2009, IGI Global, distributing in print or electronic forms without written permission of IGI Global is prohibited.

Well-designed software can also detect problems associated with data processing activities. For instance, if a sequence of cash receipts or payments are being processed and a number is repeated, then the system should identify this action and highlight the situation. One reason for enacting this security mechanism is that this may highlight situations of fraud - other reasons may be for missing items or even for legitimate circumstances. For instance, when a cheque is cancelled it will typically not be processed in the system. If the user of a system is informed of this then the user can bypass any alert by the computer software that there could be a potential problem.

For this reason, many organisations do not cancel or delete invoices - they will always be able to access a copy of the transaction. They instead provide credit notes that can be used to (effectively) cancel an invoice or modify it if its details are erroneous. This assists the organisation in maintaining a detailed audit trail that can be used to track and authenticate the status of invoices, given that once created, they then *must* be processed by the system.

Computer software also assists with the monitoring of organisational data output. In most instances this ensures that the output falls within expected and acceptable pre-determined limits or boundaries. The reasons associated with this type of activity generally can be attributed to detecting fraud. However, this type of alert mechanism can also be important in exception-type circumstances, flagging events such as excessive overtime being worked during a peak period. These 'exception' scenarios are provided by the system, often to managers, who can then follow up looking for explanations as to what has happened. This might be especially important to small businesses as they grow their number of employees and the owner/ manager does not have the resources to maintain a comprehensive oversight of operations.

With respect to their Web presence, small business operators are likely to be interested in the level of visitor views, 'click-throughs' or traffic that is generated – either on their own Website (especially if they are charged for excess traffic) or with associated third-party sites – where they need to be able to determine the amount of business that is generated from them. Output reports generated by Website hosts or third party Websites can be a very important source of unusual traffic patterns.

Blocking Inappropriate Content

It is common for businesses to prevent access to certain Websites by implementing software that filters and assists in blocking these sites. These Websites might be seen as having inappropriate or offensive content - that are deemed to distract employees. Such sites may be pornographic or even entertainment sites that may reduce organisational productivity. Arguably, the business needs to be aware of

Copyright © 2009, IGI Global, distributing in print or electronic forms without written permission of IGI Global is prohibited.

their legal and societal responsibilities with respect to the type of content that can be inadvertently or mistakenly accessed by employees.

Online Banking

One of the most common forms of online transactions that are increasingly being adopted by small businesses is online banking. Many small business owner/managers see online banking as a cost effective and efficient way in which to conduct business. In modernised countries, it can be anticipated that many small businesses will adopt online banking as a way to make and receive payments - certainly more so than with online shopping carts. It is important for a small business to ensure that the bank it is dealing with has a number of processes in place to protect the security and privacy of small business funds and transactions.

Detection

A small business is highly likely to be using e-mail as an important communication mode and is consequently exposed to potential risk from any number of attacks associated with e-mail-linked computer viruses. As mentioned earlier, later versions of operating systems, such as Windows, have a number of security features built into them (such as firewalls) to assist in preventing malicious computer attacks on unsuspecting Internet users. However, the transmission mechanisms associated with rogue computer viruses often do circumvent security control measures to cause malicious damage to files or to be a time wasting nuisance. For these reasons, it is important that the small business has *up to date virus protection* software. As with firewall software, this software operates in the background all of the time that computers are switched on. They are programmed to search for and detect unusual patterns or to specifically detect the signature behaviour of known viruses and other destructive software. It is important to ensure that virus protection software is regularly updated - new viruses are being detected regularly and virus protection software is updated on such a basis to combat this.

It is vitally important that small business employees understand that a computer attack can also occur at the personal level where other Internet users making themselves out to be legitimate businesses and seek important business information. A common and wide-spread way that is this is done is by using a misleading and dishonest process called *phishing*. Phishing occurs when a business receives an e-mail from what appears to be a legitimate online partner, for example a bank, or quite commonly, an online auction service such as eBay™, requesting that details of account user name or password details be confirmed by 're-entering' them on what turns out to be fraudulent Website. The main way to combat this is to *be*

Copyright © 2009, IGI Global, distributing in print or electronic forms without written permission of IGI Global is prohibited.

vigilant, were small business employees should be trained not to enter sensitive details requested through *any e-mail* that is received - no matter how authentic the e-mail looks.

A more complex form of deception occurs where someone sets up an online presence to pose as a legitimate business, existing or otherwise. However, there are checks in place, known as *digital certificates (or signatures),* to help to verify that a business that is being dealt with online actually is the business they claim to be. Described simply, a business can obtain a digital certificate from a well-respected third party (for example, VeriSign® is a global corporation that provides such products. In Australia, Australia Post is one of these third parties). The digital certificate usually is set up to operate when a user visits the Website or attempts to purchase something online. It operates in the following manner:

- When a consumer visits the Website or online order area of the business Website, they are sent the digital certificate file automatically.
- That file is then transferred to the 'respected third party' – that verifies that the business is who they claim to be by matching the certificate with the business name.
- If there is no match, the consumer is notified by a message from the third party that there is a problem with the digital certificate. If there is a match then the consumer is directed to the intended Web page.
- The consumer's Web browser manages this process – if everything is fine the user is mostly unaware that the process has occurred.

From the point of view of the small business, it can set up a digital certificate through a respected third party. It also helps from a *governance* and transparency aspect, as the business can advertise on its Website that it is protected by particular types of digital signatures, credit card payment security and so forth.

Limit, Recover, and Rectify

When anti-virus software is working effectively it will detect the presence of potentially harmful software. However, if such software has taken hold, then virus protection software can also perform the task of ridding the computer system of the virus (*cleaning* the system) or also remove its effects from data and program files that may have been affected. Where it cannot effectively rid the system of harmful files, it may *quarantine* them (remove access to them by the system). In other words, although the virus may have breached the initial security protocols that the business has in place, its presence has been *detected* and its affect is *limited.*

Copyright © 2009, IGI Global, distributing in print or electronic forms without written permission of IGI Global is prohibited.

Another way to limit the effect of harmful files such as viruses is to reduce the number of computers that are connected to the Internet or networked to each other. Sometimes the inconvenience of not having a computer directly connected to others on a network is reduced by the extra security of having important files being more secure.

Of course, sometimes there may be a loss of important computer files. This is where the benefits of a regular and comprehensive backup strategy become important and allow the business to continue activities with minimal disruption. In the case of computer programs, restoring the program can usually be achieved by reinstalling it. In the case of data files, the last backups can be reinstalled. In the case of Websites, the Website backup as it was last stored can be reinstalled.

Finally, if some sort of problem does occur, then it is important to *rectify* the situation and ensure that it does not occur again. Whatever measures, if any, were in place were inadequate and so should be modified to ensure that a repeat does not occur.

BALANCING THE RISKS

There are many different levels and types of computer security and protection that a small business can consider for its computer files. Security risks are exacerbated once the business decides to operate in the online environment, even if it is only to send and receive e-mails. All of a sudden its systems may be targets for unwanted and malicious Internet-based visitors. Some protections, which we will summarise later, are obvious choices because they provide a great deal of protection for a small investment, or are already incorporated into operating systems software. Others to be considered are:

- Educating and informing employees on the various aspects of computer and Internet security and any related protocols.
- Being aware of the security levels of third party Website hosts and third party Websites.
- Deciding whether or not to operate standalone computers (and perhaps losing some efficiencies because of it), and
- Thinking about business continuity aspects, such as whether or not to have backup Websites in place

All require an investment of resources and possibly a loss of efficiencies, for the purposes of increasing or maintaining security levels. The small business owner/manager needs to weigh up the likelihood of particular unpleasant events occurring

Copyright © 2009, IGI Global, distributing in print or electronic forms without written permission of IGI Global is prohibited.

Table 1. Risk management model (adapted from Schnieder 2007)

| | | Impact on Business (Cost) | |
		Low	High
Probability of Occurrence	High	Contain and control	Prevent
	Low	Ignore	Insurance or backup plan

and the cost of introducing initiatives to stop them from happening, or if they do occur be able to limit and recover the impact. Only then can a decision be made as to what is a sensible, cost effective and efficient strategy for combating them. One risk management model (refer Table 1) for determining the type of action that should be considered for different types of security risks has been proposed by Schneider (2007).

The model suggests that most potential events that are likely to disrupt business continuity and performance should be assessed in relation to their likelihood of occurrence and impact on the business. Those disruptive events that are more likely to occur and will potentially have a serious impact on business operations should be prevented. Conversely, some events that are likely to occur, but have little impact on the business should be contained and controlled. Events that are irregular, but could have a significant effect on the business if they do occur, should certainly be covered by insurance, but perhaps also be addressed in the business continuity plan. Events that are unlikely to ever occur and have a low impact on business operations in all reality should be ignored.

PRIVACY

Most small businesses are already used to dealing with information about their customers. It is important that customers are convinced that anything they divulge to the business is secure (as we have already discussed). However, in the online arena it is also good practice to assure customers that their information will also be kept *private*. It is quite common for larger businesses to include a *privacy policy* on their Website, indicating what will happen with sensitive information that may be gathered via the Web presence. For instance, businesses may have a policy stating that they will not sell or divulge customer information to any affiliated, or indeed, third-party marketing company. The privacy policy is usually positioned in a prominent part of the Website and it is imperative that the policy informs current and potential customers of the manner that the company will protect the information that customers share with the company (See also the relevant section on Website design in Chapter VII for details on aspect of Website implementation). For the

Copyright © 2009, IGI Global, distributing in print or electronic forms without written permission of IGI Global is prohibited.

small business operator who might use a third party Website to gather information about customers (say, through an online shopping cart on a portal), there should be some provision for accessing their privacy policy via that particular Website. If a business gathers information from having a portal exposure, then the privacy policy of the portal also needs to be available to customers.

Copyright Law

Copyright law is designed to protect the rights of the owners of creative works. It is designed to stop actions like the illegal copying and passing on of music or software files without some reward for their use being returned to the creator. Infringements such as the ones that have been mentioned here are fairly easy to identify. However, small business owner/managers need to be careful that they have permission to use any images, graphics or other material that may be components of their own Website, but have originated from another source. Note that it is generally suitable to have a link to other creative works, whilst in some countries permission needs to be requested. In various parts of the world copyright automatically applies upon creation of the work. If a small business owner/manager is looking to protect something that has been created within the business, it could consider taking out more binding protection, such as a patent or trademark. Again, it will important to seek information on the applicable laws and jurisdictions that apply in the countries that a business' target audience is located.

Import/Export Issues

As suggested already, the importing or exporting of goods based that are associated with Internet transactions and sales brings a new set of issues for the small business operator that should be investigated. These include:

- What actually constitutes a contract in different countries?
- How will customs laws affect any transactions?
- How will the logistics for physical goods be handled?
- What about product returns?

One of the challenges encountered in the implementation of a Web presence that might be associated with exporting goods is that the business may have little or no control over the location of its customers - accessing a global audience is after all one of the touted benefits of a Web presence. Consequently, the business might find itself having to deal with queries from places it had not even considered - and will need to have a strategy in place for how to deal with and follow through

Copyright © 2009, IGI Global, distributing in print or electronic forms without written permission of IGI Global is prohibited.

these customer queries. If a small business is actually *planning* to export goods to a particular country it may consider setting up a separate Website or Web presence for that country. Note that this would involve extra setup and maintenance costs.

OUR PREVIOUS STUDIES

From our collective studies we have not conducted research that has examined issues that was specifically related to security and privacy issues associated with the small business Web presence. Most of the material in this chapter comes from our own experiences as Internet-engaging consumers and information systems academics that have kept abreast of the latest developments in these areas. However, there were some observations that we are able to make from individual comments that were made by participants in some of the studies we have conducted.

Accountant_07

Interviews with Australian accounting practices revealed that there were differing levels of security across the practices in relation to transferring file data. Some swapped data files via e-mail, although a number had secure facilities in place to transfer client files. Some customers had access to online portfolios, secured by a password. One general theme that came out of the interviews was that most of the practices were happy with what they were currently doing – and would only look to extend the services that they offer when their clients requested it and *they could be assured of the security of their data.*

Outer_06

In this study of small business and community-based organisations (CBOs) uses of the Internet, most of the concerns were about data security and were raised by the CBOs, who complained about the lack of ICT support available when systems crashed or the Internet 'went down'. It was felt amongst a few CBOs in this study that younger members were better equipped to deal with these sorts of issues than older, less ICT savvy, members.

Tourism_04

This study of 32 metropolitan and 23 rural small tourism businesses produced some interesting single cases that were related to aspects of this chapter:

Copyright © 2009, IGI Global, distributing in print or electronic forms without written permission of IGI Global is prohibited.

- One business did not have a secure credit card facility – requesting clients to send their credit card details to them via regular e-mail.
- A number of businesses indicated that they only receive credit card payments via fax, not via the Internet. Some of these businesses did use online banking for payments and receipts.
- One interesting comment made by a participant was that the Internet provides the opportunity for employees to download 'inappropriate' content.
- In an example of BCM, one technically minded business owner hosted a Website within the business premises. To counter the potential of the Website server 'crashing' this owner also ran a backup server. The backup server could be switched to in the event of any problems to allow for seamless continuous Web presence operation for customers.

Wineries_PhDsurvey_04

This research PhD investigated Internet adoption by small to medium size (SME) wineries. The study developed an e-business model that identified activities relating to customer credit card transaction security. It was reported that an important consideration by many winery owners interviewed was that the winery Website needed to have a secure ordering feature - a feature that was associated with the purchasing endpoint for customers after an e-mail marketing campaign. The study found that various winery owners were highly conscious of the fact customers used credit cards to purchase products via their Websites. For example, one winery used the services of a third party company that not only provided Website security implementation for its Website sales, but also assisted the winery to claim a series of government endorsed taxation benefits. Another group of wineries used the online security service provided by a regional wine-industry portal, which was specifically established to allow these wineries to share resources such as secure e-business ordering - a task that would otherwise have fallen to individual wineries.

Other Studies

Information Security and Continuity in Small Businesses in the US (Keller, Powell, Horstmann, Predmore, & Crawford, 2005)

This article examines the security practices of 18 small businesses in a US City. In this study, 'small business' was taken to mean any business with less than 500 employees. Two thirds of the participating businesses that were interviewed had less than 250 employees. Whilst businesses of this size might seem beyond the

Copyright © 2009, IGI Global, distributing in print or electronic forms without written permission of IGI Global is prohibited.

scope of this book, it is still useful to examine their practices as over 80% of the businesses gave their business data a high value and it should perhaps be expected that they followed sound practice in protecting this asset.

Over half of the businesses noted that their main threat was from employees within the business – however, a factor of relevance to very small businesses is that the interviewees noted that this threat may not be intentional, but more likely from human error or accident. The next major areas of threat identified were from 'trojans' or computer viruses and hackers. Only one quarter of the businesses believed these to be a direct threat to the business – perhaps because of security measures that they already in place but possibly as they had not been affected directly by these threats.

One interesting aspect of the article is that it presents a series of 'best practice' activities that could be followed by small businesses to protect their systems and data – many of which have already been listed in this chapter. Whilst the businesses performed at differing levels for each of these, it may be useful to list the suggestions that they make (Keller et al., 2005):

- Install and properly configure a firewall
- Update software (to ensure the latest security threats identified by vendors have been rectified)
- Protect against viruses, worms and trojans
- Implement a strong password policy
- Implement physical security measures to protect computer assets
- Implement company policy and training
- Connect remote users securely (for instance, through a virtual private network)
- Lock down servers (for instance, limit what they can do and who has access to them).
- Implement identity services (to detect intruders).

Of the businesses that were interviewed, only e-mail virus protection and a firewall were implemented by all of the businesses.

Although the study did not directly address the idea of a business continuity plan, the interviewees were asked if they had an emergency action plan to recover lost information. Half of the interviewees indicated that they had such a plan, with a third suggesting that had a plan but that it was not fully developed.

Copyright © 2009, IGI Global, distributing in print or electronic forms without written permission of IGI Global is prohibited.

Legal Issues Associated with the Personalisation of Internet Applications in Europe (Schubert, Kummer, & Leimstoll, 2006)

In other chapters of this book we have discussed the notion of the use of computer and Internet based systems to profile customers. Schubert et al (2005) examine some of the legal issues associated with such practices by examining some scenarios that might be faced by SMEs when they implement such systems. The authors conducted a longitudinal study that commenced in 1999 in Switzerland and discuss the different laws that exist in Switzerland and the European Union that affect different aspects of such activities (such as laws relating to contracts, unfair competition, civil law, criminal law, protection of trade marks, data protection and so forth). One of the observations made in the article is that this situation is made more complex as businesses (even SMEs) engage with customers outside of their own region as new laws and interpretations come into play.

In a number of scenarios, the authors examine the following issues (amongst others):

*   A business would like to know how often pages are visited and the order in which pages are requested. Is this (anonymous) access permissible?
*   What if the business starts tracking Internet addresses with customer identities? [and subsequently traces these back to companies].
*   What if Website visitors are asked to offer an opinion about products or services – is it permissible to make this public (eg put it on the Website)?
*   What if the business wishes to publish content from *other sources* on its Website (the example the authors give is environmental protection information)?
*   If a business allows customers to use an online login facility, what measures does it have to take to store and use their personal data legally?
*   It may be possible for the business to build a profile of customers on the basis of various interactions they may have. What are the legal implications for storing these profiles?

The simple fact of the matter is that, according to Schubert et al (2005), the laws in some areas are stronger than others. For instance, they suggest that, in general, Swiss (and European) law related to data protection is *much* stronger than American law. The authors also suggest that the situation is more complicated when, as is the case with many SMEs, their Website is hosted externally (for instance, with their ISP).

Copyright © 2009, IGI Global, distributing in print or electronic forms without written permission of IGI Global is prohibited.

Summary of Our Studies and Other Studies

Some interesting aspects related to this chapter have come out these studies. Most small businesses that talked about securing data were aware of the need to develop strategies to manage this. These ranged from setting up secure systems themselves or using third party portals that had these checks and balances already in place. Another strategy was to avoid the *need* for credit card security by only allowing customers to fax credit card details to the business – something that we found to occur with many businesses throughout our studies. Most small businesses that discussed data security did show an awareness of the need to have suitable systems in place – with some admitting that they did not have the expertise to manage this. A few businesses had adopted strategies that did not appear to be too secure! Although not specifically asked, there was some evidence that backing up of files did occur, but it was not seen as a high priority in some businesses. Certainly, there was no evidence of recognition of the role that business continuity planning or governance could play in the Web presence in relation to the use of those terms – but there was some evidence to indicate that a small number of businesses are thinking about some longer term implications of policies that would fit into these categories.

TENETS – LESSONS FROM THE CHAPTER

There are a number of lessons from this chapter that can be applied by small businesses when considering the most appropriate means of hosting their Web presence. These are listed in Table 2.

CONCLUSION

Collectively this chapter serves to inform the small business operator on aspects of ICT governance, business continuity and security. In general, small business needs to be aware of the importance of managing any business risks associated with the failure or disruption of their ICT and Web presence and of the ethical and cultural implications of their actions. Furthermore, risk management involves adopting and implementing preventative measures in order to ameliorate the disruption of business activities should technology fail. Indeed, this chapter highlighted that risk management is an important business element that allows a firm to continue its operations in the times of unexpected adversity. The chapter also examined various issues associated with computer and Internet security, predominantly in relation to ensuring that a small business operator would be confident that not only its own

Copyright © 2009, IGI Global, distributing in print or electronic forms without written permission of IGI Global is prohibited.

Table 2. Governance, security, and privacy issues for small businesses

Theme	Feature/Factor	Consideration
Risk Management	Prevent	• High risk of occurrence, High impact • Put employee procedures in place – eg do not open executable files in email • Equipment – surge protectors, uninterruptible power supplies (UPS), restricted access (eg locks) • Software – virus protection; firewall • Check for encryption processes in transactions or secure communications • Put encryption processes in place where necessary
	Detect and Contain	• High risk of occurrence, Low impact • Put employee procedures in place – eg backup, offsite facilities • Software – virus protection, password protection • Check third party website backup processes • Check for identity verification • Put identify verification processes in place
	Manage	• Low risk of occurrence, High impact • Consider implementing aspects of a business continuity plan • Think of having an emergency backup website to switch to
	Ignore	• Low risk of occurrence, Low impact • No action
General	Privacy	• Implement a privacy policy • Check third party website privacy policies
	Cultural	• Design websites in a manner that is suitable for the diverse audiences it is targeting
	Copyright Law	• Gain permission to use website elements that are not owned by the business. • Consider protecting website material that has been created within the business with a patent or trademark. • Seek information on the applicable laws and jurisdictions that apply in the countries that a business's target audience is located.
	Import/Export Issues	• Be aware that Internet-based transactions and sales brings a new set of issues for the small business operator that should be investigated • Businesses may need to deal with geographically dispersed clients and will need to have a strategy in place for this.

information was protected, but that customer information derived via its Web presence was also safe and secure. Also explored in the chapter were aspects of Web presence that related to customer information privacy, applicable copyright law to Website material and import/export issues that may allow a business to deal with geographically dispersed clients.

Copyright © 2009, IGI Global, distributing in print or electronic forms without written permission of IGI Global is prohibited.

REFERENCES

Burgess, S., & Hill, R. 2004. Corporate Governance in Small Businesses. In *Standards for Corporate Governance: Companion Volume* (pp. 47-54). Australian Standards Association, Sydney, Australia.

Davison, A., Burgess, S., & Tatnall, A. (2003). *Internet Technologies and Business.* Data Publishing and Arramlu Publications, Melbourne, Australia.

Frenzel, C. W., & Frenzel, J. C. (2006). *Management of Information Technology.* 4th edn, Thomson Course Technology, Canada.

Haksever, C. (1996). Total quality management in the small business environment. *Business Horizons, 39*(2 (Mar/ Apr), 33.

Hill, R., & Burgess, S. (2003). Issues in Business Continuity Management.In M. Khosrow-Pour (Ed.), *Information Technology and Organizations - Trends, Issues, Challenges and Solutions: Proceedings of the 2003 Information Resources Management Association Conference.* Philadelphia, PA. Hershey, PA: Idea Group Publishing.

Hofstede, G. (2001). *Culture's Consequences: Comparing Values, Behaviors, Institutions, and Organisations Across Nations.* London: Sage Publications.

Holtsnider, B., & Jaffe, B. D. (2001). *IT Manager's Handbook: Getting your new job done.* Morgan Kaufmann.

Kaufman, J. (2005). *Unraveled: Culture and Web Design.* Kaufman, Joshua. Retrieved: 1/1/2008.

Keller, S., Powell, A., Horstmann, B., Predmore, C., & Crawford, M. (2005). Information Security Threats and Practices in Small Businesses. *Information Systems Management, 22*(2), 7-19.

Marcus, A. (2003). User-Interface Design and China: A Great Leap Forward. *Interactions, 10*(1), 21-25.

Marcus, A. (2001). Cross-Culture User Interface Design for Work, Home, Play and on the Way. *Association for Computing Machinery Special Interest Group (SIG) in Documentation Conference* (pp. 221-222). Santa Fe, New Mexico, USA: ACM.

Marcus, A., & Gould, E. W. (2000a) Crosscurrents: Cultural Dimensions and Global Web User-Interface Design. *Interactions, 7*(4), 33-46.

Copyright © 2009, IGI Global, distributing in print or electronic forms without written permission of IGI Global is prohibited.

Marcus, A., & Gould, E. W. (2000). Cultural Dimensions and Global Web User-Interface Design: What? So What? Now What? *Proceedings 6th Conference on Human Factors and the Web*. Austin, Texas: ACM.

Mitroff, I. (2001). *Managing Crises Before They Happen*. New York: AMA-COM.

Powell, T. (2002). *Web Design: the complete reference*. 2nd edition edn, Osborne/McGrawHill, Berkeley.

Schneider, G. P. (2007). *Electronic Commerce*. 7th edn, Course Technology, Boston, MA.

Schubert, P., Kummer, M., & Leimstoll, U. (2006). Legal Requirements for the Personalization of Commercial Internet Applications in Europe. *Journal of Organizational Computing & Electronic Commerce, 16*(3), 203-221.

Turban, E., Leidner, D., Mclean, E., & Wetherbe, J. (2008). *Information Technology Management: Transforming Organisations in the Digital Economy*. 6th edition ed. New York: John Wiley & Sons.

Würtz, E. (2005). A cross-cultural analysis of Websites from high-context cultures and low-context cultures. *Journal of Computer-Mediated Communication, 11*(3), Electronic Journal available http://jcmc.indiana.edu/vol11/issue1/wuertz.html.

Zahir, S., Dobing, B. A., & Hunter, M. G. (2003). Analysis of the cross-cultural dimensions of national Web portals. In S. Kamel *Managing globally with information technology* (pp. 36-49). Hershey, PA: IGI Publishing.

Copyright © 2009, IGI Global, distributing in print or electronic forms without written permission of IGI Global is prohibited.

Chapter X
Evaluating Web Presence Success

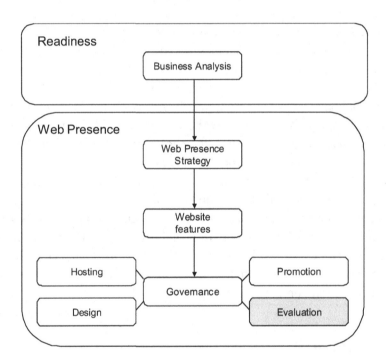

INTRODUCTION

This chapter examines the notion of how the success of a small business Web presence can be assessed. In doing so, there is initially a discussion of how a small business could classify its ICT expenses and attempt to match these outlays with

Copyright © 2009, IGI Global, distributing in print or electronic forms without written permission of IGI Global is prohibited.

any expected revenue streams. The latter part of the chapter, discusses the different approaches a small business operator can use to investigate and evaluate the success of its Web presence.

THINK ABOUT WEB PRESENCE SUCCESS EARLY

It is important for a small business owner/manager to start thinking about the success of the Web presence, and how that will be measured, when the Web presence is being initially considered – that is, at the time when the decision is being to made to actually have a Web presence. This may not be possible for many small businesses that already have some type of Web presence, but many of the concepts that will be discussed here can also be applied retrospectively.

We discussed the different strategies that can incorporate ICTs in Chapter IV, as well as discussing some techniques that can be used for ICT investment appraisal. In this chapter we will expand on that discussion.

Most small businesses have traditionally viewed their ICT investments from a *cost* perspective. That is, any ICTs have been considered as being a business adjunct that assists in *improving operational efficiencies* - without necessarily contributing directly to *adding value* to the products or services.

When talking with small businesses, one thing that we have noticed in our recent research projects is that the majority of them want to talk about their use of the Internet, be it about the power of e-mail as a communication medium or the development of their Web presence. In recent times there has been a notable and *consistent* reference by small businesses to their ICTs as if the technology directly relates to various elements of their products or services – thus, we have noticed a shift in focus in relation to the role that ICTs can play.

ICT EVALUATION

In previous chapters we have stressed that it *is* important to consider why any investment might be undertaken by a small business - an issue that needs to be considered reasonably early on in the decision-making process to adopt ICTs.

With respect to ICTs, the small business operator will predominantly invest in this type of technology allowing them to improve and enhance:

- **Communications:** Provides a conduit to facilitate information and message flows between the business and important partners,

Copyright © 2009, IGI Global, distributing in print or electronic forms without written permission of IGI Global is prohibited.

- **Operational efficiencies:** Perhaps through lowering costs or delivery faster business processes),
- **Sales turnover:** Potentially through added value, and/or
- **Information quality:** That contributes to more informed decision making.

Clearly, the introduction of a Web presence, as an ICT, can assist the business in any or all of these noted areas. However, as we have previously encountered in the other chapters of the book, this all comes at a cost. There are obvious expenses, such as the direct cost of hosting and maintaining the Web presence, possible costs in relation to the amount of traffic that might be generated from being online and the cost of equipment (such as modems). There are also the less obvious expenses - such as the time taken by employees to maintain (update) content on the Web presence. As with other business expenditure, it is important to keep an eye on these expenses. Moreover, it is necessary to know the potential costs that can be incurred with a Web presence (such as costs for Website traffic) so that there are no unpleasant surprises after the Web presence has been implemented.

There are various reasons for keeping control of ICT expenditures in the small business environment - allowing the operator to have some idea of what the costs will be and importantly, having a means of measuring them. Some of these reasons are:

- There is a legal (and often) corporate reason for doing so. Most small businesses have to file regular business returns (such as taxation returns).
- Its does provide some control over the current activities of the business and helps to assist with planning for future activities. Most importantly, it helps the business to set the price for products and services it will be selling.
- It does help to explain unexpected occurrences – for instance, a cost 'blowout' that may occur due to increased Website activity may not be perceived as a problem if there has also been increased sales as a result of this activity.

An important thing to remember when measuring the success of a Web presence is that investments associated with online activity that reflect success can be measured in a number of ways. This multiple view of what success embodies needs to be considered by the small business operator - one that will include more factors than just revenue and expenses to be evaluated.

Another consideration that small business owner/managers need to be aware of is that not all of the benefits and costs associated with ICT investments may be *quantifiable*. For instance, how is it possible to measure the business benefits that arise from a system that provides more accurate or new forms of information that assists with important decision making? Ahituv and Neumann (1990) have suggested

Copyright © 2009, IGI Global, distributing in print or electronic forms without written permission of IGI Global is prohibited.

an approach similar to the following that could be followed when determining ICT benefits and costs:

1. The most ideal situation is to be able to express them in dollars.
2. Where this is not possible, measure them in a quantifiable manner that can be *converted* to dollars. For instance, if a new system results in the saving of employee hours it might be possible to convert these to dollars and cents by working out how many hours are saved and then multiplying these by an hourly rate to get an amount in dollars.
3. Where it is not possible to convert them to dollars at least try to *quantify* them by some measure. For instance, if a new system delivers faster information for decision making – *how much* faster is that information delivered (such as, we are now getting our information *two days* earlier)?
4. Where this is not possible, try to describe the benefits and costs and fully as possible.

At the end of this process, all of this information is provided to decision makers to help them determine how successful a system is (if it has been implemented) or could be (if they are considering investing in it).

In the next section of the chapter we will examine the factors affecting the expense side of the ICT equation.

Classifying ICT Expenses

In this section we will examine how some larger businesses classify their ICT expenses and consider those techniques that may be useful in the small business environment. However, it is initially useful to consider some of the different types of expenses that a business can incur.

Fixed and Variable Costs

A *fixed cost* is a cost that will be incurred by a business irrespective of the level of business activity that occurs. From a Web presence viewpoint, an example of a fixed cost would be a Website hosting service that charges one annual price to host the business Website. Another example is where an ISP charges a set fee per month (perhaps as part of a contract) to allow a business to access e-mail and search for information on the Internet – irrespective of the number of e-mails that are sent or the amount of traffic incurred during Web searches.

Copyright © 2009, IGI Global, distributing in print or electronic forms without written permission of IGI Global is prohibited.

A *variable cost* is a cost that varies according to some type of business activity or transaction. For instance, if a small business has a shopping cart facility set up with a third party provider, it might be charged a set fee *per transaction*. Variable costs are often the easiest to consider when matching up with a Web presence where the number of sales are a measure of success. If mostly variable costs could be matched directly against sales then it is easier to work out what margin the business makes per sale.

Even so, if fixed and variable costs can be directly related to a particular sale item then it is relatively easy to determine the level of sales that are needed to put the business into a profit situation – that is, where the (sales price less variable costs) multiplied by the number of sales equals or exceeds the level of fixed costs. We will now examine a simple example of this.

The example in Figure 1 shows the effect over a financial period where a business sells a single product at a price of $2.50, incurs a variable cost per each unit sold of $1.10 and has fixed costs of $5,000 for the period. The graph shows the effect on fixed costs, total costs and sales revenue with different levels of sales (as represented on the horizontal axis). As expected, the *fixed costs* line remains constant at $5,000 for the entire period. However, for every unit sold, total costs increase by $1.10. Thus, when sales reach 2,000 units, total costs are $7,200 (that is, fixed costs of $5,000 plus $2,200 variable costs [calculated by multiplying 2,000 units sold by $1.10]).

If the business does not sell any units at all, it makes a loss of $5,000 (the amount of fixed costs which are incurred, no matter what). Its variable margin per sale can be calculated by subtracting the variable costs ($1.10) from the sales price ($2.50) per unit sold. To avoid a loss, the business must sell enough units so that its total variable margin exceeds its fixed costs. In other words, the 'breakeven' point can be calculated by:

Figure 1. Example of sales revenue vs fixed/ variable costs

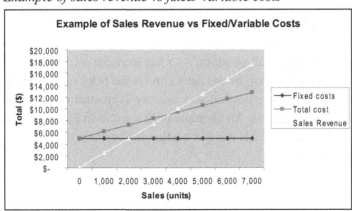

Copyright © 2009, IGI Global, distributing in print or electronic forms without written permission of IGI Global is prohibited.

Number of units to sell to reach breakeven = fixed costs/(sales price – variable cost per unit)

That is: 5,000/(2.50 – 1.10), which is 5,000/1.40, which equals 3,571.43 units.

Obviously, the business is not going to be selling 3,571.43 units. If it sells 3,571 units it makes a very small loss. If it sells 3,572 units it makes a very small profit. What the business might conclude is that it needs to sell approximately 3,600 units to reach a breakeven point. The breakeven point is represented in Figure 1 where the *sales revenue* line intersects the *total cost* line.

Of course, this example is quite a simple one and does take into account a number of factors that we are about to discuss, plus others that we will not discuss (such as product returns, different pricing strategies for different customers, depreciation and taxation effect, and so forth). However, it is useful to explain the concept of fixed versus variable costs.

However, life is not always (or often) that simple. There are a number of things to complicate this somewhat simple model of costs. The first one is that not all costs can be easily classified as being fixed or variable. Some costs have both fixed and variable components. For instance, a Website hosting service might charge a fee of $1,000 per month to host a Website, but then an extra $100 per month for each gigabyte (gb) of traffic on the Website. Although the cost of hosting can be easily divided into a fixed and variable component, the variable costs *do not* relate to directly to the sale price, but to Website traffic levels. There *may* be some relationship between the level of Website traffic and the level of resultant sales, but how to work this out (if there is any)? If there is a relationship, it is possible, but it starts to get complex.

The next level of complexity occurs where the hosting service charges on a *sliding scale,* charging different amounts where different levels of traffic are achieved. For instance, the hosting service may charge $1,000 per month for hosting, and then provide 5gb of traffic with that for free. Upon reaching 5gb of traffic, the business is charged $500. Upon reaching 10gb of traffic, it is charged $1,000 and so forth. The difficulty here is that the business is charged the same amount for 6gb of traffic as it is for 9gb of traffic – so has to make some type of determination of what traffic levels will be so that it can set the price of its offerings. To add a level of complication, the hosting service may even start to offer discounts for higher levels of transactions. An example of this is credit fees, where lower rates can sometimes be negotiated if it is known that the business might generate a large number of transactions.

Copyright © 2009, IGI Global, distributing in print or electronic forms without written permission of IGI Global is prohibited.

These types of costs are often known as *semi-variable costs*. As has been seen, not only do they contain some type of fixed and variable mix, the variable component may not vary according to sales levels.

To give an idea of the complexity involved in keeping track of the costs associated with setting up a Web presence, one of the authors (Burgess 2001) examined the costs for small businesses associated with setting up different types of Websites, examining a number of different options (such as using a free Web hosting service, services offered by specialist ISPs and online options offered by other businesses). It turned out that different service providers were optimal depending upon the type of Website that was required. For instance, for a simple brochure style Website, the free service was the most cost effective. However, once the site requirements became more complex, such as with online ordering and payment options, other service providers became more attractive – and the choices amongst these even varied according to the number of sales transactions that were made. This is because some of the services had higher setup (fixed) fees, but lower 'per transaction' fees. Thus, if there were a small number of transactions it was better to select the providers with the lower setup fees. However, as the number of transactions increased it was better for the small business to select the provider with the higher setup costs but lower per transaction fees. Other costs that emerged were specific fees for setting up online shopping carts and the fees that the banks charged for credit card transactions. This study also examined Websites that were tailored specifically for small businesses – which were generally more expensive – but of course can be tailored specifically for the business.

Now, we do not wish to make this all too complex for small business owner/ managers to keep control of, as that would defeat the purpose of this exercise. But it is useful for owner/managers to have an idea of the types of costs that can occur to give them an idea of how they might be able to deal with them and perhaps to suggest to them that they should look very closely at all of the costs associated with setting up a Web presence and match them with the type of Web presence they would like to have.

Matching ICT Expenses to Revenue

How does a business classify its ICT expenses? Should they all be just grouped together? Should expenses related to the online presence be separated from expenses related to more traditional ICT usage, such as word processing and accounting? Should ICT expenses related to a particular marketing strategy be assigned to only the revenues resulting from that specific strategy? Our experience tells us that the traditional approach that small business owner/managers use is to group all or most of the ICT expenses that can be identified into a single unit of cost - treating this

Copyright © 2009, IGI Global, distributing in print or electronic forms without written permission of IGI Global is prohibited.

amount almost as a fixed cost. Some businesses have even avoided the irregular cost of purchasing a new computer every few years by leasing their ICT equipment - which, depending on where the small business is located (and if the option of leasing is even available) can have different impacts on the business profitability by making the expense a direct cost rather than an expense based on depreciation of ICT assets.

However, we do know that small business operators tend to view their use of the Internet, and their Web presence in particular, as something different from other traditional uses of ICTs, so it might be useful to consider the different types of ways they can classify these expenses for the purpose of determining how successful they are.

We hope that if we have pointed out one thing in this book, it is that the cost of ICTs and a Web presence in particular goes beyond just the cost of equipment and 'connecting up'. Many large businesses divide their ICT costs into a number of different categories, such as ICT infrastructure, ICT maintenance and special business projects that incorporate ICTs.

ICT infrastructure and *ICT maintenance* costs relate to those ICT costs that are considered to be vital for operational aspects of the business. Such costs often cannot be traced to a particular product being sold or marketing campaign being conducted. For instance, most small businesses will have one or more computers that run word processing, spreadsheet and accounting software applications. These computers will be used for common operational activities irrespective of any other business activities that may relate to new product development, service offerings or any marketing campaigns. If the computers are networked together (as this is seen as being essential for business operations) then the hardware and software required to set up the network is regarded as being ICT infrastructure. Expenditure on 'office' type software, accounting software and protective software (such as for virus protection), could also be treated as infrastructure. If the business brings in a consultant to do things like 'keep the system' running, make sure the network is operational, update virus software and so forth, then this could also be considered as a maintenance expense. Usually a business will be able to make some type of reasonable guess at the level of ICT infrastructure and maintenance costs in a specific year, particularly if they have a hardware replacement schedule or maintenance contract in place should a problem arise. The typical classification of most ICT infrastructure and maintenance costs is that it is probably suitable for small businesses to continue to treat them as fixed costs and worry about covering them (with other fixed costs) by making enough sales for their total variable margin to offset them.

In larger businesses, the measurement of 'success' related to ICT infrastructure can be difficult to quantify – as direct sales do not result from their use (of course,

Copyright © 2009, IGI Global, distributing in print or electronic forms without written permission of IGI Global is prohibited.

it is usually accepted that some benefits will indirectly result from these activities as they lead to improved communication, better decision making and so forth). So, how do larger businesses measure their success? It is usually done in a combination of different ways, such as:

- How well overall yearly costs relate to the budgeted cost.
- Whether the system is performing as expected (that is, there are no bottlenecks caused by things such as slow computer processing).
- Whether employees are willing to use the system and are comfortable using it.
- Whether there are identifiable business benefits - benefits such as accessing new types of information that facilitates management decision making, or providing information much faster than previously, or improving intra-organisational communications.

In very small, or micro businesses, the owner/manager may typically have some notion of how their computing investments might be performing. In the slightly larger small business - say, with ten or more employees - the manager may have to rely on office personnel to provide the feedback on the operation of the computer system. Whilst small businesses will not need to keep control of ICT infrastructure costs and performance at the level of their larger counterparts, it is still important for them to consider some of the points we have raised here.

The other major type of ICT cost that a business can encounter is when they use ICTs to conduct specific business projects. The example previously given related to a marketing campaign that the operator might also be able to relate to activities such as a specific product or service releases or even the launch of a Website. In larger businesses these types of projects are often championed by someone outside of the ICT department and supported by ICTs. Of course, the likelihood of different departments or sections existing in a small business is unlikely with a typical small business have employees that are skilled across a number of areas of the business. Where computing-based projects can be directly related to increased sales it may be possible to identify marginal gains or losses associated with the project - allowing an assessment using some of the techniques documented in the Business Strategy and Planning chapter - techniques such as payback period, net present value and/or internal rate of return.

The key with these projects is that they assume that the ICT infrastructure is already in place within the business and thus any changes that the new initiative brings can be measured according to any incremental sales that are achieved and incremental costs that are incurred. The reason why this can fit well with a Web presence is that it *may* be possible to identify incremental sales gained via the Web

Copyright © 2009, IGI Global, distributing in print or electronic forms without written permission of IGI Global is prohibited.

presence (such as those through a shopping cart) to be mapped with some of the incremental costs of having Web presence (that is, those ICT costs that are incurred in addition to the usual infrastructure costs). Consequently, there is opportunity that these incremental cost/sales associated with the Web presence can be directly compared to determine the marginal contribution of the initiative. Note that we stated it *may* be possible to identify incremental sales – if the Web presence also leads to increased sales via traditional means then it may be more difficult to assess its incremental contribution. For instance, if a customer researches information about a particular product on a Website and the purchases it via a retail outlet it may be difficult to establish what contribution the Website made. Of course, the other similarity between the Web presence in a small business and similar types of business ICT projects in larger businesses is that the existence of the Web presence usually relies on the small business having some ICT infrastructure already in place (such as computers and modems) to link with the online world.

The bottom line is that for some small businesses the revenue and expenses involved in setting up a Web presence may be considered as a business ICT project and it may be possible, at least to some extent, to work out its incremental contribution to the business.

When asked about the contribution that ICTs make to their business, small business owner/ managers in the past have typically said they make a useful or adequate contribution. In our recent studies we have found, as small business owner/managers are keener to talk about the effects of the Internet on their businesses, more of them are talking about their ICTs (especially e-mail use) as being *essential* to their business. However, to finish up this section, it may be worth examining the reasons why ICT projects often fail in larger businesses that we have also observed in small businesses:

- *Lack of planning.* The business has introduced ICTs without adequately thinking about what they are actually intending to use them for.
- *Inadequate risk analysis.* This is more related to the previous chapter. The business has not considered the types of things that can go wrong when ICTs are introduced and thus not had adequate plans in place when problems occur.
- *Underestimating cost and the time taken to implement ICTs.* We have already addressed this problem enough in this book.
- *Lack of adequate specifications.* It is important to make sure that the solutions that are being considered are adequate enough for what the business desires. For instance, ensure when signing a long term Website hosting deal that provision is made for adequate Website traffic.

Copyright © 2009, IGI Global, distributing in print or electronic forms without written permission of IGI Global is prohibited.

- *Lack of skills.* All of the pieces are in place for the project to succeed, but the business has not devoted enough employee time, or employees lack the skills, to manage the ICTs effectively.

MEASURING WEB PRESENCE SUCCESS

As previously indicated, small business can achieve a range of benefits after the successful adoption of ICTs. Some of these benefits include (Barba-Sánchez et al 2007):

- Enhancing the productivity and effectiveness of some business processes.
- Encouraging adoption of new organisational, strategic and/or managerial models.
- Opening up new markets.
- Improving the level of skills within the business (for example, through training for ICT use), increasing efficiency and efficacy.

The discussion in previous sections has predominantly (but not exclusively) discussed the identification of ICT costs so that they can be matched in some way against revenue to determine the contribution of ICTs. However, as we pointed out, this is not always an easy thing to achieve.

We feel that it is important at this stage to briefly revisit the earlier stages of the book and remind the reader that the reason for a Web presence (and any ICT usage) should be able to be traced back to the business aims – which may not necessarily be dominated by profit motives. In businesses where one of the major aims is to maintain or improve the lifestyle of the participants, it is quite reasonable to assume that any extra time gained by the business through the efficiencies of ICTs might not be reinvested in further profit making activities – but perhaps in activities such as taking more time to read a book or relax in a hammock!

Measuring Success of ICTs in SMEs

We do know from our own research that small businesses generally do not often go out of their way to assess the benefits of their own ICT usage. We have already mentioned that benefits are difficult to measure, whilst costs may be difficult to identify, categorize and subsequently quantify.

Much of the preceding text in this chapter has aimed at identifying and matching ICT benefits and costs that can be quantified in dollar terms. However, as was noted earlier, not all benefits and costs fall into this category.

Copyright © 2009, IGI Global, distributing in print or electronic forms without written permission of IGI Global is prohibited.

In a review of literature related to measuring the benefits of ICTs in small businesses, Burgess (2002) identified three methods or approaches that have traditionally
been used to evaluate their success:

- *Measures of system usage.* These measures centre on examining data that
  has automatically been generated from ICT systems – such as the number of
  transactions generated, the number of reports generated and so forth. Systems
  usage is perhaps the easiest to measure, but does not always relate to improved
  productivity or performance.
- *Impact upon organisational performance.* As we have already stated, this
  can be difficult to measure as ICT systems are often integrated with other
  organisational factors (such as improved businesses processes) that can affect
  performance. One of the ways that small businesses can get around this is
  to treat ICT infrastructure and maintenance costs and ICT specific business
  project costs separately. For many small businesses, treating all ICT costs as
  infrastructure or maintenance (fixed) costs is an adequate manner in which
  to treat them.
- *Measures of user satisfaction.* This is the most common method used to assess the level of ICT success – by asking users or even owner/managers their
  opinion of the success of a new system. However, such measures are tied to
  expectations. Users or owner/managers with low expectations of a system may
  rate its performance higher than those with higher expectations of the benefits
  that can be provided. Many research projects that have attempted to evaluate
  the success of ICT projects have surveyed the information satisfaction levels
  of the owner/ manager (Caldeira and Ward 2002).

Measures of systems usage and user satisfaction cannot necessarily be easily
quantified in dollar terms. Other benefits that a Website might offer, such as improved
flexibility for customers in placing online orders or increased value for products and
services provided by improved online product support, are not easily measurable.
As mentioned earlier, Ahituv and Neumann (1990) suggested that the next step is to
try to measure benefits and costs in some way that can be *converted* to dollar terms.
For instance, when purchasing, customers might be asked if any of the Website
features contributed to them making the decision to purchase – perhaps providing
an estimate of the sales gained though the addition of a particular Website feature.
Perhaps the introduction of an online product catalogue that is linked to the business
product database might provide benefits in that some employee time is saved from
having to update details on the Website. It might be possible to quantify this time
into hours and subsequently into dollars saved. If this cannot occur then Ahituv
and Neumann suggest that it is useful to measure the benefit or cost in *some way.*

Copyright © 2009, IGI Global, distributing in print or electronic forms without written permission of IGI Global
is prohibited.

An example of this is a measure of systems usage. More potential customers may be accessing a Website due to improved features – although it may not be possible to translate this to direct (quantifiable) benefits it is useful to know what new levels of Website patronage there are (more on this in the next section).

Specific Measures for a Web Presence

There are some measures that are specific to a Web presence other than directly measuring the revenue that small businesses can adopt to assist them to evaluate the success of their Web presence. As we have seen in earlier chapters, many Web presence features and promotion activities are closely interlinked with each other - some having a dual role of assisting with business activities and also promoting the business at the same time. There are various other sophisticated techniques that can be used, but here we will list some of the simple and effective techniques that can be used:

- **Hit counter:** One of the most common techniques is to place a 'hit counter' on the Website. These counters measure the number of visitors to a Website site. An ISP can usually arrange this for you inexpensively. *However, 'hits' is a crude measure and is often not highly valued.* It can, however, provide a small business with an indication when there is a surge of interest in the Website. For instance, a small business owner/manager might want to judge the effect of a promotion campaign that involves the Website.
- **Traffic log file analysis:** A more sophisticated technique is to analyse the activities on a small business Website through the use of software that examines traffic log files. Traffic log files can be supplied by ISPs. The files look quite complex, but ISPs can typically direct their clients to software that can analyse the files and provide them with information such as when (time and date) Web surfers have visited their Website, what typical paths they have taken through the Website (that is, which pages they have visited and the order they have taken), which pages are more popular, and which outside Website they have come from (such as a search engine, third party portal and so forth). This last feature is particularly useful if the small business has set up features on other Websites that links potential visitors to their Website. Sometimes your ISP will provide their clients with these reports as they run the analysis software themselves. Small businesses should approach ISPs to help them with these statistics – but otherwise would probably source external expertise in setting this up (after that it is quite easy to use). If the small business uses the services of any third party Website as part of its Web presence then it should request (or even demand) that these or similar reports are provided so that

Copyright © 2009, IGI Global, distributing in print or electronic forms without written permission of IGI Global is prohibited.

it can analyse its traffic through those services. More recently, applications such as Google™ Analytics (http://www.google.com/analytics/) have become available to help small businesses determine what traffic is flowing through their Websites (amongst other services they offer).

- **Ranking in search engines:** The idea behind this measure is that the business tries to maintain a high ranking in popular search engines by incorporating key words into the Website (refer Chapter VIII) or by paying for a sponsored link to appear on the search engine. In both instance the idea is to be ranked higher when users type certain combinations of words into the search engine.
- **Treat Web presence sales and costs as an ICT business expense:** See the discussion of this earlier in this chapter.
- **Ask your customers:** Sometimes your customers may purchase the products and services of a small business *after* they have read about them on its Web presence. Small businesses should take the opportunity to regularly ask 'offline' customers about their Web presence – perhaps through a survey or a few questions when they make a purchase or even through online or offline promotions where they are offered an incentive in return for a little information!
- **Time saved:** It is possible that the Web presence may help to save some employee time. For instance, a small business may find that its employees have more free time to pursue other business activities because it has added a Frequently Asked Questions section to its Website, or put extra information there about its products and services. The small business owner/manager should regularly check with employees to see if particular Website features that have been adopted have had an effect on their day-to-day activities (positive or negative).

OUR PREVIOUS STUDIES

Accountant_07

In our interviews with accounting practices we spent some time discussing with them how they measured the success of the Websites. The different ways of measuring success was often dependant on a particular practice's rationale for developing the Website. Most practices suggested more than one way of measuring the success of the Website. These are summarized in Table 1.

It is interesting to note that the creation of new business was generally not regarded as a determinant of success on its own. Some practices, for example, usually gain new clients from partner referrals. For these practices, *positive feedback*

Copyright © 2009, IGI Global, distributing in print or electronic forms without written permission of IGI Global is prohibited.

Table 1. Determinants of success

Determinant	Small Practices	Medium Practices
Number/Tracking of Hits	36%	57%
Number of new clients	55%	29%
Client Feedback	45%	29%
Number of new employees	27%	29%
Number of new enquiries	0%	29%

from current clients was deemed to be a more accurate measure of the Website's success. Another partner commented that their Website's success is, amongst other factors, judged by the Website's capacity to *discourage* individual clients who do not match their business target group. This saves them time by not having to deal with their queries!

For another suburban firm, success was measured more simply: "If success is sending information to clients, then we are successful". Moreover, one practice did not monitor the success of its Website at all: "Conducting actual business and doing it well is more important to us, even if we do get the occasional remark about our Website."

Both small and medium sized practices employed a number of strategies to measure the success of their Websites.

Tourism_04

We asked our 59 interviewees in small tourism enterprises in metropolitan and rural Australia specifically about how they judged the success of their Websites. The most common form of measure was the level of increased custom, followed by customer feedback, the effect the Website had on normal business bookings and even the number of *hits* on the Website.

Here are some typical comments that were made by interviewees. Note that although we only asked about their Website, there were some instances where the interviewees referred to third party sites (the extended Web) as part of their Web presence:

- "We don't have a sophisticated measuring system hence we rely on guess-work."
- "It is very hard to measure the success of the Website. You can't tell where customers found out about us. I never measure the success by the number of hits because they don't really mean anything. You may have hundreds of hits a day but if you don't have any bookings they mean nothing".

Copyright © 2009, IGI Global, distributing in print or electronic forms without written permission of IGI Global is prohibited.

- "I can track where people found out about the business through the enquiry form but haven't had time to analyse the data".
- "I don't know whether sales increase is associated directed from the Website. I don't have a proper plan to measure it."
- "Our consultant provides us with statistics on the measurement of the success of Website once a fortnight and a report in the form of a bar chart of all statistics monthly. The statistics include: ranking of our homepage, number of hits and number of inquiries via the internet".
- "We have a 'how did you hear of us' on our online form and have found that many people say [*popular search engines mentioned here*]"
- "Our ISP has comprehensive summaries – hits, countries people come from, which link they have come from, browser type and Windows version"
- "It is much quicker on the Web - saves phone time"
- Reduced labour time because we can now get off the phone and tell people to look at the Website"
- "Our ISP provides statistics – how long people stay on each section of the Website"

We also asked interviewees a simple question - Do you think the site was successful? Over 80% of interviewees in both rural and metropolitan areas felt that their Website was successful. Some typical comments were:

- "Within 48 hours from when the Website was set up we had two enquiries from US. I was astounded"
- "A lot of work is done over the Internet rather than manually. It saves a lot of time and labour".
- "What I hoped would happen did not happen"
- "I have almost given up on the Website. Intermediaries [third party Websites] have taken over".

Other Studies

How Different Website Goals can Affect the Determination of Success (Schaupp, Fan, & Belanger, 2006)

In this study the authors carry out a study of the factors that lead to the determination of Website success. An interesting aspect of the study from the point of view of this chapter is that the authors recognise that success can be very difficult to determine. In the first instance, they suggest that the determination of success may vary from whichever stakeholder's viewpoint is taken – the user of the Website or

Copyright © 2009, IGI Global, distributing in print or electronic forms without written permission of IGI Global is prohibited.

the provider of the Website. Also, the goals and objectives of the Website might mean that the notion of its success can vary. The example they provide is that the goals of an e-commerce Website might be to sell products and maximise profits, whereas the goal of a search engine would be to quickly gather relevant links in the timeliest manner.

Schaupp et al (2006) suggest that from the business perspective the definition of success is the ability of the Website to create ongoing relationships with customers, and that customer satisfaction levels in relation to use of the Website will play a role in determining its overall success.

The study outlined in this paper attempts to build on other well-known information systems models that have been used to determine systems success to identify the factors that may lead to Website satisfaction by customers and the eventual intention to reuse the Website. In doing this they surveyed the users of two different types of Websites (with two different objectives) – and information search Website (where the purpose of the Website is to allow searches for specific types of information - 199 survey responses) and an online community Website (where the purpose of the Website was to allow users to gather and share information on topics of interest – 1837 responses). The main finding of the research (carried out using structured equation modelling), was that there *were differences* in the factors that lead to overall Website satisfaction and subsequent intention to re-use the Website.

For both Websites, the quality of information and the perceived effectiveness of the Website were factors that lead to Website satisfaction. However, *system quality* was only identified as an important factor in the information search Website – highlighting the need for a Website tat was easy to use. In the case of the online community Website, *social influence* was identified as an important factor – where the perceptions of the users' peers were seen to be an important factor in satisfaction and subsequent reuse of the Website.

One of the major findings of this research project is that Website developers need to consider the goals and objectives of the Website before considering how to measure its success.

Updating an Information Systems Success Model for E-Commerce (DeLone & McLean, 2004)

In this article, the authors consider how their own well-known model for measuring the success of information systems might be applied in the e-commerce era.

They suggest that the popularity of e-commerce has not changed the basic fundamentals of economics – long term success or failure is determined is determined by the ability to generate positive net revenues and the fundamental role of ICTs is still to facilitate business transactions and provide relevant information to decision

Copyright © 2009, IGI Global, distributing in print or electronic forms without written permission of IGI Global is prohibited.

makers. They do suggest that customers (internal to the business and external) are now included as decision-makers.

From this point of view, the authors maintain that their model can still be applied. Three factors, *information quality, system quality and service quality* will affect one of both of *intention to use/actual use* and *user satisfaction,* each of which can lead to *net benefits* from the system. The model is more complex than this, but this explanation will be enough for us now, as the interesting aspect from the viewpoint of this chapter is that the authors identify the types of e-commerce factors that can make up information quality, system quality and service quality. They suggest the following (DeLone and McLean 2004):

- *Information quality* covers Web content – which should be **personalised, complete, relevant, easy to understand and secure** – to encourage prospective buyers to make purchases and return later.
- *System quality* measures the desired characteristics of the system. These include **usability, availability, reliability, adaptability and response (download) times.**
- *Service quality* relates to the **level of overall support** provided by service providers. Poor support of users (as customers - internal or external to the business) will translate into lost customers and lost sales.

The items listed in boldface type help to highlight those factors that can help to contribute to overall Website success. The authors go on to present two case studies showing how the new e-commerce environment can be measured using the various aspects of their model.

Summary of our Studies and Other Studies

One of the interesting aspects that came out of these two studies is the observation that a variety of techniques were used to judge the success of the Web presence. These ranged from relatively involved or structured techniques through to a more intangible approach - intuition or a 'feel' about how successful the Web presence was. We found that there were a small number of businesses that judged the success of their Web presence against what their initial goals or aims - some evidence that businesses are considering overall Web presence strategy in their planning. Another common observation was that many businesses found it quite difficult to actually measure the success of the Web presence - which is something that we have alluded to in this chapter. Finally, there were a number of instances where small businesses were surprised by the impact of their Web presence on the business - in some cases these were pleasant surprises and involved queries from customer

Copyright © 2009, IGI Global, distributing in print or electronic forms without written permission of IGI Global is prohibited.

markets they had not considered. More negative experiences included some cases were a minimal number of new customers were attracted to the business after initiating a Web presence.

TENETS – LESSONS FROM THE CHAPTER

There are a number of lessons from this chapter that can be applied by small businesses when considering how they should measure their Web presence success. These are listed in Table 2.

CONCLUSION

This chapter discussed how a small business might measure the success of its Web presence. It is our observation that many small businesses lack an awareness of how to go about evaluating their Web presence and ICT use. Moreover, a central tenet in this chapter should be one of emphasising the importance of applying some form of evaluation process to a business's ICT adoption and use. Indeed, we commenced the chapter by highlighting that the small business operator should clearly thinking about how the success of the Web presence will be measured as early as

Table 2. Measuring Web presence success issues for small businesses

Chapter topic	Factor	Consideration
Be Prepared		• Think about how the success of the web presence investment will be determined as early as possible – certainly before the Web presence is implemented and hopefully before any contracts are signed!
ICT investments	Business aims	• Think about how the Website will specifically address the aims of the business – and design the success measures around those aims
	Quantify	• Convert web presence benefits and costs into dollars where possible • If not, try to measure the benefit or cost in some manner
	Classifying ICT expenses	• Consider the types of web presence expenses that occur – are they fixed, variable or semi-variable? If they are variable, do they vary according to sales or some other measure?
	Type of ICT expense	• Are the web presence expenses being considered as ICT infrastructure and maintenance costs or as ICT business project costs (or perhaps even a combination of these)?
Measuring Web Presence success	Identify tools to help measure website performance	• Website 'hit' counters • Log file analysis to track website traffic • Search engine ranking • Treat Web presence expenses as ICT business expenses • Employee time saved • Survey customers

Copyright © 2009, IGI Global, distributing in print or electronic forms without written permission of IGI Global is prohibited.

possible in the implementation process. The chapter then continued to highlight and discuss some of the methods and techniques that could be used to determine how ICT costs and revenue might be calculated. The cost-revenue evaluation can at times be difficult to achieve. Finally, we offered some specific hints as to how the success of the Web presence might be evaluated.

This chapter is the last of Part Three of this book, which represented the Implementation and evaluation aspects of the small business Web presence.

REFERENCES

Ahituv, N., & Neumann, S. (1990). *Principles of Information Systems in Management.* 3rd edn, Wm C Brown, USA.

Barba-Sánchez, V., del Pilar Martínez-Ruiz, M., & Jiménez-Zarco, A. I. (2007). Drivers, Benefits and Challenges of ICT Adoption by Small and Medium Sized Enterprises (SMEs): A Literature Review. *Problems & Perspectives in Management,* (1), 103-114.

Burgess, S. (2002). Information Technology in Small Business: Issues and Challenges. In S. Burgess (Ed.), *Information Technology in Small Business: Challenges and Solutions* (pp. 1-17). Hershey, PA: Idea Group Publishing.

Burgess, S., & Schauder, D. (2001). Web Site Development Options for Australian Small Businesses. In M. Khosrow-Pour (Ed.), *Managing Information Technology in a Global Economy: Proceedings of the 2001 Information Resources Management Association Conference.* Toronto, Canada. Hershey, PA: Idea Group Publishing.

Caldeira, M. M., & Ward, J. M. (2002). Understanding the successful adoption and use of IS/IT in SMEs: an explanation from Portuguese manufacturing industries. *Information Systems Journal, 12*(2), 121-152.

Costello, P., Sloane, A., & Moreton, R. (2007). IT Evaluation Frameworks -- Do They Make a Valuable Contribution? A Critique of Some of the Classic Models for use by SMEs. *Electronic Journal of Information Systems Evaluation, 10*(1), 57-64.

DeLone, W. H., & McLean, E. R. (2004). Measuring e-Commerce Success: Applying the DeLone & McLean Information Systems Success Model. *International Journal of Electronic Commerce,* 9(1). 31-47

Lin, K. H. C., Lin, C., & Hsiu-Yuan, T. (2005). IS/IT Investment Evaluation and Benefit Realization Practices in Taiwanese SMEs. *Journal of Information Science & Technology, 2*(4), 44-71.

Copyright © 2009, IGI Global, distributing in print or electronic forms without written permission of IGI Global is prohibited.

Schaupp, L. C., Fan, W., & Belanger, F. (2006). Determining success for different Website goals. *Proceedings of the 39th Hawaii International Conference on Systems Sciences*, Kauai, Hawaii.

Copyright © 2009, IGI Global, distributing in print or electronic forms without written permission of IGI Global is prohibited.

Section IV
Epilogue

Chapter XI
A Look at the Future

INTRODUCTION

This chapter serves to raise an awareness of some of the more cutting edge Internet innovations and applications that may become viable and useful to the small business operator in future. The chapter focuses on some of the new and emerging forms of technologies that the authors have identified as potentially affecting the Web presence. Consequently, the topic areas and content examined in the chapter does not claim to be all encompassing or prescriptive. Some of the innovations examined are nascent and may not progress to a critical mass for general adoption, whilst others tend to be used by larger business entities, possibly requiring a re-configuration if they are to be successfully used in the small business environment. Arguably, many if not all would in some way impact on the business Web presence if they were to be adopted in future.

An examination of the adoption and use of new forms of technology and ideas - or innovations as they are sometimes referred - can be assisted by examining how the early adopters use these innovations. This was briefly discussed in Chapter IV. The concept of innovation adoption and the importance of early adopters is well documented by Rogers (1995). The Rogers' paradigm describes how innovations advance, or diffuse, through a population either to be adopted or to be rejected. The successful diffusion of an innovation generally follows the S-shaped rate of adoption when a cumulative curve is plotted. The cumulative S-shaped rate of adoption curve is depicted in Figure 1 showing the relationship between the adopters and late-adopters over a period of time. Generally, the adoption of the innovation by the early adopters results in an adoption curve that is reasonably flat. However, as more members of a business group adopt the innovation, the curve 'takes off',

Copyright © 2009, IGI Global, distributing in print or electronic forms without written permission of IGI Global is prohibited.

Figure 1. The innovation diffusion process over time (adapted from Rogers (1995))

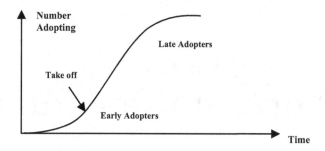

with the advent of late adopters signalling the innovation has diffused through that particular group.

Clearly, for the small business operator an indicator of an innovation that may be associated with a Web presence can be closely allied in the identification of the early adopters. The early adopters are important in the diffusion process as opinion leaders - where potential adopters look to them for advice and information, as well as best practices to emulate. Moreover, the early adopters are considered to be the individuals to investigate or analyse before using a new idea, tending to serve as role models for many others. Early adopters can be deemed to be the most important constituent in the innovation-diffusion process because they decrease uncertainty about a new idea or technology, and as a consequence convey a message of acceptance and effectiveness to peers (Rogers 1995). According to Norman (1998), the early users of an innovation provide the experience for the late adopters to observe and to learn from. Norman further suggests that even though these early users are relatively few in number, they are the drivers of a technology and can provide examples of how and why that innovation can be used. Arguably, the small business operator by conducting an examination within their own industry for the specific use of new forms of Web-related technology will identify a set of industry early adopters from which they themselves can learn from.

Small businesses have been known to be conservative in nature in relation to their use of ICTs, so many feel quite comfortable with the notion of waiting until the early adopters have been successful or otherwise. Of course, if the adoption has been successful they do not necessarily achieve the same level of benefits (often resulting in competitive advantage) that early adopters realise, but at the same time they are not taking the same risk with an unknown technology. Often, the late adopter is forced to adopt the technology as it has diffused through the majority of the industry as is regarded as a requirement by business partners or customers.

Copyright © 2009, IGI Global, distributing in print or electronic forms without written permission of IGI Global is prohibited.

The authors have identified several new or emerging areas that they believe may be important to small business operators when it comes to developments associated with respect to the Web presence. In describing these new or emerging technologies, there has been a general focus on examples of the important early adopters. The areas explored in the remainder of the chapter will include topics such as the emergence of Web 2.0, virtual worlds, Web services, mobile devices, the semantic Web, RFID and the importance of considering people issues when adopting new Web-based innovations.

WEB 2.0

The term Web 2.0 (which we have touched upon in earlier chapters) originated around 2004 when O'Reilly and MediaLive International commenced using the term to describe the perceived advent of *new types* of Websites after the dot-com collapse (O'Reilly 2005). These new type of Websites were found to be associated with technologies that in recent years have matured - becoming easier to use and access.

The key behind Web 2.0 Websites that have already become popular is that they allow users to share content – such as videos, pictures, audio files, their opinions and content – in new and varied ways. The technology itself is not really anything remarkable – but how it is being employed is. They key is that, in many instances, users are put in a position where they are able to determine how they interact with others – it is not necessarily governed by a predetermined Website design (O'Reilly 2005).

There appear to be a diverse range of Websites and Web-based applications that are associated with Web 2.0 (Lin 2007). Some Web 2.0 applications have been developed to allow a business to blend and integrate content from multiple data sources - these are known as mashups. The advent of the iPod has also contributed to the Web 2.0 phenomenon with many Websites offering complete or partially audio recordings - the podcast - as a component of their Website information. In general, Web 2.0 sites have embraced different presentation formats that allows the Website visitor and user to capture, alter and store videos online (such as YouTube), store and update information (such as Wikipedia) and provide comments via Web logs, or 'blogs', on postings associated with stories on a site. One of the aspects of Web 2.0 sites is that an individual can post different types of content (depending upon the Website) and other individuals can respond - hence, sometimes the term *social networking* Websites is used by some people when they refer to Web 2.0 sites (Knight 2007). Moreover, the opportunity that is available to individuals to post content on such sites - user-generated content - is an important value-adding

Copyright © 2009, IGI Global, distributing in print or electronic forms without written permission of IGI Global is prohibited.

feature of many of these sites. Arguably, it is the user-generated content as a primary information source, that organisers of Web 2.0 sites can leverage to gain some form of competitive advantage.

The Web 2.0 landscape with respect to new applications and ideas has numerous representations and is relatively fluid. The authors will focus on several aspects of the Web 2.0 phenomenon that have a reported application to business activity. The areas covered include the Web 2.0 activities that include wikis, podcasting and mashups.

Wikis

Wikis can be viewed as Web spaces that allow individuals to create, update and modify content about particular topics. The wiki environment is particularly conducive to collaboration between contributors and can strengthen the underlying information that is published. Wikipedia, is the best known example of how wikis operate and was created in 2001 and has become one of the largest online reference Websites.

The use of wikis as a collaborative tool has gained a certain form of acceptance by various firms (Dickerson 2004). Dickerson reports that a variety of corporations such as SAP, British Telcom and Disney have begun to use the wiki environment for activities associated with document management, project management and developing the corporate knowledge base. Firms may also benefit by using tools such as wikis as a new communication form, being a viable support service to traditional e-mail use - potentially allowing a significant component of corporate memory and content to be identified. Wikis also have a high collaborative value and can be used to facilitate participation and document sharing amongst team members. Turban et al (2008) documented the use of wikis by MicroStrategy Inc, a company that leveraged the idea in its marketing and production management area - the wiki was used by the firm as a communication tool, as well as allowing the publication of a variety of documents, marketing material and customer queries.

Challenges/Opportunities for Small Businesses

One of the key strategies for small businesses to take advantage of Web 2.0 and wikis could be to list with third party Websites that allow their users to generate their own content. This is already beginning to happen in the tourism industry, where Website visitors read other visitor-generated tourism reviews that can be potentially use in deciding to book a travel product. A similar path is being followed by the music and publishing industries, where many retail Websites encourage listeners/readers to self-publish their own reviews or comments about products. In the future, it may

Copyright © 2009, IGI Global, distributing in print or electronic forms without written permission of IGI Global is prohibited.

eventuate that it becomes commonplace for product support to be provided on a MySpace or a Wikipedia type page - where information on products and services, such as how to use them effectively, are provided by both the seller and the users of the goods. This is already happening online, but in the form of *frequently asked questions* and *bulletin boards* rather than by using Web 2.0 forms of technology.

Podcasts

The recent use of the term *pod* or *podcast* is derived from the introduction of Apple's iPod - a popular mobile digital device that has undergone numerous updates and spawned innovative ancillary support services. Podcasting is an activity that allows the recording or distribution of audio using the Website as the primary access point. Podcasts are easy to produce, can be composed with reasonably rudimentary facilities and require minimal time commitment if the data content can be sourced from existing business activities. Arguably, the audio podcast is part of the information re-packaging phenomenon - one that can be extremely relevant in promoting various aspects of a business. In effect the podcast provides an opportunity for people to access desirable Website information content and download the appropriate file to be stored for future use. Indeed, the use of the podcast can be viewed as extending the business value of Website content to the mobile non-Internet environment. The podcast has also been adapted to a new form in some organisations such as traditional media and information content providers (eg television and newspapers firms) where their Websites make availability audio slide shows, video clips and interviews for Website viewing/listening - or to be used later, potentially in a non-Web-enabled setting after being downloaded.

Challenges/Opportunities for Small Businesses

Podcasts may provide an opportunity for small businesses to extend the services they offer to their customers. For instance, what previously may have been a direct marketing e-mail newsletter may in future incorporate a regular audio podcast on new product releases that current and potential customers can subscribe to. As with Web 2.0 and wikis, podcasts might be able to even provide information on how to use the product. The difference between these methods of delivery and traditional means are that the podcasts involve video and audio descriptions rather than the traditional written text and pictures typically used now with product support. Of course, the small business will need to have access to new skills to produce these podcasts - needing to balance the time taken to develop them against the benefits that are provided.

Copyright © 2009, IGI Global, distributing in print or electronic forms without written permission of IGI Global is prohibited.

Data Mashups

The term mashup refers to a Web-based application that draws data from diverse sources, presenting the output in an integrated manner. The data mashup concept is comparable to a similar activity undertaken in the music industry - where the mixing of different tunes and melodies allows the production of a standalone new piece of music. The potential use of data mashups within the business enterprise has been recently reported. For example, Gruman (2006) indicates that an aircraft engine manufacturer used the mashup concept to draw from several internal data sources to allow employees to access integrated information that was associated with parts re-ordering and service history. Another example of a business mashup by Gruman relates to a real-estate business that was able to integrate their client data with e-mail alert information, allowing property match-ups. Arguably, the use of mashups is still in an infancy stage, however several application areas in which mashups can be used have been suggested (Merrill 2006). One of the application areas for mashups is geographical mapping. Indeed, the most commonly encountered example of how data mashups are used in the Web environment is the co-visualisation of location data with geographical maps. The advent of free access to Google™ Maps was the impetus for making this type of mashup popular. Geographical maps are an important value-adding feature that can be embedded within a Website page allowing various business and organisational locations to be displayed. It is within this context that many firms - both large and small - use geographical maps. Mapping facilities and access directions have become important piece of information associated with contacting and visiting certain types of businesses. The small business operator may need to consider this form of mashup integration as part of its Web presence sooner rather than later - mapping mashups appear to be emerging as an expected Website implementation feature in many Websites.

Challenges/Opportunities for Small Businesses

In Chapter V we discussed the types of situations where small businesses would put a map showing their location on their Website. Mashups provide an extension of this concept - allowing the user to access more information than they can gather from a static map on a Website.

In some aspects, mashups might be seen as being the 'new' generation of portals, in that they involve the gathering of content from different sources into one area. From this point of view, small businesses wishing to engage with third party Websites in the future may find themselves dealing with mashup sites rather than portals.

Copyright © 2009, IGI Global, distributing in print or electronic forms without written permission of IGI Global is prohibited.

VIRTUAL WORLDS

The concept of a virtual world has evolved to a point where Web-based technology can be used to simulate an electronic real-world environment allowing people to be active users of this space (LaMonica 2007). Virtual worlds provide an interactive three-dimensional forum for real-world individuals/groups to communicate, interact and collaborate. There are numerous examples of Web-based virtual worlds that cater to an assortment of different age groups and demographics. For example Habbo® Hotel and Gaia Online™ are virtual worlds for teenagers, Club Penguin™ is owned by Disney and provides a virtual environment for pre-teens, whilst Red Light Center, as the name indicates, is a virtual environment for adults. One of the well-known and popular virtual worlds is Second Life® (SL) that was established in 2003 by Linden Research. SL has its own currency (Linden dollars), established residents (otherwise known as 'avatars'), and a myriad of virtual firms as well as real-world companies that have an established SL presence. Some of the real-world companies that have presence in Second Life are the bigger corporations that have shown an initiative to part of this type of environment. The importance of real-world business presence in a virtual world environment should not be treated as unrealistic or with hyperbole. Gartner, one of the leaders in global IT research, suggests that by the end of 2011, some 80 percent of Internet users will have some form of second life non-gaming activity in a virtual world - a statistic that Gartner indicates will also apply to the Fortune 500 group of companies (Gartner 2007). Indeed, with such a high proportion of users that may be engaged in this form of virtual activity, businesses need to be aware of the potential opportunities that may become available as the virtual world environment matures. Furthermore, by keeping a watchful eye on real-world companies that have a business presence in the virtual world environment, it may be possible to potentially gauge how various aspects of general business Web presence might evolve in the future.

Some of the business activities that could be undertaken in virtual worlds are now examined - they may be nascent, however they are potentially illuminating. SL is used as the source for these examples due to its popular and predominant position as a virtual world environment. Selective examples of business presence and activities in SL include:

- **The Dell Company:** The global PC producer established SL retail stores that allow virtual world customers to examine products in the interactive virtual environment. Customers have an opportunity to click through in real-time to the Dell Website and use the electronic commerce system to actually order PCs that are subsequently delivered to their real-world home. Dell's virtual

Copyright © 2009, IGI Global, distributing in print or electronic forms without written permission of IGI Global is prohibited.

world presence and business activities appear to be another manner in which they are able to engage their customers (Del Conte 2006).

- **American Apparel:** One of the first major real-world firms to establish SL activity to allow the citizens of SL to purchase their products for use in the virtual world environment (Fitzgerald 2007). Moreover, the company has found that being in SL has not been expensive.

- **Sears:** One of the largest home appliance retailers in North America, allows residents of SL to design kitchen layouts with their appliances to get an understanding for how they may look (Kirkpatrick 2007). Arguably, there is an assumption that the virtual-world showroom experience that Sears provides for customers will translate into real world outcomes.

- **Starwood Hotels:** Have used the virtual world environment as a vehicle to prototype, test and market a new hotel design - the virtual hotel prototype in SL being based on one designed in the physical world. It is reported that the company was able to observe how SL residents moved through the new design space to see what preference they may have had for hotel furniture, colour combinations and layout (Reena 2006). Comments from SL residents on the new design proposal were encouraged through an online blog - blog entries that were subsequently used to design a new version of the virtual and real-world accommodation (ElectricArtists 2007).

- Carmakers such as **Toyota** and **GMH (Pontiac)** have opened SL dealerships allowing residents to test drive and purchase virtual-world replicas of real-world motor vehicles. The attraction for many buyers of the replicas is that they are able to customise a vehicle in a manner that would be relative expensive if they were doing this in the real-world situation. Although, the carmakers charge a minor fee for this virtual activity, the primary benefit is one of establishing corporate brand recognition and promoting a motor-vehicle culture in SL (Hobson 2007).

- Various large educational institutes use SL to deliver part of their classroom content with Harvard University allowing classes to be taken in SL for credit (Gronstedt 2007).

Challenges/Opportunities for Small Businesses

Arguably, many of the above examples allow a business to explore marketing and branding activities in a virtual world environment that can be considered commensurate with promoting the real-world business. It is highly conceivable that a small business entity could easily mimic many of these larger business activities. Indeed, the small business manager may consider how some form of virtual world activity might assist in consolidating or expanding their existing physical world business.

Copyright © 2009, IGI Global, distributing in print or electronic forms without written permission of IGI Global is prohibited.

WEB SERVICES

The adoption of Web-based services can be generally considered as a larger business activity. However, there is an increased propensity for such services in future to extend beyond the larger business domain and be re-configured for use in the small business sector. Web services, sometimes known as e-services, can be considered to be (Turban et al. 2008: 62):

...business and consumer modular applications, delivered over the Internet, that users can select and combine through almost any device..

The encyclopedia Website, Wikipedia, describes e-services as "the provision of services on the Internet" (with the 'e' referring to 'electronic') (Wikipedia Contributors, 2006). Stafford (2003) suggests that experts have not yet come upon a clear definition of what e-services actually are. One reason for this, as Stafford argues, could be attributed to the range of specialities involved in the delivery of e-services. For instance, e-services could be those services that can take place without buyer involvement, such as automatic collection of road tolls as a car passes through a tolling booth (Bolton 2003).

However, other authors suggest a more narrow definition of Web services. For instance, Hsu and Chiu (2004: 359) describe e-services as "highly specialized electronic services" for users and suggest that they include "support services such as consulting, outsourcing, Website design, electronic data interchange, payment transfer and data storage backups".

Web services can occur between government, business and consumer and, as Chui et al (2005) suggest, from business to business. Despite the potential for complexity in e-service developments, Chui et al claim that the majority of e-services are available through interactive Web pages in HTML. It has reached the stage where the *quality* of e-service delivery in some areas is becoming an issue when buyers are considering using the services of a business.

These modular or software applications are an important mechanism that can facilitate cross communication and data exchange between business Websites. In effect the use of Web services allows for closer integration of disparate applications within the company or between affiliates of the company - with the Internet being used as the delivery medium. Indeed, some of the well-established online retailers such as amazon.com provide a myriad of different Web services for their associates as well as third-party providers (Mueller 2004). This type of services potentially makes available assortments of data to Website owners derived from the amazon.com Website that can be used to enhance a company's own set of products or services.

Copyright © 2009, IGI Global, distributing in print or electronic forms without written permission of IGI Global is prohibited.

The foundation of Web service delivery is based on the use of XML (Extensible Hypertext Markup Language) that allows for content to be formatted so that it can be subsequently transferred between one Web-based application to another (Stair et al. 2008). Other technology components of Web services delivery include:

- **Simple Object Access Protocol (SOAP):** SOAP provides a set of specifications that allows the appropriate communication and data exchange between business partners and consumers.
- **Web Services Description Language (WSDL):** WSDL is a means for Web-based applications to be described.
- **Universal Discovery Description and Integration (UDDI):** The UDDI can be viewed as the mechanism by which Web services can be listed in an Internet directory. This listing facilitates the discovery of relevant and desirable Web services by prospective business users.

The significant benefit and strength of Web services is that a business is able to access various solutions that are applicable to their information technology requirements, avoiding having to have specific software developed either in-house, or by a consultant. The concept of Web services is also premised on a value-adding notion, where commercial firms that specialise in offering Web services are able to more readily incorporated the latest innovations into an application - more so, than if it were developed in-house. Arguably, this appears to be one of the reasons that Web services are being increasingly adopted as a viable means for accessing Web-based applications. Many companies have made use of Web services that has allowed them to not only improve and streamline their business process, but also position them in providing improved supplier and customer services.

The literature provides examples of a variety of benefits that various firms have derived from their Web-services experience. Joss (2004) alludes to the adoption of a customer relationship management (CRM) system based on Web-services that allowed the implementing firm to avoid the normal process of developing the solution in house - a scenario that potentially would have disrupted service delivery for the company concerned. Hoffman (2007) reports on a travel company that was able to increase its online bookings as a result of adopting a Web service that facilitated accessed to travel data from an affiliated company. By using the Web service, the travel company found that transaction costs were lower and that dealing with customers was more efficient. Anthony and Donaldson (2004) describe the use of Web services by the Burrell Communications Group. Burrell implemented a Web service that that allowed out-of-office employees seamless access to a variety of office based files and documents from any of a number of Web-enabled applications - be it mobile telephone, hotel-located PC or personal digital assistant (PDA). Previ-

Copyright © 2009, IGI Global, distributing in print or electronic forms without written permission of IGI Global is prohibited.

ously, the company's on-the-road personnel were required to carry a cumbersome laptop with them, loaded with appropriate software to access the company's office network. Arguably, the implementation of Web services has made the environment of employees working in the field more flexible and conducive to achieving effective outcomes for the firm.

J.P. Morgan Chase (USA) and the Nationwide Building Society (UK) are financial services companies that have adopted Web services to assist them with business activities (Pallatto 2002). The J.P. Morgan group reported that Web services allowed them to quickly bring together and publish a broad and diverse range of relevant investment information on the corporate portal. This investment information was already available, however, it needed to be sourced from different content providers - an issue that arguably could be viewed as being labour and time intensive. A key benefit of using the Web service was that the information content delivered via the portal was unified and functional. The bank's customers and employees are reported as finding that the portal acted as a single point of Web presence, compared to the fragmented access framework that previously existed. Pallatto (2002) further describes the benefits of adopting Web services by the Nationwide Building Society in the United Kingdom - allowing the company to identify new Internet-based mortgage business. The company was able to use various business-to-consumer Web service tools that reviewed customer mortgage applications sourced from an intermediary - the Web service assisted the company with the decision-making process that allowed Nationwide Building Society to further examine particular mortgages of interest. Turban et al (2008) describe the use of Web services at Merrill Lynch - a leading financial management company. Merrill was able to leverage its Web services with its vast infrastructure allowing modern applications to function within the intricate mainframe environment. One of the many Web service based application that was introduced allowed clients to make real time enquiries via a Web browser - an activity that today can be considered to be the norm when it comes to online banking. The benefits realised by Merrill included being able to dispense with purchasing new hardware and the re-coding of existing mainframe software - benefits that translated into substantial savings.

Challenges/Opportunities for Small Businesses

From the examples given it can be seen that Web services are an important utility that allows companies to realise numerous worthwhile benefits. The examples also illustrate that these services today tend to be used within the domain of the larger organisation. However, it is likely that as Web services become more adaptable to the small business environment, these services will become a viable and beneficial tool that will form another facet of Web presence for the small business operator.

Copyright © 2009, IGI Global, distributing in print or electronic forms without written permission of IGI Global is prohibited.

MOBILE DEVICES AND THE WEB

The Website has become an important tool in the business environment that allows an organisation to not only extend its market reach, but also improve the richness of its consumer information - breaking the limitations of the information reach-richness paradigm associated with pre-Internet business communication models (Evans and Wurster 2000; Schneider 2007; Sellitto 2008). The Website will often evolve with time to reflect its needs and the demands of prospective and existing customers (although this has not always been the case with small business Websites). Arguably, the small business Website that has been designed appropriately should have a certain element of functionality that allows the business to easily address new technology issues associated with mobile devices. Mobile devices are popular and their functionality has extended beyond the general use of voice communication. Indeed, mobile-device behaviour appears to have developed to the extent where owners use such devices (W3C 2006; Turban et al 2008):

- To be connected by devices that are permanently *switched on* allowing the user to be contactable 24/7, especially using the cheaper and concise text messaging tools.
- For *personalization* where the use of electronic calendars, reminders and a diary of events allows a user to specifically tailor schedules and contact requirements,
- As an accurate *location finder* and *recorder*, achieved by the incorporation of geographical mapping and camera functionality, and
- As a dexterous one-handed *fashion item* - made popular by the advent of the Apple iPod and the subsequent marketing that followed.

E-mail and Website access with a mobile device is currently less popular due to various limitations associated with the cost of data transfer, slow download times and small screen display (although there are some signs that perhaps this is gradually changing). Notwithstanding these issues, and given the spread of mobile and/or portable computing, a small business' Website may need to be developed in future to display and operate on portable handheld devices. Indeed, consumers today have numerous handheld devices that embrace mobile characteristics that include phones, personal digital assistants (PDAs) and the lightweight portable laptop that has wireless connectivity. Hence, the hardware for accessing Website-published information may have already been adopted by a business' potential customer base.

Access to the Internet via mobile devices has been possible for a while, albeit in a limited and restricted capacity. Furthermore, all businesses, not just small businesses will need to be aware of this form of Web presence and it can be assumed

Copyright © 2009, IGI Global, distributing in print or electronic forms without written permission of IGI Global is prohibited.

that with improved screen resolution, expanding signal bandwidth and enhanced functionality of devices, that mobile Web presence will become a consumer expectation - potentially replacing or substituting Website viewing on the desktop computer. Arguably, all business operators should have viewed their current Website on a mobile handheld device to see how the content renders and displays. Surprisingly, few will have undertaken this exercise, and may not understand the consequences of potentially missing out on being able to access an important market of consumers that are increasingly more dependent on such devices.

Within the general Web development community, the leading group that provides an open forum for discussion on the development of appropriate and viable mobile Web access is World Wide Web Consortium Mobile Web Initiative (W3C MWI). The W3C has recognised that the increasing popularity of mobile Website access has inherent problems that relate to poor technical interoperability and Website usability (W3C 2007). The W3C MWI by bringing together key players in the mobile device environment - players that include the content providers, browser vendors and mobile operators - hopes to document a series of good practices that will improve access to the mobile Web.

The W3C documents the many advantages of the mobile Web (being able to access Websites using mobile devices) that include the following:

- The concept of the mobile Web fits in with the original concept of the Web in that information can be gathered when people decide they need it - and not when they return to the '*fixed-Web*' available via the desktop computer. For the business this may allow on-the-fly mobile access to business information and services by a consumer in any location and at anytime - consequently, business information becomes a ubiquitous feature in the eyes of the consumer.
- The widespread adoption of handheld mobile devices is vast when you consider the collective number of these items currently in operation. Furthermore, given that direct access to the Web will not be associated with any wiring infrastructure, as inherent in the desktop scenario, it can be anticipated that mobile Web access will result in an increase in the reachable audience. One of the commonly anticipated benefits of adopting Internet technologies by small businesses was the increased number of potential consumers that the business could market to - making the small business Website mobile-device operable, further increases this audience potential.
- The mobile Web offers broader geographical access to audiences in developing countries. Given that mobile phone diffusion outstrips computer adoption in developing countries it can be assumed that Web-enabled mobile devices have the potential to provide Web access in geographical areas that currently have no access.

Copyright © 2009, IGI Global, distributing in print or electronic forms without written permission of IGI Global is prohibited.

The W3C MWI series of good practices that will improve user experience and access to the mobile Web have been postulated to address some of the following challenges in the mobile Web environment (W3C 2006):

- **Presentation:** The commonly developed and implemented Website page places a high value on presentation and will not always display appropriately on mobile device displays. This poor display makes the user experience unsatisfactory and can be attributed to the limited size of the mobile device screen size that may cause the need for considerable scrolling, loss of page layout and content to be distorted. In an endeavour to assist the mobile-device user with improved Web access a good practice is to use consistent styles throughout the Website.
- **Input:** Input into mobile handheld devices is sometimes restrictive - small keys and the lack of a mouse tends to impede confident input - when compared to using the desktop computer with its larger and more versatile input methods. Consequently, mobile input can impact on accurate typing of Web addresses and filling of forms, with typing tending to be cumbersome, slow and error prone. Not all mobile devices may have a 'back' button (used to return to the previous screen), which can impede navigation.
- **Bandwidth:** Slow connections and fixed data delivery modes are associated with some mobile devices. As such, Web page downloads can be slow, especially if they have many images and/or have large files. Just as traditional desktop Website implementation aims at fast Web page download as a definitive design issue - fast and expeditious Web page retrieval is a feature that also holds in the mobile environment.
- **Advertising:** The commercial Web advertising model associated with mobile devices can be different to that encountered when navigate the Web on a desktop computer. In the mobile environment, pop-up and large advertising banners do not work well - due to the smaller screens on mobile devices. Commercial advertisers need to alter their *modus operandi* with respect to mobile Web presence.

Challenges/Opportunities for Small Businesses

The number of operating mobile devices is growing quickly and the technology is constantly evolving. Groups like the World Wide Web Consortium Mobile Web Initiative (W3C MWI) provide an environment for developing rules, guides and good practices to improve the user experience with respect to delivering the Web on mobile devices. Moreover, the small business operator in considering mobile-Web presence will need to examine their current Website implementation to see how it

Copyright © 2009, IGI Global, distributing in print or electronic forms without written permission of IGI Global is prohibited.

should be adopted to the mobile environment. Operators need to be aware of the immense opportunities that may be available to increase client reach by having mobile Web presence.

RADIO FREQUENCY IDENTIFICATION (RFID)

One of the emerging technologies that will invariably impact on the small business sector is radio frequency identification (RFID). RFID became prominent when Wal-Mart - the large US retail conglomerate - requested that its top suppliers use RFID technology with products that were shipped to the company (Sellitto et al 2007). Wal-Mart, by mandating the use of RFID technology, provided the impetus for future and progressive use of this technology in other sectors of the supply chain. For the small business operator, it can be assumed that as larger firms use this technology more widely, there will be a diffusion effect so that smaller entities will also be required to adopt RFID.

RFID technology is implemented in the form of tags or labels that contain a microchip - the tags having the capacity to be attached to almost any object. Each tag's microchip is able to store large amounts of information about an object, making it powerful substitute for the commonly encountered barcode. Indeed, RFID microchips can hold some 40 times more information than barcode technology (Singh 2003) - hence, there is an increased mechanism to provide a greater amount of relevant information about products that may be warehoused and shipped. It has been suggested that the RFID system of technology will eventually replace the barcode as various signal exchange standards and implementation costs are overcome. RFID technology can be used with transportation palettes, containers and boxes - however, the technology is also being encountered at an individual product level. It is in the tagging of individual products where RFID holds major potential for business (Sellitto et al 2007).

The RFID system works on the premise of a signal and data-exchange between tags and readers - akin to barcode technology - however, unlike scanning a barcode, line-of-sight is not required with RFID technology for data exchange. Ongoing developments with RFID tags using high frequency transmission modes has led to tags being read from greater distances and with relatively high reliability. RFID tags can be passive types, where a reader is needed to record and capture the prewritten information on the tag (Want 2004). Another form of RFID tag is one that is termed active - these tags include an energy source allowing data to not only be transmitted to a reader, but also to be collected data from other electronic objects, or indeed, the immediate working environment of the tag. Arguably, as the cost of RFID implementation is reduced, businesses will find that RFID-captured data will

Copyright © 2009, IGI Global, distributing in print or electronic forms without written permission of IGI Global is prohibited.

be seamlessly transmitted to the company's enterprise wide computing system - a system that will be invariably networked with other business systems.

It is within the domain of this seamlessly capturing of RFID-derived data and its subsequent storage, that the potential use of the Web can be envisaged as a future utility to enhance business operations. Several examples can be use to illustrate this.

Batchelor (2007) reports the use of passive RFID tags by a Californian vineyard. The business uses RFID tags throughout vineyard as well as a series of active sensor pads. As the workers move throughout the vineyard, they are able to use their hand-held readers allowing them to electronically record exactly where grape sampling has occurred, where vines have been pruned and any particulars that may be associated with these activities. The sensors are used to capture vineyard environmental factors such as temperature and air humidity levels - factors that impact on grape growing activities. Collectively, the RFID tags and sensors provide information about the vineyard that can be accessed by vineyard managers and operators via secure login on the business Website - a form on Website implementation that has data feeds originating from an RFID associated application. Arguably, the Website is a form of internal Web presence (intranet) that allows for quick and efficient dissemination of important information to vineyard decision makers.

RFID technology can also be used to track and capture data about a product throughout its lifecycle - factors that will assist with product identification, history and potential recovery. Product recovery provides important management challenges for leaders across the manufacturing supply chain. Sometimes product recovery can be difficult in that there can be little or confusing information associated with goods that are returned to a store, need to be re-manufactured, or are set to be recycled. Kulkarni and colleagues (2005) provide a case study of how networked RFID technology can provide a complete information set about a product throughout its lifecycle. This concept of a networked RFID system fits in with the concept that electronic tags are not designed to hold a complete set of information about a product, but need to act as unique pointer to a greater repository of information about that product (Wyld 2006). In effect the unique information and identifier associated with the RFID tag becomes a form of URL pointer to the Website/database where richer information about an item can be found. As items move through the various stages of their life cycle, different types of information will be created, whilst existing information may be updated. For example, when an item is manufactured, the date of production and a serial number will be created. At the retail stage, the sale date, price and customer details are now available. In the post-retail sales stage for the item, any warranty claims, replacement parts (for larger items) are new pieces of information that can be collected about an item. Consequently, the use of RFID tags in a networked environment assists with the centralised updating and access

Copyright © 2009, IGI Global, distributing in print or electronic forms without written permission of IGI Global is prohibited.

of product information - information that is attributable to the different phases of product manufacture and use (Sellitto et al 2007). Arguably, the Website and the data repository (database) associated with product lifecycle information will become an integral component of any future Web presence for businesses that may use RFID systems in this manner.

Challenges/Opportunities for Small Businesses

As was mentioned earlier, it may be that some small businesses may need to adopt RFID to just stay in business - especially if forced to by a large buyer (or even supplier). Although such an adoption may cause an upheaval, there have been instances in the past where small businesses have reluctantly adopted newer technologies (such as Electronic Data Interchange) and actually found that there were unexpected benefits - such as long term cost savings and streamlining of business processes. There are no doubts that RFID technology provides richer information to the business - providing the RFID application can be justified from a business case point of view, there may be some potential for small businesses. For some small businesses, the fact that they have established relationships with larger trading partners might provide enough of a business case to adopt RFID!

THE SEMANTIC WEB

The semantic Web has been a commonly written about topic in the last ten years or so, its origins being with the World Wide Web Consortium (W3C). As the umbrella group for Website protocol development, the W3C is the united and directing body that addresses the objectives and ongoing development of the semantic Web (W3C 2008). The advent of the semantic Web provides an important mechanism for structuring information published on the Web - improving the online conditions and functionality for all who maintain a Web presence.

The semantic Web is not different to the World Wide Web but an extension of it - one that promotes data sharing based on set of predefined relationships. The significant value of the semantic Web is that it allows existing Website content to be easily read and processed through computer-to-computer interaction. Many applications associated with the semantic Web are based on agreed data classification protocols that allow computers to seamlessly search aggregated and present information that is derived from the existing Web environment (Gammack et al). These data protocols, or resource description frameworks (RDF) - also examined in Chapter VIII under Website design - facilitate the mapping of data on a Web page to specified themes or meanings that reflect the way that human beings tend

Copyright © 2009, IGI Global, distributing in print or electronic forms without written permission of IGI Global is prohibited.

to interpret that data - underpinning a consistent approach to categorising Web-published information. Furthermore, the RDF provides the rules of how machine dependable software needs to interpret Web-located data - hence, the notion of computer–to-computer interaction as a functional aspect of the semantic Web. In examining issues associated with the semantic Web, the theme of ontologies is encountered. Semantic Web ontology, according to Davies et al (2006), allows the conceptualisations associated with a domain of interest to be documented and specified - something that arguably establishes the interpretation rules to be used by a computer. Davies and colleagues provide salient cases of how various semantic methods and ontological approaches have been used. One case focusing on the judicial Spanish system reported a semantic Web project that was found to have been useful in improving the knowledge management skills of newly commissioned judges. In another case, a major telecommunications carrier was able to use semantic Web technologies that partially led to the re-use of available services allowing the company to dynamically implement a system in a resource-affective manner.

The current intricacies associated with semantic Web technologies and the commensurate benefits that are realised by users are generally applicable to the large business environment. Like many of the other innovations proposed in this chapter, it is likely that small business entities will be the last to potentially adopt them, given their skills and resource limitations. However, Pollock (2008) argues a business case for promoting and adopting semantic Web activities indicating that the benefits include:

- The empowering of individuals through increased opportunities to share information - an activity that can lead to new business capabilities.
- The reduction of expenditure on business information technology activities that is directly attributable to a more simplified approach to data integration.
- An altered basis for enterprise-wide software implementation as more vendors consider semantic Web specifications as part of their product development.

Daconta et al (2003) suggest that the semantic Web can be used in a diverse range of business activities that include decision support for personnel, organisational information sharing and the identification of strategies that can be appropriately articulated to reflect the corporate vision. Much of the value associated with implementing semantic Web activities is that the organisation is able to tap its hidden knowledge base - a knowledge base that already exists, but is obscurely embedded in many of its disparate databases and repositories. The W3C (2007a) lists and describes a set of case studies that reflect the diverse areas in which semantic Web applications can be used. The business application focus areas include business-

Copyright © 2009, IGI Global, distributing in print or electronic forms without written permission of IGI Global is prohibited.

to-business, e-government, organisational portals and data integration - with all cases defining the value of using a semantic Web approach.

Challenges/Opportunities for Small Businesses

Many of the business benefits and activities associated with the semantic Web fall within the adoption-domain associated with medium and large sized businesses. However, it is likely, that as the semantic Web becomes more broadly used and refined, many applications will also become more adaptable to the small business environment. As such, semantic Web activities and business benefits will eventually become a viable proposition for small businesses to consider - an issue that potentially will shape their Web presence.

SMALL BUSINESS COLLABORATION AND WEB PRESENCE

Traditionally, small business operators have valued opportunities that allow them to closely engage and network with other small businesses. These network links can be formal, as reflected through having membership of a representative business body or association. Much of the information exchanges that may occur in such networks are structured and documented. Links can also be informal in nature in that they invariably embrace loosely structured professional or social business meetings - allowing for more subtle and tacit forms of information exchanges.

Given small businesses' affinity for networking amongst other smaller firms, it makes sense that this type of collaborative behaviour may also extend to the online environment, as we have suggested in Chapter IV. Indeed, a Web presence can potentially make the small business highly visible in the online environment, allowing it to potentially engage in activities that strengthen ties with other small businesses or partners. Some of these activities may involve participating in virtual enterprises, Web portal presences and/or online collaborative networks. Indeed, Guniš and colleagues (2007) report on a project that highlights how collaborative tools can be implemented within a company, allowing the firm to undertake operations such as production and product development in an electronic form - allowing the company to closely collaborate with partners to embrace elements of a virtual enterprise. The authors identify through their project titled *RIVEM* (Research and Implementation of the Virtual Enterprise Model) that small businesses have only just commenced to exploit technological solutions in this environment. The portal environment can also provide important value adding collaborative features for small businesses. One of the many functions of an online portal is to foster community building (Eisenmann 2002) - an activity that potentially allows a small business to

Copyright © 2009, IGI Global, distributing in print or electronic forms without written permission of IGI Global is prohibited.

collaboration virtually through having a Web presence. Arguably, portal features that embrace chat facilities, message boards, instant-messaging services, online greeting cards, and other interactive Web services are fundamental elements of a portal's service provision. Collectively, these features contribute to promoting community-building activities that are commonly encountered in the Web portal environment. The small business entity can utilise these relationship-building activities to formally or informally develop closer ties with other businesses that may also have portal presence. It is envisaged that many of the social networking activities associated with Web 2.0 sites will also provide opportunities for small business to both formally and informally interact - potentially strengthening business ties. The value and promise of virtual collaboration for small business entities has been described as a form of virtual communities-of-practice (Petter *et al.* 2007). Petters and colleagues (2007) highlight how collaborative tools can facilitate learning in the small business workplace. They investigated the use of online platforms and social software applications amongst small tourism operators that facilitated cooperation and collaboration - overcoming constraints that were typically associated with time and location. The authors indicate that by identifying the learning needs of a small business in the physical world tends to be an important step in allowing them to participate in virtual communities-of-practice.

Challenges/Opportunities for Small Businesses

Small business managers have valued opportunities that allow them to closely engage and network with other small businesses - networking activities that can have a formal and informal nature. The authors propose that networking opportunities that are reflected in small business collaborative behaviour can also extend to the online environment. Indeed, a Web presence can potentially make the small business highly visible in the online environment allowing it to potentially engage in activities that strengthen ties with other small businesses or partners. Some of these activities may involve participating in virtual enterprises, Web portal presences and/or online collaborative networks. The small business operator should be aware of the potential value of networking opportunities in the online environment and the commensurate benefits it may bring.

PEOPLE ISSUES WHEN CONSIDERING EMERGING WEB PRESENCE IN FUTURE

The previous sections of this chapter have focussed on some of the newer forms of technological innovations that may potentially be useful to small businesses in

Copyright © 2009, IGI Global, distributing in print or electronic forms without written permission of IGI Global is prohibited.

creating and expanding their Web opportunities. In describing these new or emerging technologies, there has been a general focus on the importance of early adopters in the small business environment - adopters that provide examples for other small business operators to emulate. However, part of the processes associated with the adoption of any new technology can be directly attributable to the individuals that manage, or who may be employed in the small business. Indeed, small business operators and their working personnel will have a diverse level of technological skills, socio-economic backgrounds and educational achievements that will shape their views toward the adoption of innovations. These characteristics are integral to how newly proposed Web presence technologies are perceived - perceptions that contribute to a decision-making process that will lead to either successful uptake or rejection of the technology. For example, small business operators will have different management styles that will impact on the adoption of any new idea associated with Web presence. If managers perceive the benefits associated with new technology as imparting relative business advantage, then this will shape adoption behaviour. If small business management styles are conservative or uninformed then the value proposition associated with an innovation can shape negative attitudes. Not all small business managers will have the same approach to running a business - some will focus on expansion, some will be happy to maintain the status quo, whilst others will be influenced by lifestyle choices. Arguably, each different management approach will directly impact on individual perceptions associated with the uptake of new or emerging Web-based technologies. Furthermore, given the limited resources available to small business, their will be a reluctance to undertake training to upgrade skills with respect to information technology - hence, any new approaches or applications associated with the Web presence must be ideally easy to understand and use. For most people, innovation complexity has been shown to be an inhibitor of adoption, whilst application simplicity can shape a person's attitude toward potential uptake of an innovation.

Another issue that small business operators may encounter in their consideration of some of these newer technologies is the opportunity to trial and observe the application in a small business environment. The importance of business networks - albeit formal, social or informal - becomes an important factor with respect to observing how innovations can be used before adoption. Small business networks are renowned for the manner in which reciprocal activities can occur allowing members to share and learn from the experiences of the collective group. Arguably, the small business operator that has an opportunity to access and interact with an appropriate group of small business peers will be well positioned to garner relevant information about emerging and new innovations. Moreover, this interaction can provide the small business manager or owner the chance to ask questions, and seek an invitation to examine first hand how new Web-based technology may

Copyright © 2009, IGI Global, distributing in print or electronic forms without written permission of IGI Global is prohibited.

function in an ancillary business. Indeed, networking opportunities can provide a confirming experience for individual small business operators - as a precursor to making an informed decision to either adopt or reject some of the new Web-based innovations.

Challenges/Opportunities for Small Businesses

Small businesses operators need to be aware of their own personal characteristics, as well as those of staff, as potentially limiting factors in any future Web presence endeavours. Indeed, small business managers and their employees will have a diverse degree of technological skills, socio-economic backgrounds and educational levels that will directly impact the adoption of new innovations. These characteristics will tend to shape individual perceptions of newly conceived or proposed Web technologies. Hence, the small business operator needs to have the conviction to be able to acknowledge these types of business limitations when considering some of the new forms of technologies in future.

TENETS – FUTURE LESSONS FROM THE CHAPTER

The small business operator needs to be aware of constantly emerging technology, as well as the advent of recent innovations that have the potential to assist them in consolidating and enhancing their Web presence. Several forms of emerging or maturing technologies were examined in this section and it was proposed that the small business operator needed to be aware of the potential benefits of these. The following table summarises that main themes of this chapter and provides a useful guide for the small business operator.

CONCLUSION

This chapter has focussed on some of the emerging and newer forms of innovations and technology. The chapter functions to raise awareness for the small business operator of how these might be consider in future. Some of the Web-based applications covered in the chapter are nascent and require a suitable adoption period before reaching a critical mass. Other applications examined are commonly used in a large business environment and will need to be re-configured and modified for use in the small business domain. The chapter's content was broadly derived with the areas explored dealing with aspects of Web 2.0, virtual worlds, Web services,

Copyright © 2009, IGI Global, distributing in print or electronic forms without written permission of IGI Global is prohibited.

mobile devices, RFID and the importance of considering people issues when adopting new Web-based innovations.

The small business operator should also be aware of the early adopters within their own business sector of new forms of technologies - the early adopters tend to generally identify a technology shift to the use new ideas within a specific group.

Table 1. Potential technological considerations for small business to consider

Heading	Awareness and expectation value
Web 2.0	Three areas were examined under the Web 2.0 heading - Wikis, podcasting and mashups. Wikis can be viewed as a web space that allows content to be created, updated and modified. Businesses can use a wiki as a collaborative tool, a new communication form or to publish business documents to facilitate cross-company information sharing. The podcast is part of the information re-packaging phenomenon that allows business customers to access desirable website content for use in a mobile non-Internet environment. The term mashup refers to a web-based application that draws from diverse data sources to present information in an integrated manner. Mashups appear to still be in an infancy stage, the commonly encountered example of a mashup is the way that business location is co-visualised with maps. Given that location information is associated with potential customers contacting and visiting a business, small business operators should consider this form of mashup integration as part of its future web presence.
Virtual Worlds	The concept of a virtual world has evolved where web-based technology can be used to simulate an electronic real-world environment allowing residents to inhabit this space. Virtual worlds embrace technology that provides an interactive three-dimensional forum for real-world individuals/groups to communicate, interact and collaborate. The examples taken from Second Life are generally those of larger businesses and relate to marketing and branding opportunities in the virtual world environment. However, conceivably small business could emulate some of these virtual world activities in an endeavour to promote, consolidate and/or expand their business.
Web Services	Web services can be considered to be important in facilitating cross communication and data exchange between individual business websites allowing closer integration of disparate applications within the company or between affiliates of the company. Again the examples given tend to be used within the domain of the larger organisation. However, it is likely that as web services become more adaptable and scalable to the small business environment, these services will become a viable and beneficial tool that will form another facet of web presence for the small business operator.
Mobile Devices and the Web	Access to the Internet via mobile devices has been possible for a while, albeit in limited and restricted capacity. Businesses will need to be aware of this form of web presence and it can be assumed that with improved screen resolution, expanding signal bandwidth and the enhanced functionality of devices that mobile web presence will become a consumer expectation - replacing or substituting website viewing via the desktop computer. Clearly, the website is an important marketing, sales and communication medium for small business. However, small business operators should be aware of the potential of also making their web presence functional in an environment were mobile devices are becoming the norm.
Radio Frequency Identification (RFID)	One of the emerging technologies that will invariably impact on the small business sector is radio frequency identification (RFID) - a wireless and mobile technology that has been adopted by some larger businesses. Much of the adoption by larger business has been due to mandating by affiliates (Wal-Mart is the classic example) and for the small business operator, it can be assumed that as larger firms use this technology more widely, there will be a diffusion effect forcing smaller entities to also adopt RFID.

continued on the following page

Copyright © 2009, IGI Global, distributing in print or electronic forms without written permission of IGI Global is prohibited.

Table 1. continued

Heading	Awareness and expectation value
The Semantic Web	Business benefits that have been associated with the semantic web include the ability to empowering individuals through the increased sharing of information, the reduction of IT expenditure and decision support activities. Arguably, many of these business benefits fall within the adoption-domain associated with medium and large sized businesses. However, small business operators need to be aware that many applications will also become more adaptable to the small business environment - an issue that potentially will shape their web presence.
Small Business Collaboration and Web Presence	Small businesses have an appreciation and preference for networking amongst their own kind. Given this observation, it makes sense that this type of collaborative behaviour should also extend to the online environment. Indeed, web presence can potentially make the small business highly visible in the online environment and act to potentially engage in activities that strengthen ties with other small businesses or partners. Some of these activities may involve participating in virtual enterprises, portal activity and/or online collaborative networks - activities that need to be on the small business radar.
People Issues When Considering Emerging Web Presence in Future	The impetus for the adoption of any new technology, or ideas for that matter, will be shaped by the individuals who manage, or those that are employed in the small business. Small business managers and their operational personnel will have a diverse degree of technological skills, socio-economic backgrounds and educational levels that will directly impact the adoption of up-and-coming innovations. Consequently, small businesses operators need to be aware of their own personal characteristics, as well as those of staff, as potentially limiting factors in any future web presence endeavours.

Traditionally, it is the early adopters within an industry sector that will discover how new technologies can be most appropriately be used.

REFERENCES

Anthony, R., & Donaldson, S. A. (2004). Build a Better Business. *Black Enterprise, 35*(3), 136-143.

Bacheldor, B. (2007). RFID Helps California Crops Grow. *RFID Journal* (04/01/2007), [http://www.rfidjournal.com/article/articleprint/2944/-1/1/], Retrieved: 24/11/2007.

Bolton, R. N. (2003). Marketing Challenges of E-Services. *Communications of the ACM, 46*(6), 43-44.

Chiu, D. K. W., Kok, D., Lee, A. K. C. & Cheung, S. C. (2005). Integrating Legacy Sites into Web Services with Webxcript. *International Journal of Cooperative Information Systems, 14*(1), 25-44.

Daconta, M., C., Obrst, L. J., & Smith, K. T. (2003). *The Semantic Web: A Guide to the Future of XML, Web Services, and Knowledge Management.* New York: Wiley.

Copyright © 2009, IGI Global, distributing in print or electronic forms without written permission of IGI Global is prohibited.

Davies, J., Studer, R., & Warren, P. (2006). *Semantic Web Technologies: Trends and Research in Ontology-based Systems.* West Sussex, UK: Wiley.

Del Conte, N. T. (2006). *Dell to Sell PCs on Second Life.*

[http://www.pcmag.com/article2/0,1895,2059016,00.asp], Retrieved: 10/1/2008.

Dickerson, C. (2004). Is Wiki Under Your Radar? *InfoWorld, 26*(45), 26.

Eisenmann, T. R. (2002). *Internet Business Models: Texts and Cases.* New York: McGraw-Hill Irwin,.

ElectricArtists (2007). *Aloft in Second Life: A Developers Report.* ElectricArtists, Retrieved: 8/8/2007.

Evans, P., & Wurster, T. (2000). *Blown To Bits: How the New Economics of Information Transforms Strategy.* Boston, MA: HBS Press.

Ferris, C., & Farrell, J. (2003). What Are Web Services? *Communications of the ACM, 46*(6), 31.

Fitzgerald, M. (2007). Does Your Business Need a Second Life? *Inc. Magazine, 29*(2), 83.

Gammack, J., Hobbs, V., & Pigott, D. (2007). *The Book Of Informatics.* South Melbourne, Australia.

Gartner (2007). *Gartner Says 80 Percent of Active Internet Users Will Have A "Second Life" in the Virtual World by the End of 2011.* Gartner, Retrieved: 8/1/2008.

Gronstedt, A. (2007). Second Life: The 3D Web World is Slowly Becoming Part of the Training Industry. *T+G, 61*(8), 44-49.

Gruman, G. (2006). Enterprise Mashups. *InfoWorld, 28*(31), 19-23.

Guniš ,A., Šišlák, J., & Valčuha, Š. (2007). Implementation of Collaboration Model Within SME's. In P. F. Cunha & P. G. Maropoulos (Eds.), *Digital Enterprise Technology: Perspectives and Future Challenges* (pp. 377-384). Springer.

Hobson, N. (2007). Should businesses get a Second Life? *KM Review, 10*(1), 5.

Hoffman, T. (2007). Sabre's Web Services Journey. *Computerworld, 41*(2), 27-28.

Infographic (2004). RFID: How Technology Works. *MIT: Technology Review,* (March), 79.

Copyright © 2009, IGI Global, distributing in print or electronic forms without written permission of IGI Global is prohibited.

Joss, M. W. (2004). Web Services in Theory and Practice. *EContent, 27*(6), 30-34.

Kirkpatrick, D. (2007). It's Not a Game. *Fortune, 155*(2), 56-62.

Kulkarni, A. G., Parlikad, A. K. N., McFarlane, D. C., & Harrison, M. (2005). Networked RFID Systems in Product Recovery Management. *Proceedings of the International Symposium on Electronics and the Environment* (pp. 66-71). New Orleans, USA: IEEE Computer Society.

LaMonica, M. (2007). *IBM: Like the Web, Virtual Worlds Will Become Business Friendly.* C|Net new.com, Retrieved: 8/8/2008.

Liang, W., Huang, C., & Chuang, H. (2007). The design with object (DwO) approach to Web services composition. *Computer Standards & Interfaces, 29*(1), 54-68.

Lin, K. J. (2007). Building Web 2.0. *Computer, 40*(5), 101-102.

Meng-Hsiang, H., & Chao-Min, C. (2004). Predicting electronic service continuance with a decomposed theory of planned behaviour. *Behaviour & Information Technology, 23*(5), 359-373.

Merrill, D. (2006). *Mashups: The new breed of Web app: An introduction to mashups (IBM developerWorks),* [http://www.ibm.com/developerworks/library/genres], Retrieved: 10/1/2008.

Multimedia-Victoria (2007). *Would Your Business Benefit From a Second Life.* Multimedia Victoria & Acumentum Pty Ltd, Melbourne.

Norman, D.A. (1998). *The Invisable Computer.* Boston: MIT Press.

O'Reilly, T. (2005). *What Is Web 2.0: Design Patterns and Business Models for the Next Generation of Software,* Retrieved: 1/1/2008.

Pallatto, J. (2002). Web Services Deliver. *Internet World, 8*(10), 32-36.

Petter, C., Reich, K., & Helling, K. (2007). Social Software and the Establishment of Virtual Communities of Practice in the Tourism Sector. *eLearning Papers, 1*(5), 1-7.

Pollock, J. (2008). *A Semantic Web Business Case.* WC3, [http://www.w3.org/2001/sw/sweo/public/BusinessCase/], Retrieved: 13/8/08.

Reena, J. (2006). *Starwood Hotels Explore Second Life First.* [http://www.businessweek.com/innovate/content/aug2006/id20060823_925270.htm], Retrieved: 14/1/2008.

Copyright © 2009, IGI Global, distributing in print or electronic forms without written permission of IGI Global is prohibited.

Rogers, E. (1995). *Diffusion of Innovations,* 4th Edition ed. New York: Free Press.

Sellitto, C. (2008). E-mail Marketing and Website Subscription Features. *The International Journal of Technology, Knowledge and Society, 4*(1), 200-212.

Sellitto, C., Burgess, S., & Hawking, P. (2007). Information Quality Attributes Associated with RFID Supply Chain Benefits. *International Journal of Retail & Distribution Management, 35*(1), 69-87.

Snell, J. (2002). *Automating business processes and transactions in Web services.* IBM, Retrieved: 2/1/2008.

Stafford, T. F. (2003). E-Services. *Communications of the ACM, 46*(6), 26-28.

Stair, R., Moisiadis, F., Genrich, R., & Reynolds, G. (2008). *Principles of Information Systems.* Nelson Australia, South Melbourne.

Turban, E., Leidner, D., Mclean, E., & Wetherbe, J. (2008). *Information Technology Management: Transforming Organisations in the Digital Economy.* 6th edition ed. New York: John Wiley & Sons.

W3C (2007). *Mobile Web Initiative.* World Wide We Consortium (W3C), Retrieved: 2/1/2008.

W3C (2006). *Mobile Web Best Practices 1.0.* World Wide We Consortium (W3C), [http://www.w3.org/TR/mobile-bp/#UserGoals], Retrieved: 2/1/2008.

Want, R. (2004). RFID: A Key to Automating Everything. *Scientific American, 290*(1), 56-68.

Wikipedia contributors (2006). *E-Services,* [Homepage of Wikipedia, The Free Encyclopedia], [Online][http://en.wikipedia.org/wiki/e-services?oldid=89231885], Retrieved: 5/5/2007.

Wyld, D. (2006). RFID1001: The Next Big Thing for Management. *Management Research News, 29*(4), 154-173.

Copyright © 2009, IGI Global, distributing in print or electronic forms without written permission of IGI Global is prohibited.

Appendix
What Led us Here?

INTRODUCTION

This Appendix provides a brief overview of our PhDs - all of which involved re-search into small business adoption and use of ICT and Internet technologies. In effect, we felt that this appendix might provide some insights into how this book has evolved and the way that the various chapters have been ordered.

In the case of Stephen and Stan's PhDs, they particularly targeted small busi-nesses, whilst Carmine's PhD involved research into wineries in Australia – and involved a heavy emphasis on SMEs. More importantly, each of our PhDs involved the development of frameworks which have informed the outline of chapters in this book, and significant background material which have contributed the book's contents. Each of us will discuss a little of how the PhD has lead us to where we are today.

OUR PHDS

Stephen Burgess

I studied my PhD at Monash University, in Melbourne, Australia between 1998 and 2002. Although I studied part-time for the most part, I was able to complete within that time as I already had been doing some research (and teaching) in rel-evant areas and I was fortunate enough to get two useful sabbaticals – in 1999 I had six months leave to conduct a round of data collection. In 2001 I was granted a a similar period to write up the thesis. My supervisor was Professor Don Schauder,

Copyright © 2009, IGI Global, distributing in print or electronic forms without written permission of IGI Global is prohibited.

a member of the then School of Information Management and Systems. I had been researching and presenting conference papers in the area of small business use of ICTs since the mind 1990s, so was interested in pursuing that topic. I also knew I wanted to do *something* about small business use of the Internet, as the use of the Internet in business had captured my attention in teaching and research. After quite a few meetings with Don trying to work out a topic, he came up with a suggestion that sparked my interest – to examine the 'value added' aspects of Internet use by small business. For years I had been teaching about different approaches that businesses could take in employing ICTs to add value to their offerings. The models that I championed in class, encouraging businesses to match their ICT use to their business strategy and to take a strategic approach to ICT in general - became a theoretical foundation that I could use as a basis for my PhD. The next few sections briefly describe how this turned out. Even now, the influences of this can be seen in this book with the early emphasis on business investigation and strategy before considering the more technical aspects of implementing a Web presence.

PhD Summary

The aim of my thesis was to develop a practical model that would assist small businesses to use the Internet to interact with customers - specifically through their Website. In the thesis I classified any business with one to twenty employees as being 'small'. In developing the model, the intention was to take into account the specific characteristics of small businesses and to use common steps that had been identified in previous strategic ICT models as a basis for the development of the model.

When looking at the specific characteristics of small businesses, it is important to note how they differ from larger businesses, especially in their use of ICTs. Some of these ways are the lack of formal planning and control procedures when implementing ICTs, the lack of available resources (money and time) to devote to assessing ICT investments and the general lack of formal ICT training.

At the time, I noted that the use of ICTs by small businesses was usually based around administrative and operational applications (or as a reaction to something a competitor has done) rather than strategic or proactive applications. Small business attitudes to e-commerce were similar to their attitudes to ICTs in general. Small businesses had concerns about available resources and expertise to realize the advantages of e-commerce. They needed to be able to address the technical needs required to set up and maintain an Internet presence. The reasons that small business adopted electronic commerce were not that different from their reasons for using any type of information technology: that is, reduced costs, they were reacting to another organization's advantage or they were forced to by a larger partner.

Copyright © 2009, IGI Global, distributing in print or electronic forms without written permission of IGI Global is prohibited.

In order to develop the initial model for investigation, it was necessary to examine the effect of ICTs on businesses. It has been known for over two decades that ICTs can add value to a business' products and services. Hoffman and Novak's (1996) communications models for marketing in a hypermedia environment were used to identify some of the differences between traditional forms of advertising and advertising on the Internet. The Communication marketing channel, representing the exchange of information, was identified as being the channel where value was more likely to be added using the Internet.

It was shown that the steps that various models followed to identify strategic ICT ideas could be classified into three stages. These steps were the conducting of a business investigation, determination of business strategies based upon the investigation and the identification of strategic ICT opportunities based upon those strategies. A number of models specifically designed for the use of electronic commerce were organized into this framework. Again, this book follows this basic ideal.

At this stage, it was possible to design the initial conceptual version of the model.

This study had a number of characteristics that related it to interpretivist and post-positivist research and was divided into two major phases.

Phase One used a Web based discussion list as the data collection tool in a form of Delphi study designed to refine a conceptual model to assist small businesses to establish business-to-consumer interactions on the Internet. As is typical with such qualitative studies, a small sample of six academics participated in the data collection. A Web discussion list was the basis for the conduct of the first Phase of this study. An expert panel was assembled to comment upon the preliminary model, which was introduced at the start of the Phase and was refined throughout the Phase.

The model was refined as a result of the discussion that occurred in the Web discussion list. The following points highlight the major observations made during the first Phase of the study.

- The importance of using an easy to understand method for business investigation.
- The need for communication and consultation with external stakeholders at an early stage.
- The need to determine how the success of the Website will be evaluated *at the time* of designing the Website.

Phase Two of the study involved the use of three micro focus groups of small business consultants to refine the initial version of the applied model which had been developed from a combination of the conceptual model refined in Phase One

Copyright © 2009, IGI Global, distributing in print or electronic forms without written permission of IGI Global is prohibited.

and literature related to the applied model. An emphasis was placed upon those techniques that would lead to a model that was useful to small businesses. In preparing the model for this Phase, a procedures manual and accompanying spreadsheet software application (used for storing the results of small business analyses and making recommendations) were prepared. A key aspect of this phase was the use of the small business consultants, which provided a real, practical emphasis to the research. The main themes coming out of the focus groups were the need for simplicity of operation of the model for small businesses and the need to match the model to actual situations faced by small businesses.

The model proposed and developed in the PhD was based upon the major steps in other ICT models (such as Barton and Peters, 1991; Porter and Millar, 1985) and e-commerce models (for instance, Al-Moumem and Sommerville, 1999; Marchese, 1998). It represented at the time an attempt to address the specific needs of small businesses by guiding them through a proper planning process that was relatively easy to comprehend. The key was that it was meant to offer an organized process by which owner/managers could assess their competitive position, the needs of their customers and the level of resources available within the business and develop their Website strategy around this analysis. In doing this they would develop their own planning and technology skills and, where needed, the technology skills of their employees.

The purpose of the model was to guide small businesses from the planning process to setting up their Website and was based on the notion that small business owner/managers should think about the *business first* and the *Internet technology second*. The model outlined an iterative process based around a business investigation of internal and external influences on the business, formulation of Website strategy, identification of Website features, decisions relating to method of Website implementation, Website promotion and the evaluation of Website success. Figure 1 represents this conceptual model.

The initial business investigation involved a modified SWOT (Strengths, Weaknesses, Opportunities and Threats) analysis, which has been traditionally used in the marketing or economics areas of the business. An analysis would be performed on the various areas of the organization to identify current or potential strengths and weaknesses when compared with other competitive forces. Then, actual or potential opportunities to gain strategic advantage or threats to the organization's well being were identified (Kotler et al., 1989). This analysis provided the basis for making sound business decisions about the proposed Website presence, based upon the business situation.

As part of the SWOT analysis, the internal and (some) external forces within the business were examined. Internally, the resources in relation to time, money and expertise were considered, as well as the characteristics of the goods and/or

Copyright © 2009, IGI Global, distributing in print or electronic forms without written permission of IGI Global is prohibited.

Figure 1. A model to assist small businesses to interact with customers on the Internet (source: Burgess, 2002a)

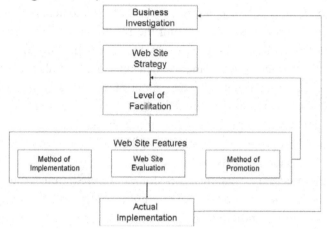

services of the business. The overall business strategy was also examined, as a business wishing to grow in size may require a more 'aggressive' Web strategy than a business that is satisfied with its existing customer base. Finally, the planning and technology skill level of the owner/manager and technology skills level of employees was determined. It is this final step that empowered the business to make appropriate, strategic decisions about their Website and provided them with the capability to achieve them. Where skill levels were inadequate the deficiencies were to be addressed by appropriate training, introduction of skilled employees or the use of skilled consultants. Externally, the Websites of competitors were examined, as well as the ability of customers to access the firm's Website.

Other steps of the model after the business investigation referred to identification of the firm's overall Website strategy, what Website features they were going to implement (facilitation), what method they used to implement these features (Website hosting), how they promoted the Website and how they evaluated its success.

My Work Since Then

Whilst the model provided some use for small businesses, it had two major shortcomings:

- It did not take into account the likelihood that many small businesses will change their Websites over time.
- There are now a number of different ways that small businesses can have a Web presence beyond their own Website – I labeled these the 'Extended

Copyright © 2009, IGI Global, distributing in print or electronic forms without written permission of IGI Global is prohibited.

Web'. In these instances small businesses will typically have Websites, but may choose to also (for example) provide their details on industry, regional or community portals or use the facilities of a general portal to allow them to sell their goods.

The purpose of the updated version of the model is to meet the challenge of providing an appropriate planning tool for small business Website content in this new environment. So, how can the model be updated to reflect the need to take into account that small businesses will probably alter their Websites over time and allow the business to consider what features of the 'extended Web' will be used? Figure 2 represents the author's attempt to update the model to take these considerations into account.

The updated version of the model includes:

- The removal of the 'strategy' section from the earlier version of the model. This is now incorporated into the business investigation (SWOT) as it was already considered in that section anyway.
- There are now two entry points into the business investigation phase. The first is where the business will be setting up a Website for the first time. A detailed SWOT analysis will be needed here. The other entry point is where the business has already been through the model once and has set up a Website.
- The addition of a 'Website audit' in the business investigation phase. This takes

Figure 2. The updated model (adapted from Burgess, 2008)

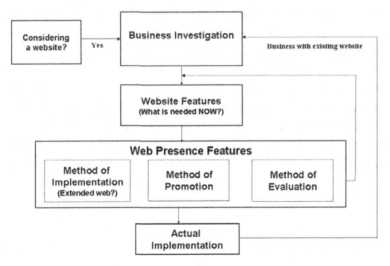

Copyright © 2009, IGI Global, distributing in print or electronic forms without written permission of IGI Global is prohibited.

into account that the business that have already developed a Website (perhaps quite a simple one) and may be considering changes to that Website.

- In the Website features stage, the decision of what features are to be placed on the Website is re-evaluated each time the model is applied. The business may decide that it wants a particular feature on its Website, but can also decide if it wants it NOW (or perhaps that it might be desirable in the future).
- The 'method of implementation' phase has a step that includes consideration of the Extended Web. That way, if a business has decided to implement say, a shopping cart feature, it can consider the use of a shopping cart on an external portal if it decides it may not be suitable (or may even be too difficult to implement) on its own Website.

The next challenge facing the author was how to incorporate this 'conceptual' version of the model into a new 'practical' version that can be used by today's small businesses. As mentioned earlier – the current preferred technique for this is to develop a handbook that will lead the small business owner/manager through the SWOT analysis and then present them with the possibilities that are available to them, allowing them to make informed decisions based upon where they stand in the marketplace and where they wish to be.

Stan Karanasios

I commenced my PhD in early 2004 and completed it in late 2007 under supervision of Dr Stephen Burgess, whom I have also worked alongside on many projects that have informed this book. My interest in the area of small business began during my Honours year at Victoria University and grew during my time spent living in developing countries in 2003. During my time away I developed an interest in the challenges faced by small businesses in developing countries in adopting and using the Internet. Whilst conducting my PhD I was drawn into many relevant projects focusing on small business and ICTs. I also spent some time at the United Nations at a program for young researchers interested in development. This program provided a basis for understanding concerning global development and a new perspective on the role of small business against the backdrop of globalisation and the information society. As has been noted on a number of occasions in this book, small businesses are numerically the dominant form of business throughout the globe and play a major role in economic development. Henceforth it is important that they are armed with the necessary knowledge to allow them to prosper in an ever changing and information based economy.

Copyright © 2009, IGI Global, distributing in print or electronic forms without written permission of IGI Global is prohibited.

PhD Summary

The purpose of my thesis was to develop a framework to assist small tourism businesses in making decisions about e-commerce. It was intended that the framework would provide small tourism businesses with an instrument that would allow them to systematically audit their business environment and provide a flexible approach to how best exploit the opportunities created by the Internet. It was intended that the framework would take into account the specific characteristics of small businesses in developing countries and the specific characteristics of the tourism industry. When looking at the characteristics of small businesses in developing countries, it is important to note that they operate in quite different environments to their counterparts in the developed world. Some of these characteristics are:

- They are resource poor.
- They suffer from information scarcity.
- They are affected by external forces which they may have no control over.
- They have basic technology needs, are informally run, and often employ family members.
- They have trouble gaining access to capital, which is often obtained from family members.
- The political environment is not conducive to small businesses and often favors larger businesses.
- They operate in informal sectors and avoid any form of formal registration.
- They face restrictions concerning accessing qualified human resources.

The study was divided into two major phases. Phase One involved a discussion with experts conducted through a Web based discussion list. A preliminary version of the framework was introduced at the start of the phase and was refined throughout the discussion. Based on the expert panel discussion the framework was refined and prepared for Phase Two of the study. Phase Two involved an investigation of small tourism businesses in a developing country context. The countries selected were Malaysia in South East Asia and Ecuador in South America. The two countries were selected based on a number of decisive factors, such as e-readiness ranking and development indicators. It was also desirable to select two countries with different characteristics such as culture, religion, government type, and so forth. In total twenty-six small tourism businesses participated. Based on the data gathered during the field a final version of the framework was produced. A number of significant findings were uncovered in this data collection phase. Some of these were:

Copyright © 2009, IGI Global, distributing in print or electronic forms without written permission of IGI Global is prohibited.

- Owner/manager readiness is one of the most relevant determinants of e-readiness. In fact, e-commerce adoption depends on how the owner/manager makes sense of available resources and the forces that surround the business.
- Owner/managers found ways to mitigate certain obstacles and deal with environmental constraints
- The tourism industry is highly competitive and market forces have fostered the adoption of the e-commerce.
- Government readiness can act as an adoption facilitator as well as provide many barriers to adoption.
- Despite the different levels of e-readiness and development experienced by both countries, small tourism businesses in both samples exploited the Internet in similar ways.
- The overall business and ICT environment acts as an adoption controller, controlling many aspects of readiness.

The Final Version of the Framework

The final framework (shown in Figure 3) is based on the data gathered in both phases of the study. The framework suggests that before the e-readiness assessment there

Figure 3. The e-readiness framework (source: Karanasios, 2008)

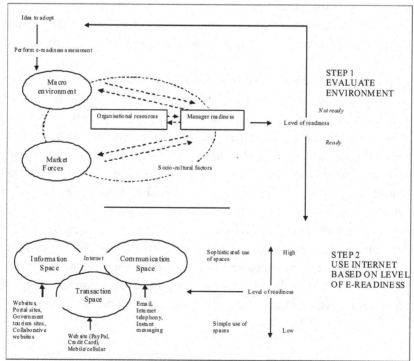

Copyright © 2009, IGI Global, distributing in print or electronic forms without written permission of IGI Global is prohibited.

is a precondition that there needs to be the idea to adopt. After performing the e-readiness step the enterprise can decide to exploit the Internet in light of the level of e-readiness, or if the enterprise decides they are not 'ready', not to proceed with adoption. After auditing the business environment the framework suggests that an enterprise progress on to exploiting three simple spaces (as per Angehrn 1997/8).

In the e-readiness step (Step 1) there are four contextual areas. The framework shows that the macro environment, market readiness and organisational readiness are all related with the owner/manager's readiness. That is, how these contextual areas influence the readiness of an enterprise is dependant on how the owner/manager is able to manage and contend with these variables.

Concerning the three spaces (Step 2), it was found that small tourism businesses exploited the spaces in a number of different ways. The Information Space was exploited through individual and group Websites, the use of third-party Websites such as tourism portals, and through government tourism Websites. The Communication Space was primarily used for e-mail, however there was some use of Internet telephony and instant messaging. The Transaction Space was the least used (only two small tourism businesses used this space) and was used for Credit Card and third party service payments.

Table 1 illustrates how the framework can be applied to small tourism enterprises. It provides a practical guide to e-readiness that is based on the rigorous framework developed in this study.

My Work Since Then

During my PhD (and since) I have worked on numerous projects, most notably a large government funded project that examines the impact of ICT projects in rural communities. A key point from this project that is relevant to small businesses is that small businesses located in rural and regional areas are likely to encounter the most difficulties concerning access to reliable and adequate infrastructure and the necessary support services such as Website designers. I aim to build on my PhD further in the future to examine the impact of a Web presence on small businesses located in regional areas, an area that has received little attention. My current project has taken me to Leeds University in the UK to work on a project involving mobile technology. Looking forward, mobile technology is likely to increase in its use in all domains of life (like the Internet) and it is an area that small businesses should be prepared to venture into to remain competitive.

Copyright © 2009, IGI Global, distributing in print or electronic forms without written permission of IGI Global is prohibited.

Carmine Sellitto

Shortly after commencing my career as a university academic in 2000, I became acutely aware of the importance of gaining a PhD qualification as an integral qualification - an award that was associated with scholarly recognition by peers, students and university administrators. Hence, out of vocational necessity, and based on my interests at the time in the area of Website development and e-commerce I commenced the *PhD journey* in early 2001. I undertook my PhD between 2001 and 2004 under the supervision and mentorship of Professor Bill Martin from the School of Information Technology, at RMIT University, in Melbourne, Australia. My thesis was titled *Innovation and Internet Adoption in SME Wineries: An e-Business Best Practice Model* and used the Australian wine industry as the basis for the research. The Australian wine industry is viewed as an important global success story exhibiting important business and economic characteristics that embraced innovation, entrepreneurship and collaboration. Indeed, the collaborative nature of the local wine industry, and the wineries in particular, allowed me to gain immense support during the study resulting in the PhD being completed in less time than anticipated. Moreover, the research thesis won the 2004 RMIT University student innovation award within the business portfolio.

The exposure to many micro and smaller sized businesses in my PhD was responsible for stimulating an increased interest to research and engage this sector further. Consequently, in recent years I have been able to undertake further research into small business use of ICT and the Internet across groups that include small medical practices, home-based micro businesses and smaller tourism enterprises. Furthermore, the value of researching this sector has allowed me to incorporate relevant case studies and examples of how small businesses adopt and use ICT in my teaching. Indeed, some of my undergraduate and postgraduate lectures that focus the use of technology by small businesses generate some of the greatest discussion amongst students. I have noted that many Management Information Systems (MIS) publications either omit, or pay a cursory acknowledgement, to aspects of small business use of ICTs. Hopefully, the content material in this book might serve as an informative resource for academics that wish to incorporate a small business topic or component in some of their classes.

PhD Summary

On a general level, the PhD's investigation of a specific industry addressed a call from the Australian National Office for the Information Economy (NOIE 2000) that by examining a specific industry or group, a deeper understanding of Internet adoption and implementation would occur. Moreover, the literature on SME adoption of

Copyright © 2009, IGI Global, distributing in print or electronic forms without written permission of IGI Global is prohibited.

ICTs, although growing, remains well behind other investigations of ICTs in larger organization, with Burgess (2002) reporting that SME peer-reviewed ICT publications representing only a relatively minor proportion of the all publications in the information systems literature. Hence, my thesis also documented and contributed an important element to the peer-reviewed ICT literature - a contribution that was associated with SMEs. The PhD explored Internet adoption by SME wineries in the State of Victoria (Australia) and developed an e-business practice model based on the experiences and perceptions of an early group of Internet adopting wineries. It was argued that Victoria provided a representative microcosm of the Australian wine cluster, and being the State with the greatest number of small wineries would aptly serve as a test-bed for the study. A mixed-method research design was employed, yielding quantitative and qualitative data that allowed winery Internet adoption patterns to be determined. Informative, relevant and pertinent case studies based on individual winery adoption patterns were subsequently used to propose an e-business practice model. The adoption of the Internet as a technological innovation by wineries was viewed from a pro-innovation perspective that assumed this type of technology was highly desirable and beneficial for wineries to adopt. As such, the Rogers (1995) paradigm was used in the research as a framework to identify participants and allow results to be discussed within the realms of *adopter innovativeness* and *innovation-decision making* constructs. The contributions of the research undertaken in the PhD addressed several areas and are highlighted in the following sections.

Contribution of the Diffusion Innovation Approach to Early Adopter Identification

A diffusion innovation study examined archived data associated with wine industry groups (wineries, suppliers, associations and distributors) for their degree of Internet adoption. By using reliable historical records, the research addressed a criticism commonly directed at the Rogers methodology on diffusion innovation - because it is time reliant - many diffusion studies fall victim to adopter recall leading to degrees of bias or erroneous results. Rogers (1995) alludes to historical records being an ideal way of overcoming this adopter recall criticism. By using reliable archival records, the study addressed this criticism of Rogers' methodology and provided a concrete and practical example of this aspect of Rogers' theory. Furthermore, archival records allowed the accurate identification of an early group of Internet adopting wineries, an aspect of the PhD that may not have been otherwise possible if the research had used a different approach.

Copyright © 2009, IGI Global, distributing in print or electronic forms without written permission of IGI Global is prohibited.

Contributions of the Industry Survey

The results of the study's Internet adoption survey allowed winery e-business applications to be gauged at a particular point in time. The survey questions reflected various aspects of Internet adoption reported in the general information systems literature, however, a concerted effort was made to draw from the work of various authors that had examined Internet technology adoption and use amongst wineries. The survey achieved a significant and notably response rate of 30%. Consequently, an important outcome of this aspect of the PhD was documenting a methodology for conducting survey research in the wine industry - an industry that has specific peculiarities that can, and often does, impact on respondent returns.

The PhD proposed that researchers, when surveying small wineries, needed to be aware of three practical areas that can potentially influence and/or impact survey response rates. These practical areas embraced six factors and addressed the following:

- **Survey design:** Factors that influence and contributed to high response rates included survey length, stakeholder engagement, and an open-ended return-by-date,
- **Preliminary testing of the survey:** The important factor here was found that a relevant and typical number of entities are used in the pilot testing stage, and
- **Implementation of the survey:** Where the distribution and timing of the survey is a significant factor in elevating response rates. Feedback of survey results is also an important factor in this highly collaborative industry.

The factors identified tend to be influenced by the seasons under which the wineries operate as well as the high degree of data collection/ compliance that occurs in the industry. The compliance issue is significant in that wineries generally need to complete numerous compulsory surveys - on average about two per month - which inhibit the completion of what may be perceived as non-essential surveys. Documentation of use of the survey instrument for improving winery response rates was accepted as a methodological research note in the International Journal of Wine Marketing - a noted peer-reviewed outlet (Sellitto 2006).

Contribution of the Case Studies

The investigation of early adopters provided concrete industry examples in the use of e-business pertinent to winery operations and activities - allowing a winery e-business practice model to be proposed in the PhD. Each case study also represented

Copyright © 2009, IGI Global, distributing in print or electronic forms without written permission of IGI Global is prohibited.

an empirically based contribution to the nascent and growing Internet literature that recorded the perceptions and behavior of a specific industry sector. Moreover, each case study reflected the values of a business that had pioneered the use of the technology in the wine sector. Collectively the case studies provided the data foundations that allowed the critical evaluation of the e-business phenomenon amongst Australian wineries, which was subsequently used to formulate new theory in the form of an e-business practice model. The case studies can also be considered to be a set of stories detailing the specific individual motivation for Internet adoption and the appropriate implementation of the technology over a period of time - hence, providing a form of longitudinal glimpse of the Internet technology adoption within the winery environment. The PhD identified a set of emergent Internet business experiences or practices (themes) that relate to why the technology was adopted and in which areas of the wine business they were used. The research provided a unique description of a winery's practices associated with Internet technology adoption across *four e-business domains* - technical, e-mail, Website and B2B. This case study component of the PhD was the initial starting point on which the foundation of the e-business model was formulated. It was noted that some of the winery operations utilized e-business practices across several domains, whilst other activities tended to involve the use of a practice within a specific domain. A summary of the four e-business domains and their application focus (operations and activities) is depicted in Figure 4.

Contribution of the E-Business Practice Model

The PhD identified e-business practices that encompassed four areas deemed to be technical, e-mail, Website and B2B domains - all of which were associated with winery operations and activities. By linking e-business practices to winery business activities the context for proposing an e-business practice model became winery operations orientated rather than technology focused. Consequently, the synthesis of the e-business practice model in the PhD embodied several spheres of activity that collectively reflected e-business adoption by the winery Internet champions. The spheres of activities that compose the model in which wineries engaged in e-business were:

1. **Winery management of Internet technology:** The activities in this sphere tend to reflect the way that wineries had formally recognized the importance of the Internet, elevating it to a relatively important management activity in the winery business environment. The relevant management operational areas included:

Copyright © 2009, IGI Global, distributing in print or electronic forms without written permission of IGI Global is prohibited.

Figure 4. Summary of identified winery operations and activities across four e-business domains (source: Sellitto, 2004)

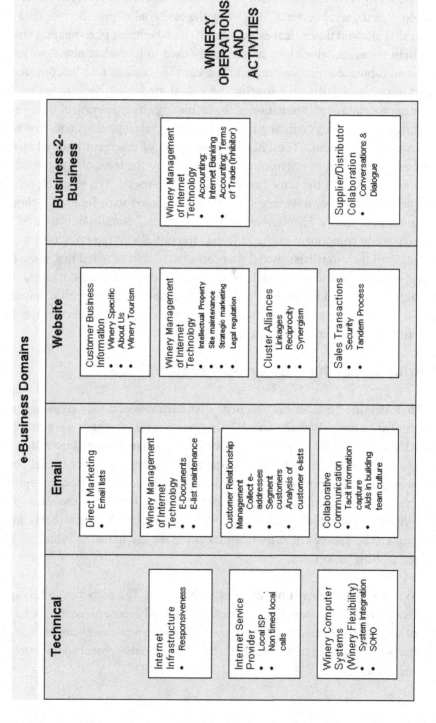

Copyright © 2009, IGI Global, distributing in print or electronic forms without written permission of IGI Global is prohibited.

- Winery accounting & winery computer systems
- E-mail lists and electronic documents
- Website maintenance
- Strategic marketing of the e-business activity

2. **Wine cluster collaboration:** This sphere encompassed numerous winery activities that utilized e-business practices to promote and foster positive collaborative interaction amongst wine industry partners as well as intra-organizational co-operation. Hence, the winery activities grouped in this sphere include:

- **Collaborative communication:** These activities occurred between wineries and amongst winery employees - an activity that had a tacit information exchange dimension associated with it, and
- **Cluster alliances:** Such activities occurred between trade partners and/or ancillary groups and other wineries - alliances that are manifest electronically by hypertext Website linkages that were either reciprocal or synergistic in nature.

3. **Direct wine-customer interaction:** This sphere reflected activities that are customer centric, allowing the winery to effectively inform the customer, **promote** the winery and its wine, manage the relationship with the customer and secure customer sales. The importance of the winery's direct sales customer was identified in all of the winery case studies where the management of customer interaction was an integral and sometimes crucial activity for the profitable operation of a winery. The activities that were part of this sphere of operation included:

- Direct marketing using a permission strategy.
- Customer Relationship Management in specifically identifying diverse customer groups, and
- Sales transactions that were achieved via the winery's secure ordering Website.

4. **An external environment:** That encompassed factors that influenced the adoption of e-business practices. These factors acted as either enhancers or inhibitors of e-business - such factors being outside the control of the winery and ones that tended to determine certain winery behavior or requirements. These factors were found to be associated with regulatory bodies - bodies that direct issues such as government taxation and legal regulations associated with alcohol sales.

The various spheres of operations and their interaction are depicted in Figure 5.

The proposed winery e-business practice model incorporates a dynamic component and a feedback loop, which determines the degree of winery e-business adoption to be gauged in each operational area or sphere. This feedback process

Copyright © 2009, IGI Global, distributing in print or electronic forms without written permission of IGI Global is prohibited.

Figure 5. A winery e-business practice model reflecting winery operations and activities (source: Sellitto, 2004)

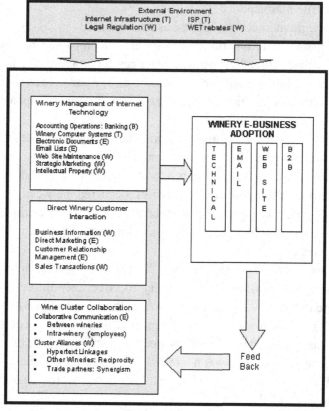

(Legend for e-Business domains associated with winery operations or activities: T - Technical, E - E-mail, W - Web Site, and B - Business-to-business [B2B])

utilizes metrics associated with the four e-business domains (technical, e-mail, Website and B2B) that allows wineries to evaluate their standing with respect to each proposed sphere of operation. The model's evaluation process is one of allowing wineries to become aware of the e-business procedures *in their industry* that have been adopted and been shown to influence tasks and activities in certain operational areas of the winery. Thus, the nature of the model allows wineries to compare the standing of their own Web presence to that of the early Internet adopting wineries - the industry relevant Internet champions. Furthermore, the evaluation process over time can allow both positive and negative e-business experiences to be recorded, allowing each of the winery spheres of operations to be modified.

Copyright © 2009, IGI Global, distributing in print or electronic forms without written permission of IGI Global is prohibited.

My Work Since Then

The research associated with the PhD has been broadly disseminated with articles having been published in journals and presented at international peer-reviewed conferences. Subsequent work undertaken since the completion of the PhD has been in the area that relates to cluster aspects of the wine industry.

During my research, I made the observation that various regional wine industry dynamics facilitated a highly collaborative environment in which wineries functioned and existed - one that was very similar to industry clusters. Industry clusters or agglomerations tend to comprise the important businesses or groups of industries that represent a sphere of strong cross sector interdependency or interaction - allowing these groups to benefit from synergies. The PhD identified a regional wine portal that allowed a set of small wineries to interact and share resources using Web presence. Post-PhD research that examined portal Web features suggested that the workings of the portal reflected the 'downstream' activities of the cluster with a strong representation of wine tourism related features. The identified portal features and their interrelationship are depicted in Figure 6.

In general, the strong tourism aspect of the portal (regional news, events and information) supports the notion that wineries and their activities are important to regional tourism. Tourism associated services such as accommodation providers and restaurants are an integral part of the portal - a facet that is also present in the real-world cluster. Part of this online strategy by the wineries tends to be one

Figure 6. Winery portal-cluster features (adapted from Sellitto & Burgess, 2007)

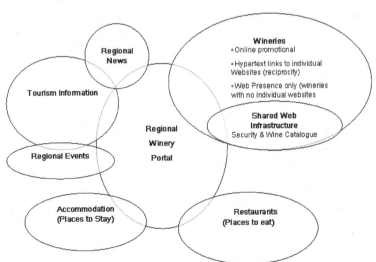

Copyright © 2009, IGI Global, distributing in print or electronic forms without written permission of IGI Global is prohibited.

of cooperation in enticing regional visits - promoting local vacations and dining. Moreover, the portal listing of wineries side-by-side allows potential customers to plan a regional excursion or holiday - visits that tend to incorporate a number of wineries in the itinerary. Furthermore, in considering these portal features, it was argued that they tended to mimic the real world cluster characteristics that I had early used and proposed as a cluster diagram in the work I had originally documented in my PhD. In the real-world industry cluster there appears to be an importance on distributors and retailers for selling, however the portal tends to reflect a reliance on the direct sales method used by the wineries. The portal was found to assist the wineries to share infrastructure in the form of common cataloguing systems, secure transaction facilities and provided an Internet-based resource framework that is commonly reported as a benefit of portal presence. In this piece of research it was proposed that the winery portal was indicative of a *virtual cluster* that appeared to mimic the real-world cluster.

CONCLUSION

We hope that this chapter has given some insight into the theoretical foundation behind the organisation of this book. We think it serves to illustrate the extensive theoretical background that each of us has in the area and the commonality of purpose that we possess in our desire to represent the issues that we consider to be important in the development of the small business Web presence. Although the language of much the book, the majority of which is academic in nature, may not necessarily appeal to small businesses directly, we hope that the messages in this part of the book translate, through the research of other academics and ourselves and those practitioners and consultants that may read the book - through to their small business constituents to benefit their Web presences.

REFERENCES

Al-Moumem, S. & Sommerville, I. 1999, "Marketing for E-Commerce", *Proceedings of the 10th International Conference of the Information Resources Management Association*, Hershey, PA, ed. M. Khosrow-pour, Idea Group Publishing, Hershey, PA.

Angehrn, A. 1997/8, "Designing mature internet business strategies: The ICDT model", *European Management Journal*, 15(4): 361-369.

Copyright © 2009, IGI Global, distributing in print or electronic forms without written permission of IGI Global is prohibited.

Barton, P.S. & Peters, D.H. 1991, "A Synthetic Framework for describing the use of Information Technology for Competitive Advantage", *Proceedings of the 1991 Australian Computer Conference*, Adelaide, Australia, Australian Computer Society: 47-62.

Burgess, S. 2008, "Determining Website Content for Small Businesses: Assisting the Planning of Owner/Managers", *International Journal of Knowledge Management Studies,* 2(1): 143-161.

Burgess, S. 2002, *Business-to-Consumer Interactions on the Internet: A Model for Small Businesses,* School of Information Management and Systems, Monash University.

Burgess, S. 2002, "Information Technology in Small Business: Issues and Challenges" in *Information Technology in Small Business: Challenges and Solutions,* ed. S. Burgess, Idea Group Publishing, Hershey, PA, USA: 1-17.

Hoffman, D.L. & Novak, T.P. 1996, "Marketing in Hypermedia Computer-Mediated Environments: Conceptual Foundations", *Journal of Marketing,* 60(3): 50-68.

Karanasios, S. 2008, *An E-Commerce Framework for Small Tourism Enterprises in Developing Countries,* Victoria University.

Kotler, P., Chandler, P., Gibbs, R. & McColl, R. 1989, *Marketing in Australia,* 2nd edn, Prentice-Hall, Victoria, Australia.

Marchese, L. 1998, "Brand Recognition", *Internet World 98: Proceedings of the Australian Pacific Conference,* NSW, Australia, Kirby Network Associates.

NOIE 2000, *Taking the Plunge 2000: Sink or Swim?* Commonwealth of Australia, (National Office for Information Economy), Canberra.

Porter, M.E. & Millar, V.E. 1985, "How information gives you competitive advantage", *Harvard Business Review,* 63(4): 149.

Rogers, E. 1995, *Diffusion of Innovations,* 4th Edition edn, Free Press, New York.

Sellitto, C. 2006, "Improving Winery Survey Response Rates: Lessons From the Australian Wine Industry", *International Journal of Wine Marketing,* 18(2): 150-152.

Sellitto, C. 2004, *Innovation and Internet Adoption in SME Wineries: An e-Business Best Practice Model,* School of Information Technology, RMIT University.

Sellitto, C. & Burgess, S. 2007, "A Study of a Wine Industry Internet Portal" in *Encyclopedia of Portal Technologies and Applications,* ed. A. Tatnall, Information Science Reference, London, UK: 979-984.

Copyright © 2009, IGI Global, distributing in print or electronic forms without written permission of IGI Global is prohibited.

About the Authors

Stephen Burgess has research and teaching interests that include the use of ICTs in small businesses (particularly in the tourism field), the strategic use of ICTs and B2C electronic commerce. He completed his PhD in the School of Information Management and Systems at Monash University. His thesis was in the area of small business interactions with customers via the Internet. He has received a number of competitive research grants in these areas. He has completed several studies related to Website features in small businesses and the functions of Websites over time. He has recently edited two books and special edition of journals in topics related to the use of ICTs in small business and been track chair at the ISOneWorld, IRMA, Conf-IRM and ACIS conferences in this area.

Carmine Sellitto is a member of the School of Management and Information Systems at Victoria University in Melbourne, lecturing in the area of Management Information Systems, Internet technologies, and e-business. He gained his PhD from RMIT University where he was awarded the Business student prize for PhD innovation. Dr Sellitto has also published widely on topics associated with e-business, information management and technology, Website analysis, tourism and IT, Internet-marketing, information quality and small business technology adoption. His articles have appeared in the *Australasian Journal of Information Systems, Information Technology and Management, Journal of Information Technology and Tourism, International Journal of Retail & Distribution Management, Journal of Information Science* and the *Journal of the American Society for Information Science and Technology*.

Stan Karanasios completed his PhD at the School of Information Systems at Victoria University, Australia in the area of small business and ICT adoption in developing countries. His research involved performing field research in Ecuador and Malaysia and developing recommendations for successful ICT adoption. He has also participated in a United Nations programme at the Palais Des Nations in Geneva in 2006 and published a number of journal articles. In addition to his PhD, Stan has worked for Monash University and RMIT University School of Business IT in the areas of e-government, rural development, small business innovation and capacity building. Recently, Stan joined the AIMTech Research Group at Leeds University in England as a research fellow and is working on a project that examines innovation in UK Police Forces and research surrounding future evolutions of wireless technologies in Europe. His interests include innovation in public and private organisations, ICTs and development, and the effective use of ICTs in small business.

Index

Copyright © 2009, IGI Global. Copying or distributing in print or electronic forms without written permission
of IGI Global is prohibited.

Copyright © 2009, IGI Global. Copying or distributing in print or electronic forms without written permission of IGI Global is prohibited.

Copyright © 2009, IGI Global. Copying or distributing in print or electronic forms without written permission
of IGI Global is prohibited.